# A HISTORY OF
# HEBREW CIVILIZATION

# A HISTORY OF
# HEBREW CIVILIZATION

BY

ALFRED BERTHOLET

PROFESSOR OF THEOLOGY IN THE UNIVERSITY OF
GÖTTINGEN

TRANSLATED BY

THE REV. A. K. DALLAS M.A.

GEORGE G. HARRAP & COMPANY LTD.
LONDON        CALCUTTA        SYDNEY

*Published 1926*
*by* GEORGE G. HARRAP & CO. LTD.
*39-41 Parker Street, Kingsway, London, W.C. 2*

*Printed in Great Britain at* THE BALLANTYNE PRESS *by*
SPOTTISWOODE, BALLANTYNE & CO. LTD.
*Colchester, London & Eton*

# TRANSLATOR'S NOTE

NO modern book of similar size provides such a luminous background to the Old Testament as Professor Bertholet's *Kulturgeschichte Israels*, a version of which is here presented to English readers. Older works, like Dr W. M. Thomson's *The Land and the Book*, while still useful, are in many respects out of date, and readers of the Old Testament will be glad to have a book that presents the latest scholarship on the subject. All who are interested in the ancient literature of that people whose genius for religion has so enriched the world, that "strange people who could never be done with God, nor God with them," and especially all who are engaged in teaching that literature in church or synagogue or school, will find here one of the best possible commentaries. It is the work of a master of the subject, and it will whet the appetite of all who read it for that history of the religion of Israel on which Professor Bertholet is understood to be at present engaged.

The author writes from the critical standpoint, and this is one of the most valuable aspects of his book. When the Hebrews invaded Palestine they came from the nomadic life of the desert into the midst of a civilization that was already old, and the reader of these pages will understand better than before the nature of the syncretism that resulted, and will appreciate more clearly the work of the Hebrew prophets and the problems they had to face.

An essential merit of the book is found in the abundant references to the Old Testament literature, and every student of the Bible will admire the skill with which these have been marshalled and used. Much time has been spent in verifying these and other references for the translation. In some cases, where a knowledge of the Hebrew text is involved, the translator has endeavoured to explain the reference.

From personal experience in the Bible department of George Watson's College, Edinburgh, the translator would add that teachers will find here aid, welcome because adequate, in their endeavours to explain the life and thought reflected in the pages of the Old Testament.

In the early chapters much is made of the significance of proper names, and the forms used have been carefully chosen with a view to indicating derivation. The spelling is therefore in some cases at variance with the familiar one.

A. K. DALLAS

RHYND LODGE
SEAFIELD, EDINBURGH
*September* 1926

# PREFACE

WHEN some years ago, at the invitation of Messrs Vandenhoek and Ruprecht, I undertook to write a history of Hebrew civilization, as a kind of supplement to their edition of annotated selections from the Old Testament,[1] I did not dream of all that was going to delay the carrying out of the work. First there was a double change in my own sphere of labour ; then came the War and all that followed it. Under the conditions that prevailed the work of printing could proceed only intermittently. I trust that the inequalities of the work due to these hindrances will not be too perceptible.

My purpose was to give, in as readable a form as possible, an account of the conditions of civilization in Palestine. In order not to interrupt the text all references to authorities have been relegated to footnotes. In the work itself I was anxious to bring out the dependence of Israel's civilization on the land in which it was achieved, and this involved showing its relation to the contemporary Oriental life. The chief mistake of those who are unfamiliar with the subject is that they show an involuntary tendency to bring to their reading of the Old Testament the completely different conditions of to-day. This temptation must be overcome. We must also abandon the idea that Israel was isolated and shut off from the rest of the world. In Palestine there was an intermingling of the most varied influences—Egyptian, Babylonian, Hittite, and even those of the Western world. To estimate correctly the relation of these to each other and their conjunct significance for Israel is one of the most difficult tasks, and one which perhaps will never be completely accomplished. Excavation work has cast much new light on the civilization of Palestine at the time of the Hebrew invasion. It has been my endeavour to utilize this as far as possible. Kittel, in the latest editions of his *Geschichte Israels*, has led the way in this regard, and I gladly acknowledge that I have learned much from him. For the rest, the matter of the

[1] *Die Schriften des Alten Testaments in Auswahl* (Göttingen, 1921–24).

7

book covers to some extent the same ground as is usually covered by books on the archæology of Israel—I should mention specially those of Benzinger and Nowack—but of course a book that is professedly a history of civilization must needs enter more fully than a manual of archæology has to do into the historical evolution.   I have tried to give special attention to the intellectual and spiritual elements of Hebrew civilization, and so the literary history of Israel, which is usually treated in separate theological works, has also been included.   The expert will see that, in this section of the work, I have to some extent followed the guidance of Professor Gunkel.   Last but not least, I have included the religion of the Hebrews—not so much the religious antiquities as the religious life.   It is one of the merits of the man to whom (as an overdue offering on his seventieth birthday) this book is dedicated [1] that he has laid emphasis on the interdependence of religion and civilization.   I hope this book will help to make clear how greatly the understanding of Israel's religion is aided by a study of its civilization.

A. BERTHOLET

WENGEN
  BERNESE OBERLAND
    *September* 1919

[1] The original work is dedicated " To my teacher, Bernhard Duhm, in token of lasting gratitude."—TRANSLATOR.

# CONTENTS

## BOOK I

### BEGINNINGS OF A SETTLED CIVILIZATION IN PALESTINE

## BOOK II

### ISRAEL'S CIVILIZATION IN PALESTINE

# ABBREVIATIONS

*AA : Archäologischer Anzeiger.*

*Agh : Aghâni.*

*AR : Archiv für Religionswissenschaft.*

*GGA : Anzeigen der Königlichen Gesellschaft der Wissenschaften zu Göttingen.*

*GGN : Nachrichten der Königlichen Gesellschaft der Wissenschaften zu Göttingen.*

Hastings, *RE : Encylopædia of Religion and Ethics*, 1908 ff.

*KAT :* Schrader, *Keilinschriften und Altes Testament*, 3rd edition, 1903.

*RGG : Die Religion in Geschichte und Gegenwart*, 1909 ff.

*TBAT : Altorientalische Texte und Bilder zum Alten Testament*, edited by H. Gressmann, 1909.

*ZatW : Zeitschrift für die alttestamentliche Wissenschaft.*

*ZDPV : Zeitschrift des Deutschen Palästinavereines.*

*ZE : Zeitschrift für Ethnologie.*

*ZDMG : Zeitschrift der Deutschen Morgenländischen Gesellschaft.*

The abbreviations for the names of the Biblical books are those usually employed.

# A HISTORY OF HEBREW CIVILIZATION

## BOOK I
### BEGINNINGS OF A SETTLED CIVILIZATION IN PALESTINE

### CHAPTER I

#### THE LAND OF PALESTINE AND ITS POSSIBILITIES FOR CIVILIZATION

IN his work on the Indo-Europeans in prehistoric times[1] Rudolph von Ihering coined the expression " Geography is latent history." The truth contained in this expression is specially relevant to a study of the development of a national civilization. The inhabitants of a territory are bound to conform to its peculiar requirements. The more varied a territory is the greater are likely to be its effects in calling out the adaptability of its inhabitants. Special adaptability has distinguished the Jewish people throughout their history, and this fact is perhaps our best justification for beginning our study of Hebrew civilization with the question, " What possibilities for cultural progress did the land of Palestine present to its inhabitants ? "

Referring to the natural catastrophe to which Palestine owes the peculiar form of its surface, Ankel[2] speaks of an " unsuccessful attempt of nature to extend the Mediterranean Sea farther to the east and south-east." Is it not very suggestive that it was what Science calls a failure that substituted for a sea the land which was destined to be the cradle of the most precious religious possessions of mankind ? That catastrophe, which took place at the end of the Tertiary Period and at the beginning of the Diluvian, had as result the formation of a series of clefts, running north to south, of such depth and size that the western

[1] *Vorgeschichte der Indoeuropäer* (1894), p. 97.
[2] O. Ankel, *Grundzüge der Landesnatur des Westjordanlandes* (1897), p. 48.

portion of the mighty chalk mass which formerly stood at the eastern end of the Mediterranean Sea broke off and became an independent formation.[1]  The deepest cleft is that formed by the Jordan valley and the Dead Sea.  This cleft, again, is the continuation of the depression which runs between Lebanon and Hermon [2] and, farther north, between Lebanon and Anti-lebanon.  In Lebanon the western mountains reach their greatest height.  The snow-covered peaks, visible from afar, rise to nearly 10,000 feet.  The surface of the Dead Sea is 1300 feet below the level of the sea.  When we realize that Palestine comprises these tremendous differences of altitude we can imagine what variety of cultural possibilities is involved.

In the main, Palestine is hill-country.[3]  Whether one enters it from Egypt or from Babylon one must 'go up' to Palestine, and the ancients, whose journeys were made on foot or riding, were, as Old Testament forms of expression show, very keen to appreciate facts of that kind.  The main mountain ridge runs north to south, falling much more steeply on the east side, toward the Jordan valley, than on the west side, where, between the mountains and the sea, plains extend throughout the broader southern two-thirds of the country.  Valleys of varying length and depth cut this ridge from east to west, and, as a natural result, the great roads of communication from north to south were built at the upper or at the lower end of these valleys, and therefore either followed the crest of the ridge or ran along the sea-coast through the plain.

The deepest cut is the valley, widening to an actual plain (13 miles long by 8 miles broad), through which the Kishon flows.  This great plain, called the plain of Jezreel, or the plain of Megiddo, or simply "the plain," is the natural boundary between the north and the centre of the country.  Here, of course, the main roads of communication intersect, and on that account the plain inevitably became the scene of the decisive battles which were fought for its possession.  The high ridge running from Lebanon begins at some distance from this plain, passing gradually into the plateau that bounds the plain on the north.

---

[1] Buhl, *Geographie des alten Palästina* (1896), p. 13.

[2] At "the entering in of Hamath," Num. xiii, 21, and frequently.

[3] The common explanation of its name "Canaan" as 'lowland' cannot be maintained.  The name "Palestine" is due to a transference of the name of the land of the 'Philistines' (Pelescheth) to the whole country.

This plateau is the fertile district of Galilee. South of the plain the mountain ridge rises once more, thrusting out a bold spur in Carmel, westward toward the sea. In the fertile plateau of Samaria or the mountains of Ephraim it reaches only a moderate height. It rises higher—reaching an average height of 2500 to 3000 feet—in the mountains of Judah. This Judean plateau becomes increasingly desolate and infertile as it runs southward into the so-called Negeb, until it again falls gradually to the southern desert. Its eastern slopes, toward the Dead Sea, are very wild, but on the west the so-called Shephela provides a transition to the undulating plain of Philistia, which is the southern continuation of the more level plain of Sharon. The low coastline to which these plains extend forms here and there real dunes, which possibly gave rise to the proverbial simile, " like the sand of the sea for multitude," but it affords no such facilities for shipping as are found in the north of Palestine, where the mountains, coming down directly to the sea, form natural bays. It would, however, be unwise to draw conclusions from the condition of the southern coast to-day as to its condition in ancient times, for there is some geological proof that the sea once stood higher at that part and retired only gradually. Besides, it must be kept in mind that the ships of the ancients were of much less draught than our modern vessels.

The Dead Sea is only a remnant of a sheet of water that was once, in very ancient days, much larger and higher. Sand and layers of shells on the edges of the great Jordan depression leave no doubt that the Jordan valley was once the bed of an extensive inland lake. This lake, under the increasing drought of the region, has been evaporated, and what was the bed of it now serves as a channel for the Jordan. Three or four streams unite to form the Jordan, and the resulting river traverses the marshy but fertile plain of Huleh, in which lies the small, shallow lake of the same name, usually, but erroneously, called the Lake of Merom.[1] From this point the river fights its way through broken country, falling about 700 feet in the stretch of 10 miles to Lake Gennesareth, whose surface covers 72 square miles. From this point to the Dead Sea the Jordan traverses three times the

---

[1] It cannot be said with certainty where the " waters of Merom " really were where Joshua gained the victory described in Josh. xi, 5 ff. : perhaps near the present-day village of Meron in Upper Galilee.

distance as the crow flies. That is to say, in this part of its course it makes innumerable windings. Of themselves these windings would be an obstacle to navigation, but in addition there are rapids, from which the river is popularly, but probably erroneously, supposed to have received its name—Haj-jarden, the " descender." In view of all this, as Wellhausen has justly said,[1] the Jordan cannot be called the 'life-stream' of the country. It is hardly more than a deep drain. Its banks recede in two rising terraces. In spring the lower terrace is flooded in places, and thereafter it becomes covered with vegetation of such luxuriance that the beauty of the Jordan banks is proverbial.[2] In summer fords are more numerous. One of these, near Jericho, formed the means of access for the inhabitants of Jerusalem to the other side of the Jordan. In this region the Jordan valley widens into what is really a plain, the so-called Ghor, famous in ancient times for its fertility.[3] Palms grew here in great beauty, and owing to this Jericho itself bore the name of " Palm Town." But all this luxuriant life comes to a sudden stop, and it is not without cause that the Dead Sea bears that name. The water is so strongly impregnated with salt and other mineral ingredients that no life save that of certain microbes can exist. The density of this water seems deliberately to repel every living thing. Josephus [4] relates that when Vespasian visited the lake he ordered several men who could not swim to be thrown into it with their hands tied behind their backs. All of them remained floating, as if forced to the surface by a wind. The deathly stillness which broods over this sheet of water, together with the celebrated play of changing colours, lends to the Dead Sea charms of another kind, upon which, however, it is not the business of the historian of civilization to dilate.

The country east of Jordan, called in the Bible Gilead in the wider sense,[5] has as its natural eastern boundary the great Syrian-Arabian desert, and on the west is cut off (although

---

[1] Wellhausen, *Israelitische und Jüdische Geschichte* (1907), p. 2.

[2] See Jer. xii, 5, xlix, 19, 1, 44; Zech. xi, 3.

[3] See, for example, Josephus, *Wars of the Jews*, IV, viii, 3.

[4] Josephus, *Wars of the Jews*, IV, viii, 4. See also Tacitus, *Hist.*, V, 6.

[5] See Deut. xxxiv, 1; Judges xx, 1; 1 Kings iv, 19; Ezek. xlvii, 18. In the narrower sense Gilead denotes the region between the so-called mountains of Gilead (south of the Jabbok) and the Jarmuk; but the use of the word is altogether indeterminate.

rivers as a rule connect rather than divide) from the country on the other side by the great depth of the Jordan valley. Taken as a whole Gilead (the land east of Jordan) is a plateau seamed here and there by valleys of varying depth running east to west, and containing isolated mountain ranges. It contains also, especially in the broad northern part, extinct volcanoes and extensive lava fields. Stony ground alternates with fertile land, and the latter with its luscious pastures and good soil encourages cattle-breeding and the raising of cereal crops.

In attempting to gain an idea of what Palestine really had to offer to its inhabitants it is natural to start from the well-known words that it was "a land flowing with milk and honey." [1] But we must be careful in drawing what might seem inevitable inferences from this expression. In itself it might, of course, be simply a poetical description of Canaan as a land whose rich pastures greatly favoured the yield of milk-giving animals, and in which the vine and other fruit-trees bore an exceptional abundance of fruit. (Honey, in Hebrew *debasch*, includes not only the honey of bees, but also fruit-honey, which is still called *dibs* by the Arabs.[2]) Or the expression might be taken as a metaphorical description of a "country which produced fruits rich as milk and sweet as honey." [3] But it is noticeable that the same combination of milk and honey reappears elsewhere. "The presence of Bacchus on earth is shown by various marvels, among others that milk and honey flow spontaneously to refresh the thirsty : the earth flows with milk and with nectar of the bees ; so it seems to the priestesses of Bacchus, when they are conscious of the presence of the God." And Usener, from whom these words are taken,[4] has shown by a series of examples that an abundance of milk and honey is a part of the ancient conception of the home of the gods, or the similar abode of the blessed, Paradise, or the place of the Golden Age.[5] In this sense milk and honey are repeatedly mentioned in later Jewish

---

[1] See Exod. iii, 8, 17, xiii, 5, xxxiii, 3, and often.

[2] See S. Krauss in *ZDPV*, vol. xxxii (1909), pp. 151–164.

[3] Such is the paraphrase of Deut. xxvi, 9, as given in the *Midrash Tannaim* of Deuteronomy (ed. by Hoffmann, 1909), p. 173. See *ZDPV*, vol. xxxiii (1910), p. 45.

[4] From the essay, "Milk and Honey," in the *Rheinisches Museum für Philologie*, new series, vol. lvii, p. 177.

[5] *Op. cit.*, p. 192.

literature, in which ancient thoughts find an echo.[1]  But the Old Testament passages in which the verse appears are always connected with the thought of the deliverance of Israel from Egypt, and it is easy to understand that Canaan is thus contrasted with the land of Egypt and with the desert as a kind of ideal land of the gods—as a land of promise.[2]  In view of these considerations the expression—which is not of Hebrew, but perhaps of Babylonian origin [3]—hardly justifies us in drawing far-reaching conclusions as to the actual fertility of Canaan. But apart from that there are many other passages in the Old Testament which extol the merits of Palestine as a spacious, beautiful land, with " brooks of water and fountains and lakes that spring out of valleys and hills, a land of wheat and barley and vines, and fig-trees and pomegranates, a land of oil-olive and honey, a land where one can eat without scarceness, where there is no lack of anything, a land whose stones are iron and out of whose hills brass can be dug." [4]  But if we are to interpret aright these passages, which are mostly found in Deuteronomy, we must not forget that they were written at a time when Israel was about to lose her beloved land, and that at such a moment its advantages were likely to be prominent to her view.  All the same, even if some deduction has to be made from the value of the Biblical testimony, we have evidence outside the Bible that corroborates in all essentials the impression that has always been derived from it.  Not to mention Josephus,[5] who is never tired of praising the fertility of Palestine, especially Galilee and the district round Jericho, we can appeal to classical writers, such as Tacitus ; [6] and of a much older date (1780 B.C.) we have in the remarkable travel-notes of an Egyptian, Sinuhe, who was compelled by circumstances to reside for a time on the high lands of Palestine, a remarkable passage [7] describing the

---

[1] See Slavonic Enoch, viii, § 5, Sibyllines, Book III, 744 ff., Book V, 281 ff. These late passages also throw light upon the famous Immanuel prophecy in Isaiah where Immanuel himself and those about him are to eat cream and honey (Is. vii, 15, 22).  Both involve a prophecy of salvation.

[2] Stade in *ZatW*, vol. xxii (1902), p. 323.

[3] *KAT*, p. 526.  According to Babylonian ritual texts a mixture of honey and thick milk is frequently used at the consecration of new idols.

[4] Deut. viii, 7 ff.  *Cf.* Deut. iv, 21, xi, 10 ff.

[5] *Wars of the Jews*, III, iii, 2-5, x, 8, IV, viii, 3.

[6] *Hist.*, V, 6.

[7] *TBAT*, vol. i, p. 213.  The date of the Sinuhe narrative is about 200

fertility of the region where he chose to live.[1]  " There were
figs and grapes and more wine than water.  Honey was abundant
and oil was plentiful, and all sorts of fruit hung on the trees.
There were wheat and barley and numberless flocks and herds
of all kinds."  There can be no doubt about it—Palestine's
fertility must have deserved very high praise.  Still further
corroboration is found in local names like Carmel, " Field of
Fruit," Beth-lehem, " House of Bread," Beth-hackerem,[2] " House
of Vineyards," Beth-phage,[3] " House of Figs," Beth-haggan,[4]
" House of Gardens," En-gannim,[5] " Garden of Springs,"
Nahal-eshcol,[6] " Valley of Grapes," and many others.  To be
sure, Palestine is poor in the *humus* that arises from the decom-
position of vegetation.  That is due to the dry climate.  All
that would form *humus* turns to dust, and is blown away by the
strong wind in the intense disintegrating heat of the sun.  But
interspersed with the stretches of bare rock there are other
regions which are covered with loamy, disintegrated soil—the
so-called *terra rossa* of the chalk districts—and in these human
labour, although necessary, was not applied in vain.[7]

When the passage already quoted from Deut. viii makes
special mention of brooks and wells and lakes as among the
desirable features of Palestine it expresses a correct appreciation of what *water* means in a land like Palestine.  It seems,
however, to imply—inaccurately—that the country contained an
abundance, or even a super-abundance, of water.  It would be
more correct to say that the opposite was the case.  As regards
lakes, the Lake of Galilee is the only one worthy of mention.
The feeling of the time when vigorous life still throbbed round
its shores is reflected in the Rabbinic words, " Jahveh made
seven lakes, but the Lake of Gennesareth is His favourite."[8]
Of wells and brooks we have evidence in the numerous local

years later than the time with which it deals.  Sinuhe is a supposed member
of the retinue of King Sesostris I (1980–1935 B.C.).
  [1] Possibly east of the Sea of Tiberias.  See Kittel, *Geschichte des Volkes
Israel* (1916), vol. i, p. 72, *note* 1.
  [2] Jer. vi, 1 ; Neh. iii, 14.
  [3] Matt. xxi, 1 ; Mark xi, 1 ; Luke xix, 29.
  [4] 2 Kings ix, 27.
  [5] Josh. xv, 34 ; a different one, Josh. xix, 21, xxi, 29.
  [6] Num. xiii, 23, xxxii, 9; Deut. i, 24.
  [7] See Schwöbel, *Die Landesnatur Palästinas* (1914), vol. ii, p. 7.
  [8] See also Josephus' description in *Wars of the Jews*, III, x, 8.

appellatives in the Old Testament compounded with *en*, 'well' or 'spring,' and *nahal*, 'brook,' and mention should also be made of the famous hot springs of Tiberias[1] and Kallirrhoë,[2] which in later times were used for curative purposes.[3] But there were other wells and brooks that betrayed the hopes that men placed in them. The deceitful brook, the waters that fail, is a familiar figure of poetical prophetic speech;[4] for in contrast with the perennial stream[5] the Palestinian was familiar with another, which contains water only in the rainy season.[6] Very much, therefore, depends on the rain, and in spite of all the damage that may be done by its torrential downpourings it is among the best blessings known to men that Jahveh opens the reservoirs of the heavens to give the land rain in its season.[7] The religious mind finds here one of the great advantages of Palestine over Egypt. In Egypt men had themselves to undertake the laborious work of irrigation, using foot-driven wheels to draw the water from the canals for their fields. In Palestine such labour is necessary only for the smaller vegetable gardens. In all other cases irrigation is provided by the goodness of God, and "when the rain falls from heaven, then the land drinks water."[8] How constant a theme of thought and speech the rain must have been is shown by the fact that the Hebrew language, in addition to several general words for 'rain,' has special names for the various kinds of rain—for the early rain in October and November, for the winter rain, lasting from mid-December to the end of March, and, finally, for the latter rain at the end of March and in April. And the timely coming and a sufficient measure of these various phases are indispensable requisites for the fertility of the soil,[9] for the summer season is such that the rain is dried up to the last drop. At that season rain and thunderstorm are extremely rare.[10] Specially dreaded is the hot south-east wind, the sirocco,[11] which almost

---

[1] Josephus (*Antiquities*, XVIII, ii, 3 ; *Wars of the Jews*, IV, i, 3) calls them Ammathus, which is perhaps Hammath (*i.e.*, "the Hot Spring"), Josh. xix, 35.

[2] They were frequented by Herod the Great in his last illness.

[3] For other hot springs see Buhl, *op. cit.*, pp. 45 and 119, and *cf.* Gen. xxxvi,24.

[4] Jer. xv, 18 ; Is. lviii, 11.  [5] Deut. xxi, 4; Amos v, 24.

[6] 1 Kings xvii, 7 ; 2 Kings iii, 16 f.  [7] Deut. xxviii, 12, xi, 14.

[8] Deut. xi, 10 f.  [9] Deut. xi, 14; Amos iv, 7; Hos. vi, 3; Joel ii, 23.

[10] 1 Sam. xii, 17 f. ; Prov. xxvi, 1.  [11] The word is Arabic, *sharki*, "eastern."

18

in a moment burns up all vegetation. It is to this that the well-known words of Deutero-Isaiah apply, that " all flesh is as grass, and all the goodliness thereof as the flower of the field," withered before the breath of Jahveh.[1] Indeed, drought, fire, and failure of the crops, with famine as a necessary result, are familiar afflictions of the country.[2] Therefore all possible measures are taken to find moisture and coolness. This is the explanation of the preference for the western slope of the mountains—that which faces the sea—over the eastern slope, with an exposure toward the desert and its drought. A north exposure is preferred to a southern one, because it is less open to the parching rays of the sun.[3] The chief refreshment of the thirsty land in the rainless season is the dew, which is sought from God as another most precious divine blessing,[4] as abundant, if possible, as the dew that falls on Hermon,[5] where the roof-tiles drip with it.[6] Here also we may gather from the metaphors used how highly the refreshment given by it was valued.[7] But, after all, it is water which is looked upon as a refreshment beyond compare [8]—an eloquent testimony that Palestine was really poor in water. The expression that may be heard there even to-day, " Water is the gift of God," is more than a figure of speech ; it expresses what is very keenly and consciously felt.[9] Palestine has always been one of the countries in which water had at times to be bought with money,[10] and where one would more readily give a thirsty man a bowl of milk than one of water.[11] All the more keenly had water to be toiled and fought for, and this was one of the respects in which human toil was necessary to make good Nature's shortcomings and to open up the country to civilization.

Besides drought, there were other plagues under which the land suffered. There is fairly frequent mention in the Old Testament of hail.[12] But a far more dangerous enemy of the

---

[1] Is. xl, 6–8.
[2] Deut. xxviii, 22 ; 1 Kings viii, 37 ; Amos iv, 9 ; Hag. ii, 17 ; 2 Chron. vi, 28.
[3] See Schwöbel, *Die Landesnatur Palästinas* (1914), vol. i, p. 35.
[4] Gen. xxvii, 28 ; Deut. xxxiii, 13.   [5] Ps. cxxxiii, 3.
[6] Theodoret says so.   [7] Hos. xiv, 5 ; Mic. v, 7.
[8] Is. xxix, 8, lv, 1 ; Jer. ii, 13 ; Matt. x, 42.
[9] See L. Bauer, *Volksleben im Lande der Bibel* (1903), p. 185.
[10] Lam. v, 4 ; Num. xx, 19.   [11] Judges v, 25.
[12] Is. xxviii, 2, 17, xxx, 30, etc.

crops were the frequent plagues of locusts.[1]  What these meant
to the inhabitants of the country can be seen in the numerous
names by which they were known.   In the Old Testament there
are eight or nine of these.[2]  Zoology has now demonstrated the
existence in Palestine of more than forty species, although not
all of these are injurious.   But it was to the injurious kinds
that unpleasant memories were attached.   There is the vivid
description in Joel, chapter i, where they appear in irresistible
numbers, as destructive as a hostile army.   Gardens and vineyards, fig-trees and olive-trees, were devoured by them ; [3] indeed, the other trees were not safe from them either, because
they destroyed the bark.   The terrible thing about them was
their numbers [4]—so great that they darkened the sun [5] and
covered the ground yards deep.[6]   " As numerous as locusts " is
a well-known proverbial expression.[7]   Deliverance from them
is brought about by a strong wind, which drives the whole
swarm into the sea.[8]   Even then there is a drawback ; an
intolerable stench may arise on the seashore from their decom-
posing bodies.[9]   Another danger, even greater if possible, is
threatened by smaller enemies—the midges, or gnats, whose
bites cause the chief illness of Palestine, malarial fever.[10]

Besides these smaller creatures, large animals became at
times a plague.   That Jahveh did not drive out the Canaanites
before the invading Israelites is said by a Biblical writer to have
been due to the fact that otherwise wild beasts would have
multiplied too greatly.[11]   And we are told that after the deporta-
tion of Israel from the northern kingdom such a multiplication
took place, to the detriment of the new colonists ; lions caused
great devastation among them.[12]   It is remarkable how much
we hear of lions in the Old Testament.   This animal is mentioned
about a hundred and thirty times—a clear indication that the
inhabitants of Palestine were familiar with it.   Safe lairs were
provided for it by the jungle growths along the Jordan banks,[13]

---

[1] 1 Kings viii, 37; Amos iv, 9, vii, 1.

[2] It is uncertain whether all these names denote different species of locusts
or only different stages of development.

[3] Amos iv, 9.   [Joel i, 7.—TRANSLATOR.]

[4] Nabum iii, 15.          [5] Joel ii, 10.          [6] Exod. x, 15.

[7] Judges vi, 5, vii, 12.          [8] Exod. x, 19.          [9] Joel ii, 20.

[10] See Canaan, *Aberglaube und Volksmedizin im Lande der Bibel* (1914), p. 4.

[11] Exod. xxiii, 29.          [12] 2 Kings xvii, 25.          [13] Jer. xlix, 19.

and it was apparently not till the time of the Crusades that the
lion was finally driven out of the country. Bears too were
dangerous, not only to the flocks,[1] but also to human beings—
at least to children.[2] The rage of a she-bear robbed of her
whelps was a proverb.[3] The bloodthirsty wolf was also a source
of dread.[4] He has his home in the desert.[5] The leopard, too,
known for his speed,[6] lurks by the wayside,[7] as do also numerous
snakes, that "sting with the tongue," [8] and were condemned, on
account of their cunning ancestor, to eat dust.[9] Special foes of
the vineyards are the foxes, that spoil the vines by their burrow-
ings.[10] Thus it is one of the familiar contrasts of the blessed
latter days that men will dwell in peace with the wild beasts.[11]
Sometimes, however, the latter are conceived as being entirely
extirpated.[12]

Palestine is exposed to a still more elemental plague than wild
animals. It is a centre of tectonic earthquakes. An earthquake that left a specially deep impression on the Hebrews was
that which took place in the reign of the Judean king Uzziah
(779–740). From it, indeed, other events were dated.[13] Another,
which took place in 31 B.C., is said by Josephus in one passage[14]
to have killed 30,000, in another passage [15] at least 10,000,
people. The terror caused by these earthquakes is still reflected
in the eschatological expectation, according to which Jahveh's
appearance in judgment is to be accompanied by earthquake.[16]

In respect of climate Palestine cannot be said to be less
favourably situated than other countries of the northern sub-
tropical region. Of course, its great differences of altitude
occasion great climatic variations. The coast-plain, the hill-
country, and the depression of the Jordan are usually regarded
as three separate zones. The coast-plain has, of course, a
higher temperature than the hill-country, while the temperature
of the Jordan valley is actually tropical. The clearest indication of how closely these separate zones touch each other is

[1] 1 Sam. xvii, 34.    [2] Amos v, 19; Lam. iii, 10; 2 Kings ii, 24.
[3] 2 Sam. xvii, 8; Hos. xiii, 8; Prov. xvii, 12.    [4] Ezek. xxii, 27.
[5] Jer. v, 6.    [6] Hab. i, 8.    [7] Hos. xiii, 7.
[8] Ps. cxl, 3; Job xx, 16.    [9] Gen. iii, 14; Mic. vii, 17; Is. lxv, 25.
[10] Song of Songs, ii, 15.    [11] Is. xi, 6–8; Hos. ii, 18.
[12] Lev. xxvi, 6; Ezek. xxxiv, 25.    [13] Amos i, 1; Zech. xiv, 5.
[14] *Wars of the Jews*, I, xix, 3.    [15] *Antiquities*, XV, v, 2.
[16] Is. xiii, 13, xxiv, 19; Ezek. xxxviii, 19; Mic. i, 4; Ps. xviii, 8, 16, cxiv, 4, 6.

found in the statement that on one occasion a lion which had wandered out of the Jordan valley into the mountains was caught in a snowstorm.[1] Snow is not uncommon on the mountains in Palestine. This might, indeed, be inferred from Old Testament expressions in which anything white is regularly compared with snow.[2] Modern observers tell us that on the average there is snow two years out of three, and owing to the lack of roads the snow is a considerable obstacle to traffic.[3] Even the winter rain is sufficient to prevent a gathering in the open air.[4] In summer, in contrast to the dreaded sirocco already mentioned, the north and west winds are welcomed. The coolness which they bring makes it possible to be in the open, especially toward evening,[5] so that, at that time, in genuine anthropomorphic fashion, God Himself can walk in His garden.[6] But these winds are also favourable to agriculture. The fresh breeze sweeps the chaff from the threshing floor,[7] and thus gives welcome assistance to the labour of the husbandman. The differences between the temperature of day and night are great.[8] The course of a single day resembles the course of the year, with its strict separation between summer and winter. In the sub-tropics these are the only two seasons. It may perhaps be said that these great variations of temperature were calculated to rear a physically strong race, capable of withstanding varying external conditions and suitable as colonists on foreign soil.

The passage in Deut. viii, 9, already quoted, might seem to imply that Palestine is rich in minerals. That, however, is not the case, and this one point alone shows how idealistic are the descriptions of the country in the Book of Deuteronomy. There was ore in North Edom (south of Palestine) and also in Lebanon. This must have been the source of the ore which David captured in great quantity from the Syrian cities.[9] In Idrīsī's *Geographia*, composed in 1154 B.C., we read that near Beirut there was a mountain with a mine of good and easily worked iron, from which large quantities were taken and delivered to the Syrian

---

[1] 2 Sam. xxiii, 20; 1 Chron. xi, 22.      [2] Exod. iv, 6; Num. xii, 10, etc.
[3] Schwöbel, *Die Landesnatur Palästinas* (1914), vol. i, p. 30.
[4] Ezra x, 13.      [5] Song of Songs ii, 17, iv, 6.
[6] Gen. iii, 8.      [7] Hos. xiii, 3; Ps. i, 4, xxxv, 5; Job xxi, 18.
[8] Gen. xxxi, 40. Properly this passage should from the context deal with conditions in Syria, but it is clear that the author is thinking of Palestine.
[9] 2 Sam. viii, 8.

cities.[1] There is an old mine east of Jordan on Jebel Mirad, near Burmeh, about six miles north of the Jabbok, where the brittle red or brown or violet sandstone contains a large admixture of iron ;[2] and in Rabbath-Ammon, the ancient Ammonite capital, the later Philadelphia, the iron sarcophagus of King Og of Bashan is said to have been shown.[3] This so-called " iron bed," [4] 12 feet broad and 27 feet long, must really have been a natural rock formation of basalt. The basalt from east of Jordan supplied the cities in that district with a really first-rate building material. It is largely used still for the manufacture of millstones.[5] East Jordan, Edom, Lebanon are the districts we have mentioned. That is to say, we have to pass round the frontiers of Palestine and even to cross them to find the stones of iron and the hills of brass of which Palestine is said to have been so full. Of much more importance practically to the inhabitants was the clay marl from the Jordan and also from the coastal district. This gave an abundant supply of material for the development of a prosperous pottery industry. And this clay, mixed sometimes with straw,[6] was also used, in the form of air-dried bricks, in house construction ; but this material was so little able to resist the unfavourable weather that we have here a sufficient explanation why certain towns and villages in the district have disappeared without leaving a trace. A more durable and more beautiful material was found in the limestone of the mountains. In prosperous times, when " the bricks are fallen down," houses were rebuilt of hewn stone.[7] The Dead Sea and its environs gave their own contributions—asphalt, salt, and sulphur. Of these the most important was salt, and it was so important that Ezekiel, who expects the water of the Dead Sea to be completely cured by the blessed effects of the future Temple well, makes special exemption, in the interests of salt-production, of several ponds and pools.[8] Crystalline salt is meant here—salt obtained by evaporation of the strongly saline water, and precipitated along

[1] *ZDPV*, vol. viii (1885), p. 134.
[2] Buhl, *Die sozialen Verhältnisse der Israeliten* (1899), p. 72.
[3] Deut. iii, 11.
[4] See Schwally in *ZatW* (1898), p. 127, *note* 3.
[5] Buhl, *Die sozialen Verhältnisse der Israeliten* (1899), p. 6.
[6] Exod. v, 7, 10–13, 16, 18.     [7] Is. ix, 10.     [8] Ezek. xlvii, 11.

the shores of the Dead Sea. At the southern end of the Dead Sea there is also actual rock salt, and through the slow, melting action of the rain natural formations are caused in which popular fancy sees petrified human beings, after the fashion of Lot's wife.[1] Josephus [2] gives some curious details as to how asphalt is obtained. "At many places the Dead Sea casts up black masses of bitumen, resembling both in shape and size headless bulls. These float on the water. The lake workmen approach and catch hold of these coagulated masses and draw them into their boats. When the boats are full it is not easy for the men to cut the masses in the boat loose from the rest, because they cling tenaciously till they are loosened by the menstrual blood of women and by urine. These are the only solvents. This asphalt or bitumen is used, not only in shipbuilding,[3] but also for medicinal purposes, and is therefore mixed with many medicines."

With regard to the flora of Palestine, there are, corresponding to the three climatic zones already mentioned, three sharply marked divisions. First, the tropical vegetation of the Jordan valley, which corresponds roughly to the vegetation of Nubia. Characteristic plants here are the date-palm, the papyrus, which grows abundantly in the small plain of Huleh, the true balsam plant, which is found in the neighbourhood of Jericho,[4] and a rubber-yielding acacia, etc. Second, the Oriental desert-vegetation, especially on the mountains of Judea, with its characteristic prickly bushes, several kinds of thistles, and quickly fading spring flowers—just the place for the breeding of cattle, mainly sheep and goats. Third, the Mediterranean flora of the coast and high ground, corresponding in the main to the flora of other countries bordering on the Mediterranean, with vines, figs, pomegranates, olives, luxuriant grain crops—in a word, the very soil and place for agriculture and silviculture. Of trees, which were mainly used for building purposes, we may mention the cedar and cypress, oak, terebinth, sycamore and wild olive, acacia, and white poplar. Of these the sycamore (mulberry fig-tree) is the commonest, just as the cedar is the finest. The same people who use hewn stone instead of bricks use cedars

---

[1] Gen. xix, 26.    [2] *Wars of the Jews*, IV, viii, 4.
[3] Of course for caulking.
[4] Josephus, *Antiquities*, XV, iv, 2 ; Pliny, *Natural History*, XVI, 135.

instead of sycamores.[1] Cypress wood was considered to be specially durable, and so in the picture of the noble ship used by Ezekiel [2] to represent the city of Tyre the beams are of cypress from Senir [3] and the oars are of oak from Bashan.[4] Externally the terebinth resembles the oak, but it is unrelated to it. It is akin to the so-called turpentine-tree, and is valued for its sweet-smelling wood, while its fruit, a small oval nut, yields an excellent edible oil. There were other trees, known and valued for their resin, especially the mastic and the styrax, and these resinous trees were so numerous and so generally grown that their produce formed a popular article of export, that of Gilead being most highly esteemed.[5] Apart from these trees, Palestine is not rich in timber. At the present day only 3·2 per cent. of the land west of Jordan is wooded.

The question arises whether conditions were not very different in this respect in ancient times. The frequent use of the ordinary word for 'forest' (*jaar*) in the Old Testament does not necessarily imply this, for this word often means not a wooded mountain, but simply low shrubs or a thicket; [6] and therefore we must not read too much into place-names like Kirjath-jearim ("Forest City"), Har-jearim ("Forest Mountain"), and others of the same kind. A more important indication is that Joshua could advise the tribe of Joseph, which had outgrown its allotted territory, to move higher up into the mountains and there clear the forest; [7] or that as late as Nehemiah's time there was a Jewish forester in the royal service to control the timber-supply around Jerusalem.[8] But an ancient testimony from a source [9] outside of the Bible is even more instructive. The hieroglyphic papyrus Golénisheff tells of the eventful

---

[1] Is. ix, 10.  [2] Ezek. xxvii.

[3] According to Deut. iii, 9, Senir is the Amorite name for Hermon.

[4] The northern portion of the country east of the Jordan.

[5] Gen. xxxvii, 25.

[6] *Cf.* the instructive parallelism in Is. ix, 18—thorns and thistles—forest thickets.  [7] Josh. xvii, 15, 18.

[8] Neh. ii, 8.  For the amount of timber around Jerusalem see Ezek. xxi, 2, where Ezekiel puts his threat against the city into the metaphor of a burning of the forests of the south.  Apart from a few olive-trees the surroundings of Jerusalem are at present quite bare.  For the disappearance of the timber there all those who besieged the city at various times must share the responsibility, not least the Romans.  See Josephus, *Wars of the Jews*, V, xii, 4.

[9] *Cf.* Guthe, *Palästina* (1908), p. 75 ff.

25

journey of an Egyptian, Wen Amon, to the seaport Dor in Palestine, which was well known in ancient times, the modern Tantura, 16 miles south of Carmel. The Egyptian had come to buy from the local prince building timber for Egypt, which has always been poor in timber. In his negotiations with the Prince he appeals to the fact that the Prince's father and grandfather had in former days sold timber to the Egyptians. These trade relations took place (according to the date given in the papyrus) about 1150–1100 B.C. As things are to-day, a deal in timber at that place would be simply unintelligible. On the heights, and still more in the valleys of the Carmel region, there is even now forest,[1] but no one could imagine that it could be exploited for trade purposes. In fact, timber is so scarce in Palestine that all strong planks and beams have to be imported, mainly from the Southern Alps. East of the Jordan one can still observe how the stock of timber—and in Bashan and Gilead there is still a considerable amount of forest—is being reduced by the bad management of the inhabitants. Where the ground has been ploughed one sees trees with their branches cut off, or their trunks seriously injured. They are in the farmer's way; therefore they must come down. As he has no tools with which to fell the trunk, he is reduced to destroying the tree by degrees. The smaller branches are cut off, and fire is laid to the stem once or twice, or as often as is necessary to weaken it to such an extent that it can be broken off.[2] In Lebanon it is a common thing to see herds of goats eating all the saplings, but no one interferes. The only forest that is now surrounded with a high wall in order to protect the young saplings is the famous cedar forest. All this seems to justify the supposition that in ancient times Palestine was more richly wooded than it is to-day. As late as the time of the English Richard Cœur-de-Lion we find mention of a forest in the plain of Sharon, north-west of Lydda, the last remnant of which are now the oaks north-west of Jaffa and west of Nablus. But even at the best the amount of timber in Palestine at any time cannot be put high. There never was anything that could be called a developed forestry or knowledge of timber, such as is found in countries where timber abounds. The best proof of the comparative

[1] Apart from the Nazareth district, Carmel is the only region west of Jordan that contains any timber to-day.　　　　[2] *Cf.* Is. vi, 13.

poverty of the country in this respect is the fact that very little wood was used for fuel.[1] Thorns [2] and thistles were used instead, and the usual fuel was animal dung.[3]

Taking together all that has been said, we are forced to the conclusion that agriculture and cattle-breeding are the chief possibilities offered by the country of Palestine. With regard to the latter, it should be added that we must not be misled by the frequent occurrence of the word (Hebrew *midbār*) usually translated " desert." It has been said that the Arabian Desert is so fertile that the owner of numberless camel herds could not wish for better land.[4] With some qualification the same could be said for the southern and western parts of the desert of Judea, especially in ancient times. For sheep and goats at least they afford abundant pasture.

After all, however, owing to the position of the country as a whole, the inhabitants of Palestine were forced to supplement their agriculture and cattle-breeding by turning to trade, and, indeed, to foreign trade. The geographical position of Palestine made it the natural passage-way for the great trade-caravans. From of old the land was intersected by the chief caravan-routes which connected Babylon and Egypt, the centres of civilization of the ancient world. One main route, coming from Egypt, ran along the coast to Carmel,[5] and divided there into two lines. One followed the coast as far as Phœnicia, the other crossed the plain of Jezreel to the Jordan valley, and either followed that valley northward to North Syria or turned eastward from the Jordan valley and ran to Damascus. The other great main route, starting from Elath on the Red Sea, ended at Damascus, traversing the entire land east of the Jordan. This was the so-called " king's high way " [6]—that is, military road. From it branch-roads led to the land west of the Jordan, of which one crossed the Jordan at Jericho, and led both to Judea and to Samaria. From the Red Sea there was also an independent branch, leading to Hebron in Southern Judea, where it met the route coming from the Nile delta. In short, all the conditions

---

[1] But see Num. xv, 32 ; 1 Kings xvii, 10 (though Sarepta is in Phœnicia) ; Is. xxvii, 11 ; Ps. cxx, 4.     [2] Eccl. vii, 6.     [3] Ezek. iv, 15.
[4] J. Euting, *Tagebuch einer Reise in Inner-Arabien* (1896), vol. i, p. 142.
[5] Hence called *via maris* during the Middle Ages. For its history see *ZDPV*, vol. xli (1918), p. 53.     [6] Num. xx, 17, xxi, 22.

were present to promote a vigorous transport trade. It is all the more important to emphasize this, because there are statements, even in the Old Testament,[1] which tend to give the impression that Israel was, so to speak, cut off from the world, and that the people lived entirely apart, far from all contact with the rest of mankind. Josephus also speaks of the exclusiveness that distinguished the Jewish manner of life, and points out that in olden days the Jews had no dealings with the Hellenes such as had the Egyptians, who introduced import and export trade.[2] But although they had no dealings with the Hellenes their intercourse with Orientals—Egyptians, Babylonians, Arabs, etc. —was all the more intimate, and for a proper understanding of the conditions of civilization we must see how impracticable it is to think of the ancient nations as isolated and how erroneous it is to imagine that the inhabitants of Palestine were dependent on themselves alone. Karl Ritter[3] long ago pointed out pertinently and with truth the two sides of the life of Palestine. " Made difficult of access by deserts and sea, secure among its rocks, ravines, and mountains, without charm, without wealth, without anything to attract foreigners . . . without navigable rivers or other natural advantages," Palestine could not but favour a native development exclusive of outside influences ; but, on the other hand, alongside of this isolating influence, Palestine allowed of " all-round intercourse with the then predominant civilizations of the ancient world, intercourse by trade and by language, by sea and by land, with the Arabian, Indian, Egyptian, and also with the Syrian, Armenian, Greek, and Roman civilizations, in the very centre of them, both in space and time." The striking thing in these words, which are perfectly accurate, is that in enumerating the civilizations in the midst of which Palestine lay geographically and chronologically there is no mention of Babylon. To Babylon would be ascribed to-day, and with justice, the first place in the list. But Ritter's Berlin lectures, out of which his work on geography grew, were delivered in 1820 and onward. At that time no one had any idea of the influences of Babylonia on Palestine. But the fact that something—in fact, a great deal—was even then known about the civilization of Palestine may be a warning to

---

[1] Num. xxiii, 9.    [2] *Against Apion*, I, § 12.
[3] *Erdkunde*, Part XV, § 1, p. 10 f.

those who maintain that all that was good in the civilization of Palestine came from Babylon. What Ritter says about an exclusively native development is in one aspect less than the truth. It understates the case. The separate regions, west of the Jordan and east of the Jordan in particular, and also the south and the north portions of the country west of the Jordan itself, were cut off from each other in such a way that the life of the people was restricted to very small districts. This is a point of great importance for the understanding of the political life of Israel. Not only did it retard and make difficult the growth of an enduring, unified state ; it made it ultimately impossible.

It was not merely material merchandise that entered the country by the trade-routes of Palestine. There is never commercial intercourse without an intercourse of thought, and whenever and wherever tangible wares are exchanged there is also an exchange of wares intellectual and spiritual. On the same roads by which wares entered the land wares went out of the land, wares—and men. The roads by which in bygone days the Hebrews themselves came into Palestine, on which foreign merchants were ever coming and going, bringing the produce of other lands, were the same roads by which at a later time the Jews themselves were to leave their land in order to barter wares in other lands and, getting more and more deeply engrossed in trade, to settle down permanently in them. The "door of the nations," as Ezekiel (xxvi, 2) once called Jerusalem as the point through which the caravans had to pass on their way to the world-market of Tyre, had only to be opened wider in order to become for the Jews themselves the door of departure to dwell among the nations. Thus the geographical position of Palestine became, ultimately, the reason for the Jewish *diaspora* (dispersion).

In one respect the country offered no encouragement to its inhabitants—viz., in respect of art. " The mountain tops unwooded and bare, the slopes only partially cultivated, the plains bare of flowers and grass except in spring, at other times brown and parched, all vegetation dead in autumn and winter—that makes a drab picture, uninteresting and wearisome to look upon. Whence was the husbandman in Palestine to learn what beauty means ? " [1] The writer of these words, who knows

[1] Benzinger, *Hebräische Archäologie* (1907), p. 19.

Palestine well, goes on to ask where in such a land was there room for the blithe deities of the Greeks ? The cheerful figures of the Olympians grew up on quite other soil. But in the religious sense also Palestine exerted its own peculiar influence. It is perhaps its very greatest educative peculiarity that, being a country whose fertility is so completely dependent on the rain, it casts its people absolutely and decisively on the goodness of heaven ; and those who are familiar with the conditions that prevail in rural life testify that the more dependent man is for the prosperity of his labours on nature and on natural phenomena against which he is absolutely helpless, the greater is the devotion to God that fills his heart. So the picture of the husbandman waiting for his "precious fruit" till it receives "the early and latter rain" (James v, 7) is the picture of the devout Palestinian saying to his God, " I will not let thee go, except thou bless me " (Gen. xxxii, 26).

# CHAPTER II

## CIVILIZATION IN PALESTINE BEFORE THE COMING OF ISRAEL

### I. INTRODUCTORY

WITHIN recent years there has been a great widening of the horizon for the study of the civilization of Israel. So long as our only sources of information were written sources, the limits of our knowledge were more or less determined by the dates to which it was believed these documents had to be ascribed, and both Criticism and Hyper-criticism took care that these dates should not be put too far back. Most of what could be said about the civilization of the people who were in Palestine before the coming of Israel was limited to what could be read between the lines of Hebrew literature. To-day the stones speak, and the splendid results of the first excavations in Palestine justify us in hoping for even finer results in the future. Outside of Palestine also, especially in Egypt, Babylonia, and Assyria, and more recently in Asia Minor, in Boghaz-Keui, the capital of the ancient Hittite Empire, the spade of the excavator has produced results which shed a completely new and undreamed-of light upon prehistoric Palestine.

While excavation work in Egypt goes back to the closing years of the eighteenth century and in Mesopotamia to the year 1843, that in Palestine is much more recent. It was English excavators who made the first successful start. Their first efforts, about 1860, aimed at the exploration of the foundations of Jerusalem, and down to the present time repeated attempts have been made to accomplish it. A change of purpose and a new start date from 1890, when, under the auspices of the Palestine Exploration Fund, Sir Flinders Petrie, already well known from his excavation work in Egypt, began to dig in Tell el-Hesi,[1] probably the ancient Lachish, the important fortress in the Jewish Shephela.[2] He was succeeded by Frederick Jones Bliss,

[1] Sir Flinders Petrie, *Tell el-Hesi* (London, 1891).
[2] Lachish was formerly a Canaanite royal city (Josh. x, 3). It was captured by Joshua (Josh. x, 31–32, xii, 11) and became Jewish (Josh. xv, 39). Rehoboam

31

who carried on till January 1893 the work so brilliantly begun.[1] In 1898–1900—in the interval his attention had been turned to excavations in Jerusalem—he undertook, along with R. A. Stewart Macalister, the examination of four other mounds in the Shephela—viz., Tell es-Safi, perhaps the ancient Philistine city of Gath,[2] Tell Sakarije, perhaps the Old Testament Aseka,[3] Tell Sandahanna, the ancient Mareshah,[4] and Tell ed-Judejide.[5] The next great success of the English work of excavation was the exploration, since 1902,[6] by Macalister of Tell Gezer, the oft-mentioned fortress Gezer [7] at the foot of the Jewish hill-country. Of German excavators Hermann Guthe,[8] under the auspices of the German Palestine Society, did successful work at Jerusalem in 1880, and their interest was renewed in 1902, when they chose as their sphere of work the north of Palestine, the plain of Megiddo. Ernst Sellin, then professor at Vienna, now in Berlin, supported by the Vienna Academy of Science and by generous private helpers, began in 1902 and 1904 to explore Tell Ta'annek, the Old Testament Taanach.[9] This beginning[10] was followed in 1903–5 by the excavation by G. Schumacher of Tell el-Mutesellim,

fortified it (2 Chron. xi, 9 ; cf. Mic. i, 13).  It was besieged by Sennacherib (2 Kings xviii, 14, xix, 8) and later by Nebuchadnezzar (Jer. xxxiv, 7).  King Amaziah of Judah was slain here by conspirators (2 Kings xiv, 19).  In post-Exilic days it is mentioned in Neh. xi, 30.

[1] F. J. Bliss, *A Mound of Many Cities, or, Tell el-Hesi Excavated* (London, 1894, 1898).

[2] For Gath see 1 Sam. v, 8, vi, 17, xxvii, 2 ff. ; 1 Chron. xviii, 1 ; 2 Chron. xi, 8 ; 2 Kings xii, 17 ; Amos vi, 2.

[3] Josh. x, 10, xv, 35 ; 1 Sam. xvii, 1 ; 2 Chron. xi, 9 ; Jer. xxxiv, 7 ; Neh. xi, 30.

[4] Josh. xv, 44 ; Mic. i, 15 ; 1 Chron. ii, 42, iv, 21 ; 1 Macc. v, 66 ; 2 Macc. xii, 35.

[5] Bliss and Stewart Macalister, *Excavations in Palestine, 1898–1900* (London, 1902).

[6] R. A. Stewart Macalister, *The Excavation of Gezer, 1902–5 and 1907–9* (3 vols., London, 1912).  More popular, *Bible Sidelights from the Mound of Gezer* (London, 1906).

[7] Formerly a royal Canaanite city (Josh. x, 33, xii, 12), it remained Canaanite till Solomon's father-in-law, Pharaoh of Egypt, conquered it and gave it to his daughter as dowry.  Solomon fortified it (1 Kings ix, 15).  It played a special part in times of war against western foes (2 Sam. v, 25), also in the days of the Maccabbees (1 Macc. iv, 15, vii, 45, ix, 52, xiii, 43, etc.)

[8] Guthe, "Ausgrabungen bei Jerusalem," *ZDPV*, vol. iv (1881), pp. 115–119, vol. v (1882), pp. 7–204, 271–378.

[9] Josh. xii, 21, xvii, 11, xxi, 25 ; Judges i, 27, v, 19 ; 1 Kings iv, 12 ; 1 Chron. vii, 29.

[10] E. Sellin, *Tell Ta'annek* (Vienna, 1904).

the ancient Megiddo.[1] From 1907 onward Sellin turned to the excavation of Jericho.[2] In the following year the American expedition sent out by Harvard University began work at the ancient city-mound of Samaria.[3] The English scholars pursued their work in the south-west, and began to dig in 1911–12 at Ain Shems, the ancient Beth-Shemesh, about halfway between Jerusalem and the coast.[4] Supported once more by the Vienna Academy, Sellin began in 1913 the excavation of Shechem,[5] near the village of Balata. All these undertakings have been temporarily stopped by the War.

It is no mere accident that almost all the excavation sites mentioned above bear the name "Tell." "Tell" in Arabic means " hill," and the " hills " in question are hills of a peculiar kind. Their profile, which is almost rectilinear, and the peculiar stair-like formation of their sides, distinguish them even at a distance from any natural formation, and give the impression that the site which they cover is artificial. In spring the fresh robe of green which covers them distinguishes them still further from the bare natural mountains. For the uninitiated perhaps the most surprising result of the uncovering of these mounds of ruins is the almost amazing certainty with which the several layers can be made out, so that in most cases we have to do with a perfectly

[1] Josh. xii, 21, xvii, 11 ; Judges i, 27, v, 19 ; 1 Kings iv, 12, ix, 15 ; 2 Kings v, 27, xxiii, 29 f.; 1 Chron. vii, 29 ; 2 Chron. xxxv, 22 ; Zech. xii, 11. See also *Tell el-Mutesellim*, by Schumacher (Leipzig, 1908).

[2] Sellin and Watzinger, *Jericho, die Ergebnisse der Ausgrabungen* (1913).

[3] The final report is still unpublished. (?)See, however, Kittel in *Theologisches Literaturblatt* (1911), Nos. 3 and 4, and Thiersch in *ZDPV*, vol. xxxvi (1913), p. 49 ff.

[4] Josh. xv, 10 ; 1 Sam. vi, 12 ff.; 1 Kings iv, 9 ; 2 Kings xiv, 11, 13 ; 2 Chron. xxviii, 18. See also Thiersch in *ZDPV*, vol. xxxvi (1913), p. 60 ff., and vol. xxxvii (1914), p. 61.

[5] *Anzeiger der philosophischen-historischen Klasse der kaiserlichen Akademie der Wissenschaften zu Wien* vom 4. März (Jahrgang, 1914, No. VII). Comprehensive accounts of recent explorations will be found in Hughes Vincent, *Canaan d'après l'exploration récente* (Paris, 1907) ; Thiersch, " Die neueren Ausgrabungen in Palästina " in the *Archäologischer Anzeiger zum Jahrbuch des Archäologischen Instituts* (1907–9) ; Gressmann, *Die Ausgrabungen in Palästina und das Alte Testament* (" Religionsgeschichtliche Volksbücher," 3rd series, No. 10), 1908 ; Thomsen, *Palästina und seine Kultur in fünf Jahrtausenden* ("Aus Natur und Geisteswelt," No. 260), 1908 ; Thomsen, *Kompendium der palästinensischen Altertumskunde* (1913), § 3 ; Karge, " Die Resultate der neueren Ausgrabungen und Forschungen in Palästina " (*Biblische Zeitfragen*, Nos. 8 and 9) ; Macalister, *A History of Civilization in Palestine* (1912) ; Kittel, *Geschichte des Volkes Israel*, 3rd edition, vol. i, Book I, ch. iv.

definite number of sites superimposed one upon another. For example, in Tell es-Safi three ' layers ' can be made out ; in Tell ed-Judejide four ; in Gezer five; in Tell el-Mutesellim eight ; in Tell el-Hesi there are eight layers and in addition three ' sub-cities.' The fact that the individual layers can be so sharply distinguished is not simply the result of violent destruction by an enemy's hand, although that was a common enough occurrence ; it is due to the perishable character of the ancient limestone used in building and to frequent carelessness in laying the foundation of the structures. The absolute necessity of good foundation-work in Palestine, where violent winter storms soften the ground far down, and where strong winds can raze a building to the ground, is familiar to us from the closing words of the Sermon on the Mount (Matt. vii, 24–27 ; see Ezek. xiii, 13 f.). How fatal, under such conditions, careless building can be was seen a few years ago at Nazareth, when twenty-five houses collapsed in a wild rainstorm.[1] Who knows whether the terrible sight exposed at an excavation in Taanach was not due to a similar cause ?   In a house that had collapsed was found the dead body of a mother (so at least it may be supposed from what follows), with five children, from four to sixteen years of age.   Beside the mother was a knife, and round her stood vessels such as were usually employed for containing food.   She was probably engaged in preparing a meal when the catastrophe happened.[2]   On the skeleton were the woman's trinkets and amulets in the usual array, not one of them missing, whereas, had it been a case of hostile attack, the robbers would hardly have failed to carry off the jewellery.   On the floor was found a bronze figure of the goddess who was supposed to be the tutelary deity of the unfortunate family !   When houses collapsed the clay of the walls, intermingled with the accumulated refuse in the streets—the dirt of the streets is proverbial in the Old Testament [3]—gradually formed a layer covering a whole civilization, and this furnished the foundation for a new one.   But how could the key be found for an approximately chronological determination of the various layers ?   It is an extremely fortunate case when one comes upon a find which can be exactly dated, like that, for example, at

---

[1] See Furrer, *Wanderungen durch das heilige Land* (1891), p. 308.
[2] Of course it might also have been an earthquake.
[3] *Cf.* Is. v, 25, x, 6 ; Mic. vii, 10 ; Zech. ix, 3 ; Ps. xviii, 42.

# CIVILIZATION IN PALESTINE

Lachish, a letter containing names known from other sources ; or that at Samaria, an alabaster vase with the name of Osorkon II of Egypt (874–853 B.C.).  Points more or less fixed, at least for the upper limit of time, are provided by numerous scarabs, whose age can to some extent be determined from Egyptian finds.  In other regards, in Palestine as elsewhere, the material of the utensils found—stone, bronze, iron—give the broad guiding lines for the chronology.  It should be noticed, however, that the absence of metals in Palestine caused flint to be employed to a somewhat later date than was the case elsewhere.  In particular, however, it is a thorough study of the development of ceramics, the comparison of it with foreign ware whose age is known, some of it imported and some of it imitated in Palestine, that supplies the chief means for the approximate dating of the layers to which the pottery fragments belong.  The sole indication that the earliest layer has been arrived at is when the excavations reach the bare rock.  This, however, takes us back to the Stone Age, and at this point the obscurity that broods over this prehistoric period begins to be illumined, even in Palestine.

## 2. THE PREHISTORIC PERIOD

The soil of Palestine, like that of other lands, has yielded an abundant harvest of hewn flints.[1]  The most ancient finds in the vicinity of Jerusalem, and on the high grounds on both sides of the Jordan, point back to the oldest period of the Paleolithic Age.[2]  Is it merely fortuitous that the legendary races of giants, the " Rephaim " of primeval days, of which Hebrew tradition speaks, are said to have lived just in those districts from which these finds chiefly come—viz., in the plain named after them, the plain of Rephaim, south-west of Jerusalem,[3] and in the region east of the Jordan [4] ?  The favourable climate seems to have permitted these early inhabitants to live in the open.  Judging

[1] See Blanckenhorn, " Über die Steinzeit und die Feuersteinartefacte in Syrien-Palästina," *Zeitschrift für Ethnologie*, vol. xxxvii (1905), pp. 447–468, and the same author in *ZDPV*, vol. xxxv (1912), p. 134 ff.

[2] They correspond to those called Chellean in the wider meaning.  The main type of the period is the almond-shaped axe.

[3] Josh. xv, 8, xviii, 16, etc.

[4] Deut. ii, 11, 20 f., iii, 11 ; Josh. xii, 4.

from finds belonging to the later Paleolithic Age,[1] human settlements spread gradually over the slopes into the valleys and over the coast-plain. The inhabitants were hunters and fishermen, living on their spoil. They lived in grottos and caves,[2] perhaps also in primitive huts made of branches or the skins of animals.[3] Examples have also been found of clothing made of skins stitched together as well as possible with bone needles. Spinning was of course as yet unknown. Pottery too was still unborn, nor is there any trace of agriculture or cattle-breeding. But perforated shells supply the most ancient witness of primitive adornment, which is, in this period, still of an amuletic character.[4]

The first appearance of smoothed or polished stone instruments, specially axes and chisels, is characteristic of the Neolithic Age, although perhaps not of the very beginning of it, for we have to reckon with a long transition period from Paleolithic to Neolithic. Pottery now begins, still entirely done by hand, without the use of potter's wheel and without ornamentation. The later Neolithic Period, with which, thanks to the excavations at Gezer, we are better acquainted, shows progress all round. The cave is still man's natural dwelling. The most extensive discoveries of such caves were made at Mareshah, but these subterranean dwellings with numerous apartments—in one single cave Macalister once found no fewer than sixty ' rooms '—cannot yet be definitely dated. Some of them are of tremendous size— up to 125 yards long by 26 high. At Gezer Macalister minutely examined forty-four of these caves. Everywhere there is evidence of how man by his art gradually adapts to his expanding

---

[1] They correspond to the Mousterian and Lower Solutrian or Eburnian, and those in the Antelia cave on Lebanon correspond to the Magdalenian, although, of course, they do not attain the perfection of the French Magdalenian.

[2] It has been usual to explain as " inhabitants of caves " (Hebrew *hôr* = cave) the name Horite given to the earlier inhabitants of Edom, who occupied the cavernous mountain land south of the Dead Sea (Gen. xiv, 6, xxxvi, 20 ff. ; Deut. ii, 12, 22). But this etymology is probably late and artificial. More correctly the name Horites should be connected with the Egyptian name for Southern Syria, Haru ; Hugo Winckler's identification of the Horites with the Charri (Aryans ?) of Boghaz-Keui is doubtful in view of the Semitic character of Horite proper names. (Kittel, *Geschichte des Volkes Israel*, 3rd edition, vol. i, p. 38 ff.)

[3] Their animals included the European bison, fallow deer, ibex, unicorn, Syrian bear, and the wild pig.

[4] Amulets are usually perforated in order to be worn on the person.

needs all that Nature presents to him in inadequate form. The walls of his cave-dwelling he adapts to his requirements with a stone axe. Intelligent thought is revealed in the formation of the approach to the dwelling. A few steps show the way, and the entrance hole is left as small as possible. Through it enters the only light, and so the cave is poorly illumined. In the cave-dwellings at Megiddo, however, lamps were placed in niches in the walls in order to light up the interior. Sometimes two or three of the caves in Gezer were connected with each other by a door. In a few cases it was clear that the inhabitants had taken the trouble to lead away the rainwater, while again in another cave was found a cistern which served to collect it. As a rule, the soft limestone offered no special difficulties even for primitive tools. In a cave at Gezer were found on a frieze, made by smoothing the upper part of the wall, primitive scratchings of animal figures, among them cows, buffaloes, and stags. These, however, could not stand comparison with corresponding figures of Phœnician or Spanish cave-dwellers.

We are also able to see the beginnings of house furniture. We find pieces of small flint knives, which might be used for cutting up meat, saws, scrapers, axes, and chisels ; also spinning-whorls, which show that the first attempts at spinning had now been made ; and, again, fragments of simple clay vessels, whose weight and porosity betray the want of skill. A primitive artistic impulse can, however, already be seen. Importance begins to be attached to the shape of the vessels, and the attempt is apparent to make the things used in daily life more pleasing by ornamentation. The manufacture is still entirely done by hand. The marks of finger pressure are still perceptible even on the better specimens. The ornamentation is at first a mere matter of lines—lattice form, ladder form, chessboard arrangement, and undulating lines—scratched in the smoothed clay with sharp or toothed stone tools, or laid on the clay with coarse red colour on a yellowish-white ground. In the custom of carrying several vessels connected by a cord we see the origin of the so-called string moulding as a common ornament on the neck of the vessels.[1] Halfway down, the original knob is replaced by the

---

[1] The cord holes on many of the vessels also show that it must have been customary to hang them up on cords.

waved moulding as a more comfortable handle. Stone plough-coulters and sickle-blades reveal the beginnings of agriculture, chiefly in cereals. For grinding the corn primitive mills were used, consisting of a circular stone across which a cylindrical stone was moved to and fro. The discovery of bones of sheep, goats, cows, and pigs, and perhaps asses, shows that some amount of cattle-breeding was conjoined with this agriculture. Sometimes the excavators found whole heaps of stones laid together in layers. They were probably used in the preparation of food. They were heated in the fire, and after the fire had gone out the meat or dough was laid on them, or they were thrown hot into the water in which the meat was to be boiled.[1] Others were probably used as missiles against wild animals or human enemies. It was therefore in all likelihood no accident that in Megiddo two hundred stones were found lying in a heap beside a fortified tower. For other defence against foes outside, so far as such defence could be necessary on steep, inaccessible rocks, there were low stone walls, with a rampart in front, consisting of hard-beaten earth and escarpment of stone. Such walls can only mean that the protection of the cave has been abandoned, and, as a matter of fact, here and there were found traces on the naked rock of primitive huts of clay, straw, and reeds.

The Neolithic inhabitants of Gezer were in the habit of burning their dead. Among Macalister's most interesting discoveries is a primitive cave-crematorium, whose chimney had been artificially cut through the rock. The smoke-blackened walls and the thick layer of ashes on the rock-floor, containing numerous remains of bones, still testify to the original purpose of this cave. Among the bones, in addition to many clay vessels which probably contained what was necessary to satisfy the material needs of the deceased—an indication that a certain continuance of life was ascribed to them—was found an animal bone, perforated, and therefore probably an amulet. A stone-idol found in the same cave, in all likelihood an amulet also, is almost similar to one found at Megiddo. Head and trunk are indicated merely by saw-cuts in the soft limestone. The head of a similar idol from Tell es-Safi is more clearly defined. As a further commentary

---

[1] For this custom *cf.* Jacob, *Altarabisches Beduinenleben nach den Quellen geschildert* (1897), p. 90.

on the religion of these Neolithic inhabitants we have bowl-shaped depressions, discovered on the rock-surface at various localities, especially at Petra,[1] the ancient Edomite city,[2] and the later capital of the Nabateans. In some places they are fewer, in others more numerous—in Gezer, for example, on a rock-surface 28 yards by 26 yards were found no fewer than 83 of them ; in Tell el-Judejide on a surface of 50 yards by 38 yards more than 100 of them. Some are narrow, some wide—in Gezer their diameter varies from 6 inches to 3 yards ; some are round, some rectangular, some deep, some shallower—the shallowest in Megiddo measure slightly over an inch in depth. Sometimes they are large enough to form pits and allow entrance to the cave situated beneath the rock. Frequently also they are interconnected by gutters. In short, there can be no real doubt that they are artificial, although there are also found irregular depressions which are most simply explained as natural formations. These depressions have been the subject of vigorous scientific discussion.[3] It is at least certain that they frequently served purely secular purposes, either as holders for rainwater or as mortars in which corn could be crushed, as oil-presses or wine-presses, as food troughs or washpots, or even as holes for posts used in the erection of huts. At the same time, in view of ethnological parallels it cannot be denied that in many cases they had some connexion with religious cult. The system of gutters already mentioned seems to indicate that they were occasionally used to contain drink offerings, which were meant to be thus conveyed to a being living inside the stone or in the ground.[4] It may have been a thirsty spirit of the dead—the dead were believed to suffer specially from thirst—or it may have been an actual earth-spirit [5] (and sometimes the distinction between the two is not clearly defined). This is, of course, a

---

[1] Cf. Dalman, *Petra und seine Felsheiligtümer* (1909), pp. 61, 81, 140, 222 ff., etc.

[2] For the identification of Petra and Selah (2 Kings xiv, 7) see Eduard Meyer, *Die Israeliten und ihre Nachbarstämme* (1906), p. 388 f. Gressmann's opinion, which is different, is given in his commentary on 2 Kings.

[3] Cf. Kittel, *Studien zur hebräischen Archäologie* (1908), and Gressmann, " Dolmen, Masseben, Napflöcher " in *ZatW* (1909).

[4] Judges vi, 20.

[5] Torge in *Seelenglaube und Unsterblichkeitshoffnung im Alten Testament* (1909) gives various references.

natural explanation in those cases where the depressions are found at the entrance to a burial cave, but even then it is still an open question how far the offering has a sacral character— *i.e.*, to what extent it is properly speaking a sacrificial offering. This interpretation may possibly find support in the fact that similar bowl depressions are found in the vertical surfaces of the stone. It is possible, as some have held, that these are imitations, made for votive purposes, of the original horizontal ones. Also the discovery of numerous pig bones in the Gezer cave beneath the rock with eighty-three such depressions shows that cave to have been a sanctuary. As in Babylon and in ancient Greece, so in Palestine the pig seems to have been a favourite sacrificial animal, and this perhaps explains why the later Hebrews, from their Jahvistic standpoint, considered the pig unclean ; just as in its turn the Christian Church discouraged the use of horseflesh because the horse was the sacrificial animal of our own heathen Germanic forefathers.

A similar significance has been given to those 'dolmens' which, though not so numerous in the country west of the Jordan, are found in great numbers east of the Jordan.[1] But the normal shape of these—two lateral stones, closed at the ends by stones, enclosing a rectangular space narrowing toward one end and covered by a stone slab or slabs [2]—seems to suggest that they are nothing but imitations of grave-chambers in the rock, " stonerooms," and were therefore originally graves. If this be really the case, it is natural that they are more numerous east of Jordan, because there are in that district no such rock-graves as occur in the country west of the Jordan. On the floor-stone we again find the bowl depressions, and in this case there can hardly be any doubt about their real purpose—viz., to hold drink offerings

[1] See the instructive conspectus of the megalithic monuments of Palestine given in the map contained in Vincent's *Canaan d'après l'exploration récente* (Paris, 1907), p. 395. See also Mader, " Megalithische Denkmäler im Westjordanland " in *ZDPV*, vol. xxxvii (1914), pp. 20–44. Von Gall in his *Altisraelitische Kultstätten* (p. 83 and p. 91) considers as dolmens the large stone heaps in the Valley of Achor (Josh. vii, 26) and near Ai (Josh. viii, 29).

[2] Hence the illusion of the altar table. In West Europe also some scholars insisted that the dolmens were Druidical altars, but the opinion is now abandoned. This does not mean, however, that the seven altars in the Balaam story (Num. xxiii, 1, 14, 29) may not have been ancient dolmens. Some scholars maintain that it is still possible to find proofs of identification.

# CIVILIZATION IN PALESTINE

to the dead. Certain stone cairns [1] may also be prehistoric graves, and the same is possibly true of the cromlechs (stone circles), of which we are reminded by the number of places in Palestine called Gilgal, which means "Stone Circle." [2] Even to this day the Bedouins to the east of Jordan are fond of forming stone circles round their graves, if only to keep away wild animals. But the fact that these same places were in historical times important places of worship makes it likely, when we keep in view the well-known conservatism that prevails in connexion with such matters, that these burial-places as such were centres of worship, and that it was therefore perhaps from them that the places in question derived their sacred character. I do not venture to decide whether the worship of the dead had any connexion with the menhirs, large unhewn or roughly hewn monoliths, mostly found, not together in numbers, but singly. They may just as likely have been looked upon as the abode of some other spirit than that of a dead person. It is difficult for us to grasp the idea of an intimate connexion between a stone and a *numen*, but it is quite common, especially in Near Asia. For example, Clement of Alexandria says of the Arabs in so many words that they worshipped the stone. Later on we shall find further evidences of such a conception, and its prevalence in Palestine down to this day is illustrated by an interesting statement by Sir Flinders Petrie in his *Researches in Sinai* (1906), p. 136. "A piece of ground between two houses in Bureyr was fenced in front with a stone wall, and all untrodden, tangled with weeds. At one side was a hollow in the wall, with a stone shelf across it, which at once reminded me of the shelves in

---

[1] " Burial mounds are called ' cairns ' when their constructive material consists of small stones " (Hastings, *RE*, vol. iv, p. 467*a*).

[2] In addition to the Gilgal between Jericho and the Jordan, the modern Tell Gelgul, there was at least one other, the Gilgal where Elijah and Elisha gathered their adherents together (2 Kings ii, 1, iv, 38) and whose degraded form of worship was later condemned by the prophets (Amos iv, 4, v, 5 ; Hos. iv, 15, ix, 15, xii, 11 ; see also Deut. xi, 30). It is uncertain whether this was the modern Gulegil, east of Shechem, or Gilgilja, south-west of Shiloh. But the stone circles of Palestine are not confined to the places named Gilgal. Graf von Mülinen mentions a cromlech in the Carmel district. " Nearly seventy yards in diameter, it is much larger than other monuments of the same kind. It consists of two rows of huge upright stones, many of them five feet wide and two feet in thickness. Through the centre of the circle ran a path paved with flat stones, perhaps a *via sacralis*." (*ZDPV*, vol. xxxi (1908), p. 39.)

similar hollows in the prehistoric temple of Hagiar Kim in Malta. On this shelf was a conical stone, the lower block of a Roman mill. I inquired why it was there, but no one would tell. We happened afterwards to find another such Roman millstone in the excavations at Lachish, but I left it at the camp when we closed the work. After travelling for some days, my donkey man (who was from Gimzu) turned the conical stone out of his saddlebag to my great surprise, and said that he could not take it all the way home. I asked him why he had taken it at all, and of what use such a stone could be, to make it worth while to load his beast with it for a two or three weeks' journey. The only answer I could get was that it was 'a good stone.' " [1]

Besides the megalithic holy places, and perhaps connected with them, there are other structures of a cyclopean nature—viz., prehistoric roads, like those which, as early as 1818, struck the English travellers Irby and Mangles near the ruins of Main in Moab, and those which were recently discovered by Graf von Mülinen in the Carmel district. The latter describes them as follows : " On both sides rose walls 4½–5 feet thick and more than 5 feet high. The outsides of these walls consisted of upright stones ; the space between was filled with smaller stones. The space between the walls—the actual road—was levelled, but not paved, and averaged about 19–22 feet in width. According to the nature of the ground where it ran it was as wide as 26 feet or narrowed down to 16 feet. In a few places it narrows to between 9–12 feet. The track was for the most part straight, even when considerable ascents had to be negotiated, so that it was in places exceedingly steep. In size and strength the road might even have served to protect armies marching along it. At certain places, where it opened up into what may have been settlements, it was a fortification as well. At other places we find, not double road-walls, but single boundary walls consisting of similar orthostats." [2] Graf von Mülinen claims as another prehistoric fortress the so-called "pulpit fortress," also in the Carmel district. [3] Similar structures are found east of

---

[1] *Cf.* Curtis, *Ursemitische Religion im Volkesleben des heutigen Orients* (1903), p. 90 ff.

[2] *ZDPV*, vol. xxxi (1908), p. 27. See also *ibid.*, p. 46, regarding the connexion of this road with a place of worship.     [3] *Ibid.*, p. 108 ff.

Jordan. The finest portion of wall still existing is in Irbid. The east side of the Tell, which is almost flat on the top, is faced by a wall of boulders about 105 yards long, and as high as seven layers of the Tell, the single stones of the wall being about 7 feet long.[1]

The first impression made by these megalithic and cyclopean structures is that they were the work of a tall and strong race of men. It is no wonder that the Israelites thought that their forefathers were giants.[2] They shared this belief with other races—some ancient and some still existing. The ancient Germans spoke of giants who in primeval days built the huge walls in the country,[3] and to this day the Kanuris, the inhabitants of Bornu in Central Africa, have stories like this : " The aborigines were idolaters, but Allah had bestowed on them a great stature. They were able to pluck the fruits from the highest palm-trees, and when they lay down to sleep their bellies towered up like hills. They could reach Lake Chad in a day and a half, and return next day with an elephant or a hippopotamus under their arm for supper. But Allah had endowed them with small intelligence, and they were poor fighters, so, when the people from the North and from the East came, they were defeated and driven into the wilderness."[4] Now, the bones found in the cave-crematorium in Gezer indicate a small race. Does that mean that we have to assume more than one race for these ancient times in Palestine ? There is another consideration that might lead us to answer this question in the affirmative. Whereas the ancient inhabitants of Gezer burned their dead, these dolmens, these megalithic structures, presuppose the custom of interment. It is, of course, not impossible that one and the same race may have alternately or even simultaneously practised the customs of cremation and burial, but in this instance it is surely more natural to suppose that it was a case of different contemporaneous or successive races. Judging from the bones discovered in Gezer, the cave-dwellers there were non-Semitic.

[1] Thiersch and Hölscher in *Mitteilungen der Deutschen Orientgesellschaft*, vol. xxiii (1904), p. 30.

[2] *Cf.* Num. xiii, 33 ; Deut. ii, 10 f., ix, 2 ; and see what was said about the Rephaim on p. 35, *supra*.

[3] *Cf.* Chantepie de la Saussaye, *Lehrbuch der Religionsgeschichte* (1905), vol. ii, p. 564.

[4] Hanns Vischer, *Across the Sahara* (1910), p. 564 f.

Also two representations of troglodyte heads in burnt earth, the one from Gezer and the other from Kirjath-jearim,[1] show very prominent jawbones. Must we, then, claim as Semites the creators of those megalithic structures, which are probably later than the small troglodytes of Gezer? This would be a hasty conclusion. These two facts—first, that dolmens are very frequent among the Indo-Germanic peoples, and, second, as is proved by recent Hittite discoveries, that Aryans passed through Asia Minor [2]—might rather suggest that Indo-Germanic peoples in their migrations left behind them traces of their passage through Palestine.[3] But there is also an argument against this supposition. Megalithic structures like those that have been mentioned cannot possibly date from a brief occupation by foreign nations : they must have been built by a people permanently settled in the country.[4] But can we assume that Indo-Germanic peoples were long settled in Palestine? Or must we suppose another race, a mixture of Hittite and other peoples of Asia Minor? These questions can only be stated. We have as yet no data for an answer. We should also require from the philological side an exact demonstration of the origin of the non-Semitic local names which are so numerous in Palestine.[5] Perhaps this is true even of the name Jordan itself. The only statement that can meantime be made with safety is that non-Semitic peoples were present in Palestine in prehistoric times. Were they there at the same time as Semitic peoples? This has been quite definitely asserted, especially for South Palestine, in reliance upon the witness of Egyptian monuments. It is perhaps correct, but we are still far from having achieved certain results.

There is equal uncertainty as to the dates of the period. The dates assigned to the beginning of the Early Neolithic Period

---

[1] See the illustrations in Hughes Vincent's book already mentioned, *Canaan d'après l'exploration récente*, p. 155 f.

[2] Especially the occurrence of the names of Aryan deities—Mitra, Varuna, Indra, Nasatya, in documents from Boghaz-Keui (Winckler, in *Mitteilungen der Deutschen Orientgesellschaft* for December, 1907, p. 51).

[3] *Cf.* Kittel, *Geschichte des Volkes Israel*, 3rd edition, vol. i, p. 46 ff.

[4] Graf von Mülinen in *ZDPV*, vol. xxxi (1908), p. 46.

[5] The name "Jordan" should perhaps be included among these. Cf. *supra*, p. 13 f. It recurs in Crete and in Elis. See Eduard Meyer, *Geschichte des Altertums* (1913), vol. i, Part II, § 476, note on p. 705.

vary from 10,000 B.C. down to 5000 or 4000. And the Late Neolithic has been put as early as 5000 or 4000 B.C. or as late as 3500. On the other hand, it is about the beginning of the third millennium that we find ourselves to some extent on historical ground, so that till that time there is at least 1000 years at our disposal in which to date those various early works of human construction which we have discussed.

## 3. THE HISTORICAL PERIOD

It used to be thought that, previous to the appearance of Israel in Palestine, only one stratum of population had occupied the country, but to-day opinion has changed, or, rather, scholars are now less hasty in giving an opinion. It is one of the most assured results of recent investigation that the ethnological conditions of Palestine in the days previous to Israel were far more complex than most people were inclined to believe.[1] Another opinion once prevalent must also be given up, that the names Amorites and Canaanites denote the same people, with perhaps the single difference that Amurru (the land of the Amorites) means specially the north of the country and Kinahna (Canaan) the south.[2] It is more probable that Canaanite and Amorite were names for successive strata of the population, and that the Canaanites were the later comers, who partly subjugated the more ancient Amorites, drove them to the hills, and as the dominant race gave their name to the country. Needless to say, the transitions from the Amorite to the Canaanite period are very indefinite, because the migrations which brought about the final conditions in which we find them are to be measured, not by years or decades, but by milleniums. And we must not be understood to be insisting on the strict meaning of these two names if in what follows we distinguish between an Amorite and a Canaanite period. We mean only that the historical period, anterior to the coming of Israel, falls for our purpose into two sections, and the dividing line between them falls, roughly, in the middle of the second millennium B.C.

---

[1] Cf. Böhl, *Kanaanäer und Hebräer* (1911), p. 19.
[2] It was Böhl who made this quite clear in the above-mentioned work.

# HISTORY OF HEBREW CIVILIZATION

## (a) The Amorite Period (up to c. 1500 b.c.)

Even those who claim that they can push back the coming of the Semites into Palestine to a time earlier than 2500 b.c. must at any rate admit that the country seems to have gained its character as an actually Semitic territory not earlier than about 2800 b.c.[1] What gave it this character was the invasion of the Amorites. The significance of the appearance of this people in Palestine becomes clear when we consider that the ruling race of Babylonia, at least at the time of the first Babylonian dynasty, the dynasty to which Hammurabi belongs, is to be claimed as Amorite. The question as to the origin of the Amorites must receive the same answer as the question about the origin of the Semitic peoples in general. The almost universally received opinion that the original home of the Semites was in the Arabian peninsula still has against it certain linguistic arguments, of which the most important are these. A primitive Semitic word existed for 'a perennial river,' and there is no such thing in Arabia, whereas each Semitic language has formed its own word for 'mountain.'[2] Must we not therefore rather seek the original home of the Semites in a plain traversed by rivers, such as Mesopotamia? And, seeing that the word for 'sea' is also probably a primitive Semitic word,[3] should their home not be sought in that part of Mesopotamia which is near the sea? If this be the case, we are brought to the neighbourhood of the Persian Gulf. According to the decision made on this question, opinions will also differ as to the region whence the Amorites came. Either they advanced from the Arabian peninsula northward, the main stream turning westward to Palestine and Syria, and a smaller one bending eastward to Mesopotamia; or, coming from the Persian Gulf, they advanced across Babylonia westward to Syria and Palestine. There are even grounds for the supposition that the wave of Semitic peoples came from the North southward.[4]

However that may be, we do not require to postulate this

---

[1] Kittel, *Geschichte des Volkes Israel*, 3rd edition, vol. i, p. 59.
[2] *Cf.* Guidi, " Della sede primitiva dei popoli Semitici " (*Atti della reale Accademia dei lincei*, Rome, 1879), and Jacob, *Altarabisches Beduinenleben* (1897), p. 28.
[3] Jacob, as above.
[4] *Cf.* Procksch, *Die Völker Altpalästinas* (1914), p. 11.

racial affinity in order to find the threads of connexion between Mesopotamia and the "Land of the West." The bond between them lay deeper. "Any state, spreading from the Euphrates and the Tigris and outgrowing its territory, is bound, if it is not to be surrounded on all sides by the civilizations of Europe and Near Asia, to try to reach the coast of the Mediterranean. This necessity commits it to the conquest of the Phœnician coast of the Mediterranean, and then, of course, in order to prevent an interruption of its communications, it could not afford to leave the hinterland, North-west Syria and Palestine, in other hands." [1] Lugalzaggisi, the first great conqueror who ruled over Babylon (*c.* 2600 B.C. at latest), boasts that his god had smoothed the way for him to the upper sea—*i.e.*, to the Mediterranean. Sargon of Agada (*c.* 2500), the story of whose exposure provides a parallel to that of Moses,[2] even "crosses the sea of the West, conquers the land of the West to its furthest bound, reduces it to one united sway, and erects his statues in the West"; [3] and his son Naram-Sin continues his father's work, and assumes the title of "King of the Four Parts of the World." Not long afterward Gudea of Lagash reports that he has procured cedars of Amanus (Song of Songs iv, 8)—*i.e.*, Antilebanon—for the building of his temple and great stones from the mountains of the Land of the West. Five hundred years later the Elamite Kudur-Mabuk, father of a Larsan king who was defeated by Hammurabi, is still found calling himself Master (?) [4] of the Land of the West, and the same title was assumed by Hammurabi himself,[5] in order that it might be an inheritance for his line.[6] All this is an illustration of the ancient Babylonian influences that were at work upon Palestine.

[1] Lehmann-Haupt, *Israel, seine Entwicklung im Rahmen der Weltgeschichte* (1911), p. 1 f.

[2] The text of the legend can be seen in *TBAT*, vol. i, p. 79: "My poor mother conceived me. She brought me forth in secret, placed me in a wicker basket [?], sealed the door with pitch, and gave me to the river, which was not large at the time [?]. Then the waters bare me up," etc.

[3] This probably refers to a campaign that came as far as Cyprus. King in his *History of Sumer and Akkad* (1910), p. 235, *note* 1, takes a different view.

[4] The translation of *adda* is not certain.

[5] His date is given by Eduard Meyer as 1958–16. Ungnad gives 2130–2088 B.C.

[6] *Cf.* the inscription of Ammiditana, *c.* 2000, *TBAT*, vol. i, p. 108, "King of the land Amurru."

But contemporaneously with these Babylonian influences, or even earlier, Egyptian influences were also at work. According to the Palermo Stone, there was an expedition of forty ships to bring cedarwood from Lebanon in the reign of Snofru, a king of the Fourth Dynasty (*c.* 2840–2680). From the mausoleum of Sahura in Abusir (south of Cairo) comes a relief representing the return of the Egyptian fleet from the Lebanon district in the days of the second king of the Fifth Dynasty (*c.* 2680–2540 B.C.). Prisoners, recognizable as Semites by their beards and hair, as also by the loincloths reaching to their knees, are being forced by the Egyptian crews to join in a shout of homage to Sahura. Under King Pepi of the Sixth Dynasty (*c.* 2540 B.C.) we hear of an actual expedition against Palestine, concerning which the tomb-inscription of a certain Wen, a creature of the King,[1] contains the following : " When it was reported that there was a rebellion among the barbarians of the Land of the Gazelle's Nose,[2] I sailed over in ocean ships with these troops, and I landed at the end of the heights of the mountain range,[3] in the north of the sand-dwellers." [4] And even earlier expeditions, spoken of in the same tomb-inscription, cannot have halted in the territory of the " sand-dwellers," against whom the expeditions were directed, because we are told *inter alia* that fig-trees and vineyards were destroyed and fortresses dismantled. This must refer to Palestine, and we ought to be grateful for the reference, because this passage is probably the earliest documentary proof we have of the culture of figs and vines in the country. How far these expeditions were attended by lasting results we do not know. From Gezer we have at least one scarab from the time of the Sixth Dynasty. It was not until the Twelfth Dynasty that the claims to the overlordship of Palestine were more vigorously pressed. It is in this period that we come upon the already-mentioned tale of Sinuhe,[5] which presupposes a busy commerce between Egypt and Palestine.

---

[1] *TBAT*, vol. i, p. 234 f.

[2] Palestine probably owed this name to the Carmel promontory.

[3] Does this mean Dor, south of Carmel, where, as the papyrus Golénisheff tells us, Wen Amon the Egyptian landed about 1100, or is it Haifa or Jaffa ?

[4] This is a name for the Bedouins in the north-east of Egypt.

[5] Of course, for our purpose it makes little difference if that tale reflects the conditions of the time, two centuries later, in which it was written down. See *supra*, p. 16, *note* 7.

# CIVILIZATION IN PALESTINE

In his flight Sinuhe meets a Bedouin chief, who knows him from a former stay in Egypt.[1] The prince under whose protection he finally settles has Egyptians at his Court, who give him a favourable account of Sinuhe, and this prince mentions, as one of the advantages to be derived from a stay at his Court, that Sinuhe will there hear Egyptian spoken ! Further, there seems to have been a steady messenger-service between north and south. Sinuhe boasts that the messenger who travelled northward from Egypt or went southward to the Court stayed for a time with him. And even in the foreign land he does not fail, when occasion offers, to praise his Egyptian god Month. Thus completely does he continue to be an Egyptian even when he is in Palestine, and yet he succeeds so well in winning the regard of the Semitic people around him that on one occasion, when an enemy appears, " every heart is on fire for him." Two generations later, under Sesostris II, the grandson of Sinuhe's king Sesostris I, an Asiatic Bedouin sheik (whose name Absha has quite a Hebrew sound),[2] with thirty-seven of his subjects, brings green eye-salve to Egypt, either as an article of commerce or as a token of homage. To the same period belongs a monument of an Egyptian official found in Gezer. A natural inference from this would be that there was a regular suzerainty of Egypt over Gezer. Judging from grave finds, Gezer seems at that time to have contained an actual Egyptian colony. To these people would belong the numerous scarabs which date from the Twelfth Dynasty. The mighty Sesostris II, of this same dynasty (c. 1887–1849 B.C.), penetrated even further into Palestine. The inscription of one of his adjutants says : " His Majesty marched northward in order to overthrow the Asiatic Bedouins. His Majesty reached a region called Sekmem. His Majesty returned safely to his palace, after Sekmem had fallen, along with wretched Syria, while I led the rear guard." [3] It is tempting to see in this otherwise unknown Sekmem the well-known Shechem. But it occupies so central a position in Palestine that, if it actually fell on this occasion, the expedition of Sesostris would be still more significant. No permanent advantage resulted from these campaigns, even although the Twelfth

---

[1] *Cf.* Abraham's stay in Egypt, Gen. xii, 10 ff.
[2] *Cf.* Abishai, also Abshai, 2 Sam. x, 10, 1 Chron. ii, 16.
[3] *TBAT*, vol. i, p. 235.

Dynasty gained other successes against the Asiatics. The Thirteenth Dynasty was far inferior to it, and itself fell (*c.* 1700) before the Asiatic Shepherd-kings, the Hyksos.[1] They poured over the land from the North, and forced it under their powerful sway, and the kinship of these Hyksos with the Palestinians gave additional encouragement to mutual influences.[2] The excavations of Gezer have given us scarabs of the Hyksos King Chian, who assumes the title " Ruler of the Lands."

In this way, in continual alternation, the claims of Egypt and Babylon to the possession of the country of Palestine cross each other, and this means, of course, that influences emanating from both of these great world-powers affected its civilization. Naturally Egyptian influence was stronger in the south, and that of Babylon in the north. Generally speaking, however, during the Amorite period the balance was distinctly in favour of Babylon. It is difficult to make out how far there was at this time an actual suzerainty of Babylon. Nominally it did exist, although it was from time to time challenged by Egypt. Whenever the strength of the great powers was crippled it meant an opportunity for the local potentates, who pursued their petty, selfish interests inside their fortified cities and behind their castle-walls. On the whole, however, they were under the wholesome pressure of a certain diplomatic etiquette, and were perhaps also moved by common interest, and they seem to have got on tolerably well with each other. " One country handed me on to another," says Sinuhe in his itinerary, as if the best relations existed between the various territories.

None of these foreign civilizing influences, however, is comparable with that of the powerful personality of Hammurabi. In this respect he reminds us of Alexander the Great, and there was an additional element in his favour. To the peoples of

[1] It is perhaps safer not to call the Hyksos Semites. The name is patently non-Semitic. According to the latest opinion the Hittites, who invaded Babylonia in the eighteenth century, and the peoples of Asia Minor, who commenced their migrations about that time, were the actual originators of the movement which began in the north and east and spread over Syria and Palestine and thence over Egypt. *Cf.* Kittel, *Geschichte des Volkes Israel*, 3rd edition, vol. i, p. 91 ff.

[2] Eduard Meyer (*Geschichte des Altertums*, 3rd edition, vol. i, Part II, § 306, p. 319), on the basis of the isolated statement in Num. xiii, 22, which connects Hebron with the Egyptian Tanis, a supposed capital city of the Hyksos, suggests that Hebron was a centre of their power.

Palestine he was not, like Alexander, a complete foreigner, but an 'Amorite,' and therefore related to them by race, even although there were many with whom he did not come into personal contact. His most brilliant achievement, a great testimony to the justice of which he boasts, is his law-code,[1] which, after nearly 4000 years, was brought again to the knowledge of an astonished world when in 1901 the French excavations in Shushan disclosed the great boulder of diorite with a copy of the law of Hammurabi. It is not Hammurabi's work in the sense that it was something completely new. Indeed, in its details it is evidently only the writing down of an existing law of custom, but, viewed as a whole, it is Hammurabi's achievement. It reduces the law of custom, distinctly if not quite completely, to a systematic form which reveals a genius for organization in the service of humanity, as well as an amazingly developed sense of justice, deeply felt, though of course conditioned by its time. " In order that he who is strong may not do violence to him who is weak, to guide widow and orphan on a way that is right, I have written my precious words on my monument in Babylon, in Esagila, in the temple whose foundation is as firm as heaven and earth, in order to give justice to the land, to give law to the land, and to lead the oppressed by a right way "—thus Hammurabi expresses himself in the epilogue of his inscription. His law is adapted to the conditions in Babylon, and these were very different from those in Palestine. Hammurabi's code is meant for a people that has outgrown the stage of simple natural life, and indicates a time when trade and industry had permeated all classes.[2] But it is abundantly clear from the most ancient code of Israel that Palestine was far from being unaffected by Hammurabi's law, whether that law entered in actual copies into a land politically dependent on Babylon or whether some of its provisions found their way thither in the free oral exchange of ordinary life. The law of Hammurabi is only one part, by chance known to us, of the

---

[1] Translation of it in *TBAT*, vol. i, pp. 140–171 (Ungnad). See also Winckler, "Die Gesetze Hammurabis" (*Der Alte Orient*, vol. iv (1906), p. 4); and the same author's *Die Gesetze Hammurabis in Umschrift und Übersetzung* (Leipzig, 1904).

[2] See Hans Fehr, *Hammurapi und das salische Recht, Eine Rechtsvergleichung* (1910), p. 2 f.

intellectual civilization with which the Palestine of that time must have been fertilized by Babylon. How valuable this was is only fully apparent when we come upon certain facts of later times. To explain the readiness with which these Babylonian influences were received we may again point out the close affinity which connected the Palestinians of the time with the dominant strain in Babylon. The contemporary Egyptian influences seem to have been confined to the periphery of the country and to have affected more the externals of life. This impression is confirmed by the excavation results, so far as these bear on the period before us. They also allow us a deeper look into the cultural life of the time.

Caves have ceased to be dwellings—at least, for the living : they have become the resting-places of the dead. They are also used as cisterns, as storerooms, as places of refuge in times of need.[1] The ruins of the prehistoric settlements have been levelled and used as sites for new dwellings, because the natural advantage of the old sites, the open high position or the bluff (where two or three sides are steep and only the fourth side abuts on the ridge which forms the site), were unwillingly given up.[2] The new dwellings are stronger.[3] There is, of course, a very great difference between the dwellings of the common people and the castles of the king and his nobles. It is mainly in the latter that the actual progress of civilization can be judged, and it is in them, too, that we see clearly the foreign influences that were at work, both Babylonian and (in the south) Egyptian. The people still build their frail houses and huts of clay, using no stone save for the foundation. It was unhewn stone, and the joints were filled in with smaller stones. In other cases, as is shown by the example from Jericho, handsome structures could be built with unburnt clay. But they do not stop at unburnt clay. Bricks of various sizes [4] were baked, and stamped with a sort of factory mark, a pottery mark in the

---

[1] Judges vi, 2 ; 1 Sam. xiii, 6.

[2] Examples of bluffs are Megiddo, Gezer, Tell es-Safi, Samaria ; examples of isolated heights are Taanach, Lachish, and Jericho. See Karge, *Die Resultate der neueren Ausgrabungen und Forschungen in Palästina*, p. 28.

[3] On the subject of defensive building generally see Billerbeck, *Der Alte Orient*, vol. i (1903), p. 4.

[4] 'Standard' sizes were, of course, made also (Sellin and Watzinger, *Jericho*, p. 58).

form of some letter.[1]  In order to strengthen these clay structures wooden beams, when such were available, were fitted in between the various layers of clay.  That, at least, is the simplest explanation of the large amount of wood-ash found in certain ruins.  Apart from these, the chief building material for castles is plain stone, sometimes also brick, so that a brick wall crowns an underbuilding of stone, as, for example, in the castles at Megiddo.  The ability to work stone shows perceptible development.  In the so-called Intermediate Castle of Megiddo the underbuilding is composed of three layers of stone.  The lowest layer is made of flat quarrystones laid almost horizontally. The stones of the second layer are tilted to the left, those of the top layer to the right, so that the result is a structure comparable to the Roman *opus spicatum*.[2]  There is another type of building, using polygonal stones, of which we have a specimen in the West Castle at Taanach.  The smooth surface and the splendid preparation of the stones betray the skill now reached. Even more complicated work was undertaken where special strength was desired, as, for example, on the west side of the same castle.  The retaining wall has been built in four receding stories.[3]  It was desired to make the west side of the more recent castle in Megiddo specially strong.  This was achieved by means of a moat 6 yards deep and $4\frac{1}{2}$ feet wide at the top. In this same castle we also see an advance in technique in the increased strength and greater regularity of the stone work, and the clay of the brick superstructure is better worked than in former times.  Special mention should be made of a primitive vault, discovered at Megiddo, with something of the pointed arch in its shape.  It is all the more remarkable because, although it has been built without the assistance of any other tool than a bronze or flint hammer, it is as strong as any building of our own day.  It has sustained for centuries, up to the moment of excavation, a weight of roughly 135 tons.[4]  This once more reveals unmistakable Babylonian influence, and recalls the conical vaults at Sippar.[5]  The vault covers a burial chamber, and there is a second one, the walls of which are consolidated into a barrel-shaped vault, which ends in a huge stone with a

---

[1] See the illustration in Vincent, *Canaan d'après l'exploration récente*, p. 33.
[2] Cf. *Tell el-Mutesellim*, vol. i, p. 12.     [3] Sellin, *Tell Ta'annek*, p. 48.
[4] *Tell el-Mutesellim*, vol. i, p. 14 f.     [5] Vincent, *op. cit.*, p. 260.

conical opening in the centre. Although this opening may in some cases have been intended to permit the offering of food to the dead, it also hints how attempts were being made to solve the problem—otherwise neglected—of illuminating an interior. There was found in Taanach a clay tube or pipe tapering from both ends toward the centre, and the explanation given—probably correctly—on the basis of analogous examples from Babylonia and Assyria, is that it was meant to admit light from above.[1] Openings in the walls for windows hardly seem to have been known at this period. The roof of the castle must have been flat, and consisted of wattles and hard-beaten earth laid upon wooden cross-beams resting on pillars of stone or wood.[2] The floor consisted of hard-trodden earth, and the fireplace was a depression in it lined with stone.

The castle-buildings, with their dwelling-rooms and store-rooms, were usually grouped round an open courtyard. To our ideas, the dimensions of the rooms were more than modest. The West Castle of Taanach is instructive in this respect: 20 yards long and 23 yards broad, its superficial area is about 460 square yards. This is divided into nine rooms (apart from a small vestibule), a long rectangular corridor, and a large main space with a water-cistern in the centre (probably the castle court). Sellin, who excavated the castle, estimates that the average superficial area of these rooms is not quite 3 square yards.[3] This seems to be an error, but even the corrected result, between 4 and 5 square yards,[4] is still surprisingly small.[5] If the great ones of the city were content with so little, we can only imagine what was considered sufficient for the common people.

The art of masonry, which produced such creditable results in the castles, shows to still greater advantage in the erection of the city-walls. The growth of the community in such centres as Megiddo and Taanach made it necessary to carry the city-wall over the edge of the hill and down to the foot of it. This, of course, necessitated a greater strength in the construction of the wall. In return there was the advantage that it could be

---

[1] Or was this pipe a primitive chimney? *Cf.* the chimney of the cave-crematorium, *supra*, p. 38.

[2] See Sellin and Watzinger, *Jericho*, p. 45.      [3] *Ibid.*, p. 47.

[4] Kittel, *Geschichte des Volkes Israel*, 3rd edition, vol. i, p. 168, *note* 1.

[5] I make it even larger. On Sellin's plan the walls of the rooms vary from a little more than 2 yards to 5 yards at most.

supported by the hill, and it naturally assumed a terraced form. In Megiddo the actual wall consisted of a terraced brick structure 7 or 8 yards—in some places 9 yards—in thickness. The foot of the wall rested on a projecting base of unhewn boulders, these also being arranged in receding steps. In front of this base was a glacis consisting of small stones and clay trodden hard and covered with a coat of plaster. This arrangement not only made an approach more difficult ; it also facilitated the shedding of water and kept the wall dry. The entire structure was topped by a ring of stone, so that the wall when complete had the enormous height of 34 feet. To strengthen it still further, buttresses tapering upward were superadded, and at intervals rectangular towers with very massive foundations projected, affording a safe position for its defenders, who were also protected by battlements and palisades. In Gezer towers of this kind stood at regular intervals of 30 yards. In Lachish there were even bastions containing enclosed spaces. A different type of construction, going back perhaps to Egyptian models, is seen in the circumvallation of Jericho. In the main it dates from this period—perhaps a little later [1]—and the structure is dominated by one idea, that of defensive strength. The wall is double. There is a strongly built inner wall (about 4 yards thick) and, running parallel to it at a distance of 4 yards, an outer wall not so thick, both consisting of clay bricks resting on a foundation of quarrystone.[2] There are, besides, turret fortifications.[3] When we remember that the higher (the inner) wall rose to a height of 100 feet above the valley we can understand the fear that was felt by the invading Israelites when they saw fortified cities of this kind " as high as heaven."[4] And then there were the gates and bolts.[5] The number of gates was kept as low as possible—Jericho seems to have had only one—and they were so constructed as to make it as difficult as possible for any enemy to enter the city. The excavations in Gezer have revealed two gates, one of which, broken into the wall at right angles, passes through a long tower. The other, although straight, has an ascending entrance

---

[1] The foundations of the interior double wall extended beyond a bed of brick belonging to an older building.
[2] Sellin and Watzinger, *Jericho*, p. 21 f.     [3] *Ibid.*, p. 23.
[4] Deut. i, 28, iii, 5 ; Num. xiii, 28.     [5] Deut. iii, 5.

way, 14 yards long, but only 3 yards wide. In construction also it shows remarkable features. The gate-wall is of stone, lined with air-dried bricks, and on the inside this lining is in places panelled with large stone blocks. The spaces between these form niches, which probably were meant to serve a defensive purpose.[1]

We ought, however, not to entertain exaggerated ideas of the area thus enclosed by the walls of a city. In those cities which have already been excavated it in no case exceeds 225 acres, and even these dimensions belong to a later period. The site occupied by ancient Jericho is only a little larger than that of the Colosseum at Rome.[2] Such dimensions are intelligible only if we conceive the streets and lanes to have been extremely narrow. But they are in keeping with the dimensions already given for the dwellings ; and it is well known that the cities of classical antiquity were in this respect very similar. Troy could have stood in one of the courts of the Louvre !

One of the main requirements of any settlement in Palestine was the water-supply. Of special interest in this connexion is the plan of a tunnel discovered in Gezer. It was about 76 yards long, and led through the rock of the eastern slope to a spring which, now dry, lies 42 yards below the present level and 30 yards below the then level. Niches at the side were used to hold lamps, and the path must have been much used. The eighty steps leading down to the well are greatly worn. It is an amazing piece of work, especially when we remember that it must have been carried out with nothing but stone tools. It is no wonder that it so greatly impressed the later inhabitants of Gezer that they were wont to say that the ancient Flood began from the hill of Gezer and returned to it at the close. Nor was this Gezer tunnel the only one of its kind. From the ancient keep of the Jebusites on Mount Zion the " way of Ophel " led to the Virgin's Spring,[3] and there were similar arrangements at Jibleam [4] and at Megiddo.[5] In Jericho the outside wall enclosed the abundant spring Ain-es-sultan.

---

[1] This arrangement of niches recalls Ezekiel's description of the gates of the Temple at Jerusalem (Ezek. xl, 6 ff.).
[2] Sellin and Watzinger, *Jericho*, p. 21.
[3] See *ZDPV*, vol. xxxvi (1913), pp. 10–14.
[4] Palestine Exploration Fund, *Quarterly Statement*, 42 (1910), p. 107 ff.
[5] *Tell el-Mutesellim*, vol. i, p. 161 f.

# CIVILIZATION IN PALESTINE

The efforts of private individuals to secure water are seen in the numerous cisterns, and these not only collected water, but became in course of time the resting-place of many objects of antiquarian interest ; jugs, bowls, female trinkets, and all the other things that fell into the cisterns when people were fetching water have been faithfully preserved at the bottom !

Next to the water-cisterns, the most important domestic requirements were the oil- and wine-presses. They leave no room for doubt as to the occupation of the inhabitants. They are evidently engaged in agriculture, and it will be recalled that the travel report of Sinuhe [1] and the report on the campaigns of King Pepi [2] both make mention of vines and fig-trees, of oil and grain. Where possible, a depression in the rock was used for these presses. Where that was not available, a stone was hollowed out, and the liquid was conducted through a hole into several settling basins, and from these direct into a jug-shaped cistern for permanent storage.[3] In other cases the liquid, when ready, was stored in jugs. Jugs of a larger size, or, if necessary, cisterns or entire rooms, were used for storing grain. The corn-mills were, in principle, the same as they had been [4]—flat slabs of basalt curved at one end, and rolling-pins of basalt or of hard limestone of elongated oval shape. Others of daintier construction were dye-mills of black limestone, consisting of a lower part in which a conical hole had been worked and an upper part with a round plug so carefully ground to fit the hole that the colour meant for ceramic work could be ground very fine after the addition of some liquid.[5]

Cooking-stoves have been found in great numbers. The most ancient ones, made of thick, badly mixed, red-brown clay, and built in with stone, are nothing but round containers. Into these were put not only the fuel, but also the material to be cooked. To this day the fellaheen construct their stoves in this same primitive form. One of an exceptional kind was found in Taanach, with a double wall, the space between the walls being meant to hold the fuel.[6] Another of peculiar con-

---

[1] See *supra*, p. 16.    [2] See *supra*, p. 48.

[3] For example, the carefully prepared oil-cistern in the North Castle at Megiddo (*Tell el-Mutesellim*, vol. i, p. 73).

[4] See *supra*, p. 38.    [5] *Tell el-Mutesellim*, vol. i, p. 64 f.

[6] Sellin, *Tell Ta'annek* (1904), p. 49.

struction was found in Lachish. Its inside width was more than 6 feet and the wall was 27 inches thick. It contained narrow passage pipes, branching in all directions, opening below into the fire chamber and conducting the hot air upward inside, so that the heated air was protected against external cold, and the glowing heat within was concentrated as much as possible.[1] The purpose of this stove is not quite clear. Close beside the ovens were frequently found utensils made of basalt, evidently the furnishing of a kitchen, or perhaps of a pottery: hollowed-out basalt blocks used as mortars, etc., cooking utensils of dolorite, with their round cavity resting on a shaped base with three or four feet.[2] That considerable demands might sometimes be made on a kitchen in those days is evident again from Sinuhe's report: "My daily food was bread, and I had wine every day, boiled meat and roast goose: also game from the desert, caught in snares and brought in for my use, besides what my own hunting dogs caught. They made for me a great deal of . . .[3] and milk prepared in all sorts of ways." A burial-urn containing leg-bones of poultry, as well as the bones of a child, was found in Taanach, and the nature of this provision for the dead testifies to the use of poultry as food.

With regard to the small articles found, one is struck by the large extent to which flint articles continue to appear well into the Bronze Period. There are scrapers, knives, chisels, saws, hammers, etc. Evidence of improved skill is shown by the manner in which a chisel edge has been sharpened. Weights, evidently belonging to a weaving loom, are of stone (basalt or limestone or brown ironstone), and of course also of clay. The spinning-whorls too are of stone or clay, sometimes of bone. This is clear evidence that spinning and weaving have been taken up, and if we may draw a conclusion as to the customs then prevailing in Palestine from the clothing of the caravan going to Egypt under the leadership of the before-mentioned Absha [4] it was no longer merely a loincloth that was worn, but long garments reaching from the shoulders to the knees, made of dyed cloth trimmed with braid and tassels. Actual shepherds

[1] Thiersch, *AA* (1908), p. 16 f.    [2] Cf. *Tell el-Mutesellim*, vol. i, p. 65.
[3] The word is wanting in the papyrus. The copyist could not make out the word in the sheet he was using. (*TBAT*, p. 213, *note* 2.)
[4] *Supra*, p. 49.

and land-workers, as may be gathered from Sinuhe's account, may, like the modern fellaheen, usually have been content with a sheepskin—the garment in which they were also laid to their last rest.[1] Sewing was still done with needles made of animal bone. Bone needlecases have also been found; indeed, bone is still a favourite material for all sorts of tools. But bronze is the usual material, and needles, nails, gimlets, studs, chisels, knives, and ploughshares, all of bronze, have been found in great numbers. The weapons also are either of stone or bronze. Along with arrowheads of flint are found others made of bronze, some of them with deadly barbs: also bronze shears and swords, and battleaxes shaped like halberds. In addition to these, the club was still a common weapon. It is shown in an Egyptian representation[2] of the siege of Netia, probably a city of Palestine, as the weapon of its Semitic defenders, and in the illustration of the caravan of Absha (already mentioned more than once) we find it along with other weapons, such as a carved wooden javelin. Mention may also be made here of three other objects in the same representation not found among the results of the excavations in Palestine—viz., waterskins, ass-saddles, and zithers.

A new chapter, and an extensive one, is opened when we turn to ceramics. The time has not yet come to write the detailed history of the development of this art in Palestine. But, thanks to the discoveries in Lachish, which have been confirmed by later finds in Jericho[3] and elsewhere, the main features of it can already be so clearly made out that it is in these ceramic discoveries that we find our main criterion for the approximate date of the various excavation strata.[4] The progress made is most evident at the point where mere pottery work begins to be an art, born of the joy produced by beauty of form and surface. Here again we meet with foreign influences, both Babylonian and Egyptian. The exterior surface of the clay vessels gradually becomes

---

[1] Referring evidently to the more expensive burial customs of Egypt, Sinuhe speaks of the Palestinian method of burial as " a wrapping in sheepskins." The clothing in which the dead were buried was presumably that which they wore in life.

[2] At Deshasheh above Fayum; see Sir Flinders Petrie, *Deshasheh* (1897), Plate 4.

[3] See Sellin and Watzinger, *Jericho*, p. 103 ff.

[4] See *supra*, p. 35.

glossier, either by simple smoothing with the hand or by polishing with a sharp tool. In the case of larger vessels a sort of pattern is produced by means of a brush,[1] with which the surface is rubbed in different directions. The surface also begins to be coloured. The design is scratched in the clay, and a mono-chrome coat of colour is laid upon it, or a coat of whitish, or bright red, or chestnut-brown colour is laid on the surface, and a design in colour is laid on the top of it. The mere line ornamentation of the prehistoric period is surpassed, although it is not yet entirely given up. The pottery workers take their patterns from nature, painting, sometimes with thick, broad lines and sometimes with finer lines, plants—the tree of life— and animals—ibexes, fishes, birds—and that too with a fidelity which reveals a fine gift of observation. Nor are they content to stop even here. Vessels or parts of vessels are made in the shape of animals—e.g., a horse-head with bridle in Megiddo, or a duck-shaped lamp in Gezer, like a smaller one found in Taanach. Of greater interest is a find at Taanach, consisting of an animal in red clay, 7 inches long and 4 inches high. It is probably a camel, on which a naked youth is mounted. Some have thought this to be a votive offering, seeing that in Arabian antiquity sacred camels play a great part, and in Cyprus votive gifts have been found showing the donors mounted.[2] Perhaps it is only a lamp. Indeed, the period with which we are dealing, as compared with earlier times, shows an advance in the shape given to the lamp. From the simple plate or bowl form it begins to develop into a closed container, which by and by has openings only for the wick and for filling. Peculiar to Palestine are the handles on the sides of larger vessels, bent upward and divided by finger-pressure. Their original purpose was, it is thought, to give assistance and security for carrying the vessel on the head, and their transference to smaller vessels was simply due to the desire for ornamentation.[3] It is possible that, toward the close of this period, Mycenæan pottery began to reach Palestine.

Toilet articles and personal ornaments of this period have not been found to any great extent ; but that does not mean that

---

[1] Sellin and Watzinger, *Jericho*, p. 103.
[2] See Sellin, *Tell Ta'annek* (1904), p. 45 ff.
[3] Sellin and Watzinger, *Jericho*, p. 104.

ornaments were little worn. It means only that unprofessional excavators—*i.e.*, thieves and robbers, ancient as well as modern —have done their work with great thoroughness. All the same, numerous kinds of ornaments have been found : bone combs, earrings, bracelets, anklets, clasps, pins, rosettes, small moons, twisted wire-work, all of gold or silver or bronze, fillets of gold foil, beads of blue, white, yellow, and green enamel, red agate, white limestone, ribbed glass, small crystalline cylinders, scent or salve bottles of clay and enamelled china, alabaster vases, thin pieces of ivory for the ornamentation of wooden boxes, bronze mirrors with enamelled handle—a collection which reminds us of Isaiah's catalogue of female toilet articles.[1] A whole collection of trinkets was found among the bones of the hapless mother who was overwhelmed in her house with her five children.[2] Sellin, who discovered them, says [3] the finest of them all is a gold finger ring, which had, in place of a seal, a small rotatory cylinder made in three parts. Similar rotatory rings have been found in Egypt and Cyprus, but they are mostly set with scarabs. Scarabs and seals of various kinds are, of course, among the commonest finds in Palestine, and the scarabs, found in great numbers, especially in the southern cities and in Megiddo, clearly betray Egyptian influence, if not Egyptian origin. There are specimens of white steatite, carnelian, yellow enamel, greenstone, blue amethyst, crystal, light blue china, green glazed clay, etc. The engravings on them are of many kinds. The most interesting is that on a seal-cylinder of black syenite from Taanach, which goes back to about 2000 B.C. It shows two figures, the deity (a Babylonian one in this case, the deity Nergal) [4] and his worshipper, and between these two the sign of the moon and other signs. Behind the deity are a star and the Egyptian so-called Nôfr sign. In an intermediate

---

[1] Is. iii, 18 ff.

[2] Sellin, *Nachlese*, p. 14, and see *supra*, p. 34.

[3] Sellin, *ibid.*, p. 14 f.

[4] Nergal (2 Kings xvii, 30) is the god of the parching sunlight, as well as god of the underworld and god of war. The chief seat of his worship was the city of Cutha, from which the Assyrian colonists were brought to Israel after the fall of Samaria. Possibly the original text of the Song of Songs (vi, 4*b* and verse 10) mentioned the " stars of Nergal " along with the dawn, the moon, and the sun. They would represent the constellation of the Twins, which appears in the two Babylonian representations of Nergal. See Winckler, *Altorientalische Forschungen*, vol. i, p. 293, and *KAT*, p. 414 f.

position behind the human worshipper we have, twice, the Egyptian sign of life and a bird below it. To the left of this intermediate column we find ancient Babylonian cuneiform writing giving the owner's name, Atanahili, son of Habsi, servant of Nergal. Here we have, in Palestinian territory, the servant of a Babylonian god, with a seal-cylinder half of whose signs are Egyptian! Could there be a clearer indication of the intercrossing of civilizations at that early date in Palestine? And the owner of the jewel was probably rather a native of Palestine than a mere Babylonian colonist, for, in the latter case, the Egyptian influence would be less intelligible. The use of the Babylonian language and writing, however, and still more the worship of a Babylonian deity, show that Babylonian influence went far deeper than the Egyptian, which affects only certain externalities of the scene. Of course, not all these seals betray foreign influence with the same clearness, and the symbols on a seal found in Megiddo—an ass being stung by a hornet—are perhaps merely due to personal observation on the part of the Palestinian seal-cutter.

A short step takes us from ornaments to amulets. The small moons mentioned in the last paragraph as having been found among the trinkets already point in that direction. In the Old Testament we read that the camels of the Midianites had small moons on their necks.[1] And in Palestine at the present day favourite horses wear an amulet of silver or ivory in the shape of a half-moon slung round their necks.[2] The animal thus adorned—and, of course, the rider also—is supposed to be under the protection of the moon-god, and that protection is needful whenever, owing to the intolerable heat of the day, travelling is done at night. The fact that the beads and pendants thus worn were predominantly blue in colour is in keeping with the fact that popular superstition in Palestine to-day decrees the wearing of blue glass beads as a protection,[3] especially against the evil eye. To this day the glance of a blue eye is most dreaded in Palestine, probably because it is rare, and no doubt it was always so. Blue beads as a protection against blue eyes are simply an example of sympathetic magic. Shells were also

---

[1] Judges viii, 21.
[2] L. Bauer, *Volksleben im Lande der Bibel* (1903), p. 199.
[3] L. Bauer, *ibid.*, p. 198.

believed to have special efficacy against the evil eye, and every living creature—man, woman, child, or even she-camel—in North Arabia wears shells round the neck.[1] Perforated shells have been found in Palestine which go back as far as the later Paleolithic Period,[2] and they recur again and again in Gezer as gifts to the dead. The amuletic character is equally apparent in the numerous perforated bones, stones, disks of clay and of metal. It is, in fact, in things of this kind that foreign influence is most apparent. Egyptian influence is specially shown by a large number of Horus eyes,[3] and by an amulet from Taanach with an Anubis head on one side. In Taanach were found a number of snake-heads, and in Gezer a miniature snake 6 inches in length, strongly resembling an article of the same kind (10 inches in length) from a small temple in Shushan.[4] We need not, however, immediately infer from this that serpents were worshipped, although we shall later meet with other traces which might suggest it. In this case it is probably simply an amulet or a talisman, for serpents were considered to be efficacious for this purpose. Glaser found in Arabia fragments of brazen serpents which, as is clear from the hole bored through the head, were meant to be hung on the person, and were therefore amulets.[5] This, of course, sets the later brazen serpent of Moses [6] in a new light. The camel-head found beside the female skeleton in Taanach is supposed by Sellin [7] to have been attached, in accordance with the usual practice, to the roof of the house as a protection, and to have collapsed along with it. Similarly, a horse-skull performed the same office on the house-roof of the ancient Germans, and a camel-skull (or part of one) can still be

[1] Musil, *Arabia Petræa* (1908), vol. iii, p. 314.

[2] *Supra*, p. 36.

[3] Horus, son of Osiris and Isis, lost an eye, when fighting with Seth, his father's murderer. The god Tot spat on the eye, and it was restored. Horus, however, gave the eye to his father to eat, and the latter was restored to life on account of this display of filial affection. The Horus eye became thenceforward the symbol of all gifts. See Erman, *Die ägyptische Religion* (1905), pp. 37 and 48.

[4] See illustrations in Vincent's *Canaan*, pp. 117 and 175. The fact that the bronze serpent of Gezer dates from the third period of the city (about 1500 B.C.) does not matter here.

[5] See Ditlef Nielsen, *Die altarabische Mondreligion und die mosaische Überlieferung* (1904), p. 190, with illustration.

[6] Num. xxi, 8; 2 Kings xviii, 4.

[7] Sellin, *Nachlese*, p. 16.

seen in use for the same purpose on outside doors in Hebron.[1]
In almost every layer in Taanach, in houses and rubbish-heaps,
Sellin found in very large numbers human and animal heel-
bones, and, as these were never found beside others, but in
groups of four or six together by themselves, he at once
guessed,[2] and rightly, that they had something to do with the game
called by the Arabs *ki'âb*, which is still played with bone dice.[3]
When the bone falls and remains in a perpendicular position
the thrower wins, and *vice versa*. This find proves the far-back
origin of this game, and, as Sellin rightly says, that origin must
be sought in the sphere of mantics. From the fall of the bone
probably an oracle was deduced—indeed, it is not impossible
that the animal to which the bone belonged was originally a
sacrificial animal.[4] Sellin is inclined to give a similar interpretation to a small Canaanite jug with sixty-six small flat, white,
heart-shaped (or bean-shaped) stones, seeing that the number
(6 × 11) was a sacred number.[5] Was it part of the outfit of a
magician? That magic was greatly in vogue in our period is
attested by the existence of a local name, Achshaph (" Magic "),
found mentioned in the annals of Thutmosis III (1501–1447 B.C.).[6]

To the end of this period belong apparently the first representations of Astarte, who was worshipped as the tutelary
goddess of women.[7] These terracottas are for the most part so
small that one might be tempted to include them among the
amulets.[8] But there are specimens in which two studs underneath the feet of the figure show that they once stood on a base,
and were therefore more probably the objects of actual domestic

---

[1] Canaan, *Aberglaube und Volksmedizin im Lande der Bibel* (1914), p. 19.

[2] Sellin, *Tell Ta'annek* (1904), p. 112.

[3] The Arab boys, when a ram was slaughtered, begged for the ankle-bones
to play with (Jacob, *Altarabisches Beduinenleben* (1897), p. 111). *Cf.* also the
Turkish game with the collar-bones of sheep, a species of game with dice
(Vámbéry, *Das Türkenvolk* (1895), p. 191).

[4] Jacob, *op. cit.*, p. 112 *note*.

[5] Sellin, *Tell Ta'annek*, pp. 42 and 112.

[6] Josh. xi, 1, xii, 20, xix, 25.

[7] The antiquity of the worship of this apparently Semitic goddess is attested
by the fact that the name of the city of Ashtaroth occurs as early as the annals
of Thutmosis. *Cf.* in the Tell Amarna letters in Winckler's edition 142, l. 10,
237, l. 21 = Knudtzon's edition 197, l. 10, 256, l. 21 (Weber in Knudtzon,
p. 1292).

[8] So Kennedy in Hastings, *RE*, vol. iii, p. 440. Paton in the same volume
(p. 186*b*) calls them votive offerings.

worship. Of this type is the Astarte figure which was found in the collapsed house in Taanach beside the skeleton of the mother with her five children.[1] This solid cast-bronze figure, 6 inches in height, shows the goddess clothed in a delicately woven garment, through which the breasts and the navel are visible. On her head she wears a crown tapering upward, and round her neck is a thick ring. Of more primitive make is a figure found in Megiddo, which has been put together by hand, in 'snow-man' fashion, out of separate pieces of clay. As these figures, however, for the most part belong to a subsequent period we will reserve a full consideration of them till a later chapter.

With regard to the religion of the inhabitants of Palestine in this period, we are mainly reduced to inferences from the later, the Canaanite period, and the line of separation between the Amorite and the Canaanite strata is, as far as our present knowledge goes, indefinite. Thus, much of what will be said in connexion with the Canaanite period will hold good for the religion of the period now before us. The one and only expressly documented name of a deity in our period is the name of the Babylonian deity Nergal. In the following period we meet with a whole series of traces of the worship of Babylonian deities in Palestine, but seeing that in this subsequent period the political hegemony definitely falls to Egypt, this worship is presumably older. This agrees with the conclusion to which we found ourselves obliged to come regarding the predominance of Babylonian influences in this period, especially in Hammurabi's time.[2]

In addition to the already-mentioned Nergal, other deities belonging to the Babylonian pantheon are found in Palestine. Among these are Shamash (in Hebrew Shemesh [3]), Sin, Nebo, Ninib, and Ramman (Rimmon).[4] On the other hand, Hadad

---

[1] *Supra*, p. 34.  [2] *Supra*, p. 50 f.

[3] But the agreement of the name (meaning " Sun ") in this case does not absolutely prove the identity of the deity.

[4] We do not raise the question whether we should include Anu on the strength of the Palestinian place-name Anaharath (Josh. xix, 19) and Lahmu on account of the name Beth-lehem. We have already (p. 17) rendered Bethlehem simply as " House of Bread." There are weighty arguments against an identification of the goddess Anath of Palestine with the Babylonian Antum or Anatu, the female companion of Anu. Mention should also be made of the Babylonian deity Sibitti (a deity closely resembling

E                                                                         65

(identical with Ramman), along with Ashera, seems to have migrated to Babylon from the west, and Dagan (Dagon) seems to have been brought both to Babylon and Palestine from his original Amorite home. The main centres in Palestine of the cult of the sun-god Shemesh (Shamash) were probably places like Ir-Shemesh [1] (" City of the Sun "), Beth-Shemesh [2] (" House of the Sun "), En-Shemesh [3] (" Well of the Sun ") ; and the hero Samson perhaps exhibits features of the same original figure.[4] The sun-god seems also to have been worshipped under the other name for the sun, Heres ; hence probably the names of the places where he was worshipped—Har-Heres [5] (" Mount of the Sun ") and Timnat-Heres [6] (" Region of the Sun "). The worship of the moon-god Sin, who was specially honoured in Haran, Abraham's starting-point, is attested by the names Mount Sinai and the wilderness of Sin.[7] Other ancient centres of the worship of the moon-god were probably Jericho, which is named after the moon (*jareach*), and Hadasha [8] (" New Moon "), in the hill-country of

Nergal, and by some identified with him), who had probably some connexion with the Pleiades (*KAT*, pp. 413, 459). Some scholars (including Paton in Hastings, *RE*, vol. iii, p. 184*a*) have even ventured to connect Sibitti or the seven Babylonian demons with the name of Beer-sheba and the name Bath-sheba (also Elisheba, Exod. vi, 23, Elisabeth, and Jehosheba, 2 Kings xi, 2). But that is doubtful. Beer-sheba means simply " Seven Wells " (Nöldeke in *AR*, vol. vii (1904), p. 341). Nöldeke (p. 344) says that till the contrary is proved we must assume a Babylonian origin for the special significance of the number seven. The similarity of *sheba*, the Hebrew for ' seven,' and *shaba*, meaning ' swear,' is certainly not accidental. Swearing is an appeal to seven gods or spirits, or a seven-times repeated appeal to one and the same supersensuous being, or even simply a sevenfold repetition of the oath formula. The Arabs, when taking a serious oath, repeat the statement to which they are swearing as often as seventy times (Wellhausen, *Reste arabischen Heidentums* (1896), p. 186). But see also Pedersen, *Der Eid bei den Semiten* (1914), p. 5 f.

[1] Josh. xix, 41, ascribed to the tribe of Dan.

[2] Josh. xv, 10 ; another of the same name, Josh. xix, 22 ; another, Josh. xix, 38, Judges i, 33.

[3] Josh. xv, 7, xviii, 17, apparently on the road from Jerusalem to Jericho.

[4] See Stahn, *Die Simsonsage* (1908).

[5] Judges i, 35, in the tribe of Dan.

[6] Judges ii, 9, on Mount Ephraim. In Josh. xix, 50, xxiv, 30, the same place is named Timnat Serach, and in the Septuagint of Josh. xxiv, 30, it is called Timnat Sachar, but these are probably intentional changes to blot out the name of the heathen deity.

[7] Exod. xvi, 1, xvii, 1 ; Num. xxxiii, 11. We should perhaps add the name of Shinab, king of the destroyed city of Adma, near the Dead Sea (Gen. xiv, 2).

[8] Josh. xv, 37.

Judah.[1] The god of writing, Nebo, or rather a sanctuary named after him, has given his name to the well-known mountain from which Moses saw the promised land [2] and also to cities on both sides of the Jordan.[3] The worship of Ninib, the god of war, is indicated by the name of a locality, Beth-Ninib (" House of Ninib "), not far from Jerusalem,[4] and by the proper name Abd-Ninib ("Servant of Ninib"), both of which occur in the Tell Amarna letters. The name of Ramman (Rimmon) [5] the storm-god appears in a whole series of Palestinian place-names : Rimmon,[6] Rimmon-perez[7] (" Rent of Rimmon "), Gath-Rimmon[8] (" Wine-press of Rimmon"), En-Rimmon [9] (" Well of Rimmon "), Sela-ha-Rimmon [10] (" Rock of Rimmon "). The symbol of this god was frequently the bull.[11] In his hand he holds a bundle of thunderbolts. His native name in the west is Hadad ; at least, this name was believed in Babylonia to be of Amorite origin.[12] Hadad must therefore have been worshipped here at an earlier period.[13] According to the Tell Amarna letters, he makes his

[1] To me it seems unlikely that Libnah (Num. xxxiii, 20 f.), in the desert of Sinai, and another town of the same name in Judah (Josh. x, 29, and often), have anything to do with l<sup>e</sup>bana, a poetical name of the ' white ' moon. Nor can it be said with certainty that the female name Sarah is connected with Sarratu, the name of the moon-god of Haran. It is difficult to say whether the name Chesil in the south of Judah (Josh. xv, 30) has any relation to the constellation of that name (probably Orion), because the texts do not agree with regard to the name.

[2] Num. xxxiii, 47 ; Deut. xxxii, 49, xxxiv, 1.

[3] To a town east of Jordan, Num. xxxii, 3, xxxiii, 47 ; to a Judean town, "the other Nebo," Ezra ii, 29, x, 43, Neh. vii, 33 ; and probably also to Nob (1 Sam. xxi, 2 ff.).          [4] There was another near Gebal (Byblos).

[5] This vocalization in Hebrew is perhaps due to a popular etymology. Rimmon means ' pomegranate.'

[6] Josh. xv, 32, xix, 7, 1 Chron. iv, 32, Zech. xiv, 10, in the south of Judah, allotted to Simeon ; also Josh. xix, 13 (Remmon), a town in Zebulun.

[7] Num. xxxiii, 19, a camp of Israel.

[8] Josh. xix, 45, xxi, 24, 1 Chron. vi, 54, a town in Dan.

[9] Neh. xi, 29, 1 Chron. iv, 32, a town in Judah or Simeon.

[10] Judges xx, 45, 47, xxi, 13, in Benjamin.

[11] It cannot be mere coincidence that one of the ancient bull images comes from Erruman (in the land east of the Jordan).

[12] In a Babylonian list of deities it is expressly said that A-da-ad is the name of this god in Amurru, the west country (see Bezold in *Proceedings of the Society of Biblical Archæology*, vol. xi, p. 174 ff.).

[13] The worship of Hadad became widespread in Near Asia, as is attested by Old Testament proper names : of various Edomite kings (Gen. xxxvi, 35 ; 1 Kings xi, 14–32) ; Ben-Hadad (" Son of Hadad "), 1 Kings xv, 18, etc., and Hadad-ezer (" Hadad is Help "), 2 Sam. viii, 3–12, are names of kings of Syria ; Henadad (Ezra iii, 9 ; Neh. x, 10) is the name of a Levitical family.

voice resound in the sky, so that the whole land trembles.[1] The identity of Hadad with Rimmon is also expressed in a late passage of the Old Testament in the name Hadad-Rimmon.[2] As wife of the Babylonian Ramman, we sometimes hear of the goddess Ashratum, or Ashirtu. This is none other than Ashera, who again is of western origin, and the antiquity of her worship in the west may be inferred from the fact that she is named in a dedication inscription to Hammurabi in which he himself is called King of the Land of the West (Amurru).[3] In this inscription she appears as the " bride of the king of heaven," as " queen of luxury and splendour," as " the merciful one, who reverently entreats her husband." An Abd-Ashirti, or Abd-Ashrati—*i.e.*, "Servant of Ashera"—is frequently mentioned in the Tell Amarna letters. Finally, Dagan,[4] of whom there are traces in Babylon from 2400 B.C. onward, and whom Hammurabi in the introduction to his law calls his " begetter," is in all probability the same deity whom we meet in the Old Testament as the Philistine god Dagon.[5] The Philistines seem to have adopted his worship only after their settlement in Canaan. The Palestinian name Beth-Dagon [6] (" House of Dagon ") is a reminiscence of his worship, and the occurrence of a proper name compounded with Dagon in the Tell Amarna letters [7] is proof that his worship goes back to the Amorite period, or at least close to it. But the form of the name, Dagan, identifies the bearer of it as the original god of grain (*dagan*). His emblem on a Phœnician seal is an ear of corn. It can have been only at a later period that he became a fish-god, as he has been represented since Jerome's day, unless this character was ascribed to him in error, on the basis of an interpretation due to a popular etymology (*dag* = fish).

But these deities above named do not exhaust the Amorite

---

[1] Winckler, 149, l. 13 ff. Hadad's name also occurs in the Amarna letters.

[2] Zech. xii, 11. Here it is probably not the name of a place in the plain of Jezreel, but the name of a deity, whose death, like that of Tammuz (Ezek. viii, 14) or Adonis, caused lamentation.

[3] *KAT*, 3rd edition, p. 432 f.

[4] *Cf.*, for what follows, Paton in Hastings, *RE*, vol. iv, p. 386 ff.

[5] 1 Sam. v, 2-7. *Cf.* 1 Macc. x, 83, xi, 4. Games in his honour were celebrated at Gaza (Judges xvi, 23 ff.).

[6] One in Judah, Josh. xv, 41, another in Asher, Josh. xix, 27.

[7] Dagan-takala, letters nos. 215 and 216 in Winckler.

pantheon. There was also a goddess Anat, whose name is attested in Palestine in the fifteenth century B.C.[1] by the local name Beth-Anat. Among the Egyptians, whom her worship must have reached at latest in the same century—for at that time she had a priesthood at Thebes[2]—she was a war-goddess. Probably she was the same in Palestine. She was perhaps of Hittite origin.[3] What other deities, of whom we either hear directly or whom we can at least infer for the Canaanite period, belong to the period we are now dealing with cannot be ascertained.

But the undoubted polytheism indicated by the deities already named cannot have wholly displaced older polydemonistic ideas. For these are found in undiminished strength in the ensuing period—conceptions of spirits living in stone or tree or spring, or on high place, and who are called, quite generally, by the name of El (meaning, perhaps, " Power "). This name is doubly attested for our period. Among the Amorite names from the time of the first Babylonian dynasty compounds with El are frequent, and in Palestine in the fifteenth century place-names compounded with El are already found.[4] For example, in the list of Thutmosis III among the districts conquered in the first Syrian expedition of the King mention is made of Har-El (" Mount of El "), also of Jacob-El and Joseph-El, two names which have been much discussed owing to their first component. It cannot be said with equal definiteness what other names were used to denote deity. Baal, for example, which might be called the classical name of Canaanite religion, occurs pretty frequently in Babylonian proper names of the

[1] In the list of Thutmosis III (1501–1447) the Beth-Anath mentioned means a town in Naphtali (Josh. xix, 38 ; Judges i, 33). There was another town of the same name (spelt Beth-Anoth) in Judah (Josh. xv, 59). Anathoth, the birthplace of Jeremiah, is called after Anath, as is also the Anati mentioned in an Amarna letter (Winckler, 125, l. 43), as well as the Anath referred to in Judges v, 6, a Canaanite oppressor of Israel. By a misunderstanding he is said to have been the father of the Israelite judge Shamgar (Judges iii, 31). Kittel takes another view, and thinks that the expression " son of Anath " conveys an encomium of warlike bravery. He is also inclined to make the name Baanah (2 Sam. iv, 2 ff.) a derivative from Ben-Ana, " Son of Ana."

[2] W. Max Müller, *Asien und Europa nach altägyptischen Denkmälern* (1893), p. 313.

[3] Von Orelli, *Allgemeine Religionsgeschichte* (1911), p. 259, and Eduard Meyer in *ZDMG*, vol. xxxi (1877), p. 716 ff.

[4] The Amarna letters also contain proper names compounded with El.

69

Amorite period, but it does not occur in the Amarna letters.[1] On the other hand, there is no lack of proofs that the deity was already in this period indicated by names expressive of kinship, such as *ab* ('father'), *am* ('father's brother'), and *ach* ('brother'). Also, the leader of the caravan of which we have spoken (*supra*, pp. 49 and 58), about 1900 B.C., bears the name Absha, and the Palestinian prince at whose Court Sinuhe settled down was called Ammienshi.[2]

The conception that a supersensuous being likes to take up his abode in a stone is fully attested by finds in layers belonging to this period.  In Taanach, for example, out of a natural rock, rising about 3 feet above the surrounding surface, had been constructed a sort of altar, to which access was obtained by steps hewn in the rock.[3]  On the upper surface was a large oval hole for sacrifice, about 18 inches in diameter, besides three small holes $3\frac{1}{2}$ inches in diameter.  All round the rock ran a deep channel, which was perhaps partly natural, but had been artificially deepened.[4]  To the same period probably belongs the primitive rock-altar which is still to be seen at Sar'a, the Old Testament Zorea,[5] probably the very one which plays a part in the story of Samson.[6]  Other common evidences of former worship are upright pillars.  The excavations have disclosed many of these.  Extreme care is, however, necessary in interpreting them.  Not every monolith found standing upright is straightway to be claimed as a sacred stone, though ultra-zealous historians of religion are apt to do so.  The excavators

---

[1] It is, however, attested in Egyptian sources as an Asiatic name of the deity Seth or Sutech (W. Max Müller, *Asien und Europa*, p. 309).

[2] Numerous names like this are found in Babylonian sources of this period : Ammu- or Hammurabi, Abiramu (Abraham).  Genesis mentions names of Palestinian contemporaries of Abraham compounded with *ab* : Shinab (xiv, 2), Abimelech (xx, 2).  Place-names compounded with *am*, like Jibleam (Josh. xvii, 11 ; Judges i, 27 ; 2 Kings ix, 27), which occurs in the list of Thutmosis III, are probably of the same kind.  Cf. *supra*, p. 49.

[3] At a later time Hebrew legislation forbade such an arrangement, " that thy nakedness be not discovered thereon " (by the deity who was supposed to be present in the stone), Exod. xx, 26.  Indeed, all hewing of stone was forbidden (verse 25).

[4] Sellin, *Tell Ta'annek*, pp. 34 and 103.  For the channel or gutter *cf.* 1 Kings xviii, 32, 35.

[5] There are several illustrations of it in Kittel, *Über primitive Felsaltäre in Palästina* (reprint from the *Hilprecht Anniversary Volume*, Leipzig, 1909).

[6] Judges xiii, 2 ff.

of Tell es-Safi [1] thought they had discovered in some pillars the remains of an ancient sanctuary, and the numerous bones of camels, sheep, and oxen found among the rubbish seemed to confirm their belief. But Thiersch [2] utterly ruined their joy over their discovery by his definite verdict that the place had only been a stall for animals! A closely analogous case was the rock-stable of Tell Sandahanna, where the appliances for tying up the animals excluded all doubt as to the purpose of the place. [3] On the other hand, wherever a place is named after a pillar, like Kirjath-nasib ("City of the Upright Stone"), mentioned by Thutmosis III among the Palestinian cities conquered by him, we have in all likelihood a sacred pillar.

But it was not only in solid stone that gods and spirits might dwell. They might also take up their abode in the open field. We may safely assume that the spirits of the field, who, to the horror of the Hebrew lawgiver, were still worshipped at a later period, [4] and after whom a place of worship was named, [5] were in our period believed to exist. At least, Hebrew legal ordinances, centuries later, confirm in their own way the existence of such conceptions reaching back to primitive times and closely connected with agriculture. The vineyard, for example, was planted simultaneously with vine and grain in order to bring it under the protection of the spirits of the field, who would otherwise be offended at being robbed of their due. [6] Again, the fruit of trees was left untouched for the first years, so that the spirits of the field might receive their due portion [7]—a custom which

---

[1] That the layer in question brings us to a somewhat later period does not affect the statement in the text.

[2] *AA* (1908), p. 369 f.

[3] The ceiling is supported by six pillars rectangular in section. The columns at Tell es-Safi were originally rectangular.

[4] Lev. xvii, 7.

[5] Bamath-has-seïrim (instead of Bamoth-hashshearim in our text) means "High Altar of the Spirits of the Field" (2 Kings xxiii, 8). They were of the nature of satyrs and fauns, and had their abode in uncultivated land (Is. xiii, 21, xxxiv, 14), the steppes, and the desert. See Hans Duhm, *Die bösen Geister im Alten Testament* (1904), p. 46 ff.

[6] Deut. xxii, 9. Similar conceptions lie behind the prohibitions to sow a field with two kinds of seed (Lev. xix, 19), to yoke together an ox and an ass to a plough (Deut. xxii, 10), or to mate them (Lev. xix, 19), or to wear garments made of wool and linen woven together (Deut. xxii, 11) or of two materials spun together (Lev. xix, 19).

[7] Lev. xix, 23–25. See my commentary *in loc.*

finds a parallel to-day in some places in the practice of not eating certain fruits before a definite day of the calendar.[1]   Or, at reaping time, a corner of the field was left unreaped in order that the spirit of the corn might not be driven out of the field, for this spirit dwells in leaves and fruits.   Again, great events and special occasions in human life, such as birth, sickness, and death, were placed under the care of other deities.   The enactment of the Jewish law that parturition makes the mother unclean is unintelligible if it is Jahveh Himself that "opens the womb."[2]   But if, according to the original view, it was done by a different *numen*, who was later replaced by Jahveh, then the matter is clear.   For one cult that which belongs to another cult is unclean.[3]   The name of the valley Jephthah-El[4] (*i.e.*, "El opens") probably indicates the worship there of a deity or spirit who assisted women to a happy accouchement.[5]   In connexion with a valley we must also remember the brook which traverses it, and take into account the prevalence down to the present day of the "primitive Semitic" custom—of which the American scholar Curtis[6] gives many examples from his own observation in Palestine—according to which women bathe in a natural stream in order to be made fertile by its Weli—*i.e.*, the holy *numen* who inhabits it.   Further, at a later time sickness—at least, leprosy—was looked upon as a "stroke of Jahveh."[7]   Here again it is unintelligible that the leper should be "unclean" in the eyes of the worshippers of Jahveh.[8]   We are driven to the same conclusion, that Jahveh has here only taken over the part of an earlier *numen*, to whose influence the incurable disease was in earlier days ascribed.   In keeping with this, we hear of curative *numina*, such as Jirpe-El ("El cures"), whose memory is still preserved in a Benjamite town of the same name.[9]   The question as to a general worship of the dead receives some light

---

[1] Haberland, in *Zeitschrift für Völkerpsychologie*, vol. xviii (1888), p. 17. Also the *Lawbook of Manu*, vol. iv, 27 f., where the Hindu is forbidden to eat new rice or new corn till he has offered the firstfruits of the harvest.

[2] Gen. xxix, 31, xxx, 22.     [3] *Supra*, p. 40.     [4] Josh. xix, 14, 27.

[5] Von Gall, *Altisraelitische Kultstätten* (1898), p. 144.

[6] Curtis, *Ursemitische Religion im Volksleben des heutigen Orients* (1903), pp. 112–115.

[7] 2 Kings xv, 5; 2 Chron. xxvi, 20.     [8] Lev. xiii f.

[9] Josh. xviii, 27, possibly identical with 'No-r-p'-a ("Healing") in the annals of Thutmosis III.

from what we know of the treatment of the dead in our period, and it is fortunate that the excavations are supplying additional information on this matter.

The practice of cremation, which is confirmed by the cave-crematorium at Gezer,[1] has in our period completely ceased, and has given place to the universal custom of burial in caves or in the earth. This is a change which took place also in Babylon— at least, in Nippur—with the invasion of the Semites.[2] The change was brought about without any intermediate stage. In the cave-crematorium at Gezer the new corpses were simply laid to rest on the ashes of the earlier dead. Of course, this new manner of disposal of the dead required greater space, and this was secured by doubling the size of the cave. It now also became necessary to guard the place against the entrance of wild beasts, and this was done by building up the former stair entrance and digging a perpendicular shaft through which the dead could be lowered into the cave. The bodies were apparently laid without any plan on the top of each other, but those of specially distinguished persons were laid on special couches of stone round the walls of the cave, and surrounded by a low stone wall. The presence of a jar containing the remains of a new-born child on a platform of stone probably points to a building sacrifice offered on the occasion of the transformation of the cave for its new purpose.

Gruesome traces of this widespread custom of building sacrifices have been disclosed by the excavations. It will suffice to adduce two specially instructive examples from Megiddo. Between the lowest layer of the foundation and the second stone base was found a jar, 3 feet long and 16 inches wide, surrounded by masonry work and crushed by the weight of the super-incumbent layers. It contained the remains of a very young child, along with a number of ceramic offerings.[3] At another place, in the North Castle at Megiddo, was found, lying diagonally across the foundation stones of the lowest layer, the skeleton of a girl of about fifteen years of age. The vertebral column had assumed the shape of the large stone on which it lay ; the feet were resting in a depression between the stones of the wall ;

---

[1] *Supra*, p. 38.  [2] *Cf.* Vincent, *Canaan*, p. 267.
[3] Schumacher, *Tell el-Mutesellim*, vol. i, p. 44 f.

the head was outside the wall, under the floor, resting on a stone which gave it a raised position, and it was surrounded by a ring of small pieces of rock.[1]  Even worse horrors of ritual murder are suggested by other discoveries, if these are correctly interpreted as pointing to cannibalistic orgies.  On the top of two male skeletons, which were lying outstretched, was the upper body of a lad of seventeen.  The lower part of the body was wanting, and careful examination seemed to indicate that it had been severed during life.  Again, there was found in a cistern the naked upper body of a girl of sixteen with the skeletons of twelve men and two youths ; a knife and an axe, found in the same cistern, seemed to corroborate the dread surmise.[2]  At the mouth of the same cistern the severed skulls of two other girls were discovered, and other severed remains of bones and skulls were found.  In one case, the top of a skull was fitted exactly into an earthen bowl, so that the savage owner was able literally and actually to drink out of the skull of his enemy.[3]

Going back to the question of the natural method of burial, a point of view forces itself upon us which we found decisive in connexion with our interpretation of the dolmens.[4]  The artificial grave arrangement is an imitation of the natural arrangement of the primitive rock-cave.  A very common type is the grave at the foot of a shaft bored in a rock.  A round shaft,[5] wider above than below, is driven to a depth of about 6 feet. From this shaft a rectangular opening leads into the actual grave, hewn in the rock and vaulted, on the floor of which the dead body is laid.  The grave-structure in Megiddo, stone-built in primitive fashion, conforms exactly to this arrangement.  The centre of it was a quadrilateral grave-chamber, of whose remarkable vaulted roof we have already spoken.[6]  From it one crawled through a passage 5 feet long to the door at the west, to which a

---

[1] Schumacher, *Tell el-Mutesellim*, vol. i, p. 54 f.

[2] But Vincent, in his *Canaan*, p. 276 ff., suggests a different explanation, and refers to the Egyptian custom of " double burial."

[3] Thiersch, *AA* (1909), p. 360.          [4] *Supra*, p. 40.

[5] Two rectangular graves in Gezer are probably Egyptian (Macalister, *Gezer*, vol. i, p. 303 ff.).  Egyptian graves in Palestine are not unusual (Vincent, *Canaan*, p. 218 ff.).  In the huge " graves of the children of Israel " at Hizme (the 'Azmaveth or Beth-'Azmaveth of Ezra ii, 24, Neh. vii, 28, xii, 29) Vincent sees imitations of the Egyptian mastabas.  *Cf.* Erman, *Die ägyptische Religion* (1905), p. 119.          [6] *Supra*, p. 53.

hewn shaft formed the secret approach from the surface of the ground. But this was not a case of a single grave. The chamber contained five corpses lying on the floor, and a sixth on a stone bench, along with numerous offerings.[1] Similar, but more primitive, was a second grave arrangement connected with this one. It was a collective grave, containing twelve dead. Peace and seclusion [2] were secured by a great stone at the grave-mouth, which was still in place when the excavators found it. In cases where no natural rock-cover was available, or where the vault of masonry could not be built, the work was done with earth or a layer of plaster surrounded by stones.[3] Where it was at all practicable graves were made in the house of the family concerned, but building sacrifices were not always necessarily involved. The practice of having the dead in the closest possible proximity to the living can be proved as late as Old Testament times,[4] and it was also common in Arabian antiquity.[5] The usual posture of the dead was sitting on the haunches, with knees drawn up.[6] To the Oriental this seemed perhaps the most natural position. It is not easy to say whether the thought of " Mother Earth," into whose womb the dead person was laid in the posture of the embryo, in order to be reborn of her,[7] was partly responsible for this, although that thought also was not unknown among the Semites.[8] Sometimes the dead were laid with the head toward the East. But the varieties of posture are too numerous for us to speak of any one regular posture.

A special method of burial was frequently used in the case of children. They were not laid in open graves, but placed, head downward, in plain jars or urns, often with knees drawn up, arms and hands close to the mouth, and the body was often bedded

---

[1] Schumacher, *Tell el-Mutesellim*, vol. i, p. 14 f.

[2] *Ibid.*, p. 19 ff.

[3] Referring to Megiddo, *ibid.*, pp. 18, 25, 58 f., 62.

[4] 1 Sam. xxv, 1, 1 Kings ii, 34, Samuel and Joab were buried in their own houses. See also Ezek. xliii, 7 f.

[5] *Cf.* the poem from the *Hamasa* quoted by Marti, *Geschichte der israelitischen Religion* (1907), p. 133.

[6] Corpses extended at full length were found in Megiddo. See *Tell el-Mutesellim*, vol. i, p. 58, *note* 6, and p. 60.

[7] *Cf.* Dieterich, *Mutter Erde*, 2nd edition (1913), p. 27 f., *note* 6.

[8] *Cf.* Nöldeke's article "Mutter Erde und Verwandtes bei den Semiten" in *AR*, vol. viii (1905), p. 161 ff.

in sand or in finely sifted earth.[1]  Such jar or urn usually
contained ceramic gifts.[2]  The urns were closed with a dish, or
two of them were fitted into each other.[3]  An entire children's
cemetery, with twenty bodies, none of which could be more than
two years old, was discovered by Sellin at Taanach.  In the
same locality he found two large jars, filled with fine sand, which
had never contained a dead body.  Presumably this was a case
of a cenotaph—*i.e.*, formal interment, practised when the body
itself was not available, in order not to prevent the spirit from
enjoying its rest.[4]  The children buried in this cemetery were,
notwithstanding the adjacent rock-altar mentioned above,[5] probably not sacrifices.  There seems to have prevailed a custom,
suggested by foreign analogies, that children up to a certain age
were buried, not in the family grave, but underneath or near
the house, or even in a place specially set apart for that purpose.[6]
The red colouring of the bone-remains found in a grave in
Megiddo also attracted attention.  Possibly the colouring is
not fortuitous.  The custom is widespread of painting dead
bodies red, the purpose being to give to the dead an external
appearance of life, in order to protect them from evil influences
which might injure them in their helplessness.[7]

It should be added that the number of dead bodies found in
the graves laid bare is far less than was to be expected in the

---

[1] Sand and earth probably symbolize burial in the ground, but possibly
the use of sand points to ideas connected with sympathetic magic, and
suggests the expectation, already referred to, that the rebirths might be
as numerous as the sand on the seashore (Gen. xxxii, 13 ; Jer. xxxiii, 22 ;
Hos. i, 10).

[2] In one case (in Taanach) a large jaw-bone. Sellin, *Tell Ta'annek*, p. 33.

[3] In one case, where the child's body had been too large to be forced into
the mouth of the jar, the bottom of the jar had been knocked off and an
entirely different bottom subsequently affixed (Sellin, *ibid.*, p. 34).

[4] Sellin, *ibid.*, p. 37.  Regarding cenotaphs (among the Greeks) see Rohde,
*Psyche* (1910), p. 66, *note* 2, p. 163, *note* 1.

[5] *Supra*, p. 70.

[6] Sellin (*ibid.*, p. 36, *note* 1) quotes a statement of Pliny (*Natural History*,
VII, 15, 72) to the effect that savage peoples did not cremate a child's body
till he or she was old enough to have a tooth.  *Cf.* Dieterich, *Mutter Erde*,
2nd edition, p. 21 ff. ; Dalman, *Palästinajahrbuch*, vol. iv (1908), p. 50, *note* 3 ;
Hastings, *RE*, vol. iv, p. 422.  It was apparently believed that this would
facilitate the child's reincarnation.  The practice of urn-burial in Egypt,
in Cnossus, and Aphidna in North Attica, and in Babylon, has now been
completely proved (Sellin, p. 96, *note* 1).

[7] Von Duhn, " Rot und Tot " in *AR*, vol. ix (1906), p. 9.

course of so many centuries. This leads us to suppose that, for the great mass of the people, there was a kind of burial which was less calculated to protect them against the destroying influences of time. Macalister found on the south side of the hill of Gezer a whole series of bottle-shaped pits in the ground, filled nearly to the top with the bones of men and of animals (camels, cows, asses, and horses), and he is no doubt right in his conjecture, seeing that no gifts were found, that these were graves of poor people who could not afford a grave of their own.[1] How many thousands of such bodies may have turned to dust in the course of the centuries !

We should greatly like to know what the people of the time thought regarding their dead. The only thing that can be said definitely is that the dead took with them into their graves all that was needed to meet the requirements of their life on earth. This is shown by the multifarious gifts which the excavations have brought to light from the various graves. The dead are conscious of hunger and to an even greater degree of thirst. They are therefore carefully supplied with food, and even more carefully with water. Near the large water-jug there is occasionally found a small cup or goblet, with which the dead person could supply himself to his heart's content with water. Sometimes the food is uncooked, sometimes it is ready for use. In Gezer was found, on top of the remains of a dish of mutton, the blade of a bronze knife, which was meant to be used by the dead man for carving the meat, and on the top of it was an inverted dish, in order, as it were, to keep the food warm. Besides food, the dead need light, and the lamp is not, as was formerly believed, a creation of the Hebrew time.[2] In Gezer and Megiddo the lamp goes back to this Amorite period, although we cannot say it was common. All sorts of household utensils and tools have been found in graves. Seals are specially frequent, and they form the transition to jewellery and trinkets. It may be enough to say that our knowledge of ancient Palestinian jewellery[3] is largely based on what has been found in graves. Even the jars buried with the dead are not exclusively utilitarian. Articles of luxury show that the dead did not wish to lack in the grave

---

[1] This helps us to understand more fully the threat to King Jehoiakim that he would be " buried with the burial of an ass," Jer. xxii, 19.

[2] *Supra*, p. 60.   [3] *Supra*, p. 59.

the things in which he took pleasure in life.[1]  Even in the grave weapons—daggers, lances, javelins—are a man's pride.  Some of the things found in children's graves can perhaps only indicate toys.[2]  It is striking to find how few of the gifts have any real religious significance.  They are mainly amulets, and the numerous camel-teeth found in the first grave-chamber at Megiddo, already mentioned,[3] are probably amulets also.  A peculiar custom, often observed, was that the things put at the disposal of the dead were in one way or another rendered useless for the purposes of this life ; the vessels have been broken, or at least holed, a kind of symbolical killing.  The same symbolical significance explains why animal-shaped vessels were made lacking the head.

It is hardly possible to decide whether the offering of such gifts can in any case be interpreted to mean an actual worship of the dead.  Seeing, however, that in these matters definite lines were seldom drawn, this significance may be read into them.  There is one consideration that seems to justify the interpretation.  At the entrance of the large cave at Gezer, which contained, superimposed upon the ashes of the earlier inhabitants, numerous corpses of their successors, stands a small stone pillar, which without any doubt had a religious significance of some kind.

### (b) The Canaanite Period (from the Middle of the Second Millennium to the Invasion of Israel)

We are entirely ignorant of the course of events by which the Canaanite population gradually gained the upper hand over the Amorites.[4]  Both Amorites and Canaanites were Semites, apparently very closely akin, and this relationship itself guarantees a certain continuity in the growth and development of the civilization.  The treatment of the dead, for example, remains essentially the same as that which has been described at length in the preceding pages.  Externally the division between the two periods is marked by the conquest of Palestine by Egypt, and it is this that justifies the division we have

---

[1] Vincent, *Canaan*, p. 213.
[2] Schumacher, *Tell el-Mutesellim*, vol. i, p. 60 ; Thiersch, *AA* (1908), p. 362.
[3] *Supra*, p. 74.      [4] *Supra*, p. 46.

made. The Egyptian conquest of Palestine meant, of course, a decided increase of Egyptian influence on its civilization. It goes without saying that this influence was specially effective in the south of Palestine.

The expulsion of the Hyksos from Egypt and their pursuit, which drew their Egyptian enemies at times over the frontiers of Palestine, were for the Egyptians the signal for an ambitious and grandiose policy of conquest. What the founders of the new Egyptian empire, the first rulers of the Eighteenth Dynasty, were able to achieve only with temporary success in the early years of the sixteenth century B.C. the powerful Thutmosis III (1501–1447) was able to turn into a definite and lasting success in seventeen Asiatic campaigns. In his very first campaign (1479) Megiddo became the gathering-place for the forces which the allied princes of North Palestine and Syria, under the chief command of the King of Kadesh, had brought together to resist Egypt. " The capture of Megiddo means the capture of a thousand cities," exclaims Thutmosis to his troops, in order to encourage them to besiege the city, in which the enemy, after their defeat in the field, had taken refuge.[1] The siege had the result the Egyptians desired. For our purpose it is instructive to read the detailed enumeration of the booty as it is inscribed on the interior of the temple of Amon built by Thutmosis III at Thebes (Karnak). Here is an abbreviated extract. " List of booty taken at Megiddo : prisoners 340, hands 83,[2] horses 2041, colts 191, stallions 6, a gold-mounted chariot with chariot-pole (?) of gold belonging to the King of Kadesh, a beautiful gold-mounted chariot belonging to . . . [Here is a lengthy gap in which other chariots, presumably belonging to the other allied princes, were named], 892 chariots of his wretched troops—all together 924 chariots ;[3] a beautiful bronze shirt of mail of the King of Kadesh, a beautiful bronze shirt of mail of the Prince of Megiddo, 200 shirts of mail of his wretched soldiers, 502 bows, 7 silver-mounted tent-poles from the tent of that prince. My soldiers took 1929 oxen, 2000 goats, 20,500 sheep. List of what the King afterward took of the

[1] For the remarkable manner in which they succeeded in doing this see *TBAT*, vol. i, p. 238.   [2] As trophies of the slain.
[3] See Nuoffer, *Der Rennwagen im Altertum* (1904). Plate 3 gives a picture of a Syrian chariot.

furniture of that prince, likewise of the property of the cities which yielded to the King : precious stones, gold, drinking bowls, a variety of vessels, a large jar of Syrian workmanship,[1] . . . vessels, drinking cups, bowls,[2] a variety of drinking vessels, large pots, 87 swords, all together 1784 *deben* of gold, . . . also silver . . . 966 *deben* and 1 *kite*,[3] a silver figure . . . with head of gold, 3 sticks with human heads of ivory, ebony, and . . . wood, gilt, 6 litters of that prince, 6 stools belonging to them, 6 large coaches of ivory, and . . . wood, the . . . wood inlaid with gold and all manner of precious stones ; the bed of that prince, gilded all over, a statue of that prince of gilded ebony, the head being of lapis lazuli, vessels of bronze and much clothing of that prince. List of the crops which his Majesty captured from the fields of Megiddo : 207,400 sacks of wheat, besides what the soldiers of his Majesty had already reaped for their own use." [4]  In other cities, again, Phœnician cities this time, they find " wine lying in the cellars like flood water." [5]  We are not surprised to find it added that " his Majesty's soldiers were drunk every day, and anointed with oil, as at festival times in Egypt."

The picture here displayed is that of a flourishing civilization, and the excavations confirm its truth. We have only to look at the storehouses discovered at Gezer, one store-chamber alone containing about 600 baskets of corn. The cultivation of grain and fruit, as well as cattle-breeding, must have reached a high stage of development. Prosperity, and even a certain amount of luxury, is noticeable in the cities, especially along the coast.

Of course, the conditions must not be exaggerated. Things were not done on a great scale. What strikes one in the Amarna letters, which are hardly a century later, is the modesty of the figures mentioned. We find one prince asking and receiving fifty men to defend his city ; [6] another requests forty ; a third twenty or even ten. A fourth writes : " Please give me six

---

[1] The word for ' jar ' means a tall, long-necked jar with two handles.

[2] The name means bowl-shaped vessels with a small foot and peculiarly curved handle.     [3] 1 *deben* = 12 *kites* = 91 grammes.

[4] The translation is taken from *TBAT*, vol. i, p. 239 f.

[5] The metaphor was naturally suggested to the Egyptian by the Nile floods.

[6] See Winckler, *Die Tontafeln von Tell el-Amarna* (1896), 268, l. 11, 83, l. 67, 150, l. 18, 151, l. 15, 154, l. 14. In Knudtzon's work *Die El-Amarna-Tafeln* these are 238, l. 11, 108, l. 67, 149, l. 18, 151, l. 15.

bows, three daggers, and three swords. If, when I march against the country of the king, you come to my aid, then I shall certainly subdue it." [1]  Besides, the numbers of the troops mentioned in the report quoted above are not very high : 2503 prisoners from the whole of Syria, 1796 of these being slaves (and the number includes women and children). The number of captured chariots points to an army of about 3000 men. [2]  Of course, it is to be remembered that armies in the ancient East were never very large. It is improbable that any Egyptian king ever invaded Asia with more than 25,000 or 30,000 men ; the usual number would be under 20,000. [3]

When Thutmosis III entered Palestine the sovereignty of Babylon over it was at most merely nominal. Indeed, it may have already been overthrown by the predecessors of that king. The foreign rule of the Cassites, who, thanks to the advance of the Hittites, had conquered their way to the royal throne of Babylon, meant the downfall of Babylon's power in the west ; and Thutmosis made it clear to the people of Palestine that the Egyptian sovereignty which he had helped to establish was to be a real one. He deliberately did his utmost to 'Egyptianize' the country. Nor was he content with setting up princes obedient to his will. From the accounts of his sixth campaign we learn that he took to Egypt, evidently for their education, the children of the princes and of their brethren, and " whenever one of these princes dies, his Majesty appoints the son of the dead prince in his father's stead." [4]  Could there be a more effective method of permeating the conquered country with Egyptian civilization than by securing that the leaders of the people should breathe the air of the Egyptian Court during their most susceptible years ?  Further, Egyptian garrisons marched into the land in order to help the growth of a feeling friendly to Egypt. [5]  At the head of these were governors, or plenipo-

---

[1] In the letter from Lachish (*TBAT*, vol. i, p. 128).

[2] *Cf.* Eerdmans, *Alttestamentliche Studien*, vol. ii (1908), p. 77.

[3] Breasted, *A History of Egypt* (1906), p. 424.

[4] *TBAT*, vol. i, p. 241.

[5] This is clear from an inscription of the successor of Thutmosis III, Amenophis II (1447-1420) : " Lo ! his Majesty received the news that some of those Asiatics who were in Jeketi had conspired to form a plot to drive his Majesty's garrison from the city and to separate themselves from his Majesty's loyal servants " (*TBAT*, vol. i, p. 244).

tentiaries, in whom the native petty princes could not fail to recognize Pharaoh's power,[1] in spite of the personal freedom of movement which was allowed them. "The whole region was under the general control of a ' Governor of the North Countries.' " [2] A document of a later period, which is interesting for its own sake, gives eloquent proof that from this time forward Egypt's suzerainty over Palestine was looked upon as regular and in order. It is a passport exactly corresponding to a similar document of to-day which a king of Near Asia of that time gave to his ambassador : " To the Kings of Canaan, the servants of my brother,[3] thus writes the King : Lo, I have sent Akia, my ambassador, to the King of Egypt, my brother, to convey to him my sympathy.[4] Let no one stop him. Conduct him quickly to Egypt and put him quickly into the hands of the . . . in Egypt. Let no violence be done to him." [5] This passport shows how international safety of travel was a matter for the diplomacy of that day. The Babylonian Cassite king Burnaburiash complains to Amenophis IV that his merchants in Hinnatuni (Old Testament Channaton,[6] in the land of Zebulun) have been attacked by men from Acco. " Canaan is thy country," he writes to him, " and its kings are thy servants. In thy country I have been subjected to violence. Keep them in order and restore the money they have stolen ; and, as for the men who have murdered my servants, kill them and avenge the blood of the slain. If thou dost not kill these men, they will commit murder again, either attacking my caravans or thy messengers, and then messages between us shall cease ; and if that come to pass, they will rebel against thee." [7] On another occasion an unknown person promises to put in order all the

[1] Kittel, *Geschichte des Volkes Israel*, vol. i, p. 103—in particular *note* 1.

[2] Breasted, p. 322.

[3] The " brother " is the King of Egypt; the kings of Canaan are his " servants " ! In the Old Testament also one king addresses or speaks of another as his brother (1 Kings ix, 13, xx, 32).

[4] This alludes apparently to the death of Amenophis III, who died in 1375 (Lehmann-Haupt, *Israel* (1911), p. 24). Weber in Knudtzon's *El-Amarna-Tafeln*, p. 1073, refers it to the death of his predecessor, Thutmosis IV, which took place in 1411. 2 Sam. x, 2, attests the practice of sending ambassadors from one royal Court to another on an errand of condolence.

[5] The passport is given in Knudtzon, no. 30, in Winckler, no. 14.

[6] Josh. xix, 14.

[7] Knudtzon, 199, ll. 10–13, Winckler, 145, ll. 13–15.

roads of Pharaoh, as far as Busruna (probably Bozra, east of Jordan).[1] Over these roads, thus made straight, passed not only soldiers and diplomats, but also traders, and care was taken that their rich wares no longer went down the Euphrates to Babylon, but were diverted to the Nile delta.[2] The vassals of the Egyptian King declare repeatedly that they guard not only the King's troops, but also the royal trading caravans. " Who am I," writes one from the south of Palestine,[3] " that I should not forward the caravans of the King, my lord ? Lo, Labaia, my father, served the King, his lord, and he forwarded all the caravans which the King sent."[4] Palestine, the natural corridor for these trading expeditions, could not fail to profit from this traffic. On the other hand, the King of Egypt was surrounded by settlements of people to whom the name Charu is given in an Egyptian inscription.[5] This name, in which we have an echo of the Old Testament name Horites,[6] is the name in Egyptian for the inhabitants of the south of Syria—that is to say, Palestinians also. The fact that such settlements existed is all the more important for us since we may take it for granted that they were not without reflex effects on their homeland of Palestine.[7]

Thus from various sides we hear of Egyptian influence on Palestine ; even in external things, such as building, there was a new impulse given. The clearest evidence of this is in Gezer, where, in place of the ancient circular walls, which had been destroyed, new ones were built, which to this day are, in places, from 9 to 12 feet in height.[8] Round Lachish also was built a new, more extensive circumvallation, and a little later a new

[1] South-east from Ashtaroth. See Weber in Knudtzon, p. 1292, and Buhl, *Geographie des alten Palästina*, p. 251.

[2] Breasted, p. 322.

[3] Weber in Knudtzon, p. 1318.

[4] Knudtzon, 255, ll. 12–19, or Winckler, 256, ll. 12–19 ; also Knudtzon, 194, ll. 20–24.

[5] On a stele erected by Amenophis III (*c.* 1411–1375). *TBAT*, vol. i, p. 246.

[6] *Supra*, p. 36, *note* 2.

[7] *Cf.* the mention in the Egyptian Wen Amon's report of the name Berket-El, which seems to have been borne by a Semitic merchant in Tanis (*TBAT*, vol. i, p. 227, *note* 2).

[8] They are 12 feet wide and built of large, irregularly hewn stones, the interstices being filled with smaller stones. Can even the primitive drainage attempts in Gezer be due to Egyptian influence ?

stronghold in Egyptian style.[1] Evidently Thutmosis and his immediate successors considered it important to give special attention to the defence of the roads of communication between Egypt and Canaan.[2] No doubt a few cities were also provided with an Egyptian palace ; at least, there is evidence of one such palace in the Syrian port of Simyra. In Byblos there was even an Egyptian temple; and a monumental hieroglyphic inscription from the west dome of Gezer indicates the existence of a large temple in Egyptian style,[3] which seems from the articles found there to have belonged to the Nineteenth Dynasty (1350–1205).[4]

This is merely the outward expression of the fact that the gods of the conquerors followed them into the conquered country, and that, as the excavations show, Egyptian gods now made their entry into Syria and Palestine : Osiris, Ptah, in particular Amon, the chief deity of Thebes, to whom King Amenophis II once sacrificed seven Syrian princes after clubbing them with his own hand.[5] Whether such violent methods helped to make the god popular in the country is more than questionable, but the traces of his worship are unmistakable. It is not always possible to tell whether the bearers of names compounded with Amon were natives of Palestine or merely natives of Egypt living in Palestine or Syria,[6] but in some cases the former alternative is practically certain.[7] The city of Byblos

---

[1] No doubt that of King Japhia, afterward destroyed by Joshua (Josh. x, 3 ff., 31 ff.). The foundations are most carefully laid in Egyptian fashion on fine sand, which was put there for the purpose (Thiersch, *AA* (1908), p. 20 f.).    [2] *Cf.* Kittel, *Geschichte des Volkes Israel*, vol. i, p. 178.
[3] Breasted, p. 322 f.
[4] Thiersch, *AA* (1909), p. 401.
[5] *TBAT*, vol. i, p. 245. This recalls the Hebrew practice called *herem*— *i.e.*, the ban—as it was carried out by Samuel on Agag, King of the Amalekites (1 Sam. xv, 33), and by others. The Philistines did the same with Saul's dead body (1 Sam. xxxi, 10). Practices like these were universal.
[6] The occurrence of Amon in proper names in the letters from Taanach (Sellin, *Tell Ta'annek*, p. 119, and *Nachlese*, p. 36 f.) does not definitely decide the question.
[7] For example, in the case of the Syrian vassal Amanhatbi and that of Pen-Amon, servant of the Prince of Byblos (*TBAT*, vol. i, p. 229) ; probably also in the case of the officer of the same name mentioned in the papyrus of Anastasius III and in that of Necht-Amon, named in the same papyrus (*TBAT*, vol. i, p. 249). Pen-Amon is presumably a compound like Peni-El (Gen. xxxii, 31) or Penu-El (Gen. xxxii, 32), meaning the "Face of El," or like Pene-Baal, "Face of Baal," often applied to the Phœnician deity Tanit, and would therefore mean the "Face of Amon." *Cf.* also Exod. xxxiii, 14 f.

(Gebal) [1] on the coast of Phœnicia seems to have been a special centre of the worship of Amon. Letters of the local prince mention him in the same breath with the Baal goddess of the city.[2] From the description by Wen Amon,[3] an Egyptian who came to Byblos as commissioner of the high priest of Amon to get cedarwood for a new temple-ship, and brought an image of Amon with him, we learn that the fathers of the King of Byblos " have sacrificed to Amon all their days." Wen Amon's account is also instructive from the manner in which the Egyptian speaks to the Syrian about Amon : " There is not a vessel on the river that does not belong to Amon, for the sea is his, and to him belongs Lebanon, of which thou sayest, ' It is mine.' Lebanon grows for the ship of Amon, the lord of all ships." In keeping with this, Wen Amon makes the Syrian speak as if he voluntarily admitted that all the art and science of his city came from Egypt. Even if the Egyptian is here ascribing to the Syrian thoughts which the latter perhaps never expressed, and which he perhaps never even entertained, still, the passage is instructive with regard to the intellectual exchange which was bound to take place in view of the constant contact with Egypt on Syrian (and, of course, also on Palestinian) territory. No doubt in the course of the centuries many an Egyptian not only entertained the thoughts to which Wen Amon gives expression, but also actually uttered them in the hearing of Syrians or Palestinians. And Syrians and Palestinians must have partially agreed with them,[4] even if we subtract from their letters to the Egyptian Court all that can be ascribed merely to sycophancy and conventional flattery. There is a letter from the Prince Abimilki of Tyre to Amenophis IV (1375-58), that remarkable reformer who sat on the throne of Egypt, and who attached great importance to the introduction of the worship of the one highest god, the " Lord of the Sun." In the beginning of one of his letters [5] the Tyrian prince soars to an actual hymn in praise of the King, in which he alludes to him

---

[1] It is mentioned in the Old Testament in Ezek. xxvii, 9, and its inhabitants in Josh. xiii, 5. On the other hand, the text in 1 Kings v, 18 is incorrect.
[2] Knudtzon, 87, l. 5, 95, l. 3, and Winckler, 67, l. 5, 110, l. 3 f.
[3] *TBAT*, vol. i, p. 228.
[4] Knudtzon, 55, l. 53 ff., and Winckler, 138 *dorso*, 18 ff.
[5] Knudtzon, 147, l. 5 ff., and Winckler, 149, l. 5 ff.

as the sun, who by appointment of the sun, his gracious father, rises day by day over the countries, giving life to all, giving the whole country peace. Here we have not merely the general recognition of the divinity of Pharaoh as the incarnation of the sun-god, such as is frequent in the form of address, to the " great King, the god,[1] the sun," in the correspondence of these Syrian and Palestinian princes with Egypt. We can hear in it something like an echo of the " new doctrine," and it is also to be observed that some scholars have claimed to find similar allusions to the " new doctrine " elsewhere—*e.g.*, in contemporary letters from Jerusalem.[2] Some scholars have even changed the names [3] in order to bring them into harmony with it.

Much more popular in Palestine than the supreme Egyptian State divinities of the rank of Amon, or Aton (this was Amenophis' name for his supreme god), was the small Bes, "one of the host of demons, who might be compared to the satyrs of the Greeks. Their task is to gladden the gods by music and dancing, or to wait upon the children of the gods. They are conceived as comical beings, and images of them are used as mirror-handles or salve-boxes ; but they also fight their enemies with knives and bows, and strangle serpents and lions. It was probably protection against evil beings which Bes was specially expected to give."[4] Among the excavation layers belonging to this period were found Hathor terracottas, statuettes of the cat-headed Bast and of her relative, the lion-headed Sechmet, also Isis-Horus groups,[5] and ushabtis—*i.e.*, small mummy-shaped figures which were buried with the dead in the belief that they would come to life in the world beyond, and undertake for them there the coarser tasks, specially field-work. The

---

[1] The usual form is the plural *ilani*, ' gods,' sometimes outdoing the immediately preceding singular *ilu*, god (Knudtzon, 151, l. 1, Winckler, 151, l. 1).

[2] See Weber's remarks in Knudtzon, p. 1025. The letters from Jerusalem are referred to in Knudtzon, 287, l. 60 f., 288, ll. 5–7, and in Winckler, 180 f.

[3] Knudtzon, 292, l. 36, 315, l. 13, 326, l. 17 (Winckler, 239, 236, 213).

[4] Erman, *Die ägyptische Religion* (1905), p. 78.

[5] No image was more popular in Egypt than that of Isis, the mother of the deity, holding her infant Horus on her lap (Erman, p. 37)—a prototype of our Madonna pictures ! It is very questionable whether the Egyptian goddess Mut should also be mentioned here, although some scholars find her name in place-names and proper names like Jarmuth and 'Azmaveth. In all these names *maveth* seems to mean ' death.' Mut (Death) was a goddess among the Phœnicians. See Eusebius, *Præparatio evangelica*, Book I, § 38.

interesting thing is that these articles were now no longer merely imported from Egypt. A clay mould was found in Gezer which had been used for the local manufacture of statuettes of Bes. Egyptian amulets also become more numerous : Horus-eyes of faience and bronze, also scarabs. A burial-urn from Tell Sakarije has restored to us the rich jewellery of a girl, all in Egyptian style : 81 beads made of carnelian, of Egyptian shape of the Eighteenth and Nineteenth Dynasties,[1] 250 beads of faience, of different colours, 4 faience scarabs, some of them from the time of Thutmosis III and Amenophis III, Egyptian amulets of faience, etc. And in this connexion we may also mention the discovery in Megiddo in a carefully sealed jar of a collection of ornaments : a large number of small beads of clay and red carnelian, amulets of green enamel, Egyptian Horus-eyes of steatite and stone, animal teeth, numerous Cyprus shells once joined to form a necklace, a fossilized snake which had been worn as an amulet, two bronze finger rings, small sheets of gold as thin as paper rolled together and impressed with leaf-ornamentation, delicately toothed fish-fins, bronze lace-work, as well as two images of Bes of green enamel, small Egyptian statuettes, and pieces of painted glass and steatite. In the urn and beside it were thirty-two other scarabs with one or two lions or the royal ring of Thutmosis III.[2] In all these there is again noticeable the strong Egyptian influence.

But it was not only Egyptian influences that were at work in this period. The West, whose products begin to appear as early as the close of the previous period,[3] now begins very clearly to make its influence felt and to fill the Palestinian markets with its wares. It is the ceramics that teach us most regarding this influence. The influence of Cyprus is evidenced by characteristic hemispherical bowls from Lachish, with ladder-ornamentation in sepia brown on pale green clay. Genuine Mycenæan potsherds are not rare. They suggest (and it is corroborated by an Egyptian picture from the middle of the fourteenth century B.C.[4] showing tribute-bringing ambassadors) that the beauty of Ægean art found admirers in genuinely Oriental

---

[1] The Eighteenth Dynasty reigned from *c.* 1580, the Nineteenth from 1350 onward.

[2] *Tell el-Mutesellim,* vol. i, p. 88 f.       [3] *Supra,* p. 60.

[4] See Breasted, Fig. 118.

territory. Among the gifts brought by the ambassadors to King Tutankhamen (1375–58) are splendid specimens of classically shaped Ægean vases, one of which is so large that it takes two men to carry it. Elegant animal-heads form the lids of the vases, and the lower, pointed end is fastened into a neat stand. This increasing importation from the West could not fail to lead to imitation of it. These imitations, of course, do not attain the excellence of the models. They are coarser and more limited. Yet progress is discernible. This is perhaps due to the fact that the use of the potter's wheel, which at an earlier date seems to have been employed only on rare occasions, now becomes in some places the regular practice. Indeed, Macalister made in Gezer, from studying the marks on the bottom of earthenware vessels, the delicate observation that whereas the potter's wheel was formerly turned from right to left it must now have been worked in both directions.[1]

Even the shape of the vessels gains in elegance, although it must not be judged by standards applicable to Greek ceramics. The jars become slenderer, sometimes with the neck so long that the clay of the jar's body has been twisted by the weight of it, giving rise to remarkable and not unbeautiful misshapes, usually called *bilbils*,[2] from the name given to them by the Arabian labourers employed at the excavations. These stand quite firmly, but the large jars taper downward to such a sharp point that, like the jars on the Egyptian representation just mentioned, they require a special stand to keep them upright. On the other hand, pots and dishes resting on low feet are mostly shallower, and made of any convenient shape. The clay has been smoothed or passed through a bath of dye, and the colouring has been mostly done in thin, vigorous strokes of monochrome, repeating a small geometrical decorative design. There are also examples of imitations of natural objects : birds, gazelles, imaginary quadrupeds, and even creatures of polyparian shapes. Of special ceramic interest are the potsherds from Megiddo, belonging probably to the thirteenth century,

---

[1] On the other hand, there is no proof that the potter's wheel was known in Jericho previous to the coming of Israel (Sellin and Watzinger, *Jericho*, p. 110). The pre-Hebrew ceramics in Jericho form a complete unit in which there is no room for additions. See *op. cit.*, p. 106 f.

[2] See Vincent, *Canaan*, p. 328, with illustrations.

on which are painted Canaanite warriors in brown-red and black pigment on flesh-coloured ground.[1] When we remember that these figures show the equipment of the very people with whom the invading Israelites had to deal, we are tempted to spend a moment in describing them. Their sole garment is a short, triangular, bright piece of breast-armour with large black bosses, the breast-armour probably of wood, the bosses of metal. In the left hand they carry a small round shield; in the right hand a hatchet or battleaxe. The only warrior whose face has been completely preserved has black hair and beard, such as we frequently find on Egyptian representations of Asiatics.[2] If from the above-mentioned picture of Asiatic ambassadors bringing tribute we may draw conclusions with regard to the dress worn, at least by people of rank, in time of peace, the difference in comparison with the previous period [3] consists in this, that the ancient cloak-shaped garment has been exchanged for a long strip of cloth wound spirally from three to six times, close fitting round the body, and kept in place by a belt tied with a large bow, the edges being bound with braid.[4]

Thus far in dealing with specimens of ceramic art we have mentioned only those on which figures have been painted; but this period also provides examples of vessels which are actually made, entirely or partly, in the shape of animals— lions, apes, ducks, pigeons, etc. Of special interest is a bowl of red clay from Tell es-Safi, with the figure of a swan swimming in it. The curved neck of the swan is seen through a triangular cut in the wall of the bowl, while the head and beak project over the upper rim, alongside of the figures of two young birds, crudely attached.[5] The excavations of Tell es-Safi give us still more important information. Tell es-Safi is in all likelihood

---

[1] *Tell es-Mutesellim*, vol. i., Plate XXIV, and p. 81.

[2] The upper lip is usually, but not always, shaven, and in some cases the hair of the head is closely cropped. *Cf.*, in addition to the pictures of Absha's caravan (referred to on p. 49 above) and of the Asiatic ambassadors mentioned on p. 87, the Leyden relief from the grave of Haremheb (1350–15), given in Breasted, illustrations 116 and 148. It shows the presentation of Asiatic prisoners.

[3] *Supra*, p. 58.

[4] See Benzinger's *Hebräische Archäologie* (1907), p. 77 and Fig. 38— princes from Lebanon felling trees.

[5] *Cf.* Thiersch, *AA* (1908), p. 371 f.

the site of the ancient Philistine city of Gath, so we here obtain a glance at the nature of Philistine ceramic work. Seeing that it is now certain [1] that Caphtor, whence, according to the Old Testament,[2] the Philistines came, was Crete, we need not be surprised to find Western influences so distinct and palpable in Philistine ceramic work that, as a whole, it must be called " a late Mycenæan sister-group to the Cyprian type which from the end of the second millennium [3] was gradually taking rigid geometrical forms." Its chief characteristic is the debased Mycenæan spiral.[4] On the other hand, the way in which animal figures are fitted into a linear space betrays special skill.

The pronounced Ægean touch which appears in the ceramics of this period is also found in the bronze articles. Needles with eyes, decorated with spiral patterns, from Gezer and Lachish are specially instructive ; also a massive double-edged axe from Gezer. Indeed, among the discoveries in Crete the double-edged axe plays an important part as one of the main objects connected with the cult. True, it is also found elsewhere [5]— e.g., among the Hittites ; and Hittite influence should perhaps be taken into account in connexion with the development of the metal-work of that time. The advance in the technique of bronze-work is perhaps best illustrated by a number of bowl-stands or basin-stands in Megiddo, one, for example, showing a nude female figure playing a flute.[6]

At the close of the period with which we are dealing we meet with the beginning of the transition from bronze to iron. It is not surprising that some have sought to connect the invention of work in iron with the contemporary invasion of peoples from the West. Perhaps, however, it is doing the Philistines too much honour to credit them with the invention of iron-work.[7]

---

[1] Cf. Eduard Meyer, *Sitzungsberichte der Berliner Akademie* (1909), p. 1022 f., and F. Stähelin, *Die Philister* (1918). ' Documentary ' attestation that the Philistines came from Crete is found in the so-called Discus of Phæstus.

[2] Amos ix, 7 ; Jer. xlvii, 4 ; Deut. ii, 23 ; cf. Gen. x, 14, corrected text. The well-known phrase " Cherethites and Pelethites " (2 Sam. viii, 18, etc.) means Cretans and Philistines, and hints at an intimate connexion between them. Cf. also 1 Sam. xxx, 14.

[3] Thiersch, *AA* (1908), p. 381.      [4] *Ibid.* (1909), p. 575.

[5] Cf. A. B. Cook, " The Cretan Axe-cult outside Crete " in the *Transactions of the Third International Congress for the History of Religions*, vol. ii, pp. 184–194.      [6] *Tell es-Mutesellim*, vol. i, p. 85 f.

[7] As Belck does in *ZE* (1907 and 1908). See my discussion with him there.

# CIVILIZATION IN PALESTINE

As a matter of fact, we are reduced to pure surmise when we try to answer the question, from what quarter iron and the knowledge of its working came into Palestine. The one certain thing is that the discovery of its technique presupposes an abundant supply and the easy accessibility of the raw materials in the country where the technique was invented.[1] Seeing that there is an entire lack of these raw materials in Palestine,[2] we must look outside for the sources of iron and iron-work. Of all the adjacent peoples it is the Hittites if not the Phœnicians[3] or the Arabians[4] or even the smith tribe of Kenites[5] to whom the invention should be ascribed. The Canaanites seem soon afterward to have used iron for their war-chariots, and to have become so expert in such work that their products were in great demand both at home and abroad. In the spurious letters of the papyrus of Anastasius IV, belonging to the first year of King Sethos II (1209–1205), three closely adjacent cities in the plain of Kishon are named as centres for the export of war-chariots and first-class chariot-parts. W. Max Müller[6] attaches great importance to this notice, because in writing exercises of this kind (that is what these pretended letters are) references are made only to manufacturing centres which were well known to every Egyptian. The district in which the cities mentioned are situated is just that district which is named in the Old Testament[7] as famous or, rather, notorious among the Israelites[8] for its "chariots of iron." Is it too bold an inference that the special feature of these Canaanite chariots lay in their use of iron? For why should the Egyptians have procured their chariot-parts from such a distance unless these possessed some advantage which the Egyptians either did not have at all or did not have in equal perfection?

[1] Blanckenhorn, *ZE* (1907), p. 364.    [2] *Supra*, p. 22.

[3] Jer. xv, 12, a very corrupt passage, speaks of the north as the source of iron.    [4] Ezek. xxvii, 19.

[5] In Gen. iv, 22, Tubal-Cain, a double name, apparently a coalescence of two figures, is said to be "father of all those that hammer bronze and iron." See Gunkel's commentary on the passage. The Kenites were originally associated with Sinai and the god of it ; the peninsula of Sinai contains very ancient mines.

[6] *Asien und Europa*, p. 153.    [7] Josh. xvii, 16 ; Judges i, 19, iv, 3, 13.

[8] *Cf.* also the fact that the excavators found in Tell el-Mutesellim a smithy with iron dross and lumps of brown clay iron ore (*Tell el-Mutesellim*, vol. i, p. 130 ff.).

Strong, however, as were Egyptian and Ægean and even Hittite influences at the time with which we are dealing, the influence of Babylon, which had been predominant in the preceding period, was still by no means exhausted. On the contrary, the traces of it found in this period testify that it still continued to possess the importance it had attained in the preceding period. Imitations of Babylonian style are still apparent even in technique. In Lachish, for example, was found a Babylonian seal-cylinder imitated in Egyptian porcelain ; and a magnificent bronze curved sword found in Gezer seems to be almost an actual copy of the sword of the Babylonian king [1] Rammannirari I (c. 1325). But there is something more important—the whole wide field of the use of writing. The great surprise connected with the discovery of the archives of the Egyptian king Amenophis IV (1375–1358) in 1897 at Tell Amarna was the fact that the correspondence of the kings of Near Asia and of the vassal kings of Syria and Palestine with the royal Court of Egypt was carried on in Babylonian writing. The contrast is striking. The Syrians and Palestinians begin each letter with the assurance that they cast themselves seven and seven times in the dust before Pharaoh. They call themselves the dust on which he treads, the footstool of his feet, his dog, and his groom. But the language in which they thus address him is neither his language nor theirs—it is Babylonian. And the same is the case with the contemporary correspondence of the Palestinian city-kings with each other. This is proved by writings found at Lachish and Taanach. So predominant must have been the influence of Babylonia on the civilization of Palestine in the preceding period that even now, when the power of Babylon beyond its own frontiers was near its close, the Babylonian language was still that of all official and diplomatic intercourse. The importance of this is in no way diminished by the fact that the language of this correspondence contains numerous Canaanite glosses. On the contrary, it is only another confirmation of the former intellectual superiority of Babylon that the language is retained even although those using it are beginning to find difficulties in mastering it. The

---

[1] Vincent, *Canaan d'après l'exploration récente* (Paris, 1907), p. 231, where cylinder and sword are both illustrated.

pains bestowed upon its acquisition are shown by the discovery of a few clay-tablets in Amarna. These prove that the scribes at the Egyptian Court employed Babylonian texts for their linguistic studies ; [1] and they also supply proof that Babylonian myths, like the Adapa myth [2]—that of the man who trifles away the gift of immortality which was to be bestowed upon him— were already, in an original form, part of the contents of an Egyptian library in the first half of the fourteenth century B.C. Nor must it be forgotten that the road from Babylon to Egypt led through Palestine, and that the scribes at the petty Palestinian Courts, no less than their Egyptian colleagues, required foreign reading matter for their studies. Who can tell what they may have borrowed for this purpose in the way of Babylonian literature ? There need, therefore, be no hesitation in giving a satisfactory answer to the question, Whence comes the knowledge of Babylonian mythical material that is found in the Old Testament ? In any case, the time is past for thinking that such knowledge must be confined to the days of the later Hebrew kingdom, or even to the period of the Exile.

But our interest in the Amarna correspondence is not confined to the proof it affords that at that time people in Palestine wrote in the Babylonian language. It also shows how large a place writing occupied in the life of the time, and in their own way the twenty-two clay tablets found in Jericho without any writing on them are evidence of the comparatively large demand that there was for writing material. Still, it would be over-hasty to conclude that writing and reading were generally diffused at that time. It must be remembered that the writings which we possess, letters, lists, and so forth, all come from official circles; that therefore the art of writing that produced them was not a possession of the common people, but only of the scribe, well trained for his official career. From Egyptian sources we know the esteem in which the scribe was held. An Egyptian father, taking his son to school to be trained as a scribe, exhorts him to be diligent, and points out that while every form of industry is beset by difficulties and dangers the office of the scribe is the

---

[1] On these tablets the Egyptian practice is followed of using large coloured full stops to indicate where words end. They are not always correctly placed, or there are inconsistencies (Knudtzon, *Die El-Amarna-Tafeln*, p. 25).

[2] Also the myth of Nergal and Ereshkigal (*TBAT*, vol. i, p. 34 ff., 69 ff.).

only one that brings honour and wealth ![1] We are not told,
but we can easily imagine, that similar thoughts were entertained in scribal circles in Palestine. And when we find a scribe
addressing his words, not to his correspondent personally, but
to the latter's scribe,[2] because the scribe is the only one who
can read what is written, it is an indication of how business was
done " over the heads " of the illiterate. And similarity of
education and of interests binds men together. The ancient
Canaanite name of the city Kirjath-sepher [3] (" Book Town ")
shows that there were certain centres for the writing fraternity.
If we give rein to our fancy we can easily picture other results.
It is easy to imagine that in such scribal towns or districts a
culture took root whose fruits are only fully seen in the days
of later Hebrew literature. Kittel [4] reminds us that the sage
Imhotep, whose proverbs were known and recited centuries
afterward, was chosen by the Egyptian scribes as their special
guardian.[5] Does that not mean that here and there in their
circles these scribes cultivated a Wisdom literature like that
which was afterward ascribed to Solomon,[6] or which we still
have in the Proverbs of the Old Testament and of the Apocrypha?
In any case, nothing forbids the assumption that what was thus
going on in Egypt found imitators in Egypt's dependency,
Palestine.[7] Besides, these scribal circles may have become the

[1] Breasted's *History of Egypt*, p. 98 f.
[2] *Cf.* the beginning of the letter from Lachish : " Say to the great one,
' thus saith Pâbi,' " etc. (*TBAT*, vol. i, p. 128), or the close of a letter of
Abdi-Hiba from Jerusalem : " To the tablet-writer of the King of my lord thus
saith Abdi-Hiba, thy servant, ' Take words, fair words to the King, my lord,' "
etc. (Knudtzon, 286, l. 61 ff., Winckler, 179, l. 61 ff.).
[3] Josh. xv, 15 f.; Judges i, 11 f. Sethe (*Nachrichten der Königlichen
Gesellschaft der Wissenschaften zu Göttingen, philosophische-historische Klasse*
(1917), p. 464, *notes 1 and 2*) has shown that there is no reason for preferring
the reading Kirjath-sopher (" Scribes' Town "). Later the town was called
Debir.
[4] See his *Geschichte des Volkes Israel*, 3rd edition, vol. i, p. 196 f., *note* 5.
[5] Breasted, p. 83.                    [6] 1 Kings v, 12.
[7] Proofs may be given in a series of proverbial or poetical forms of expression in the Tell Amarna letters (Knudtzon, 147, ll. 41–48, Winckler, 149,
ll. 41–48) : " Who listens to the King, his lord, and serves him in his place,
upon him the sun rises and good . . . returns to him from his lord's lips.
But if he hearken not to the word of his lord, the King, his city is ruined,
his house is ruined, nor does his name abide for ever in the land " (see also
Knudtzon, 153, ll. 12–14) ; (Knudtzon, 193, l. 17, Winckler, 264, l. 16) :
" But the man who does not serve, him will the King curse "; (Knudtzon,

natural centres for the preservation of many a piece of historical tradition. After all, the scribes would have charge of the archives, which could not fail to be produced by the growing requirements of a political intercourse conducted in writing. Judging from excavations in Taanach and Jericho, the Palestinian cities possessed such archives.[1] Doubtless these scribes would also have charge of the propagation of the legal decisions of the law-book of Hammurabi.[2] And, finally, this communal life of writing experts enables us to understand more easily the successful transition from the foreign Babylonian writing to a native Canaanite style.

How this new Canaanite style of writing arose is still obscure. Most light has been thrown on the subject by two recent papers of Sethe.[3] These seem to have proved successfully that the Semitic (Canaanite) alphabet had the Egyptian script both for prototype and pattern—for prototype with regard to its outward form, and for pattern with regard to its nature. A script without vowels, like the Semitic, could not have been created by a Semitic-speaking people of their own accord, whereas they would naturally make use of such if it lay to their hand ready made. In the Egyptian language ideographic pictures became automatically in course of time consonantal signs, because in view of the gradual disintegration of the language certain roots

---

195, ll. 16–23, Winckler, 144, ll. 16–23) : "The lord is the sun in the sky, and his servants wait for the words of their master as for the rising of the sun "; (Knudtzon, 214, ll. 30–33) : "Any one who hearkens not to the King's words is an evildoer in thy land "; (Knudtzon, 232, l. 12 ff., Winckler, 157, l. 12 ff.) : "Where is the man to whom the King writes and he does not obey ? " The passage (Knudtzon, 264, ll. 15–19, Winckler, 189, ll. 15–19) "If we ascend to heaven or descend to the earth, our life is in thy hands," reminds us of Amos ix, 2, or Psalm cxxxix, 7. Knudtzon, 266, ll. 19–25 (Winckler, 190, ll. 19–25) : "A brick may move away from , . ., but I shall not move from under the King's feet " (Knudtzon, 292, ll. 13–17, Winckler, 239, ll. 13–17, Knudtzon, 296, ll. 17–22, Winckler, 214, ll. 17–22). Weber (in Knudtzon, p. 1324) quotes as a parallel Is. liv, 10.

[1] Cf. what Wen Amon says about Byblos : "The King of the city ordered the annals of his fathers to be brought in and to be read aloud to me " (TBAT, vol. i, p. 227).

[2] Supra, p. 51.

[3] In the GGN (1916), pp. 88–161, and (1917) pp. 437–475. See specially (1916) pp. 104, 119, 133, 135 ff. ; (1917) pp. 455 f., 465 f. I do not think that Sethe's conclusions have been upset by Hans Bauer (Zur Entzifferung der neuentdeckten Sinaischrift und zur Entstehung des semitischen Alphabetes, 1918).

which they denoted were reduced to one consonant. An intermediate stage between Egyptian and Canaanite script is represented by some recently discovered inscriptions at Sinai. This intermediate stage employs a number of hieroglyphics selected arbitrarily without regard to their Egyptian meaning, and in this fact we have the surprising solution—viz., that the Semite, in borrowing, has taken from the Egyptian script both the spirit and the body of his own creation, but, strangely enough, has not taken them together, but separately. He has named the borrowed signs in accordance with their pictorial meaning and given them their letter-value in accordance with the principle of acrophony.[1] According to Sethe, this alphabet came to Palestine with the Hyksos in the beginning of the sixteenth century B.C., and gradually ousted the Canaanite language spoken in the country. This date would agree with Kittel's statement that the Hebrew script (which in all essentials is identical with the Canaanite) as found on clay fragments in Samaria belonging to the year 900 presupposes a considerably longer use of Canaanite writing, either on stone or bronze, on animal-skin or on papyrus ; because (as he rightly says) it is practically impossible that ink and quill pen were first used on clay fragments.[2] Large consignments of papyrus came from

[1] The customary order of the letters in the alphabet seems to have been determined to some extent by certain associations : *jod* (' hand ') is followed by *kaph* (' hollow of the hand ') ; *mem* (' water ') by *nun* (' fish ') ; *ayin* (' eye ') by *pe* (' mouth ') ; *koff* (' back of the head ') by *resh* (' head ') and *sin* (' tooth '). This order is very old, as it is the same in Greek and in Hebrew. The Hebrew order is attested by certain Psalms—ix f., xxv, xxxiv, xxxvii, cxi, cxii, cxix, cxlv—by Lamentations i–iv, and by Prov. xxxi, 10–31, and also by the cabalistic system of writing called Atbash—interchanging the first letter with the last, the second with the second last, etc., as found in Jer. xxv, 26 (SHeSHaCH = BaBeL), and Jer. li, 1, where the Hebrew LeBKaMaY becomes KaSDIM, meaning Chaldæans.

[2] Kittel, *Geschichte des Volkes Israel*, vol. i, p. 196. The cursive character of this potsherd writing also betrays a lengthy process of evolution. In the excavations at Megiddo and Lachish are found mason's and potter's marks that are of a comparatively early time, and resemble some letters of the Canaanite writing. In Gezer, it is true, treaties in cuneiform script dating from the middle of the fifteenth century B.C. have been found (*TBAT*, vol. i, p. 140), but this is due either to local retention of ancient legal custom or to the fact that Gezer had at the time an Assyrian garrison or colony. This disposes of von Gall's suggestion that David's scribe Shisha (1 Kings iv, 3) was a Cretan and the inventor of alphabetic writing. About 1800 B.C. there were already in Crete three different kinds of writing. (*Hessische Blätter für Volkskunde*, vol. x, p. 43 ff.)

Egypt to Byblos, the city from which is derived the Greek word for book (*biblion*). Wen Amon about 1100 brought to Byblos five hundred rolls at one time.[1] Probably Byblos may have carried on a trade in it, and may have supplied the adjacent country of Palestine with writing material. But papyrus was very unsuitable for Babylonian writing ; that cuneiform style of writing requires a yielding material like soft clay. How splendid a thing the invention of the Canaanite script proved to be is shown by its success. The inventors of this alphabet laid under their debt not only Palestine's near neighbours, Phœnicians, Syrians, Moabites, South Arabians, etc., but also the distant East (India), as well as the whole of the West.[2] And down to this day the very name ' alphabet ' reminds us of its Semitic origin : *alpha*, ' ox ' ; *beta*, ' house.'

Our study has brought before us the contemporary or subsequent effects of many influences—Egyptian, Babylonian, Ægean, and Hittite. As a result, the civilization of the time is of a very mixed kind, and it may fairly be asked whether this very pronounced effect of foreign influences, this lack of a really indigenous civilization among the Canaanites, does not explain why they were bound to succumb to the invading Israelites.

In keeping with this extremely mixed civilization we find an equally pronounced syncretism in the sphere of religion.[3] That the worship of the Babylonian gods which we found prevalent in the Amorite period should still continue is easily understood when we remember that at the time official correspondence was still carried on in the Babylonian language. There were, however, Egyptian deities also. They have already been enumerated.[4] Hittite deities were worshipped too. The officer stationed by Pharaoh in Jerusalem, Abdi-Hiba (or Puda-Hiba), has as the second element of his name the name of the Hittite goddess Hepa.[5] And there is evidence of an Abdi-Hiba in Taanach too.[6] There are other proper names derived from

---

[1] *TBAT*, vol. i, p. 229.

[2] The Greeks looked upon the Phœnicians as the introducers, if not the inventors, of the alphabet.

[3] See Stanley A. Cook, *The Religion of Ancient Palestine* (1908), L. B. Paton in Hastings, *RE*, vol. iii, pp. 176–188, and W. Carleton Wood, " The Religion of Canaan," in the *Journal of Biblical Literature* (1916), pp. 163–279, (1917), pp. 1–133.  [4] *Supra*, p. 84.  [5] Weber in Knudtzon, p. 1333.

[6] Sellin, *Nachlese*, p. 39, Nos. 7 and 8.

G

other gods—nature-gods like Barak,[1] god of the lightning, who is perhaps connected with the more famous Resheph,[2] and more abstract deities like Gad, the god of fortune, whose name recurs in the local name Migdal-Gad [3] ("Tower of Gad"), as well as in the identical Israelite tribal name, and in various other proper names.[4] The Old Testament (Is. lxv, 11) expressly states that this deity, as well as Meni, the god of fate, possibly also an ancient Canaanite deity,[5] was worshipped in Palestine till a late period.

A passage from one of the letters from Taanach, in which the writer expresses the wish that the "lord of the gods" might protect the life of his correspondent,[6] has led some scholars to the opinion that the Canaanite polytheism had undergone a 'monarchical sharpening' which can almost be interpreted as monotheism.[7] When we remember how warmly the princes of Syria and Palestine received the monotheistic doctrine put forth by Amenophis IV [8] it is not possible to deny offhand that ideas of this kind existed at the time.[9] But we must not forget that

[1] *Cf.* the place-name, formerly a tribal name, Bene-Berak (Josh. xix, 45), in the territory of Dan. Its modern name is still the same—Ibn Ibrak. *Cf.* also the name of the well-known Hebrew judge (Judges iv, 6 ff., v, 1). The Babylonians had also a deity Birku, frequently identified with Ramman (*KAT*, 3rd edition, pp. 446 and 451).

[2] There is direct attestation of Resheph as a deity in Phœnician and Aramaic inscriptions, and also, as a borrowed Egyptian name, in the Assyrian epithet of 'fire-god' (*KAT*, p. 478). In the Old Testament the word *resheph* means 'lightning,' and no idea of deity remains in it (Ps. lxxvi, 4, lxxviii, 48). It also means 'flame' in the Song of Songs viii, 6, and 'burning heat' in Deut. xxxii, 24, and Hab. iii, 5. Gressmann therefore suggests that he was a god of pestilence of the Canaanites. There is some support for this, because the name also occurs as that of a god of war, represented with shield, spear, and club, wearing an Asiatic fillet adorned with the head of a gazelle (W. Max Müller, *Asien und Europa*, p. 312).

[3] Josh. xv, 37. The place-name Baal-Gad (Josh. xi, 17, xii, 7, xiii, 5) is probably different.

[4] For example, 'Azgad ("God is Strong," Ezra ii, 12, viii, 12, Neh. vii, 17, x, 16) and perhaps Gaddiel (Num. xiii, 10), Gadmelek on a Hebrew seal, 'Abd al-Jadd ("Servant of God") among the Arabs, etc. Gad is also a deity known to the Syrians, Phœnicians, and Assyrians.

[5] See Nöldeke in Hastings, *RE*, vol. i, p. 661b. The ancient Arabian deity Manat bears a cognate name.     [6] *TBAT*, vol. i, p. 129.

[7] Gressmann, *Die Ausgrabungen in Palästina und das Alte Testament* (1908), p. 20; also Kittel, *Geschichte des Volkes Israel*, 3rd edition, vol. i, p. 212.     [8] *Supra*, p. 85 f.

[9] No inherent objection can be raised against the antiquity of the phrase *el eljon* ("supreme deity"). But until certain proof can be offered we must be cautious, and there is less to be said for the historicity of Gen. xiv (*cf.* verse 18 ff.), because the expression became a favourite one in later Judaism.

# CIVILIZATION IN PALESTINE

the people who used these expressions all belonged to the most cultivated section of the nation ; and a further very important question is, What do such expressions actually mean ? We may say with confidence that these are not the thoughts that gave the religious life of the Canaanites its characteristic stamp. The contrary is the case. True, their religious life, with all its polytheism, seems to have assumed an increasingly unified character ; but that character is of an entirely different kind. The Old Testament itself is a documentary source which enables us to construct a tolerably graphic picture of the religious life of the land. Think of the whole round of sensuous nature-worship into which the Israelites themselves fell after their conquest of the country, and which the ancient prophets and the Deuteronomic legislators unweariedly opposed.[1] It was a worship " on every high hill and under every green tree," [2] under oaks and poplars and terebinths with their enticing shades —a worship which Hosea, and after him Jeremiah, called " a whoring," [3] using the expression not merely in a metaphorical sense, but deliberately, in view of the unclean orgies into which this worship often degenerated. The sanctuaries harboured women [4] who were dedicated to prostitution in the service of the deity ; [5] and when Deuteronomy (xxii, 5) forbids women to wear male dress and men to wear female dress we rightly interpret these striking injunctions in the light of the statement of Servius that in Cyprus men in female dress and women in male dress sacrificed to the bearded Astarte. The infamous *galli*, known to us from the Roman religion, with their female dress and trinkets, are mentioned on a Cyprian inscription by the same technical name which we find applied in the Old Testament [6] to similar phenomena due to Canaanite influence.[7]

---

[1] Deut. xii, 2 ; 1 Kings xiv, 23 ; 2 Kings xvi, 4, xvii, 10.
[2] Jer. ii, 20.       [3] Hos. iv, 13.
[4] The *kedeshen*. Deut. xxiii, 18 ; 1 Kings xiv, 24 ; Amos ii, 7 ; Hos. iv, 14. The name is instructive ; it comes from the same stem as *kādôsh* (holy). The root idea is ' separation,' but, as we see here, this can mean something very different from moral holiness. It is often overlooked, but it is the case that morality and religion come from different sources. See *infra*, p. 110.
[5] The female deity of fertility and sensual love, Astarte, is meant. The name and the institution of male and female *kedeshen* in the service of Astarte probably came from the Babylonian worship of Ishtar. (*KAT*, 3rd edn., p. 437.)
[6] Deut. xxiii, 17.
[7] Robertson Smith, *The Old Testament in the Jewish Church.*

In fact, this orgiastic character seems to have pervaded the whole Canaanite religion. Wine-drinking—for the deity worshipped was the giver of wine [1]—and noisy music were general features of the current forms of worship. The excavations have brought to light rattles comparable to the *sistra* of the Egyptians. Distinct statements leave us no room for doubt that sensual extravagance and unbridled ecstasy were allowed full sway. Wen Amon, in his itinerary already quoted, tells what he saw with his own eyes at Byblos. When the prince of the city was one day sacrificing to his gods the deity seized one of his most noble youths and threw him into ecstasy, so that he raved the whole night through.[2] That is a striking parallel to phenomena of a later time which are well known from the history of Saul,[3] and which are usually compared to the doings of modern dervishes. All this shows the source whence such phenomena came among the Israelites. And we must also include the memorable scene on Mount Carmel,[4] where the Canaanite priests of Baal encircled the altar of their god, praying him to send rain. By dancing [5] and loud crying, cutting themselves with swords and lancets till the blood streamed down their bodies, they carried their excitement to the utmost limit. That was the way to please the god! As late as Hosea's time [6] it was a practice to cut the skin " in order to get corn and wine." The deity loved to see blood! The excavations of strata belonging to the previous period have already shown us some significant things of this nature.[7] Discoveries made in strata belonging to this period provide material of the same kind.

These excavations have also shown us what is perhaps a genuine Canaanite sanctuary—" high place " it can hardly be called,[8] seeing that it lies in a hollow between two knolls. At least, that is the interpretation given [9] to a number of striking monoliths brought to light at Gezer, eight upright unhewn pillars varying from 5 to 10 feet in height. Two are broken;

[1] Hos. ii, 7 and 8.      [2] *TBAT*, vol. i, p. 226.
[3] 1 Sam. x, 10, xix, 20.      [4] 1 Kings xviii, 26–29.
[5] *Cf.* the name, found in inscriptions, of Baal-markod (" Baal of the Dancing-ground "), near Beirut. It is from the sacred dance or procession that the Hebrew ' feast ' takes its name—*chag*.
[6] Hos. vii, 14.      [7] *Supra*, p. 73 f.
[8] Although Macalister speaks of a " high place."
[9] *Gezer*, vol. ii, p. 381 ff.

all the ten—perhaps there were originally twelve[1]—are in a line running exactly north and south. Something of a similar kind, but from a later time, has been found in ancient Beth-Shemesh [2] —a clump of five stone pillars which have been thrown down. The sacral character of these discoveries has been disputed.[3] Some scholars have pointed to Andrae's discovery [4] of a double row of stelæ in Assyria, one row consisting of twenty-eight pillars containing the names of kings, the other row of about one hundred pillars, with the names of officials and nobles of the empire. Reference has also been made to more than four thousand *ex voto* stelæ consecrated by the Carthaginian people to Baal-Ammon and to the goddess Tanit; and there are analogous finds in Cyprus. These, it is contended, prove that the pillars at Gezer and Beth-Shemesh were not connected with the cultus, but are merely monuments or memorials meant to represent the person of their founder and to ensure his future life; [5] or they were votive stelæ, "erected to the honour of the god." The question would still remain to what deity they were erected. And it is not impossible that they were erected to a deity who was conceived of as dwelling in one of the pillars.[6] Macalister, who discovered the stones,[7] noticed on one of them a number of smooth places, which reminded him of similar smooth places in the Church of the Holy Sepulchre at Jerusalem, and at other places of pilgrimage in Palestine and elsewhere, which are caused by the kisses of numerous worshippers.[8] They might even be due to repeated anointing with blood or oil. And when

---

[1] *Cf.* Exod. xxiv, 4; Josh. iv, 9, 20. The basement, with its rectangular depression, on which an eleventh pillar stood is still to be seen. The pillar itself, perhaps the best of the whole series, may have been carried off as a trophy after a defeat, like the stele of Hammurabi (Thiersch in *ZDPV*, vol. xxxvii (1914), p. 88).

[2] Palestine Exploration Fund, *Quarterly Statement*, 44 (1912), pp. 171–178.

[3] *Cf.* Thiersch, *AA* (1909), pp. 375 ff., 573 f.; *ZDPV*, vol. xxxvii (1914), p. 67; Eduard Meyer, *AA* (1913), p. 82, says it is "neither an altar nor a sanctuary"; Eduard Meyer, *Geschichte des Altertums*, 3rd edition, vol. i, Part II, pp. 421 and 423.

[4] *Die Stelenreihen von Assur* (1913).

[5] *Cf.* 1 Sam. xv, 12; 2 Sam. xviii, 18; Is. lvi, 5.

[6] *Cf.* the Phœnician El-hamman and Baal-hamman, meaning the "God" or "Lord of the Stone Pillars."

[7] Macalister, *Bible Sidelights from the Mound of Gezer*, p. 45 ff.

[8] *Cf.* 1 Kings xix, 18, and Hos. xiii, 2, for the practice of kissing the object of worship.

it was found that one of the other stones had not been quarried locally, but apparently belonged to the Jerusalem district, and, further, that on the surface of it was a notch meant to hold and keep in position the rope by which it had been dragged, the inference was easy that it was a war-trophy taken from the citadel of the Jebusites, the earlier inhabitants of Jerusalem,[1] and set up in the sanctuary before the deity just as in later days the Ark of Jahveh was set up before Dagon.[2] The presence of a cave, mysteriously built up, and thought by Macalister to be specially suitable for oracular purposes ; also a cistern-like pit, containing human and animal bones, probably the remains of sacrificial victims ; a cemetery with the skeletons of little children, probably first-born children offered in sacrifice ; and, finally, a rampart of earth, 3 yards in length, containing a large number of human skulls, but no trace of any other parts of the bodies—all these, although they are far from being a complete demonstration, seemed to confirm the sacral significance of at least the one stone, the others being a kind of " guard of honour " to it.    If this interpretation is accepted, it would also show that the Canaanite religion did not shrink from human sacrifices. There are also, it is true, evidences of a modification of this gruesome practice.    Apparently the persons selected as victims in connexion with foundation sacrifices were those who were of no further use to their fellows, an aged, rheumatic, crippled woman or a man who had lost his left hand.[3]    The remains of lamps, found at various places, are supposed to mean the complete cessation of human sacrifice.    A small clay lamp was set in a bowl, and covered by another bowl inverted upon it, all being quite new and unused, expressly made and procured for this purpose.[4]    It has been suggested that the extinguished lamp was a symbol of the extinguished life, but perhaps it had an

[1] The Amarna letters speak of actual hostilities between Gezer and Jerusalem.

[2] 1 Sam. v, 2.    The practice of carrying off sacred objects and images as trophies of war is well attested ; e.g., in the Amarna letters (Knudtzon, 55, l. 33, Winckler, 138 dorso, 18 ff.) and on the Moabite stone (l. 12).    See supra, p. 101, note 1.            [3] Macalister in the work just quoted, p. 100 f.

[4] The thought that what is used for holy purposes must not be taken for profane purposes finds expression in Num. xix, 2, and Deut. xxi, 3.    Other examples from ancient Roman life will be found in Warde Fowler's The Religious Experience of the Roman People from the Earliest Times to the Age of Augustus (1911), p. 172.

apotropaic significance—*i.e.*, in the cavity contained between the two bowls the demons who might do hurt to the human or animal inhabitants were, so to speak, imprisoned. In *The Arabian Nights* we read of a spirit being put into a bottle and securely sealed up in it.[1]

If it be correct to suppose that the stone pillar at Gezer was looked upon as the dwelling-place of the deity (Hebrew, Beth-El), it brings to mind the story of another Beth-El, where Jacob set up the stone which he had used for a pillow as a memorial (*masseba*), because the dream that came to him as he slept upon it revealed the presence of God.[2] The continuity of the conception is evident;[3] and when Jacob pours oil on this stone it throws light on the nature and meaning of the ancient Canaanite rite. The sacrificial oil is applied to the stone, that it may thus reach the *numen* who dwells in it. The oil, or the wine, may here have taken the place of the earlier offering of blood, for of course the oil (like the wine) is the specific gift of the civilized country. The offering is made to the deity because he is looked upon as the giver of oil (and wine).[4] By and by other things too are offered, fruits of the field, in the form of cakes quickly baked, tree-fruits, the flesh of animals of the flock, first-born, etc. The setting up of a stone is no longer sufficient by itself. The need is felt for a table, however primitive.[5] Sometimes the broad base in which the *masseba* is fixed is used for this purpose.

It is clear that in proportion as those sacrificial gifts which required a horizontal base became more important the altar came to be essential, whereas the *masseba*, even although it was still supposed to be in some way the dwelling-place of the deity,[6] gradually came to be a mere appendage to the altar. In some Old Testament passages[7] we find both the *masseba* and the *ashera* occupying this position. Just as the *masseba* is merely the successor of the sacred stone, the *ashera* is an imitation of the sacred tree, in which the deity was supposed to dwell, just

---

[1] Gressmann in *Die theologische Literaturzeitung* (1913), p. 829.
[2] Gen. xxviii, 16–18.     [3] *Supra*, pp. 41 and 70 f.
[4] Hos. ii, 8.     [5] When available a flat rock was used (*supra*, p. 70).
[6] An unconscious retention of the ancient idea of a deity residing in the stone is betrayed in names like Zuri-El, " El is my Rock" (Num. iii, 35), and Zuri-Shaddai, " the Almighty is my Rock " (Num. i, 6, and others), and in the frequent use of the word 'rock' with reference to Jahveh (Deut. xxxii, 4, 15, 18, etc.).     [7] Exod. xxxiv, 13, etc.

as he dwelt in the stone. The *ashera* was of wood, and in view of the perishable nature of the material there need be no surprise that not one has come down to us.[1] It is striking that it bears the same name as the deity of whom we have already spoken.[2] This identity of name gave rise to doubts as to the existence of a separate goddess of that name, until the facts became too strong to be resisted. But this identity of name cannot have been accidental. Perhaps the object of worship, set up in imitation of the tree, received its name from the fact that the *numen* worshipped in the tree was worshipped and addressed as the goddess Ashera, giver of fertility.[3] The excavations have not revealed any images of the deity beside these altars, but there seem to have been cases in which they were present. A few scattered allusions in the Amarna letters [4] are far more important than indirect inferences drawn from the existence of images in Old Testament times. These allusions directly prove the existence of such images in the times before the coming of Israel.

With regard to the situation of the sanctuaries, we have an indication in the technical name *bama*. This name describes them as " high places." [5] And it is no mere accident that we hear of a large number of Palestinian localities, places of worship, with names which are indicative of an elevated situation.[6]

---

[1] See, however, the illustration of a relief of a Semitic sanctuary from Shushan with *asheras* in Vincent's *Canaan*, p. 144.     [2] *Supra*, p. 68.

[3] Another explanation is, however, possible. Eduard Meyer considers that it is a characteristic peculiarity of Semitic religion that the objects in which the *numen* resides are dissociated from the *numen* and become separate deities. He appeals for support in his view to the example of the North Syrian Zeus Madbachos, where the great altar, the *madbach*, is itself the deity, and becomes identified with the Greek Zeus (*Die Israeliten und ihre Nachbarstämme* (1906), p. 294 f.). This would be analogous to the case of Bait-Ili (Beth-El, " House of God "), which is attested in cuneiform as God (and indeed as a Western God). See *KAT*, 3rd edition, p. 437.

[4] Knudtzon, 129, l. 51 (Winckler, 105, l. 28), 132, l. 55. With regard to the domestic images of Astarte see *infra*, p. 110.

[5] The use of *bama* for sanctuary in general, apart from its elevated position, seems to be a secondary use. See Ezek. vi, 3.

[6] The Egyptians also spoke of Baal being worshipped " on the mountains " (W. Max Müller, *Asien und Europa*, p. 309). *Cf.* also 1 Kings xx, 23, 28. Of course, any of the sanctuaries here mentioned may belong to a later time, but in view of the conservatism displayed in such matters we can hardly be mistaken if we claim those of the Hebrew era as pre-Hebrew or even Canaanite places of worship.

Such are Rama,[1] Geba,[2] Gibea,[3] Gibeon,[4] all meaning "high place"; also Mispah[5] ("Outlook"). Further, a great many mountains in Palestine appear as holy places, Hermon,[6] Tabor,[7] Carmel,[8] Ebal and Gerizim,[9] Mount of Olives,[10] Zion,[11] and, east of Jordan, Nebo and Pisgah[12] and Peor.[13] There is mention, it is true, of places of worship situated in valleys, but in these cases it was probably a well or spring to which they owed their sanctity; e.g., Beer-sheba[14] and En-Shemesh[15] ("Well of the Sun") between Jerusalem and Jericho, Gihon,[16] En-rogel[17] ("Fullers' Well"), and the "Dragon's Well"[18] close to Jerusalem, and, at the source of the Jordan, Dan.[19] In other places, again, the presence of a conspicuous tree gave sanctity to the locality. The very assonance of the names for the sacred tree, êl, êla, êlôn, alla, allôn, with the name for God, El, is not fortuitous. The most famous tree of this kind is the oak of Abraham at Hebron.[20] We also read of the "Oak of Weeping" below Beth-El;[21] of a terebinth at Ophra,[22] another at Shechem;[23] of a tamarisk at Beer-sheba,[24] and another at Rama,[25] or more accurately at Gibea, of a third at Jabesh;[26] of a pomegranate at Gibea;[27] of the palm of Deborah, between Rama and Beth-El;[28] and a special acacia (shitta) gives its name to the town Beth-hash-shitta.[29] All the same, worship at places with a natural sacred stone such as we have spoken of[30] has not been given up. To these perhaps belongs the "Stone of Help" (Eben-ha-ezer), which the narrative in I Sam. vii, 12, transfers to the worship of Jahveh. Finally, there are names of very important holy places—e.g., Shiloh—regarding which it is impossible to say definitely to what they originally owed their sanctity. Altogether, it is clear that the country throughout was well supplied with holy places.

---

[1] I Sam. vii, 17.  [2] 2 Kings xxiii, 8.  [3] I Sam. x, 5.
[4] I Kings iii, 4.  [5] I Sam. vii, 6.
[6] The name means 'holy place.'  [7] Hos. v, 1.
[8] I Kings xviii, 20.  [9] Deut. xxvii, 4 and 12.  [10] 2 Sam. xv, 30.
[11] Passim.  [12] Deut. xxxiv, 1.  [13] Num. xxiii, 28.
[14] See supra, p. 65, note 4.  [15] Supra, p. 66.  [16] I Kings i, 33.
[17] I Kings i, 9.  [18] Neh. ii, 13.  [19] Judges xviii, 29.
[20] Gen. xiii, 18, xviii, 1.  [21] Gen. xxxv, 8.  [22] Judges vi, 11, 19.
[23] Josh. xxiv, 26.  [24] Gen. xxi, 33.  [25] I Sam. xxii, 6.
[26] I Sam. xxxi, 13.  [27] I Sam. xiv, 2.  [28] Judges iv, 5.
[29] Judges vii, 22. Shittim also, meaning "Acacias," is a place of worship (Num. xxv, 1).  [30] Supra, p. 103.

The deities who were worshipped at these shrines were called by the general name of Baal. Baal, however, is not a proper name; it is a generic appellative.[1] It denotes the deity as master and owner, and if it be asked, Owner of what? the most probable answer is, Owner of the soil. Baal-worship reeks strongly of the earth. The Baal is strictly limited, territorially and locally, and it is his essential quality that he gives fertility to the region that belongs to him, that he does not withhold the fruits of the land. It is an indispensable condition that he waters it, for in Palestine all fertility depends on water. There are, however, two possibilities. Baal gives water from below—and to this day the Arabian phrase "what Baal waters" means land rendered fertile by the water in the ground, land that does not require artificial irrigation[2]—or Baal sends the rain, particularly the thunderstorm. In one word, Baal is the husbandman's god. But seeing that the farmer's prosperity is also dependent on the well-being of his cattle, his faith in Baal's efficacy is extended to include them also. Baal makes the animals fruitful,[3] and protects their young. In the fact that men look to Baal for rain and, in due course, for sunshine also we see how Baal may now and again become the god of the sky or be identified with the gods of heaven.[4] This does not mean that he was ever simply the sun-god, but that he was conceived at one time as sidereal, at another time as tellurian; and being thus bound to the soil and in touch with men, he is their helper both in their peaceful tilling of the soil and in their defence of it in war.[5] A Baal can dwell anywhere, in a single tree or in a single spring. In fact, Baal is not one god. Where he seems to be thought of as such, we are dealing with an abstraction of a later time. In his essential nature he is, speaking generally, everywhere the same, but in reality he is divided into a multi-

---

[1] This is proved by the use of the article in the Hebrew of Judges ii, 11, 13, etc.

[2] Wellhausen, *Reste arabischen Heidentums* (1897), p. 146, and also Robertson Smith, *The Religion of the Semites*, p. 70.

[3] Perhaps as being husband of Astarte, also of women. *Cf.* Num. xxv, 1 ff., and Kittel, *Geschichte des Volkes Israel*, 3rd edition, vol. i, p. 218.

[4] *Cf.* the Baal-shamem, the "Baal of Heaven," of Semitic inscriptions. In the Amarna letters the form given is "Baal in Heaven."

[5] Especially in Egypt Baal had become god of war. *Cf.* Gressmann in the *Baudissinfestschrift* (1918), pp. 199 ff. and 204.

plicity of locally differentiated figures.[1] More than one writer has sought to illustrate this by means of an analogous cultus belonging to our own day—the cultus of the Virgin. Everywhere, of course, it is the same Holy Virgin, but actually she is subjected to a more or less strong local differentiation. The Mary of Lourdes is not the same as the Mary of Einsiedeln ; the Mary of Pompeii is not the same as the black Madonna of Czenstochau. Other analogies could also be named—e.g., the modern cult of Shiva in India,[2] or the ancient Roman cult of Juno. There was the Juno of Gabii, Juno Regina of Ardea, Juno Sospita of Lanuvium, Juno Quiritis of Tibur, Juno Lucina of Tusculum.[3] There is, of course, this difference—Baal was never at any time *one* deity in the same sense as Shiva or Juno, nor *one* person in the same sense as Mary. As we have said, his essential qualities were always the same, and the analogies quoted are helpful and instructive only as examples of local differentiations of the deity. Baal, like Mary, receives a more definite appellation according to the locality of the worship paid to him. There is a Baal-Lebanon,[4] a Baal-Hermon,[5] a Baal-Tabor,[6] a Baal-Peor,[7] a Baal-tamar[8] ("Baal of Palms "), a Baal-Perazim,[9] a Baal-Hazor,[10] a Baal-Shalisha,[11] Baal-Meon,[12] Baal-Judah,[13] Baal-Gad,[14] Baal-zephon[15] ("Baal of the North "). In the example Baal-tamar we can see how the belief in Baal gradually absorbed the belief in the various ' gods ' —*i.e.*, the local and elementary nature spirits of earlier times. They still retain in many places the name El, as we see from the large number of place-names[16] which may date from this

---

[1] Hence the expression " the Baalim," Judges ii, 11, and often.
[2] Monier Williams, *Brahmanism and Hinduism* (1891), p. 107.
[3] Wissowa, *Religion und Kultus der Römer* (1902), p. 114 ff.
[4] In Semitic inscriptions.
[5] Judges iii, 3 ; 1 Chron. v, 23. According to Eduard Meyer this name is due to text mutilation, but there is no inherent impossibility in it.
[6] Zeus Atabyrios.   [7] Num. xxv, 3, 5.
[8] Judges xx, 33.   [9] 2 Sam. v, 20 ; 1 Chron. xiv, 11.
[10] 2 Sam. xiii, 23. A place named Hazor is mentioned in Neh. xi, 33.
[11] 2 Kings iv, 42. Shalisha appears in 1 Sam. ix, 4.
[12] Num. xxxii, 38, Ezek. xxv, 9, 1 Chron. v, 8, always as place-name. It must have been called Beth-Baal-Meon (Josh. xiii, 17). *Cf.* Kirjath-Baal (" City of Baal "), Josh. xv, 60, xviii, 14, for Baal-Judah.
[13] 2 Sam. vi, 2. The text gives wrongly " Baale of Judah." See preceding note.   [14] Josh. xi, 17.   [15] Exod. xiv, 2, 9 ; Num. xxxiii, 7.
[16] Jabne-El, Jezre-El, Nachali-El, Migdal-El, Gaddi-El, Peni-El, etc.

period or have been taken over from the preceding period.[1] There are also, besides the ancient names denoting relationship,[2] names corresponding to the political constitution, which gave each district a ruler, such as Melek[3] (" King"), Dan[4] (" Judge"), perhaps also Adon[5] (" Lord "). The conception of the deity as judge shows that he is beginning to be elevated above nature, and to be conceived as the protector of justice. Zedek (" Justice ") is, in fact, the name of a god of this period. It is familiar to us from proper names like Adonizedek[6] (" Zedek is my Lord"), Melchizedek[7] (" Zedek is my King"), Benzedek[8] (" Son of Zedek "). In this connexion we should also mention the Canaanite covenant god El-berith[9] or Baal-berith,[10] the god of the city of Shechem. He seems to have been the god of a confederation[11]—*i.e.*, a god with whom treaties were concluded or to whom treaty offerings were made,[12] a god who,

[1] *Supra*, p. 69.      [2] *Supra*, p. 70.

[3] In the form of Milcom Melek became the chief name of the deity of the Ammonites. The common form Moloch is due to the bowdlerizing of the Massoretes, to whom we owe the vocalization of our Hebrew text. To the consonants *m, l, k*, they supplied the vowels of the word *bosheth*, meaning ' shame,' in order to express their detestation of the name of the heathen deity. Melek appears as the name of a deity in Emek Hammelek (" King's Vale") in Gen. xiv, 17, and 2 Sam. xviii, 18, and the name shows that this valley was a sanctuary. There are other names from the time of the Amarna letters, such as Abi-milki (" Melek is my Father "), Ili-milki or Milk-ili (" Melek is my God "), and Milk-uru. Uru (" Light ") will also thus have been the name of a deity; *cf.* Uru-shalim, the ancient name of Jerusalem. But more probably it points to the existence of a god Shalem, which name occurs in that of the Assyrian king Shalmaneser. (*KAT*, 3rd edition, pp. 224, 474 f.) If there was no god called Uru, then the Arabian and Babylonian god of darkness Selem has left his traces in Palestine. *Cf.* the Old Testament names Mount Zalmon (Judges ix, 48) and Zalmonah (Num. xxxiii, 41), also Buru-Silim from the Amarna letters (Paton in Hastings, *RE*, vol. iii, p. 181*a*).

[4] *Cf.* Addu-dan (" Hadad is Judge ") in the Amarna letters. Perhaps the tribal name and place-name Dan also point to a god Dan. It would be an abbreviation, like Joseph from Joseph-El, Jacob from Jacob-El; and Mahane-Dan (" Camp of Dan ") in Judges xiii, 25, xviii, 12, would have been originally been a place of worship.

[5] *Cf.* Aduna in the Amarna letters.

[6] The name of the Canaanite king of Jerusalem (Josh. x, 1, 3). The name is formed in the same way as Adonijah (" Jahveh is my Father ").

[7] Gen. xiv, 18; Ps. cx, 4.      [8] In an Amarna letter.

[9] Judges ix, 46.      [10] Judges viii, 33, ix, 4.

[11] More naturally of a confederation between men than between God and man (Eduard Meyer, *Die Israeliten und ihre Nachbarstämme* (1906), p. 550 f.).

[12] Nöldeke, *ZDMG*, vol. xlii (1888), p. 478.

like Zeus Horkios, saw to it that a treaty was faithfully observed.[1]

Baal has a consort in the female deity Baala, or Astarte, or Ashera. Reminiscences of Baala are still found in a few place-names in Palestine, Baala,[2] Baalath,[3] Har-hab-Baala [4] (" Mountain of Baala "), Baalath-beer [5] (" Well of Baala "), Bealoth.[6] More frequently, especially in the Old Testament, the goddess appears under the name of Astarte,[7] a name which is probably derived from that of the Babylonian Ishtar.[8] It is also found in the place-name Ashtaroth.[9] The fuller name of the town, Ashtaroth-carnaiim [10] (" Ashtaroth of the Horns "), refers to the usual representation of the goddess with cow-horns, which puts her in line with the Egyptian goddess Hathor.[11] We have already [12] spoken of the older representations of this goddess found in the Palestinian excavations belonging to the close of the Amorite period ; but the majority of them belong to the Canaanite period, and they reveal not only the influence of Egypt, especially in the south, but also the influence of Babylon, Cyprus, and of the Hittites. But these foreign influences do not exclude the gradual perfecting of local types, such, for example, as are found in Taanach. Usually the goddess is shown as a figure in relief, standing on a clay slab, about 4 to

---

[1] I do not think that, when the name is thus understood, Baal-berith is an impossible figure in the Canaanite pantheon. Some have sought to evade the necessity of acknowledging him by interpreting the name as Baal of Beirut (as if *he* had any business in Shechem !), or as Baal-beroth (the " Sacred Tree " in Shechem), or as Baal-b^eeroth (" God of the Well "), after the fashion of Baalath-beer (" Goddess of the Well "), in Josh. xix, 8.

[2] Josh. xv, 29.    [3] Josh. xix, 44.    [4] Josh. xv, 11.    [5] Josh. xix, 8.
[6] Josh. xv, 24, and 1 Kings iv, 16. The plural corresponds simply to the masculine plural form Baalim (*cf*. p. 108, *note* 3) and is to be similarly explained.

[7] Judges ii, 13. Ashtoreth (1 Sam. xxxi, 10 ; 1 Kings xi, 5, 33 ; 2 Kings xxiii, 13) is another intentional change to the vowels of *bosheth* (*supra*, p. 108, *note* 3).

[8] The following shows how keen was the desire to make known the name of Ishtar. In the days of Amenophis III (died in 1375) his " brother " in Mitanni, knowing that he was old and sick, sent a second time to Egypt the captured image of the Ishtar of Niniveh, no doubt in the hope that the famous goddess could drive away the evil spirits that caused the King's illness and thus cure him (Breasted's *History of Egypt*, p. 114).

[9] Deut. i, 4.   In Josh. xxi, 27, it is called Be 'Eshterah, meaning " House of Astarte." The parallel passage (1 Chron. vi, 71) reads Ashtaroth.

[10] Gen. xiv, 5.
[11] Any reference to the ' horns ' of the crescent moon is doubtful.
[12] *Supra*, p. 86.

8 inches high. Clay moulds which were used in the manufacture of these figures have been found. Completely modelled figures are not as frequent as those on slabs. In Gezer and Taanach were found rare examples of bronze statuettes of the goddess. She appears in all sorts of attitudes. In some cases she is dressed ; in others she is naked. In some her hair falls in broad tresses over her shoulder ; in others it is caught up by a sort of tiara. Sometimes she is wearing bracelets and necklets, earrings, a girdle, and even anklets ; sometimes she is wearing no jewellery at all. In one case her head is covered by a veil, but usually she is without veil. Here her hands are striking a tambourine ; there she is holding a lotus-stalk, or an animal, probably a snake ; and again she has her hands pressed against her bosom. In most cases her female characteristics are strongly emphasized, and this gives a hint as to her real character. She is the embodiment of female fertility, the goddess of love and of maternity. Besides being worshipped as Baala, Astarte, and Ashera,[1] she was also honoured in Palestine under the name of Kadesh, a name which actually occurs [2] on Egyptian representations ; the female hierodules who were in her service probably got their name from her.[3]

In a letter found in Taanach mention is made of " the finger of Ashera." The expression is obscure, but it seems clear that it refers to something that was employed to obtain oracles. Indeed, the oracular element was in great vogue. This is shown by names like the " Oak of Prophecy "[4] and the " Terebinth of Moreh." [5] As the name denotes, the latter was an "instruction-giving " tree. How a tree oracle arose we can see from the case of David : [6] in the rustling of the mulberry-trees he hears the divine voice urging him to pursue the enemy. Who can say how old these customs were in Palestine ? [7] A spring with the

---

[1] *Supra*, pp. 65 and 104.

[2] See the illustrations in *TBAT*, vol. ii, p. 70. In this case the naked goddess is standing on a lion. The Egyptian Astarte drives in a war-chariot.

[3] Kadesh means simply " Consecrated " (see p. 99, *note* 4). Therefore the various places in Palestine called Kadesh may simply have been sanctuaries. The name does not necessarily imply that they were sites of worship of the goddess Kadesh.

[4] Judges ix, 37.

[5] Gen. xii, 6 ; Deut. xi, 30. In the second passage the plural is an intentional correction.       [6] 2 Sam. v, 24.

[7] *Cf.* the place-name Achshaph (" Magic "), Josh. xi, 1, xii, 20, xix, 25.

name En-mishpat [1] (" Well of Judgment ") suggests the ancient conception that the judicial verdict was believed to be given in the murmur of the spring—that is, by the unseen *numen* himself.[2] Consultation of the dead was in all probability practised also.  At a later time it was still practised professionally by women [3]—among whom all superstitious customs are wont to linger.  Though no clear evidence of ancient worship of the dead can be found, still there are traces.  A number of places owed their renown solely to the fact that they contained the graves of heroes, tribal ancestors of Canaanite clans, whom the Book of Judges has entitled petty " judges." [4]  The inference is at least natural that worship *was* offered to the heroes and ancestors who were buried there.  It is very unlikely that the religion of Jahveh would have so strongly emphasized the "uncleanness" of graves if it had not found these places looked upon as " holy places."

There were still other relics of primitive religion that continued to retain their influence among the Canaanite population.  Hints of animal-worship are found perhaps in place-names like " Serpent Town " [5] and " Serpent Stone," [6] for it is hardly likely that these names are merely due to the fact that serpents were found there.  Even Astarte is occasionally depicted holding a serpent in her hand,[7] and it is possible that what was itself an object of worship in earlier times had been reinterpreted and adopted into the worship of a higher *numen*.  A similar instance is found in the case of Baal-zebub, the Baal of flies, god of Ekron, in whose sanctuary oracles were apparently given in accordance with the behaviour of flies.[8]  And to a similar cause, no doubt, is to be attributed the adoption of bull-shaped

---

[1] Gen. xiv, 7.

[2] Just as Deborah imparted instruction under the palm-tree of Deborah (Judges iv, 4).  Her words were no doubt held to be inspired by the rustling of the leaves.      [3] 1 Sam. xxviii.

[4] Tola in Shamir (Judges x, 2), Jair in Camon (x, 5), Ibzan in Beth-lehem (probably in Zebulun, xii, 10), Elon in Ajalon (xii, 12), Abdon in Pirathon (xii, 15).  Whether and to what extent the plain of Rephaim (spirits?) was an important centre of religion it is now impossible to say.   [5] 1 Chron. iv, 12.

[6] 1 Kings i, 9.  Perhaps also " Dragon's Well," Neh. ii, 13.    [7] See p. 110.

[8] 2 Kings i, 2, 6, 16.  Like Zeus Apomyios this deity may have been looked upon as the driver away of flies.  For the relation between Beelzebub and Beelzebul (Mark iii, 22) see my article " Geister " in *RGG*, vol. ii, column 1223.

images,[1] and even the use of 'bull' as a name of God,[2] into the worship of Jahveh. The original element in this, and perhaps the Canaanite element, would be the worship of the bull itself as the embodiment of male strength and procreative power ; and the strong protest of Jahvism against animal-worship, such as is implied in the laws concerning food,[3] presupposes the sanctity of certain other animals in the cult of Canaanite ' heathendom.'

All these more primitive cults seem in course of time to have fallen more and more under the domination of the one Baal cult, which had more of a unified character. From first to last that was the cultus of an agricultural people, and its highest expressions were joyous celebrations which seemed to grow spontaneously out of the rejoicings naturally connected with the culture of the land and the culture of the vine. When the sickle was put into the corn,[4] at the close of the corn harvest, and especially at the close of the grape-gathering,[5] which marked the end of all harvest work for the year, the people came together for a joyous feast, in order to give to the god of the harvest the share and the thanks that were his due, and to ensure his continuing help by a meal taken together in his presence. We do not know whether the presence and co-operation of any separate priesthood was necessary on these occasions. In the more important sanctuaries, especially when a sacred oracle had to be sought and received, the participation of regularly appointed priests was probably indispensable, and allusions in the Tell Amarna letters seem to confirm this assumption.[6]

For the males of the nation there was a rite of initiation into the privileges of the cultus—viz., circumcision. The practice of performing this rite on children of tender years does not go back to very ancient times. It was originally one of those rites practised by so many peoples on those who had reached the age of puberty,[7] and it seems to have been performed by

---

[1] 1 Kings xii, 28.

[2] *Abbîr*, afterward as *abîr*, transferred to Jahveh (Gen. xlix, 24).

[3] Lev. xi ; Deut. xiv.          [4] Deut. xvi, 9.

[5] Judges ix, 27.                [6] Paton, Hastings, *RE*, vol. iii, p. 188*a*.

[7] Its former connexion with marriage is reflected in Exod. iv, 25, and Gen. xxxiv. *Cf.* the connexion between *chātān*, ' bridegroom,' and *chatana* the Arabic for 'circumcize.' See Wellhausen, *Reste arabischen Heidentums* (1897), p. 175. Puberty ceremonies are also elsewhere put forward into early years—*e.g.*, in Polynesia (*cf.* F. B. Jevons, *An Introduction to the History of Religion* (1896), p. 185). Baptism has also been similarly put forward.

one simultaneous operation on all the young men of a certain age. This is indicated by the name of the holy place at Gilgal, the " Hill of Foreskins." [1] The name means, no doubt, that the foreskins of those who had been circumcised at the sanctuary in one general celebration were buried in that hill. [2] Whether this rite had already in Canaanite times been transferred to childhood we do not know. The antiquity of this transference is attested by two considerations. It presupposes the custom of going naked, for as a religious and tribal symbol it had to be visible to all ; and it continued for long to be performed with a stone knife. [3] Another special form of consecration was that of anointing with oil. This meant either that the strength and virtues of the oil were communicated to the persons or things thus besmeared with it, or that they were in some way purified by being so anointed. [4] The anointing of the king is attested by an Amarna letter, in which Ramman (or Hadad)-nirari of Nuhassi, near Aleppo, says that Thutmosis III (*ob.* 1447 B.C.) installed his grandfather as king and " poured oil upon his head." [5] In fact, this custom is perhaps of Egyptian origin, [6] and in the Egyptian meaning of the rite it was performed for the protection of the person anointed. [7]

The anointing of a Canaanite king by an Egyptian king was still in this period the outward expression of Egyptian sovereignty. As time went on this sovereignty declined. The successors of Thutmosis III succeeded in upholding it. [8] But the possession of power gradually weakened the energy of the dominant nation, and just at the time when the advance of the Hittites from the north required a man of iron will on the throne of Egypt that throne was ascended by Amenophis IV,

[1] Josh. v, 2.  [2] Stade in *ZatW*, vol. vi (1886), p. 132 ff.

[3] Exod. iv, 25 ; Josh. v, 2. As late as 1716 the Jews in Wetterau used slate for this purpose (Andree, *Zur Volkskunde der Juden* (1881), p. 154, *note* 3).

[4] For the meaning of the anointing see Vollers, *AR* (1904), pp. 97–103, in particular p. 101 f., and Wellhausen, *AR* (1904), pp. 33–39. *Mashach*, which came later to mean ' anoint,' originally meant to stroke with the hand, and, as Wellhausen says, " all over the ancient world spiritual values are conveyed by physical contact " (p. 38).

[5] Winckler, 37, l. 4 ff., Knudtzon, 51.

[6] Erman, *Ägypten*, vol. i (1885), p. 317.

[7] Spiegelberg, *AR*, vol. ix (1906), p. 144.

[8] Breasted, *op. cit.*, p. 327 f.

H

a young dreamer, " to whom the philosophy and theology of priests was more important than all the provinces of Asia." Closely invested by the Hittites, a Syrian town close to the frontier of Palestine is found protesting that for twenty years they have been sending messengers to the King of Egypt, without receiving any answer.[1] And it was not only in the north that the royal help was denied. Thanks to the discovery of the royal archives at Tell Amarna in Egypt, containing *inter alia* the correspondence of the Palestinian princes with the Egyptian Court (the protest mentioned above is an extract from it), we get a glimpse into the chaotic condition of the political situation. The petty princes of Palestine live in mutual rivalry. The one stirs up trouble against the other ; one allies himself with a second against a third. This rivalry and dissension of course attract new invaders from the desert. To some extent they come in response to actual summons, but in other quarters we hear agitated protests against their approach. Abdichiba of Jerusalem, for example, writes to his Egyptian overlord : " At this moment the Habiru are capturing the cities of the King. No regent is left to represent my lord the King. All are being dispersed. . . . Let the King attend to his country, and let the King secure troops for the country, for if troops are not here this year, all the lands of my lord the King will be lost. . . . If troops are not here this year, let the King send an administrator, to conduct me and my brethren to the King,[2] and we will die beside the King, our lord."[3] This name Habiru, here applied to the new invaders, means, in spite of all that has been urged against the interpretation, the Hebrews. The name includes more than we understand by the Hebrews, which we are wont to make synonymous with Israelites. But the only inference to be drawn is that the invasion of the Israelites must be regarded as part of a larger movement, and can be understood only as part of a more comprehensive migration of nations.

---

[1] Knudtzon, 59, ll. 34–46.
[2] The text reads erroneously " to me."
[3] Knudtzon, 288, ll. 36–40, 48–53, 57–61.

# CHAPTER III

## THE CIVILIZATION OF THE INVADERS

ACCORDING to the account given in our sources, when Israel entered Palestine they were simply re-entering a country which their fathers had possessed long ages before. It is not the task of a historian of civilization to investigate the accuracy of that statement. There is no reason to doubt that under the veil of tradition that envelops the origins of Israel genuine historical memories are concealed, but no one can reasonably expect definite information regarding the first beginnings of that people. These lie far back at the stage of nomadic life. The ancestors of the people whom we find in Palestine at this period are Bedouins.

For our attempt to describe the civilization they brought with them there are three main sources of information. First, there is the Old Testament itself. The Israelites there portrayed are, it is true, no longer Bedouins, but pictures of their former life as such are found in the Old Testament descriptions of some of their ancestors, and, to an even greater extent, in the descriptions of the neighbouring peoples related to them. A second source of information is the native literature of these kindred peoples, especially the Arabs, and there are now excellent collections of the relevant literature which are very useful in this connexion.[1] The third source is found in descriptions of Bedouin life at the present day in the countries that adjoin Palestine. Some of these are in the form of detailed notes of travel;[2] some are of a more general character.[3] The two last-named sources must, of course, be used with caution. The oldest Arabian literature to which we owe our knowledge of Bedouin life was written almost 2000 years after Israel had entered Canaan; and modern descriptions of Bedouin life belong to a time 1200 years later still. Besides, Israelites and

[1] Especially Jacob, *Altarabisches Beduinenleben* (1897), and (for the religion) Wellhausen, *Reste arabischen Heidentums* (1897).

[2] Especially Doughty's *Travels in Arabia Deserta* (2 vols., 1888).

[3] Burckhardt, *Notes on the Bedouins* (1830); Jaussen, *Coutumes des Arabes au pays de Moab* (1908).

Arabians cannot exactly be said to be synonymous. But in view of the unchanging conditions which the desert presents to its inhabitants, in view of the unchanging nature of Oriental life altogether—a feature which is not easily appreciated by those who are accustomed to the changeful life of the West— these sources, though late, can still be of great service.

The Bedouins have been described as aristocrats. The description is true if pride of descent be considered a sufficient justification for the title. In the mind of the Bedouin descent or lineage takes the place that is usually occupied in the mind of a peasant by love of home.[1] Lineage means, first and fore- most, purity of blood. Indeed, it is amazing to learn the importance which the Bedouin attaches to " blood." The Old Testament has made us familiar with the thought that " the blood is the life." [2] That conception is no mere theological speculation of a later time, based on the idea that when blood pours from a wound the principle of life leaves the body. No doubt such observations and reflections were involved in the conception, but it is more naïve and more literal than that. In a hot, thirsty land all life is dependent on the rain ; a dead body almost immediately takes the semblance of a piece of dry wood. So it was natural that the soul or life should be conceived as residing in the sap or blood.[3] At this stage blood-relationship is the basis of social life. There is only one thing that can be compared with it—viz., relationship through the mother.

The mention of this brings us to the important place occupied by the mother. The Old Testament contains a number of traces which seem to indicate that among the ancestors of historical Israel the *matriarchate* was in force—that is, a child was considered to belong, not to the father's clan or family, but to that of the mother. In these primitive times the father was not definitely known. Polyandry prevailed—*i.e.*, a woman was visited by various men. Strabo [4] mentions this as prevalent among the Arabian peoples akin to Israel. Under such con- ditions only the mother knows her child, and therefore it is she who gives it its name. This practice lasted in Israel far down into the historical period, although the reason for it had long disappeared and was forgotten. But the surviving traces of it

---

[1] Jacob, *op. cit.*, p. 222.    [2] Lev. xvii, 14 ; Deut. xii, 23.
[3] Jacob, *op. cit.*, p. 143.    [4] Strabo, *Geographica*, XVI, iv, 783.

are instructive. To have one's mother cursed is felt to be the greatest possible insult.[1] No other insult touched so closely one's blood and lineage. Again, the idea that the mother was the actual link in one's descent is clearly expressed in the claim to be descended from female tribal ancestresses like Rachel or Leah. A further surviving trace of an earlier matriarchate is seen in the fact that the tent belonged to the woman. The tent to which Isaac brings Rebecca is his mother's tent.[2] Sisera takes refuge in the tent of Jael.[3] Among the Arabs, when a woman had grown tired of a man she simply reversed her tent—*i.e.*, she turned the door to the other side. When the man returned and found the tent thus reversed he knew that she wished to have nothing further to do with him.[4] Accordingly, it was not the woman's part to follow the man ; it was the man's part to follow the woman.[5] Is there not an echo of this condition of society in the familiar words, "A man shall leave his father and mother and cleave unto his wife"? [6] Finally, the fact that in primitive times it was kinship with the mother and her blood-relatives that alone was of account explains why there was no objection felt to marriage with a stepmother, or between stepbrothers and sisters, the children of another mother. Abraham expressly explains to the Philistine king that Sarah was the daughter of his father, but not of his mother.[7] Even in David's time the admissibility of such marriages was recognized. David's daughter Tamar refers her brother Amnon, when he is urging her to lie with him, to the King. She says, "He will surely not deny me to thee." [8] At the same period it was the recognized right of the successor to the throne to appropriate his father's harem. When Absalom does so on the advice of crafty Ahithophel [9] he is simply announcing that he is entering upon his father's inheritance ; and, *vice versa*, when Adonijah asks for Abishag, one of David's concubines, as his wife his brother Solomon suspects that he is aiming at the throne.[10] In none of these cases is it felt to be at all offensive in itself that a son

---

[1] 1 Sam. xx, 30.   [2] Gen. xxiv, 67.   [3] Judges iv, 17.
[4] *Cf.* the example of Hâtim Tej (F. Schulthess' edition of his *Divan*, No. LI).
[5] Judges xiv, 1, xv, 1. The so-called *çadîka* marriage is meant. *Cf.* Wellhausen, "Die Ehe bei den Arabern," *GGN* (1893), p. 470.
[6] Gen. ii, 24, also xxiv, 5 (Eliezer's fear).
[7] Gen. xx, 12.
[8] 2 Sam. xiii, 13.   [9] 2 Sam. xvi, 21.   [10] 1 Kings ii, 16 ff.

should have intercourse with his father's wives, excepting, of course, the son's own mother. Such an act offends in no way against the blood-tie which connects him with his mother. It is only at a later time, when the patriarchate had been established, that we find a law[1] forbidding such unions; but that is only another proof of the later origin of that system, and it cannot invalidate the testimony of the facts that prove the existence of an earlier matriarchate.

Finally, there is another piece of evidence which is not without value.[2] There is reason to suppose that the Hebrew word for 'clan,' *mishpachah*, is connected with *shiphcha*; in the Old Testament *shiphcha* means a female slave, or even a concubine, but, under the matriarchate, it had meant the matriarchal wife.[3] In the nomadic period the *mishpachah* seems to have been the ultimate social unit. It had a communistic life,[4] and was based on blood-relationship. It has a wider meaning, however, than 'family' in our sense. The latter would be too small to be able to face the demands made on its power of resistance by the desert and its dangers. On the other hand, the *mishpachah* is narrower than the 'tribe,' which comprises several 'clans.' Perhaps we get the best idea of it if we think of it as an enlarged family—*i.e.*, a compound unit, held together by a natural sense of kinship,[5] with the addition of those elements which have been adopted into it from outside.[6] The only association conceivable is a family association.[7] Where, therefore, the bond of blood

---

[1] Lev. xviii, 9, xx, 17; Deut. xxvii, 22; *cf*. Ezek. xxii, 11.

[2] Wellhausen upholds the opposite view in *GGN* (1893), p. 446 ff., and adduces the fact that the language has special names only for the relatives on the father's side, and that the maternal relatives have to be indicated by periphrases. But *cf*. *hāl*, 'maternal uncle,' and *ach*, 'fellow-clansman' (Paton, *The Early Religion of Israel* (1910), p. 7).

[3] This is Schwally's view. *Cf*. Lods, *La croyance à la vie future* (1906), vol. ii, p. 33.

[4] Gen. xii, 4, xlii, 37, xlv, 10, 19, xlvi, 5.

[5] The limitations of this sense depend on the extent to which the memory of ancestors reaches. According to Lamprecht, this goes back to the fifth generation (Procksch, *Über die Blutrache bei den vorislamitischen Arabern* (Leipzig, 1899), p. 24). For these five generations among the modern Arabs, the *khomse*, see Burckhardt, *Notes on the Bedouins*, p. 121. *Cf*. also from the Old Testament Exod. xx, 5, xxxiv, 7, Deut. v, 9, 2 Kings x, 30.

[6] Among the Arabs the corresponding word is *chaij*, which is the *chaj* of 1 Sam. xviii, 18; *cf*. Hebrew *'am*, although this word apparently presupposes patriarchal conditions.    [7] Doughty, *op. cit.*, vol, ii, p. 41.

or of milk is absent, and the question arises of receiving some one into association, it is done artificially. All over the world we hear of the relationship of 'blood-brother,' which is constituted by the contracting parties cutting their veins and reciprocally licking the blood that issues forth. This type of blood-relationship still exists in some parts of Arabia and in Lebanon.[1] That it also existed among the ancestors of Israel is a legitimate inference from the regular expression for making a covenant—to 'cut' a covenant. From Arabia and Egypt interesting instances are known of strangers, adults even, being received into a new kinship by symbolical suckling.[2] Whether there was anything corresponding to this among the Israelites we do not know. Among the Arabs eating together is usually sufficient to constitute a protective relationship, and a later incident from the Old Testament gives ground for assuming that this custom was known in ancient Israel also; when making a covenant with the Gibeonites the Israelites partook of the food which the former had brought with them.[3] The idea underlying this widespread custom [4] was that fellowship in eating produced fellowship of life. This is carried to such an extent among the Arabs that Zaid al-Khail refused to kill the thief who on the preceding evening had drunk by stealth out of his father's milk bowl.[5]

This brings us to the large subject of hospitality, the peculiar pride and glory of the Bedouin. For a stranger to enter a tent and partake of food there means, for him, that he comes under the unqualified protection of the owner of the tent. Even to have merely touched the tent-rope means that he is safe from any injury at the hands of any member of the clan of the tent-owner until such time as he himself renounces that protective relationship. All that we read in ancient Arabic literature of the praise bestowed by poets on the hospitality of the nomads, and of the scorn they pour on the head of the man who betrays this protective relationship, is the expression of views and sentiments which can be transferred in their entirety to the Israelites of the nomadic period. Such an act as that of Jael, who lulls

---

[1] Trumbull, *The Blood Covenant* (New York, 1885), p. 5.
[2] *Globus*, vol. lxiii (1893), p. 50.  [3] Josh. ix, 14.
[4] For its extent see Hastings, *RE*, under " Brotherhood (artificial)," vol. ii, § 18, p. 861 f.  [5] *Agh*, vol. xvi, 51.

Sisera by a draught of milk into a false sense of security and thereafter slays him in her tent,[1] must have seemed to the Bedouin not only an outrage on all good manners, but actually a crime.

On the other hand, it is clear that this unqualified hospitality toward a stranger could not last for ever. An ancient Anglo-Saxon saying occurs in the law of Edward: "Twa night gest, thrid night agen "—*i.e.*, "Two nights my guest, the third night on your own." Similar sentiments find expression among all peoples. Among the Arabs a man can be a guest, in the privileged sense, only for three days and four hours. If he stay longer he is not sent away, but he is expected to bear his share in the work and expenses of the household. It cannot have been essentially different in the nomadic days of Israel. In any case, we see here how the protective relationship accorded to a stranger might develop into that of bondsman. And what is thus true of an individual who, seeking protection, attaches himself in this way to a member of a tribe or clan, thereby attaching himself to that tribe or clan as a whole, also holds good of entire clans or remnants of tribes who are no longer able to maintain an independent existence, and who seek safety by attaching themselves to another and larger combination. This, indeed, is the main cause of the increase of certain tribes. Tribal attachments were not permanent. This is clear from the variability of their genealogies. These genealogies are the precipitate of the whole tribal history. A tribe which yesterday was small and weak is to-day numerous and strong, or *vice versa*. This is expressed in genealogical form thus : the tribe is to-day said to be the elder (or, as the Hebrew expresses it, the bigger) son or brother, whereas he had previously been called the younger (*i.e.*, in Hebrew, the smaller).

These *protégés*, who thus pass gradually from the relationship of bondsmen into membership in the tribe, are quite different from slaves. The difference between them is that while they stand to their protectors in a covenant-relation, which they may renounce at will, the slaves belong absolutely to their masters. But just because of this the slaves are part of the tribe, and it is here that the great line of demarcation between men runs—

---

[1] Judges iv, 17 ff., v, 24 ff.

between those who have no tribal relation and those who have. The lot of the 'outsider' is a desperate one. The fear expressed by Cain, that he would be driven out from "the face of the ground "[1]—*i.e.*, that he would be compelled to leave civilized territory—conveys a hint of what awaits him in the desert. The homeless fugitive roams up and down in it, and whoever meets him may slay him. A man who has been thus driven forth, a man who has either failed to secure a tribal connexion or who has forfeited it, is like a hunted animal, a prey to attack and death at the hands of men. It is inevitable. The Bedouin who attacks a wayfarer does so, not from ill-will, but from necessity. The desert, unable to support its sons, forces them to steal and shed blood.[2] He who has no tribal connexion lacks the sole protection that the desert-dweller knows. He has no one to avenge his death, and blood-vengeance is the supreme law of the desert.[3] When a man's blood has been shed it is the inviolable duty of his clan to take vengeance on the murderer, or, if he cannot be found, to take vengeance on his clan by shedding blood for blood. The passion that can be inspired by this thought is shown in the so-called Song of Lamech,[4] "a note from Israel's nomad days, a true song of the desert " :

> A man I slew for wounding me,
> A young man too for bruising me ;
> Avenged may Cain be sevenfold,
> But Lamech seven and seventyfold !

Arabian life supplies direct parallels. Imruulkais, hearing that his father has been slain, vows to abstain from all delights until he has killed a hundred Beni Asad and cut off the forelocks of a hundred of them. A similar vow to kill a hundred of his enemy's tribe is made by Shanfara, and Amr, the son of the King of Hira, burns to death a hundred men to avenge his son, slain by mistake.[5] Read strictly, the law of blood-vengeance was not supposed to demand a number of victims larger than that of those whose death called for vengeance. When this number had been secured, the matter was deemed at an end, lest occasion should be given for new vengeance. Without this

---

[1] Gen. iv, 14.    [2] Nöldeke, *ZDMG*, vol. xl, p. 175.
[3] See Merz's monograph, *Die Blutrache bei den Israeliten* (1916).
[4] Gen. iv, 23 f.   See Gunkel's commentary *in loc.*
[5] Jacob, *op. cit.*, p. 145.

limitation, the chain would have been endless. But how should hate and thirst for vengeance pay heed to strict numbers ? No doubt experiences of this kind helped to narrow the bounds of blood-vengeance. To-day it is limited to the family involved and to the fifth generation. Another limitation, which certainly goes far back, provided that those demanding vengeance might take from the murderer and his kindred a ransom, whose amount— no doubt it was originally paid in animals of the flock—gradually came to be approximately fixed. But then it was not always considered honourable to be satisfied with such a ransom. The more precious coin of vengeance was at all times blood ; nothing could surpass that in glory.

If in respect of blood the Bedouins are aristocrats, their tribal organization rests on a basis of complete democracy. At the head of the tribe stands the man (or men) who enjoys the highest respect of the tribe. Such respect involves, it is true, purity of descent, and perhaps also wealth, but it rests no less on personal qualities, such as superior wisdom, insight, and experience. But those holding this high place must not imagine that they possess despotic power. Their influence rests on the moral respect they inspire. They can command obedience only as long as they can preserve their moral authority. They are not entitled to issue orders, nor can they compel their tribesmen to do anything. In the last resort every man is his own master. The chief's authority lasts only so long as he is in agreement with the will of the tribe, and on important occasions he must find out what that will is. The prosperity and happiness of the tribal life depends on such agreement. An ancient Arabic Bedouin poem represents the relations of the chief and his tribe under the image of the tent-poles and pegs :

> A folk that hath no chiefs must soon decay,
> And chiefs it hath not when the mob bears sway.
> Only with poles the tent is reared at last,
> And poles it hath not, save the pegs hold fast.
> But when the pegs and poles are once combined
> Then stands accomplished that which was designed.[1]

The principle of tribal organization is thus the equality of the

---

[1] Al-Afwah al-Awdi, vol. ii, pp. 8–10, in Nöldeke's *Delectus*, p. 4, quoted by Nicholson in *A Literary History of the Arabs* (1907), p. 83.

members. It has been justly said,[1] " In the mouth of a heathen Arab, loyalty does not mean degrading servility towards his superiors, but loyal devotion towards his equals." That must have been the case too among the ancestors of Israel, and we must bear it in mind if we are to understand why the ancient Israelites had such an instinctive antipathy to the kingship that, as Jotham's parable[2] declares, no true man will recognize it. The picture of royal despotism which Samuel held up before the people when they asked for a king[3]—that a king would conscript their sons and daughters for all manner of services— is the exact opposite of the ideal of a chieftain cherished by the Bedouin. Moreover, his ideal presupposes a moral order which is quite distinct, although it is altogether unwritten. The Bedouin has his own code, though he knows no executive authority. Even the authority of a judge in a case that has been referred to him is merely moral. It cannot be fortuitous that the introduction by Moses of a regularly constituted judicial system is ascribed to the advice of the priestly head of a nomad tribe.[4]

The Bedouin's life is a roving one. He is like the wild ass,[5] and what that means is seen in the magnificent description in the Book of Job : [6]

> Who hath sent out the wild ass free ?
> Or loosed the bands of the untamed one,
> To whom I gave the desert for a house,
> And the salt land for a dwelling place ?
> He scorneth the tumult of the city,
> The cries of the driver he hears not.
> He scours [7] the mountains for pasture
> And searches after every green thing.

It is significant that throughout their after-history Israel loved to compare life to a road—*i.e.*, to a constant wandering to and fro. The simile is a faithful reflection of the point of view of the nomad, who has nowhere " a continuing city." At the same time, we must not strain too far the conception of his free roaming. As a rule, well-defined pasture-grounds form the pivots round which his wanderings turn, and the position

[1] By Nicholson, *op. cit.*  [2] Judges ix, 7 ff.  [3] 1 Sam. viii, 11 ff.
[4] Exod. xviii, 13.  [5] Gen. xvi, 12.  [6] Job xxxix, 5–8.
[7] Read *jatur* for *jetur*.

of these is in turn determined by the presence of water. The possession of a well is the most precious treasure that the nomad covets. The finding of one gives rise to a song of rejoicing : [1]

> Spring up, O well ; sing ye unto it :
> The well, which princes digged,
> Which the nobles of the people delved
> With the sceptre, with their staves,
> Out of the desert, a gift.[2]

It was thus, as we learn from the biography of St Nilus, who had fallen a prisoner into the hands of a nomad tribe of Bedouins in the peninsula of Sinai, that the ancient Arabs were wont to break into song when a well had been found.[3] The familiar narratives of the destruction of wells which we find in the history of the patriarchs [4] show the difficulties men threw in each other's way. To this day the Arabs destroy the wells on the roads followed by pilgrims if their demands for toll are refused.[5]

The failure of water and the resultant lack of pasture, as well as the hostile acts of rival tribes, may cause nomad bands to seek new pasture-grounds. It is a well-attested fact that Semitic nomads, compelled by famine to shift their quarters, sought permission to enter Egypt. Egyptian officials report to Sethos II in the middle of the thirteenth century B.C. : " We have allowed the Bedouin tribes from Edom to pass the Merneptah fortress of Tku [6] to the pools of Merneptah, to get food for themselves and their cattle in the great pasture-lands of Pharaoh, the fair sun of all lands." After a considerable gap in the record come the names of other tribes who passed the fortress of Merneptah.[7] The bounds of the settlements were exactly defined, and it was the business of Egyptian officials to see that the fugitives did not trespass beyond the district assigned

[1] Num. xxi, 17 f.

[2] The true meaning of this last line is due to Budde. See *Preussische Jahrbücher*, 82 (1895), p. 491.

[3] Brockelmann, *Geschichte der arabischen Literatur* (1901), p. 11. For a modern analogy, see *ZDMG* (1907), p. 232.

[4] Gen. xxvi, 15, 18.

[5] *Cf.* also Euting, *Tagebuch einer Reise in Inner-Arabien* (1896), vol. i, p. 92.

[6] Perhaps Succoth, the first camping-ground of the Israelites after leaving Egypt (Exod. xii, 37 ; Num. xxxiii, 5).

[7] Spiegelberg, *Der Aufenthalt Israels in Ägypten* (1904), p. 24.

to them. When the Egyptian oppression became too great, when it took the form of forcing the Bedouin to do unaccustomed labour,[1] of course no barriers could restrain them.

The main occupation of the nomad is, and always has been, cattle-raising. The camel was alike animal for riding and beast of burden. Perhaps nothing can give a better idea of its importance for the nomad than the part it plays in Arabian poetry. But it was equally valuable to the ancient Hebrew. According to the writer of the history of Abraham, Abraham's servant recognizes the divinely destined wife for Isaac in the maiden who carefully tends the camels.[2] Apparently the nomad of that time had no horses.[3] The animals he raises are mainly sheep and goats. First and mainly he is a shepherd, and it is perhaps to this period that later times owed their familiar image of the shepherd and his sheep, which they were so fond of using to illustrate the relation between political or spiritual leaders and those under their charge. The goats are mostly black. From their hair the Bedouin women make tent-cloth. Hence the Shulamite in the Song of Solomon can compare her sunburnt skin to the colour of the tents of Kedar.[4] Most of the necessary labour, when not done by slaves or strangers, fell to the women. In any case, it was looked down upon. As the appellative " Cain " denotes the smith, it is not impossible that the clan Cain, or the Kenites, were a tribe of desert smiths ;[5] and it may be relevant to recall that Jael, the wife of a Kenite, had at hand a hammer, or other tool of the kind, wherewith to slay Sisera.[6] To this day the smiths of the Syrian desert and of Arabia form a caste.[7] The smiths would also provide such indispensable domestic utensils as iron pots. Weapons must have been mostly imported, but the commonest, such as bows and arrows,[8] would be made by each man for himself. Of other forms of handicraft, the commonest was the manufacture of leather articles, the material being supplied by the animals of the tribe. A round

---

[1] Exod. i, 11 ff.     [2] Gen. xxiv, 14.

[3] They are not mentioned among Abraham's belongings in Gen. xii, 16. Asses and she-asses, cattle, and sheep are mentioned, but by that time, of course, Abraham was no longer a genuine nomad.

[4] Song of Songs i, 5. Kedar is a nomad tribe of the Syrian-Arabian desert, living in tents in the country toward Babylon.

[5] See Gunkel, *Genesis, in loc.*, p. 48.     [6] Judges iv, 21, v, 26.

[7] Stade, in *ZatW* (1894), p. 255.     [8] Gen. xxi, 20 ; Is. xxi, 17.

stretched skin was the most primitive form of table.[1] A piece of leather drawn together by a string passing through rings forms a bag, which is carried slung on the camel's saddle. Water [2] and corn were carried and kept in bags made of skin.[3] The same Hebrew word [4] means 'bag' and 'jug,' but there can be no doubt as to which meaning is the older. The nomad used the skin bag; the fragile vessel of clay belongs to a settled civilization. A few vessels were made from fruits hollowed out; others were probably made of wood. Hand-mills were of course always of stone, and 'grinding' [5] is the current Bedouin word for battle, whereas the settled peasant speaks of a 'threshing.' [6]

If we may speak of tent 'furniture' at all, the only article that can be so named is the camel-chair; [7] the nomad usually sits on his haunches, or lies on a straw mattress or carpet. There is, of course, also the lamp, to make up for the scanty light that enters. The Old Testament way of saying that a family has died out is their light " has gone out " or " has been quenched." [8] When the Bedouins to-day say of a man " he sleeps in the dark " they mean that he is reduced to beggary—*i.e.*, has not even money enough to buy himself oil.

We have no ancient description of the tent itself, but if it is ever legitimate to draw inferences from present-day conditions surely we may do so here. The Bedouin tent may be likened to an inverted ship-hull, only more round than elongated. The firmament of heaven, for example, can be called a tent.[9] The tent-pegs are fixed in the ground, and the roof, which rests on a number of tent-poles, is kept in position by ropes. The tent is open in front. It is little more than man-high, but the size may vary. It is usually divided into two compartments, one for the men and the other for the women. People of means may even have a separate tent for the women.[10] Tents are usually erected in rings or circles, so disposed as to utilize as far as possible the natural protection of a thorn-hedge or other growth of the kind.

---

[1] *Shulchan*, 'table,' is from the root *shalach*, 'to skin.'
[2] Gen. xxi, 14, 19.
[3] ' Neck ' and ' belly ' of the skin bag (and of the jar) were originally meant quite literally.
[4] *nebel*.    [5] [*Cf.* English 'mill.'—Tr.]    [6] *Cf.* Jacob, *op. cit.*, p. 128.
[7] Gen. xxxi, 34.    [8] 2 Sam. xxi, 17; Jer. xxv, 10.    [9] Is. xl, 22.
[10] On women's tents see also p. 117, *supra*.

# CIVILIZATION OF THE INVADERS

The familiarity with tent-life which Israel brought with them from their nomadic period was so deeply ingrained in them that even after the tent had given place to the solid house the old forms of expression still survived. To " go to one's tent " meant to return home ; to " pull up the tent-pegs " meant to set out ; and the author of the Book of Job, comparing the human body to a tent, speaks of death as the breaking of the tent-ropes.[1]

The nomad's clothing is made from the skins of the animals of the flock. The most ancient garment is the loincloth.[2] Later the clothing consists of an under garment (a more developed loin-cloth) and a cloak.[3] In special cases, as so often happens, the ancient skin-clothing continued into civilized life. The so-called sackcloth—a coarse, hairy material tied round the loins—was worn by Isaiah.[4] The same material was also the dress of mourning (perhaps a relic of the time when worship was paid to the dead). There was also the furry " prophet's mantle," which was worn even into New Testament times.[5]

The burning rays of the sun rendered necessary some form of headdress. This was the turban. Shoes were not nearly so indispensable. But a free use of jewellery—the narrative of the golden calf correctly presupposes an abundant use of it in the wilderness [6]—is not surprising, seeing that it had essentially an amuletic significance.[7] Even the animals stood in need of the protection it afforded.

The chief food of the Bedouin is milk, both goat's and camel's. It is kept in the goatskin bag. In the hot climate it rapidly acquires a sour taste, and is all the better fitted to quench thirst. Milk is the first thing that is offered to a thirsty guest.[8] Butter is made by shaking the milk in the goatskin bag.[9] Whether cheese-making goes back to Israel's nomad period is uncertain. Besides milk, the Bedouin has always other food at hand—meat from the animals of his flock. But this is not at all a frequent or common food. In fact, he is unwilling to kill an animal [10]

---

[1] Job iv, 21. But perhaps instead of *jithram* the reading should be *jethedam*, ' their tent-peg.'     [2] Gen. iii, 7.
[3] See below, Book II, chapter 1, 5.     [4] Is. xx, 2.
[5] 2 Kings i, 8 ; Zech. xiii, 4 ; Mark i, 6 ; Heb. xi, 37.
[6] Exod. xxxii.     [7] See *supra*, pp. 36 and 40 f.
[8] Judges iv, 19, v, 25.     [9] *Cf.* the drastic simile in Prov. xxx, 33.
[10] *Cf.* F. B. Jevons, *An Introduction to the History of Religion* (1896), pp. 116, 157.

except on festive occasions, and as an animal was never killed without sacrifice being offered, the same word means both to 'kill' and to 'offer sacrifice.' For the rest, the food of the Bedouin depends on the nature of the country and soil on which he happens to be encamped. He may find fruit, such as dates ; and there are tribes who live almost exclusively on milk and dates.[1] Locusts, when they can be had, are not unwelcome. They are eaten roasted or boiled ; or they are ground to powder or baked. The modern Bedouin lives chiefly on butter and flour. But flour involves the possession of corn, and that means living in or near civilized territory. In fact, the Bedouin can hardly live without the gifts of civilization. Sometimes he buys what he wants, say, oil for his lamp ; sometimes he takes it by force. What he buys he pays for with the money received for escorting a caravan in safety to the frontiers of civilized territory, or with the tribute he imposes on travellers in return for his permission to pass unmolested, or with what he compels the settled peasants to pay for the protection of their fields from the ravages of other Bedouin tribes. Only too frequently, however, he is one of the ravagers, and the most genuine type of nomad is seen in the Midianites, whose bands invade the cultivated districts and carry off what they can, with the result that the peasant, in order to save his corn from them, threshes it with the flail as best he can in the closed wine-press, instead of in the usual manner on the threshing-floor.[2] Bedouin raids, like those we read of in the Book of Judges, have been repeated all down the centuries. It is the primeval contest between the desert and civilization, which seems to be inherent in the nature of things.

Some entire tribes have yielded to the impulse to betake themselves to civilized life, but others would look upon such a change as the loss of their nomadic liberty. This is simply a repetition of what is seen every day in ordinary life ; the sole aim of one man is to rise to a higher condition, while another is content with what he has. Even a Bedouin's heart may beat faster at the sight of the attractions offered by civilized life, and a reflection of this is seen in the narrative of the sending out of the spies, who bring back bunches of grapes, pomegranates, and figs as trophies of their journey of espionage.[3]

---

[1] Jacob, *op. cit.*, p. 88.    [2] Judges vi, 4, 11.    [3] Num. xiii, 23.

The intellectual gifts of the Bedouin have been greatly exaggerated by those who indiscriminately derive the whole contents of the Pentateuch from Israel's desert life. Modern literary criticism has done much to correct this exaggeration, but the " Pan-Babylonians " have once more revived the tendency to credit the Israel of the wilderness with an intellectualism for which there is no support. Representatives of that school speak of an ancient Oriental " astral science," the very name of which shows that it is entirely alien to the richly imaginative but unreflective nature of nomad civilization. A glance at ancient Arabian poetry dispels all doubt as to the imaginative power of the nomad Semites. Unfortunately, the Old Testament contains very little Hebrew literature that goes back to the desert period. We have already mentioned the Song of Lamech and the Song of the Well.[1] We have also the Song of Miriam,[2] and some fragments of other war-songs,[3] and these relics, scanty as they are, reveal no small amount of poetic gift and creative power. The poetry of the time was, of course, entirely oral, sung by minstrels,[4] taken up by the people, and handed down from father to son.[5] No doubt professional story-tellers were also busy, although there is no definite mention of them in the Old Testament. On the other hand, the Bedouin does no writing, at least not in the literary sense,[6] but his love of music and song is shown by the ancient tradition in Genesis which divides mankind into three classes, flock-owners, musicians, and smiths.[7] And those who are here named second in order, those who play the zither and the flute, take precedence of those who work in brass and iron. In contrast to these last, the other two classes, dwellers in tents who are flock-owners and musicians, are traced back to the first wife of the ancestor.

The question as to the religion of the invaders brings us to less sure ground. They certainly came as the hosts of Jahveh ; and it is quite possible that the original meaning of Jahveh-zebaoth, " Jahveh of the War-hosts," was intended to describe

---

[1] See *supra*, pp. 121 and 124.      [2] Exod. xv, 21.

[3] Num. xxi, 14 f., 27 ff. (the latter is perhaps of a later date).

[4] *Cf.* Num. xxi, 27.

[5] *Cf.* Exod. xiii, 14 ; Deut. vi, 20.

[6] When Mohammed appeared there were seventeen men who could write, and the art of writing was still rarer among women (Jacob, *op. cit.*, p. 163).

[7] Gen. iv, 20 ff.

I

their god as the deity who stood at the head of their war-hosts.[1]
But the permanent association of Jahveh with Israel was the work
of Moses, and coincides in time with the " exodus from Egypt,"
which brought Israel to the frontiers of the civilized territory
of Palestine. What Israel brought with them from their
nomad life was, along with their faith in Jahveh, and more or
less pervaded by that faith, a religious inheritance of an older,
nay, of an ancient time, the actual contents of which it is not
so easy to determine. All the same, we may safely start with
the fact that it was the clan that constituted the ultimate social
unit of the nomadic period. Accordingly, the clan was the
original association for worship, and this character it retained
for a long time after Israel had settled down in a civilized
country.[2] The deity to whom such worship was paid stood
naturally in a special relation to the clan, and the inauguration
of this relationship was traced back to an experience of God
vouchsafed to the father or mother of the tribe. The fundamental conception of the importance of blood affected even
their religious thinking. The deity and the sib-association
that worshipped him were conceived as related in blood,[3] and
the sacrifices (among which those involving blood predominated,
the deity and the worshipper each receiving his share of it [4])
seem to have had as their main purpose the formation of that
blood-bond between the two parties, or, if that bond should
have been loosened, the restoration of it.

Some have gone even further, and have alleged that the
animal sacrificed was the deity himself. The sacrificial animal,
it is said, was originally a totem animal, and Israel's forefathers
passed through the stage of totemism.[5] Two of the essential
features of totemism were that the totem animal (except in
the ceremonial meal) must not be eaten, and that the sib-
community was named after it. The Old Testament seems

---

[1] The opinion that ' war-hosts ' refers to angels or stars or cosmic powers
must meet the objection that wherever these are spoken of as Jahveh's army
the singular *saba* is used (also in the corrected text of Ps. ciii, 21, cxlviii, 2) ;
*sebaoth* is used only of human war-hosts (*e.g.*, 1 Sam. xvii, 45), and specially
of those that came out of Egypt (Exod. vii, 4, xii, 41).

[2] *Cf.* 1 Sam. xx, 6.

[3] *Cf.* names like Abihu, Amminadab, Exod. vi, 23, and see *supra*, p. 70.

[4] The ceremonial of Exod. xxiv, 6 ff., is specially instructive.

[5] *Cf.* especially Robertson Smith, *The Religion of the Semites*.

to contain illustrations of both these features. Prohibitions against eating certain animals are contained in it, in a systematic form which was brought to a stage of absolute perfection by subsequent priestly activity.[1] Animal names which are also proper names occur with great frequency—*e.g.*, Caleb, "Dog"; Rachel, " Ewe " ; Leah, " Wild Cow " ; Eglah,[2] " Calf " ; Beker[3] and Gemalli,[4] " Camel " ; Hazir,[5] " Boar "; Shual,[6] " Fox "; Laish,[7] " Lion " ; Simeon, a cross of wolf and hyena ; Zibiah,[8] " Gazelle " ; Hulda,[9] " Weasel " ; Nun,[10] " Fish " ; Aiah,[11] " Hawk"; Jonah, " Dove "; Hagab[12] and Hagabah,[13] " Locust"; Deborah, " Bee "; and others. In the first instance, to be sure, these proper names are names of individuals, but that fact does not make it impossible to take them as the names of septs, because it is undoubted that septs were named after their actual ancestor or after an outstanding leader.[14] *E.g.*, Caleb and Simeon are undoubtedly tribal as well as personal names. But, just because the names are originally personal names, their totemistic interpretation is in no case the only possible one. For what is there to surprise us in the fact that Bedouins, living in the open, should occasionally call their children after beasts of the field or after birds ? J. L. Burckhardt[15] tells us that if a dog happened to be by when an Arab boy was born the boy was called Kelab (Caleb) ; and how readily a chance happening could decide the choice of a name is clear from examples in the Old Testament, some of them being mere jests of popular etymology. Or, again, such an animal name seemed best suited to express certain qualities which were observed in the child, or which it was desired he should have. Arabs might call a boy Qird ("Ape") because of his great imitative powers.[16] But there are other Arabian analogies which provide a superstitious background for this use of animal names. The ancient Arabs

---

[1] Lev. xi ; Deut. xiv.      [2] 2 Sam. iii, 5.
[3] Gen. xlvi, 21 ; Num. xxvi, 35.      [4] Num. xiii, 12.
[5] 1 Chron. xxiv, 15 ; Neh. x, 20.
[6] 1 Chron. vii, 36 ; *cf.* 1 Sam. xiii, 17.
[7] 1 Sam. xxv, 44 ; 2 Sam. iii, 15.      [8] 2 Kings xii, 1.
[9] 2 Kings xxii, 14.      [10] Exod. xxxiii, 11, etc.
[11] Gen. xxxvi, 24 ; 2 Sam. iii, 7.      [12] Ezra ii, 46.
[13] Ezra ii, 45.      [14] Nöldeke, *ZDMG*, vol. xl (1886), p. 158.
[15] In his *Notes on the Bedouins* (1830), p. 97.
[16] E. König, *Geschichte der alttestamentlichen Religion* (1912), p. 62.

were fond of naming their boys after repulsive animals or prickly, bitter plants, in order that no one should try to do them harm,[1] the idea being that there was a close connexion between name and creature. This might have been the meaning of such Hebrew proper names as Parosh [2] (" Flea "), Shaphan [3] (" Rock-badger "), Tola [4] (" Worm "), Coz [5] (" Thorn "). It is therefore very unsafe to infer a previous stage of totemism in Israel from the existence of animal and plant names. And the same is true of the Old Testament prohibitions of certain foods ; for, although it is undeniable that these have a religious background, their protest is just as likely to have been directed against some other form of animal-worship than totemism.[6]

There was at least one form of animal-worship in Israel's nomad period for which there is abundant evidence, but it has no connexion with totemism. In the Temple at Jerusalem up till the end of the eighth century worship was paid to a brazen serpent, whose history is traced back to the desert period.[7]

All this seems to show that it is a fallacy to trace ancient Israel's belief in the existence of a blood-kinship between deity and worshipper to a former totemism. But there is perhaps more to be said in support of the suggestion that the clan deities worshipped were the human ancestors of the clan. Many mourning customs may go back to former worship of the dead. These customs, some of them then meaningless, some of them with a new meaning read into them, continued well on into the historical period. We must be careful not to interpret all of them as definitely or exclusively religious,[8] but the habit of removing the sandals at the sight of a dead person [9]—and even in post-Biblical days Jewish coffin-bearers had to be barefooted [10] —inevitably recalls the custom of taking off the sandals when approaching holy ground.[11] And the curiously ceremonial form of the dirge [12] shows that it was really a religious ceremony.

---

[1] Wellhausen, *Reste arabischen Heidentums*, p. 200.    [2] Ezra ii, 3.

[3] 2 Kings xxii, 3, 12.    [4] Gen. xlvi, 13 ; Judges x, 1.

[5] 1 Chron. iv, 8 ; Ezra ii, 61.    [6] See *supra*, p. 112.

[7] 2 Kings xviii, 4 ; Num. xxi, 8.

[8] *Cf.* for what follows my brochure *Die israelitischen Vorstellungen vom Zustande nach dem Tode* (1914).    [9] Ezek. xxiv, 17.

[10] S. Krauss, *Talmudische Archäologie* (1911), vol. ii, pp. 64, 481.

[11] Exod. iii, 5 ; Josh. v, 15.

[12] Zech. xii, 11 ; *cf.* Amos v, 16, Jer. ix, 17.

It is difficult to attach any other meaning to the practice of cutting the body [1] than that of a method of attracting the attention of the spirit of the dead, just as the priests of Baal try by similar means to emphasize their appeal to their god. [2] It is natural to see in the practice of cutting the hair as a sign of mourning [3] a survival of an early hair-offering : it is found almost everywhere, and always in connexion with worship of the dead. [4] And the rending of the garments [5]—by no means the only form of gift to the dead—may be a survival of a former offering of clothes. The funeral feast, which is well attested for the late Jewish period, [6] recalls the well-known sacrificial feasts. Further, there were sacred graves in ancient Israel, [7] and oracles were sought from the dead just as from a deity. The place called Oboth (" Spirits of the Dead "), one of the desert stations of the Exodus, was probably a place where the spirits of the dead were worshipped. [8] When the witch of Endor calls up Samuel, the apparition is called Elohim, [9] a name elsewhere always applied to deity. It is hardly credible that that name was applied to the dead only in the Jahvist period, because the religion of Jahveh looked upon the dead and all that concerned them as unclean, so that this use of the ' divine ' name must have come down from former times. Indeed, the repellent attitude which Jahvism took up toward the dead is perhaps the best proof that they actually were, in former times, the object of worship.

From the worship of the dead it is only a step to ancestor-worship. Wherever ancestor-worship prevails special importance is attached to the possession of a posterity, preferably a male posterity, who will render to their ancestors the worship that is due. It is, of course, well known that in Israel we find a striking emphasis laid on male posterity. [10] Among other results, this led to the custom of the so-called levirate, according to which it was the first duty of the brother or other next of kin of a dead man to marry his widow, in order to "raise up seed"

---

[1] Jer. xvi, 6, etc.
[2] 1 Kings xviii, 28.
[3] Is. xxii, 12.
[4] E.g., *Iliad*, XXIII, 151 ff.
[5] 2 Sam. i, 11 ; 2 Kings ii, 12.
[6] The Epistle of Jeremy, xxxi ; Josephus, *Wars of the Jews*, II, i, 1.
[7] Gen. xxxv, 8, 19.
[8] Num. xxi, 10, xxxiii, 43.
[9] 1 Sam. xxviii, 13.
[10] See below, p. 150.

to the dead.[1] Where this custom is found outside of Israel (and it exists in India) it is expressly associated with ancestor-worship, and this provision is made for a posterity in order to assure the continuance of offerings to the dead.[2] Was it the same in Israel? Certain images mentioned in the Old Testament, such as the teraphim,[3] have also, and perhaps correctly, been interpreted as images of ancestors.

But ancestor-worship is not as a rule exclusively of a religious nature. In addition to spirits of ancestors, there are spirits of nature of all kinds. And if we were correct in speaking in the section on Canaanite religion of the worship of stones, trees, wells, and stars, the same must undoubtedly have been the case with the Israel of the same period. The Semitic peoples who occupied Palestine passed through parallel lines of development. The changes of population in Palestine were simply successive waves of kindred peoples pouring over the country. Therefore it is certain that the belief, common to all Semitic peoples, that a stone could be the dwelling-place of a divine *numen* goes back to Israel's desert period. What well and tree meant for the desert nomad it is not difficult to estimate. Robertson Smith says : [4] " To one who has wandered in the Arabian wilderness, traversing day after day stony plateaus, black volcanic fields, or arid sands walled in by hot mountains of bare rock, and relieved by no other vegetation than a few grey and thorny acacias or scanty tufts of parched herbage ; till suddenly at a turn of the road he emerges on a Wady where the ground-water rises to the surface, and passes as if by magic into a new world, where the ground is carpeted with verdure and a grove of stately palm-trees spreads forth its canopy of shade against the hot and angry heaven, it is not difficult to realize that to early man such a spot was verily a garden and habitation of the gods." And the constellations of night were also of great importance to the desert traveller, who, no doubt, preferred the greater coolness of the night for his journeys.

Again, it cannot be fortuitous that the feasts which go back to the nomad period are connected with the phases of the moon.

---

[1] *Cf.* Deut. xxv, 5 ff. ; Gen. xxviii ; Ruth iv, 3 ff. ; Matt. xxii, 24.
[2] J. Jolly, *Recht und Sitte* (1896), p. 70.
[3] Gen. xxxi, 19 ; 1 Sam. xix, 13 ; Ezek. xxi, 21 ; *cf.* Exod. xxi, 6.
[4] *The Religion of the Semites* (1889), pp. 97–98.

They were the feast of the new moon and the Sabbath, which is often mentioned in the same breath with it, and which was perhaps originally the feast of the full moon.[1] The Paschal feast also, the feast of the firstlings of the flock, a typical nomad festival, seems originally to have been a celebration in honour of the moon-god.[2] The time of its celebration and the nature of it practically prove this : it falls on the night of the full moon of the spring month (14th Nisan), and the Paschal lamb must be eaten before daybreak.[3]

But the desert is also populated by spirits which are not confined to any special dwelling-place, and to these also worship must be paid. The ritual of the later Day of Atonement tells us of a desert demon, Asasel, to whom the scapegoat is sent.[4] Perhaps this is a late adaptation of an ancient demon-worship. The numbers of these demons may be increased—*e.g.*, from the spirits of the dead, especially the souls of men who were strange even during their life, or of those who died a violent death. Hence the custom, which lasted into the civilized period, of erecting a cairn of stones over such a grave, in order to keep the dreaded spirit confined to its place ; and every one who passed that way had to add a stone to it.[5]

The result to which we thus come, that the pre-Mosaic religion was in all probability polydemonistic, is in sharp contrast to the well-known theory of Renan that the monotony of the desert taught its Semitic inhabitants to be monotheists. It would be an error to suppose that Renan intends this to be understood as praise of the Semites. On the contrary, he says that their minds were too simple and stolid to appreciate the magic and the variety, the poetry, and the romance of mythology, and that they therefore made no advance beyond the monotheistic stage. All that need be said in answer to this is that this alleged primitive monotheism is simply inconsistent with

---

[1] *Cf.* Meinhold, *Sabbat und Sonntag* (1909), pp. 7-12 ; also cf. *ZDMG*, vol. lviii (1904), p. 459. The Babylonian *sab(p)atti* means the fifteenth day of the month—*i.e.*, full moon.

[2] The text of Deut. xxxiii, 14, perhaps not well preserved, still reflects the belief in the moon's influence on fertility.

[3] Exod. xxxiv, 25.          [4] Lev. xvi, 8, 10, 21.

[5] Musil, *Arabia Petræa*, vol. iii, p. 35. A. von Wrede, *Reise in Hadhramaut* (1870), p. 266 ; *AR*, vol. xv (1912), p. 148. *Cf.* Josh. vii, 26, viii, 29 ; 2 Sam. xviii, 17.

the facts. The same criticism applies to the statement made by some Assyriologists, that the atmosphere of a monotheism which had developed from primitive Babylonian speculation spread so as to include the nomadic civilization of Israel. As if the artificial productions of a small intellectual *élite*, or even of selfish priests who in the interests of their temple and for their own gain sought to exalt the one god of the Babylonian pantheon above all other gods, could possibly have been able to exercise a lasting influence over peoples far away !

This much-vaunted monotheism of the ancient East does not even help us to understand the work of Moses. And the same may be said of the reform introduced by the Egyptian king Amenophis IV. What made Moses the prophet of a new faith was a personal experience at a holy place,[1] which constrained him, in the name of the God who thus drew near to him, to lead forth to freedom and to this God his brethren then enslaved in Egypt ; and the marvellous deliverance which they and he experienced at the Red Sea, where Jahveh "threw horse and rider into the sea," [2] set the seal upon it. By that deed the God of Sinai bound to Himself as His people the tribes leaving Egypt. Without raising the question what this God of Sinai originally was, a thunder-god, a volcano-god, or whatever else, or the question whose God He originally was,[3] it must be said that the new and permanent element in the work of Moses was that he divested the ancient God of Sinai of all the limitations attaching to a nature-god and connected Him with the history of the nation which was then being born. In this union lies the real germ of the special religious development which was the unique possession of Israel.[4]

---

[1] Exod. iii.　　　　　　　　　　　　[2] Exod. xv, 21.

[3] The " Kenite hypothesis " I can accept only in the sense that Jahveh was *also* god of the Kenites. To the view that he was originally *only* the Kenite god there are in my opinion strong objections. I cannot reduce the tradition about the " God of the fathers " (Exod. iii, 6) to a secondary adjustment of the Mosaic stories with those of Genesis. In particular it seems to me to be difficult to suppose that a man coming in the name of a completely strange god could have succeeded in inducing the Israelites to follow him. The case would be different if Jahveh was the god at least of Levi or of the Leah tribes, with (Levitical) Kadesh as one of his centres of worship. The Levitical name of Moses' mother Jochabed (Exod. vi, 20), which is compounded with Jahveh, is by no means necessarily a later invention.

[4] See the author's *Die Eigenart der alttestamentlichen Religion* (1913).

Of the utmost practical importance was the work, ascribed by tradition to Moses, that connected law and justice with the sanctuary of the new God.[1] To His "instruction," or whatever other word may be used to translate the Hebrew *torah*[2]—it originally meant oracle, and was so called from the method of its manipulation—there was thus given a decisive influence on the vicissitudes of individual and communal life which could not fail to have a telling effect on the formation and shaping of the national *ethos*.

We must not allow ourselves to be prevented from recognizing these facts by the presence of various magical features which we find in the picture of Moses. In his hand his rod is invested with powers that are no less than magical.[3] The Ark of God, a holy shrine or cabinet, owing its sanctity to its contents (probably two meteoric stones [4]), accompanies the people of the Exodus as their war palladium, which to touch, or even to be near, brings death.[5] Is it surprising that Moses did not hesitate to give a central place in the worship to this purely material object, as well as to the tent which he afterward erected to contain it? [6] It should not be forgotten that any reformation which is not to fail of practical effect cannot break abruptly with the past, but must adapt itself to it by some amount of compromise. Who can say whether this was not the sole method by which the tribe of Joseph, whose tribal sanctuary the Ark seems to have been,[7] could be induced to accept the God preached by Moses? The analogy of the black stone at Mecca, taken over into the new religion by Mohammed, is at once apparent. After all, it is just in the sphere of the cultus that magical customs show such remarkable tenacity. In the Paschal celebration the doorposts and the lintels of the house were smeared with blood [8] in order to render its inhabitants

---

[1] Exod. xviii.

[2] The probable derivation is from *jarah*, ' to cast the lot ' (see Josh. xviii, 6) or ' to shoot the arrow.' For an arrow oracle, *cf.* 1 Sam. xx, 20, Ezek. xxi, 21.

[3] Exod. vii, 9, xvii, 5, 9.

[4] Unfortunately, it has become the fashion to say that the Ark was originally " the empty throne of God," although the arguments against this view, as stated by Budde (*Theologische Studien und Kritiken* (1906), pp. 489–507), are final.

[5] 1 Sam. vi, 19 ; 2 Sam. vi, 6 ff.          [6] Exod. xxxiii, 7.

[7] It is found later on Josephite territory at Shiloh (1 Sam. i, 3, iii, 21).

[8] Exod. xii, 7.

immune from harm. At a time when tents still took the place
of houses, the same effect would be produced by the smearing
of a tent-rope. This would be a natural supposition, even if
it were not expressly confirmed by customs in Palestine that
have continued unbroken down to the present day.[1]

The cultus itself must have been marked by the utmost
possible simplicity. The picture of the elaborate and costly
apparatus attributed by the Priests' Code to the Mosaic period
cannot be reconciled with the facts. This is not only an assured
result of modern scholarship : passages from Amos [2] and Jeremiah [3] put it beyond all doubt. The blood of the sacrificial
animal was smeared or sprinkled on the sacred stone ; the gift
offering was hung on the tree or cast into the well. It is vain
to refuse to admit that human sacrifices also took place. It was
because the Egyptians tried to prevent the Israelites from
sacrificing their first-born that they paid for it with their own.[4]
Apart, however, from the so-called *herem—i.e.*, the sacrifice of
prisoners of war—this cruel custom was remitted at an early
period.[5] Preparation for taking part in the cultus consisted in
refraining from sexual intercourse and in washings.[6] Perhaps
at that time, as in modern Islam, when water was not available
the sand of the desert was a permissible substitute. Ornaments
were also put on.[7] Hence it caused no surprise to the Egyptians
when the Israelites, who were presumably going to worship
Jahveh in the desert, begged the use (or loan) of their gold and
silver ornaments.[8] This association of ornament with worship
rests on the amuletic character of ornament.[9] As an amulet the
ornament is invested with magical power. Thus Aaron demanded
the earrings of the women and children from which to make the
golden calf.[10] The calf or image, which of course must also

---

[1] Curtis, *Ursemitische Religion im Volksleben des heutigen Orients* (1903),
p. 208.

[2] Amos v, 25.        [3] Jer. vii, 22.        [4] Exod. xi.

[5] For the custom see Exod. xxii, 28 f., xxxiv, 19, Ezek. xx, 25 f. ; for its
remission Gen. xxii, Exod. xii, 23, xiii, 13.

[6] Exod. xix, 10 ; 1 Sam. xxi, 5.        [7] Hos. ii, 13 ; Gen. xxxv, 4.

[8] Exod. iii, 21 f., xi, 2, xii, 35 f. The narrator does not even try to conceal
the fact that the Egyptians were deceived by the demand of the Israelites.
This behaviour of the Israelites exemplifies the view that as toward strangers
and foreigners the same moral obligations which were required toward one's
own people were not binding.        [9] Cf. *supra*, p. 127.

[10] Exod. xxxii, 2 ff. ; similarly Judges viii, 24–27.

possess magical qualities, was thus constructed through the adding together of numerous small items possessing magical power. As a rule, the cultus of the nomad is almost entirely destitute of images, probably for the natural reason that he is averse to rendering his movements more difficult by superfluous baggage. In all cases circumcision [1] is an indispensable preliminary to taking part in worship. We have already said all that is necessary regarding its original character.[2] It is not the only tribal symbol or symbol of worship. The story of Cain, the ancestor of the nomad tribe of Kenites, who were closely akin to Israel, speaks of " the sign of Jahveh " that protects its wearer, "lest any finding him should kill him." [3] It was probably some tattoo mark on the hand or forehead (or, more exactly, between the eyebrows). This was also known in Israel [4] until a later law [5] forbade the ancient custom, but the prohibition itself is a proof that it was practised. [6]

Besides the feasts already mentioned there was also the sheep-shearing,[7] a genuine nomad festival. The question whether official priests existed in this period seems to receive an affirmative answer in what we are told of the Midianite priest Jethro.[8] Offering sacrifice, however, was not the main or sole occupation of the priest : the father of a family or the head of a clan was entitled to do so. The real significance of the priest, the *kôhēn*, is indicated by the fact that among the Arabs the *kâhin* is the seer. The chief place in religious matters comes to be taken by the man who, thanks to his gift of vision, is able to learn the divine will. When the psychical gift declines, the need of an artificial substitute is felt, and the former seer makes use of the sacred lots. Even for this special qualifications are necessary— the questions must be put in a proper way, because the required answer can be obtained only through a proper narrowing of the circle of possible answers. This is in keeping with the

---

[1] Exod. iv, 25.　　[2] See *supra*, p. 112.　　[3] Gen. iv, 15.

[4] Exod. xiii, 9, 16 ; Deut. vi, 8, xi, 18 ; 1 Kings xx, 38–41 ; Is. xliv, 5.

[5] Lev. xix, 28, xxi, 5.

[6] *Cf.* Stade in *ZatW*, vol. xiv (1894), p. 250 ff., and my article " Zur Volkskunde der alten Juden " in the *Schweizer Archiv für Volkskunde*, vol. xvii (1913), p. 11, where an attempt is made to show the connexion of the later phylacteries with the ancient tattoo marks.

[7] *Cf.* Gen. xxxviii, 12 ; 1 Sam. xxv, 4 ; 2 Sam. xiii, 23.

[8] Exod. ii, 16.

twin lots " Urim " and " Thummim." [1]  The priest is thus in the first instance the director of the sacred oracle, and he continues to be so for a long time in civilized territory,[2] before his sacrificial duties become his main task.

The ideal of life cherished by some minds was purely nomadic : to build no house, sow no seed, plant no vineyard, drink no wine.  This was the ideal which still lived, centuries later, in the minds of some enthusiasts, of the type of the Nazirites [3] and the Rechabites,[4] in the midst of civilized life.  But for the great majority the transition from the desert to civilized territory meant just this significant change of thought and life.

---

[1] *I.e.*, probably a " yes " and a " no " ;  1 Sam. xiv, 41 (LXX).
[2] Deut. xxxiii, 8.        [3] Judges xiii, 7, 14.        [4] Jer. xxxv, 6 ff.

# CHAPTER IV

## THE PERIOD OF TRANSITION

THE transition from the nomad life of the desert to settled life in civilized territory is never accomplished all at once. We have already had occasion to remark that the free roaming of the Bedouin must not be exaggerated ; that, as a rule, well-defined pasture-grounds form the pivots round which his roamings turn.[1] And there are even in the nomad's life certain approximations to the settled life of the peasant cultivator. Travellers in Arabia [2] tell us that the best valleys on both sides of the Harra near El-heyr are sown every year by Arab tribes. When the harvest is over they strike their tents, move off with their cattle, and roam about for a time in nomad fashion. And of the district of Beer-sheba it has been said : " The children of the desert know how to handle the plough. They look down upon the settled peasant ; they insist that they are on a different level ; but wherever the soil allows, they raise crops of corn. As the interval between seedtime and harvest is only a few months, their agriculture does not tie them so closely to the soil as to exclude a real nomadic life. In the dry season, the Bedouin goes with his flocks in search of pasture. But although his chief interest is undoubtedly cattle-raising, still his agricultural work is by no means small." [3] Under such circumstances we are justified in speaking of half-nomads.

In the case of Israel, even more than in that of others, there is good reason for assuming such an intermediate stage. It is very significant that our sources have preserved the memory of a lengthy stay at Kadesh,[4] a place that also figures as a great centre of worship. And, if it be the case, as the tradition has it, that the invasion took place through the country east of Jordan, this district is full of instruction for us still. There is many a peasant there to-day who can tell that his grandfather

---

[1] See *supra*, p. 123.
[2] Doughty, *Travels in Arabia Deserta* (1888), vol. i, p. 234.
[3] Rotermund im *Palästinajahrbuch*, vol. v (1909), p. 114.
[4] Num. xiii, 26, xx, 1.

was a nomad, living in tents and moving about with his flocks, while his father settled down in a place that suited him and built a modest cabin ; the peasant himself has built a house of stone, and is now permanently attached to the fields which his plough turns up.[1] Thus movable are the boundary lines between the types of life. This is evident even in what we read of the " sons of Jair." In one verse we read of their tent villages, in the next of their cities.[2] Linguistic usage is also instructive in another respect. The word [3] which formerly called the goal of their journey the ' pasture-ground ' comes to mean the ' fixed dwelling-place,' and is even finally used as a contrast to the ' desert.' The centre of the settlement is, of course, the well, and the claim to its ownership is frequently supported by a story telling how the ancestor came to possess it.[4]

This half-nomad stage is still reflected in the picture drawn in Genesis of Abraham, Isaac, and Jacob and his sons. The leaning toward settled domestic life is unmistakable. Abraham's sojourn in Mamre could almost be called permanent, although his dwelling was still a tent.[5] The chief occupation was the raising of stock, especially sheep and goats. Cattle are also mentioned,[6] but they play a subordinate part. All the same, their presence implies agriculture, and, as a matter of fact, there is a large store of flour in Abraham's household.[7] Isaac sows in Gerar, and reaps—this is certainly an exaggeration [8]—one hundred-fold.[9] Jacob prepares a dish of lentils.[10] Reuben finds the mandrakes when he is in the field in the time of harvest.[11] Joseph dreams of the sheaves with which he and his brethren are busy,[12] and when corn in Palestine fails his brethren proceed to Egypt to buy it—that is, corn is already an indispensable food.[13] It is possible, of course, that the conditions of the later

---

[1] Thomsen, *Palästina und seine Kultur* (1909), p. 23. *Cf.* the instructive juxtaposition " cities and sheepfolds " in Num. xxxii, 36. A graphic picture of the transition types of settlement in Syria and Egypt is given by H. Fischer in *ZDPV*, vol. xxxiii (1910), p. 210 ff.

[2] Num. xxxii, 41 ; Judges x, 4.      [3] *nawĕh* (Is. xxvii, 10).

[4] Gen. xxi, 25 ff. ; Judges i, 14 f.      [5] Gen. xviii, 1.

[6] Gen. xii, 16, xiii, 5, xviii, 7, etc.      [7] Gen. xviii, 6.

[8] To-day wheat yields on an average eightfold, and barley fifteenfold, in the fertile plain of Sharon (Benzinger, p. 142).

[9] Gen. xxvi, 12.      [10] Gen. xxv, 34.

[11] Gen. xxx, 14.      [12] Gen. xxxvii, 7.

[13] Gen. xlii, 2.

period when these ancient narratives were reduced to writing may have coloured some of the details here given.

The transition from the half-nomadic stage to that of complete settlement in civilized territory involved coming to terms with the population already there. This has been frequently represented as an undisguisedly and purely hostile meeting. According to this view, the invaders entered the country as conquerors, and mercilessly wiped out the inhabitants in obedience to a sacred call. This simply takes for granted that all outside the ranks of the Israelites were depraved heathens, and that to Israel, as the servant of the true God, the prime duty fell of completely extirpating this heathenism. This view is, indeed, as old as the Old Testament itself,[1] but it is only found in the writings that reflect the views of later legalism, and it is contradicted by facts which are irrefutably attested by later sources.[2] It is even shown to be erroneous by its gross exaggeration of the military successes of the invaders. Israel's actual successes in battle were mainly due to their personal superiority kindled by sacred enthusiasm ; and wherever this superiority could not prevail against the advantages derived from better knowledge of war they made no progress. Thus, in the hill-country, where the fighting was hand to hand, Israel was victorious, while in the plains, where the fortified cities lay, and where the war-chariots of the Canaanites could display their terrible efficiency, the opposite was the case.[3] As a result, the first Israelite settlements were on the high grounds, with Canaanite territory all round them in the plains. The people of Assher, for example, dwelt " in the midst of the Canaanites, who occupied the land, because they were not able to drive them out." [4] To be sure, the ancient chronicler from whom these words are taken seeks in other passages to reverse this way of stating the conditions, and says that Canaan dwelt in the midst of Israel, and that Israel, when it had grown in strength, made the Canaanites do forced labour.[5] All the same, his last word is " they could not drive them out."

The superiority of the Canaanites was first shown in the plain of Jezreel, through which the main arteries of traffic ran. The

---

[1] Deut. vii, 2.    [2] Especially Judges i.

[3] The same was repeated in the battles of the Bedouins with the Turks under Mohammed Ali Pasha. Burckhardt, *Notes on the Bedouins*, p. 236.

[4] Judges i, 32.    [5] Judges i, 27 ff.

Song of Deborah,[1] a contemporary document, gives us a clear view of the conditions that prevailed. The insecurity of movement was such that all who found it necessary to travel avoided the highway and took to roundabout paths, for the enemy was watching the main routes and was ready to fall upon anyone that passed along. The courage of the newcomers sank so low that they did not dare to face the enemy. But this intolerable oppression was followed by a great deliverance. The kindling call of an inspired prophetess roused the slumbering powers of an impulsive leader, and round him Israel's brave fighting men gathered. This great host, it is clear, was a thing of steady, gradual growth. Roused to action by the very greatness of their extremity, the common will to break the power of the enemy was born of smaller successes in various places. In the case dealt with in the poem several tribes failed to appear. They had no intention of sacrificing their own interests to the common cause. Nevertheless, battles like that immortalized in the Song of Deborah reveal the actual progress of the national idea. This national movement was at the same time religious. The warriors felt themselves animated by one spirit, and this gave them a strength that was irresistible. Their battle was the cause of the God to whom they felt united by a common faith. He came mightily to their aid and led them to victory.

The fate of the vanquished depended on circumstances. Those whose slaughter was not decreed by the *herem* (the ' ban ' that doomed them to death in honour of the god of the victors) were condemned by their human conquerors to all manner of service, from actual slavery down to simple payment of tribute.

This hostile encounter between the two peoples was, however, accompanied by a more peaceful one, which for our purpose is of far greater importance than the other. So-called Israelite communities, too weak to maintain their independence, sought the protection of a more powerful Canaanite tribe. We may simply transfer to this period what took place in Arabia centuries afterward, when a Jewish clan or sept from Medina, conscious of their weakness, placed themselves under the protection of the tribes Aus and Khazrai.[2] The fact that such relationships

---

[1] Judges v.

[2] *Agh*, vol. xix, 97. *Gîrân*, the Arabian name for those who thus became citizens for safety's sake, corresponds to the Hebrew *gêrîm*. ["Strangers."—TR.]

were established by mutual treaty in the period with which we are dealing is shown by the case of the Gibeonites.[1] It makes no difference that in that case it was Canaanites who sought protection and Israelites who granted it. The services which such *protégés* had to render to their protectors were of various kinds. They became bound for military service ;[2] had to yield up a portion of the booty which they took in expeditions undertaken in the interests of their protectors ;[3] or they were assigned a piece of land which they had to bring under agriculture ; or a piece of woodland was given them to clear.[4] According to the rule accepted everywhere,[5] this opened up for the dependent parties a prospect of acquiring property, which they could either dispose of or leave to their descendants. If fortune favoured their labours the original relationship might in course of time be reversed, and in many instances this was the case with Israel.

In proportion as the original distinction between the two parties became obliterated—and the descendant of a slave taken in war might become the heir of a childless master—mixed marriages became more frequent ;[6] and these in their turn contributed greatly to the wiping out of national distinctions and to the bridging over of differences in civilization. There are numerous examples of such mixed marriages.[7] Perhaps the most instructive is that of Judah, the ancestor of the tribe of the same name, with the daughter of the Canaanite Shuah.[8] There is no doubt that this tradition reflects the fact that this tribe had a specially large infusion of Canaanite elements. Eduard Meyer[9] goes so far as to say that it almost seems as if it contained hardly any Hebrew element at all. Such assimilation, brought about by intermarriage, is really the best explanation of the increase in numbers which we find in the statements made about the size of armies from the beginning

---

[1] Josh. ix, 3 ff.        [2] 1 Sam. xxix.

[3] 1 Sam. xxvii, 5 ff.

[4] Thus in Josh. xvii, 15, which seems to refer to an assignation of the Gilead plateau. *Cf.* Num. xxxii, 29, and Budde in *ZatW*, vol. viii (1888), p. 148.

[5] Post, *Grundriss der ethnologischen Jurisprudenz* (1894), vol. i, p. 345.

[6] *E.g.*, Judges iii, 6.

[7] See my book, *Die Stellung der Israeliten und der Juden zu den Fremden* (1896), p. 63 ff.

[8] Gen. xxxviii, 2.        [9] *ZatW*, vol. vi (1886), p. 10.

K

of the monarchy.[1] This process of assimilation, at least from
the political point of view, was to all intents and purposes
completed and ended by the political organization which was
carried through in the reign of, say, Solomon. It was only what
might have been expected, however, when, in the case of some
tribes, especially on the south and east borders of the country,
the old nomadic impulse proved too strong for them to be
included in the process. This is, probably, the reason why
Simeon and Levi, and to some extent Reuben,[2] fell back into
the obscurity that has no history.

The political victory of Israel over Canaan had as a result the
cultural subjection of Israel to Canaan. This subordination is
all the more complete the less we imagine the encounter between
the two peoples to have been exclusively one of force. As late
as the seventh century the Israelites themselves were still fully
conscious that they had acquired a civilization that was originally alien to them. They spoke [3] of " great and goodly cities
which they had not builded, and houses full of all good things
which they had not filled, and wells digged, which they had not
digged, vineyards and olive-trees, which they had not planted."
It was their task to accommodate themselves to this civilization,
and although we can hardly hope to succeed in tracing the
various phases of the development through which they passed
in the process of doing so, still the result was that they did acquire
it in spite of the resistance of those nomad-loving elements who
refused to surrender the ancient nomadic ideal.[4] The national
development simply passed these by.

Even in a purely religious respect the process of intermixture
could not be stayed. Owing to various kinds of personal
contact, due to alliances and mixed marriages, the life of Israel
was gradually and inevitably permeated by certain elements of
Canaanite civilization. But apart from that, it seems to be an
unchangeable law, verified in the history of all religions, that
religion somehow clings to the soil of a country.[5] Whoever
enters a new land is bound to do homage to the gods of it. Woe

---

[1] For more exact estimates, see Buhl, *Die sozialen Verhältnisse der Israeliten*
(1899), p. 51 ff.

[2] In Deut. xxxiii, 6, he is said to be " dying."

[3] Deut. vi, 10 f.          [4] See *supra*, p. 140.

[5] 2 Kings v, 17; Ezek. xx, 28.

to those who fail to do so! When after the fall of Samaria
Assyrian colonists were settled in the conquered territory they
knew not the worship of the god of the land, and omitted to pay
heed to it. Thereupon the angry Deity "sent lions amongst
them "[1]—*i.e.*, the destruction caused by the increasing numbers
of wild beasts in the land through which war had passed was
regarded by all as a punishment for the neglect of the deity of the
land. Such a view made it simply the duty of Israel, when they
invaded Palestine, to render to the gods of that country the
tribute they demanded. This peculiarity of religion finds still
truer expression in the case of actual sanctuaries and places of
worship. It has always been so. Conquerors locate their cultus
at the places which were sanctuaries of their conquered opponents.
Christianity and Islam did the same, and the consequences duly
appeared. In one way or another something of the ancient
temple peers out in the newly consecrated church, and something
of the former church can still be seen in the mosque. To every
place of worship there cleaves something of the character of the
rites that belong to it. And it is not only with the soil that
religion is thus closely interwoven ; it is also closely intertwined
with the daily life of the people and their ways. When newcomers try to adapt themselves to these they find they must also
adopt the pious customs and festive occasions that form part of
the daily life, however hard they may try to reinterpret these
to suit their own religion, or even to suppress them by force.

In all directions, therefore, Israel's encounter with Canaan
brought about a decided intermixture of civilizations. In the
following chapters we have to see the life that was thus produced.

[1] 2 Kings xvii, 25.

# BOOK II

## ISRAEL'S CIVILIZATION IN PALESTINE

### CHAPTER I

#### FAMILY AND DOMESTIC LIFE

##### 1. CLAN, FAMILY, AND MARRIAGE

IF we may reason from what usually takes place when a nomad people passes over to settled life, we should expect that in the case of the Israelites entire septs (families in the large sense, frequently comprising three or four generations) settled down together on a piece of territory and cultivated it in common.[1] This is apparently what did take place. The first person to meet Saul on his return from his search for the lost she-asses was his uncle.[2] To all appearance the uncle had his home there also, and the Deuteronomic law (about 621 B.C.) implies that adult brothers lived together.[3] Again, we read that Abraham and Lot, who up till then had lived together in one household, parted company, "for their substance was great, and the land was not able to bear them, that they might dwell together,"[4] or because, according to the older version,[5] "there was a strife between" their herdsmen. The causes that led to the breaking up of the clans into single families were, no doubt, of various kinds. Jacob's separation from Laban, to whose household Jacob's entire family had belonged,[6] was due to special causes,[7] and if life was lived in cities protected by strong walls there was, of course, less need than in the open desert for the additional protection against outsiders that came from dwelling together.

---

[1] See R. Hildebrand, *Recht und Sitte auf den verschiedenen wirthschaftlichen Kulturstufen* (1896), vol. i, p. 94, and O. Schrader, *Reallexikon der indogermanischen Altertumskunde* (1901), under "Familie," II. The names of ancestors were remembered to the fourth generation, as appears from the ancient genealogies in 1 Sam. i, 1, ix, 1. See also *supra*, p. 118, *note* 5, and S. Rauh, *Hebräisches Familienrecht in vorprophetischer Zeit* (1907).

[2] 1 Sam. x, 14.　　　　　[3] Deut. xxv, 5; also *cf.* Ps. cxxxiii, 1.
[4] Gen. xiii, 6.　　　　　[5] Gen. xiii, 7.
[6] Gen. xxxi, 43.　　　　[7] Gen. xxxi, 1 ff.

# FAMILY AND DOMESTIC LIFE

Suffice it to say that more and more the *family* came to be the social unit, although the ancient clan-relationship, strengthened by the habit of associated worship,[1] was not forgotten. As late as Elisha's time the woman of Shunem in whose house the prophet is lodging feels it to be the real guarantee of her safety that she " dwells among her own people." [2]

The Israelite family has now passed from the earlier stage of the matriarchate (although some traces of it still remain[3]) to that of the patriarchate. Just as the former was the reverse side of primitive polyandry, so the latter is the reverse side of polygamy. But we must at once take into account a consideration that limits the possible number of wives a man could have —the wife is her husband's *property*. To have many wives, therefore, means to be rich, or, more correctly, a man must be rich to be able to have many wives. Their number was determined by a man's wealth,[4] and a large harem was first and foremost a luxury which only the rich, the very rich—such as kings, or men who occupied positions analogous to that of a king—could afford. The seventy sons of Gideon, for example,[5] imply a considerable number of wives. The names are known of seven of David's wives.[6] In the Song of Songs[7] Solomon boasts of his " sixty queens, his eighty concubines, and virgins without number " ; and another source,[8] evidently exaggerating, credits him with seven hundred wives and three hundred concubines.[9] In these royal marriages political motives of

---

[1] 1 Sam. xx, 6.

[2] 2 Kings iv, 13, correcting the punctuation.

[3] See *supra*, p. 117 ff. Samson's marriages with the woman of Timnath (Judges xiv, 1 ff.) and with Delilah (Judges xvi, 4 ff.), and that of Gideon with the woman of Shechem (Judges viii, 31), are irrelevant here. These unions corresponded to the Arabian *çadîka* marriage (Wellhausen, *GGN* (1893), p. 470 f.), which was more a mere love-affair, a kind of parallel to the Roman free marriage. The man goes to the woman's home instead of bringing her to his. And, as is shown by Samson's case, the friends of the bridegroom are not chosen from his clan, but provided by the woman's relatives. Cf. *ZatW*, vol. iv (1884), p. 250.

[4] Among the Zet in Abyssinia there was a wife for every 100 cows a man had (*GGA* (1915), p. 462).

[5] Judges ix, 2.

[6] 1 Sam. xviii, 27 ; 2 Sam. iii, 2–5.

[7] Song of Songs vi, 8.

[8] 1 Kings xi, 3.

[9] Muhammed al-Tayib, a dyer in Bagdad, boasts of more than nine hundred (Hastings, *RE*, vol. viii, p. 470*b*). A king of Loango is said to have had seven thousand (Westermarck, *The History of Human Marriage*). Concerning such exaggerations, see below in Chapter III.

course played a part ; alliances by marriage with strong native clans or with foreign Courts added strength to the king's position.

We should not, therefore, make these exalted classes our starting-point when we begin to draw a picture of family life in Israel. Coming down from the royal Court to the common people, we find a man like Elkanah, Samuel's father, with two wives, Hannah and Peninnah.[1] The patriarchal narratives no doubt mirror the actual conditions. Lamech has two wives.[2] In addition to Sarah, who also gives her female slave to her husband,[3] Abraham marries Ketura.[4] As far as we know, Isaac had only one wife, Rebecca, but Jacob had two, Leah and Rachel, and has relations with their slaves Zilpah and Bilhah. His brother Esau, according to one account, had two wives ; according to another, three.[5] We know of only one wife of Joseph, Asnath, an Egyptian.[6]

It is clear that the polygamy thus practised was confined within narrow limits ; in reality it was little more than bigamy ; and, even so, in many cases it only meant that a man, in addition to his wife, might have as concubine a female slave. In the cases already mentioned the reason for the wife's giving her own slave to her husband was her own childlessness, and this brings us to the heart of the matter—in Israel the main purpose of marriage was the procreation of children.[7] The adoption of children, which might to some extent have served the purpose, is practically unknown in the Old Testament.[8] The high value attached to the possession of children, especially male children, is a universal feature of family life in Israel. Even a Psalmist says : [9]

> Like arrows in a hero's hand, so are sons of youth.
> Happy the man who has filled his quiver with them !

---

[1] I Sam. i.    [2] Gen. iv, 19.    [3] Gen. xvi, 1 ff.

[4] Gen. xxv, 1. According to our narrative as it now stands this was after Sarah's death.

[5] Gen. xxvi, 34, xxxvi, 2 f.

[6] Gen. xli, 45, 50.

[7] In Babylonian law this goes so far that when a wife has died without children her father has to return the price her husband paid for her (Hammurabi, § 163).

[8] But cf. Gen. xlviii, 5, 1, 23. Hammurabi's law (§ 185) regulates it.

[9] Ps. cxxvii, 4 ; see Prov. xvii, 6.

This high value attached to the possession of descendants, which has ultimately a religious basis, decides the estimation of marriage itself. Both are simple expressions of the fact that, whatever happens, the family must be carried on. No one could conceive the idea of founding a new family; the family already in existence had to be kept in being. This feeling is so deeply rooted in the family that the family itself jealously seeks to assure its own continuance.[1] In questions of marriage the family collectively has no rights. It is the business of the parents, especially of the father,[2] who is the embodiment of the family power and the family tradition, to secure suitable marriages for his children, especially for his sons; and the leanings or likings of the individuals concerned have little to do with the choice made.[3] Thus Abraham sends his faithful servant to select a suitable wife for his son Isaac,[4] and in his turn Isaac directs his son whom he should choose.[5] Judah secures Tamar as wife for his son Ger;[6] and so on. The father even selects a concubine for his son.[7] With all this, things did not go so far in Israel as they did in Babylon. In Babylon a marriage entered upon by a son without his father's consent was invalid;[8] but, although Esau's foreign wives were distasteful to Isaac and Rebecca,[9] just as Samson's Philistine wife was to his parents,[10] in both cases the marriages retained their validity.

In the cases just mentioned, what rendered the marriages unwelcome to the parents was that the wife belonged to another people. What Laban said to Jacob, " It is better that I give my daughter to thee than to a stranger,"[11] seems faithfully to express what was the general feeling—it was better that marriage should be within one's own tribe and clan; and marriage between cousins seems to have been as popular in Israel as it is among the Arabs. This is shown not only by the cases of

---

[1] See what was said on p. 133 about the levirate.

[2] In Gen. xxi, 21, the mother does it, in Gen. xxiv, 55, mother and brother; in Gen. xxiv, 50, the father's name, Bethuel, is added.

[3] Gen. xxiv, 58; 1 Sam. xviii, 20.

[4] Gen. xxiv.  [5] Gen. xxviii, 1 f.

[6] Gen. xxxviii, 6.  [7] Exod. xxi, 9.

[8] Cf. Landersdorfer, Die Kultur der Babylonier und Assyrier (1913), p. 119.

[9] Gen. xxvi, 35, xxvii, 46.

[10] Judges xiv, 3.  [11] Gen. xxix, 19.

Isaac [1] and Jacob,[2] but also by that of Rehoboam,[3] and, according to tradition,[4] Moses' parents were nephew and aunt. Circumstances, however, were stronger than the most pious wishes of parents, and no doubt marriages between relatives were more than balanced by the numerous cases of *connubium* with Canaanites.[5]

The head of the family is the father—it is he that performs the family sacrifice.[6] This privileged position of the father carried with it his lawful authority, especially in matters of civil law. *E.g.*, the father was entitled to award the birthright to some one other than his eldest son,[7] until the Deuteronomic law protested against it.[8] Without his father's consent a son could not undertake any service,[9] and a father could reduce his children to slavery.[10] He even had authority over the person of his daughter, and Lot was prepared without scruple to sacrifice his daughters' honour [11] when his reputation for hospitality was at stake. On the other hand, the father's authority to punish within his own family came in course of time under limitations. Possibly the Roman legal custom, that a father had power of life and death over his children,[12] also at one time existed in Israel; but Deuteronomy [13] enacts that when a father charges his son with disobedience the punishment of death can be inflicted only by a resolution of the elders of the city ; and perhaps it is another echo of an earlier paternal power of punishment when we hear of the provision that an unchaste daughter should be stoned to death " before her father's door." [14]

The wife's power rested on her position as mother. To become a mother was the dearest desire of the Israelite wife.

[1] Isaac's father, Abraham, is the brother of Nahor, grandfather of Rebecca (Gen. xxiv, 15).

[2] Jacob's mother, Rebecca, is sister of Laban (Gen. xxiv, 29), father of Leah and Rachel.

[3] His wife Maacha is daughter of Absalom, brother of his father, Solomon (1 Kings xv, 2).

[4] Exod. vi, 16, 18, 20 ; Num. xxvi, 59.

[5] See *supra*, p. 146.       [6] See below, Chapter V.

[7] Gen. xlviii, 17, xlix, 4 ; *cf.* 1 Kings i, 13.

[8] Deut. xxi, 15 ff.       [9] 1 Sam. xvi, 22.

[10] Exod. xxi, 7 ; Neh. v, 2.

[11] Gen. xix, 8 ; Judges xix, 24 ; on the other hand, see Lev. xix, 29.

[12] Gen. xlii, 37, *cf.* xxxviii, 24 ; Zech. xiii, 3. There were also once sacrifices of first-born.

[13] Deut. xxi, 18 ff.       [14] Deut. xxii, 21.

# FAMILY AND DOMESTIC LIFE

" Give me children, or I die," cries Rachel,[1] and no doubt a similar desire was laid, more quietly, if not less passionately, in ardent prayer before God by many a wife, as Hannah did in the temple of Shiloh.[2] There were also other and more sensual means used to secure the blessing of children. Probably the mandrakes mentioned once [3] were only one of several specifics of this kind.[4] That she might be " the mother of thousands of millions " [5] was the exaggerated formula of blessing given to the young wife on her marriage. The reason why a wife should desire children lies on the surface. It is significant that a second wife was called *sara*,[6] 'the female enemy'; in such a relationship enmity was a matter of course. The wife who had no children was, as it were, delivered by Nature into the hands of her more fortunate rival.[7] The wretchedness which inevitably existed under such conditions was great enough to induce later humane legislators to introduce protective measures. The flagrant injustice implied in the fact—and the well-known instance of Jacob shows that it was done—that, as in Babylon,[8] a man could marry his wife's sister while his wife was still alive was, by the new legislation, to be henceforth forbidden ; [9] natural sisterly feeling was to be spared at least this stab of pain. Legislators also enacted that if the two wives of a man both had children the husband's partiality for one of his wives should not be allowed to affect the father's relations to his children.[10] If a wife had no children she could still give her personal slave to her husband : the child of such a union was accounted hers. The most striking fact in this connexion is that it made no difference to the child's right of inheritance who his mother was, wife or female slave. Ishmael, the slave-girl's son, would have shared his father's inheritance with Isaac if Sarah had not prevented this by expelling Hagar and her infant.[11] Similarly,

[1] Gen. xxx, 1.    [2] 1 Sam. i, 10 ff.    [3] Gen. xxx, 14 ff.
[4] See my article " Zur Volkskunde der alten Juden " in *Schweizer Archiv für Volkskunde*, vol. xvii (1913), p. 4.
[5] Gen. xxiv, 60.
[6] The word is not only Hebrew, but common to all Semitic languages.
[7] Gen. xvi, 4, xxx, 15. Sarah had at least the advantage that she, as Hagar's mistress, could send her away.
[8] *Cf.* H. Winckler, *Geschichte Israels* (1895), vol. ii, p. 58.
[9] Lev. xviii, 18. The Anglican prohibition, based on this passage, against marrying a wife's sister overlooks the main point—" in her lifetime."
[10] Deut. xxi, 15–17.    [11] Gen. xxi, 10.

Jephthah was driven out by his brothers because they did not wish the son of a common harlot [1] to share their inheritance ; that is to say, had he remained he would have been entitled to his share. Thus the ancient Israelite had no conception of what we understand by legitimacy. The only thing that counted was descent from the father, and this is a complete expression of the fact that the patriarchate now prevailed.

The wife is of secondary importance. All that we hear of her makes it impossible for us to forget for an instant that her husband is her lord and master. His power over her may even extend to her freedom of decision in matters of religion. A late law,[2] casuistical in its nature, still speaks of vows taken by a wife, which her husband can either ratify or not, as he pleases. A husband retains full liberty of intercourse with women other than his wife : he does not thereby commit adultery. As Stade [3] has correctly put it, he cannot sin against his own marriage, but only against the marriage of another man, whereas the wife sins only against her own ; that is to say, we can only speak of adultery by a man in so far as, by intercourse with another man's wife, he interferes with that man's marriage. It is only with this other husband that he has to reckon, not with his own wife's family—at least, not in a legal sense. His wife has no ground of complaint against him at all so long as he does not defraud her of her necessary maintenance and marital intercourse.[4]

On the other hand, it is in the husband's power at any moment to send his wife away. To send her away is simply renouncing a portion of his property, for he does not get back the sum for which he purchased her. The " bill of divorce " is as simple as possible. It is sufficient for the husband to give his wife a " bill of divorce," [5] and this need contain nothing but the short statement, " She is not my wife : I am not her husband." [6] Divorce being thus made so easy for the husband, it is not surprising if he made abundant use of his privilege. This is probably the reason why Deuteronomic legislation found it needful to put obstacles in the way of unjustifiable divorce.

[1] Judges xi, 1.    [2] Num. xxx, 7 ff.
[3] Stade, *Geschichte des Volkes Israel* (1887), vol. i, p. 386.
[4] At least, the slave concubine is legally entitled to claim this (Exod. xxi, 10).
[5] Deut. xxiv, 1 ; Is. l, 1 ; Jer. iii, 8.    [6] Hos. ii, 2.

Not only did it suspend the right of divorce in some cases,[1] but it laid down the principle that a husband might not take back again his divorced wife after she had married another husband.[2] These were, of course, only slight checks on the husband's freedom of action, but the wife had no power whatever to get free from a marriage she had made.[3] She might receive a certain moral support from her family if it was powerful enough ; and this perhaps helps to explain why men preferred to see their daughters married to men near at hand, so that they might see how things went with them. For infidelity on the wife's part the punishment was death ;[4] she was stripped naked and stoned to death in public.[5]

From all this it is clear that, in connexion with marriage in Israel, we cannot speak of contractual marriage in the sense that the two contracting parties had equal, or anything like equal, rights. This, however, does not mean that marriage-contracts were unknown. We have no documentary proof of their existence till a much later time,[6] but marriage by contract reaches far back in Babylon, and Hammurabi enacts[7] that when a man has married a woman without such a contract the woman shall not be regarded as his wife. It is therefore perhaps permissible to assume that contractual marriage, in a form closely resembling the Babylonian, was also in use in ancient Israel. We accordingly give here two Babylonian companion documents of this kind.[8] The circumstances which they imply— viz., the marriage of a man to a wife and to her slave at the same time—are familiar from Old Testament narratives.[9]

The contract with the chief wife is as follows : " Arad-Shamash has taken in marriage and wedlock both Taram-Sagila[10] and Iltani.[11] If Taram-Sagila and Iltani say to their husband, Arad-Shamash, Thou art not our husband, they shall be thrown

---

[1] Deut. xxii, 19, 29.

[2] Deut. xxiv, 1–4. Hosea knows nothing of the prohibition referred to here if Hos. iii, 1 ff., refers to his former wife, Gomer. See also 2 Sam. iii, 14. The Koran, on the other hand, makes it a condition that she must have meantime married another man before her husband can take her back.

[3] It is otherwise in Hammurabi's law (§ 142).

[4] Deut. xxii, 22 ; Lev. xx, 10.

[5] See Ezek. xvi, 37 f. ; Hos. ii, 3, 10.     [6] Tobit vii, 14.     [7] § 128.

[8] Taken from Bruno Meissner, *Aus dem altbabylonischen Recht* (1905), p. 23.

[9] Jacob with Leah and Zilpah, and also with Rachel and Bilhah.

[10] The chief wife.     [11] The subsidiary wife.

from the tower. But if Arad-Shamash says to his wives, Taram-Sagila and Iltani, Thou art not my wife, they shall depart from his house and establishment. Iltani shall wash the feet of Taram-Sagila, carry her chair into the house of her god, shall dress her hair [?], and attend to her welfare [?]. She shall not open anything that is sealed, and every day she shall grind 10 *kas* of flour and bake them into bread for her."

The contract with the subsidiary wife is as follows : " Arad-Shamash, son of Ki-ennam, has taken in marriage Iltani, sister [1] of Taram-Sagila, from Shamashshata, her father. Her sister Iltani shall dress Taram-Sagila's hair, attend to her comfort, and carry her chair into the temple of Marduk. All children already born, and those whom Iltani will yet bear, shall be children of both. If she says to her sister Iltani, Thou art not my sister, she shall leave the house [?], and if Iltani says to Taram-Sagila, Thou art not my sister, a stigma shall be put upon her and she shall be sold for money. If Arad-Shamash says to his wives, Ye are not my wives, he shall pay one *mina* of silver. If both wives say to their husband, Thou art not my husband, they shall be strangled and thrown into the river." [2]

Whether contracts like these existed in Israel or not, the fact remains that the wife was entirely the property of her husband. This appears even in the manner in which he secured her. He bought her with the so-called *mohar*—that is, the sum which he paid for her to her father.[3] On the average it amounted to about 50 shekels of silver—say, about £6 sterling.[4] Occasionally, no doubt, there was bargaining,[5] and of course daughters of prominent men, or even princesses, were more expensive.[6] The money was paid at the betrothal. In law, therefore, it was the betrothal, not the marriage, that constituted the woman the wife of the husband. If a betrothed woman was violated she was treated by Deuteronomic law [7] as if she were already the wife of her husband ; and Lot's sons-in-law were looked

---

[1] In the Babylonian view two women become ' sisters ' by marrying the same husband.

[2] Another marriage-contract (from Nabopolassar's time) is given by Gressmann, *TBAT*, vol. i, p. 139.

[3] Luther was therefore wrong when he translated *mohar* by *Morgengabe*— *i.e.*, ' bridegroom's gift to the bride.'

[4] *Cf*. Deut. xxii, 29, with Exod. xxii, 16 f.    [5] *Cf*. Gen. xxxiv, 12.

[6] *Cf*. 1 Sam. xviii, 18, 23.    [7] Deut. xxii, 23–27.

upon as members of his family even before the marriages had taken place.[1] It is uncertain how far we can speak of a period of betrothal in ancient times, for the marriage occasionally took place immediately after the *mohar* had been paid.[2] The *mohar* might also be replaced by personal service, and this " marriage by service " [3] was perhaps commoner than " marriage by purchase." It is well known that Jacob served seven years for each of his two wives.[4] Such service might take the form of war-service—the taking of an enemy's city,[5] the killing of a dreaded foe,[6] etc. Saul was perfidious enough to demand from David as *mohar* for his daughter Michal one hundred Philistine foreskins ; [7] this was, of course, meant to cost him his life.

Seeing that a bride did not pass into her husband's possession without payment of a purchase-price, daughters represented a certain capital for their parents. To this day (when the purchase-price has risen in Palestine to fifteen times its former amount [8]) the birth of a daughter means a rise of credit even to very poor parents.[9] That is some compensation at least for the much greater importance attached to male issue.[10] The father was, of course, free to do as he pleased with the purchase-sum, but he was considered stingy and mean, especially when he was well off, if he did not give a portion of it to his daughter.[11] An actual dowry, however, was confined to the wealthy. An Egyptian princess brought to her royal spouse an entire city, Gezer.[12] A daughter of the desert brought to her sheik as dowry the right to a well.[13] The most usual dowry was a female slave

[1] Gen. xix, 12 ff.

[2] *Cf.* Gen. xxix, 21 ; contrast Deut. xx, 7, xxviii, 30, Jer. ii, 2.

[3] *Cf.* Post, *Grundriss der ethnologischen Jurisprudenz* (1894), vol. i, p. 318 ; also his *Studien zur Entwickelungsgeschichte des Familienrechts* (1889), p. 217.

[4] Gen. xxix, 20, 27.     [5] Josh. xv, 16 = Judges i, 12.

[6] 1 Sam. xvii, 25, xviii, 17.     [7] 1 Sam. xviii, 25.

[8] According to L. Bauer, *Volksleben im Lande der Bibel*, p. 87, it varies between 4000 and 10,000 piastres, according to the prestige of the family and the qualities, beauty, and age of the girl.

[9] *ZDPV*, vol. iv (1881), p. 63.     [10] See *supra*, p. 150.

[11] *Cf.* Gen. xxxi, 15. In Babylon in Hammurabi's time the purchase-price was retained and passed later to her children, but the husband might have the use of it, or of the interest of it, for his business (Jastrow, *Civilization of Babylonia and Assyria* (1915), p. 346). The Koran implies that it was the recognized custom that the wife received the *mahr* (= *mohar*).

[12] 1 Kings ix, 16.     [13] Josh. xv, 19 = Judges i, 15.

for the wife's personal service. Sarah had Hagar,[1] Rebecca had her nurse,[2] Rachel had Bilhah,[3] Leah had Zilpah ;[4] and in all cases the mistress had the free disposal of her slave in marriage.[5] The bridegroom might, of course, give presents to his bride,[6] but they had nothing to do with the purchase-money. These formed, no doubt, the beginnings of independent personal property of the wife herself.[7] If a man married a war-captive he was free from all obligations either toward her father or herself.[8] This was possibly the last remnant of the earlier marriage by capture, of which there is at least one trace in the Old Testament.[9] The only condition imposed by the Deuteronomic law[10] was that the husband of such a captive should allow her a month in his house to bewail her father and mother, to shave her head, to cut her nails, and to lay aside the dress which she wore as a captive.

By paying down the purchase-price of his bride the Hebrew husband acquired another worker ; for work—hard work and plenty of it—was the lot of the Hebrew wife. In her parents' house, from her girlhood, she had been brought up for this life ; and in view of her continuous exertions in a hot climate it need cause no surprise that the Eastern wife quickly grows old. But it would be a mistake to imagine that she was merely her husband's slave. Much depended, here as elsewhere, on the wife's personality. By clever, independent action a woman of strong character, say, like Abigail, might, without her husband's knowledge, successfully avert danger from her homestead.[11] Indeed, such capacity seems to have been not uncommon among Hebrew women,[12] capacity and energy.[13] A Deborah inspired a hero like Barak and a whole people to daring revolt.[14] A woman like Jael did not hesitate to take up a hammer and kill in her tent the enemy of her nation.[15] Ruth's

---

[1] Gen. xvi, 1.    [2] Gen. xxiv, 59.    [3] Gen. xxix, 29.
[4] Gen. xxix, 24.    [5] Gen. xvi, 2, 6, xxx, 3 f., 9.
[6] Gen. xxiv, 53, xxxiv, 12 ; cf. *Iliad*, XI, 243.
[7] Gen. xxxi, 16 ; 1 Kings xviii, 19 ; 2 Kings viii, 5. See also Rauh, *Hebräisches Familienrecht in vorprophetischer Zeit* (1907), p. 23. The law of Hammurabi also implies that married women could possess property of their own.    [8] Deut. xx, 14 ; cf. 1 Kings xx, 3.    [9] Judges xxi, 6 ff.
[10] Deut. xxi, 10 ff.    [11] 1 Sam. xxv, 18 ff.
[12] Typically clever women are mentioned, 2 Sam. xiv, 2 ff., xx, 16 ff.
[13] Gen. xvi, 5 ff., xxvii, 13 ff., 42 ff.
[14] Judges iv f.    [15] Judges iv, 18 ff., v, 24 ff.

' push ' and energy made her so indispensable to the wealthy farmer Boaz that he married her. There can be no doubt that, under such conditions, there was much genuine conjugal affection, and its praise has perhaps never been more beautifully sung than in the words of the Song of Songs : [1]

> Strong as death is love,
> Inexorable as Sheol [2] is jealousy. . . .
> Many waters cannot quench love,
> Neither can rivers drown it.

And if it be said that the Song of Songs is a late production, earlier narratives recount not only the touching love of an Elkanah for a Hannah, the childless wife, to whom he claims to be better than ten sons,[3] but also that of a husband like Hosea, through whose life there runs the golden thread of a great love, unworthy as was the wife on whom it was bestowed. For hearts capable of deep love like his, monogamy is the only natural form of marriage ; in fact, in that form it is to him a symbol of the relation between God and the nation.[4] The ancient account of the history of the Creation also shows how deeply rooted in the minds of the spiritual *élite* of Israel was the thought that Nature herself holds up monogamy as the only worthy conjugal relation ; and it could not fail greatly to raise the estimation in which woman was held. And it is no mere chance that in the later edition of the Decalogue a man's wife is specially mentioned as an independent entity, apart from all his other possessions.[5] Of course, in the hands of an ambitious woman this increased power might be abused for selfish ends. Bathsheba contrived by intrigues to wheedle David in his old age into promising the succession to her son Solomon, although his elder brother Adonijah's [6] claims were better founded ; and the moral earnestness of the prophets brings other charges against the luxurious women of their day.[7] Amos [8] protested against their wicked enticements to drinking and wantonness

---

[1] Song of Songs viii, 6 f.
[2] Hebrew name for the underworld.                    [3] 1 Sam. i, 8.
[4] The same figure reappears frequently ; *e.g.*, Jer. ii, 2, Ezek. xvi, 8, Is. l, 1.
[5] *Cf.* Deut. v, 18, with Exod. xx, 17. Other attempts of Deuteronomic legislators to raise the status of women are recorded in Deut. xxi, 10 ff., xxii, 13 ff., xxiv, 1 ff.                    [6] 1 Kings i, 11 ff.
[7] *Cf.* also the description of Jezebel, 1 Kings xxi, 7 ff.                    [8] Amos iv, 1.

in Samaria, and Isaiah [1] against their shameless behaviour in the streets of Jerusalem.

Numerous passages, both in the prophetic writings and in the legislative books, [2] show how pitiable was the fate of widows. These passages urge consideration and kindness toward them. There are also examples of widows dealing quite freely with property, [3] but as a rule they were excluded from inheritance. Later they were so excluded by express law, [4] and it is probable that in the early days they were themselves taken over by the children as part of the property of the deceased husband. [5] Childless widows returned to their father's house ; [6] in a later time they were quite at liberty to marry again. [7]

## 2. CHILDREN

An ancient source [8] tells, not without pride, how easily Hebrew women bore children. [9] To this day fellaheen women in Palestine give birth to their children in the middle of the road, and thereafter make their way to their distant village, carrying on their back not only the newly born child, but other heavy loads besides. [10] This may be a reason why Hebrew families are usually large.

The newly born child was not only washed, but rubbed with salt. [11] This rubbing with salt is practised in Palestine to this day, [12] and is intended to protect the child against evil spirits, as salt is popularly believed [13] to be a powerful means of defence. [14]

---

[1] Is. iii, 16–24.

[2] Is. i, 17, x, 2 ; Mic. ii, 9 ; Exod. xxii, 22 ; Deut. x, 18, xiv, 29, xxiv, 19, 21. A concrete case of oppression of a widow is given in 2 Kings iv, 1 ff.

[3] Ruth iv, 3. Micah's mother (Judges xvii, 2) seems to have been a widow.

[4] Num. xxvii, 8–11.          [5] 2 Sam. iii, 7, xvi, 21 ; 1 Kings ii, 21.

[6] Gen. xxxviii, 11 ; Lev. xxii, 13 ; Ruth i, 8.

[7] Ruth i, 9.                              [8] Exod. i, 19.

[9] According to Exod. i, 15, there were only two midwives for 600,000 Israelites in Egypt ! Difficult births are mentioned in Gen. xxxv, 16, and 1 Sam. iv, 19.

[10] Canaan, *Aberglaube und Volksmedizin im Lande der Bibel*, p. 2.

[11] Ezek. xvi, 4.          [12] *ZDPV*, vol. iv (1881), p. 63.

[13] The ancient superstition still finds an echo in the official prayer with which, in the ancient baptismal ceremony, the salt which was to be given to the catechumen was consecrated. "We pray Thee, O Lord our God, that this salt may become in the Name of the Trinity a saving sacrament to expel the evil foe."

[14] There seems also to have been a practice of rubbing the gums with date-juice ; the word *chanak* meant later ' to consecrate.'

A similar protective purpose is served by naming the child. To the ancient Hebrew a name was far more than a mere sound : it represented the nature of its bearer, and it was by no means a matter of indifference what kind of name a child received. The fact that a person is called by his name increased the importance of it. According to the popular belief, the name when uttered became an actual living entity, with power to work out its significance.[1]  In the presence of a person uttering a curse an Arab will throw a child flat on the ground, in order that the words may not touch it.[2]  It was therefore unlikely that a child would receive a name of ill omen.  On her death-bed Rachel could only call the son whose birth was costing her her life Benoni—i.e., " Child of my Sorrow " ; but this name was changed by the father to Benjamin, " Son of my Right Hand " [3]—meaning the side which brings good fortune.  It was also considered necessary that the names should be as euphemistic as possible.  It was a favourite practice to use names of which a divine name formed a part.  This was equivalent to a prayer to the deity on behalf of the child who bore the name, or, in some cases, to a magical incantation compelling divine aid.  In other cases a specially repellent [4] or misleading [5] name was chosen.  This was due to a desire to ward off dreaded beings who would bring harm.  There were cases also, as among other nations,[6] in which the name given was determined by the circumstances attending the child's birth.[7] At first it was the mother who gave the child its name,[8] but in course of time the father assumed this privilege and this responsibility.[9]  In all cases the name was a personal, not a clan or

---

[1] Is. lv, 11 ; Jer. xxiii, 29.

[2] Wellhausen, *Reste arabischen Heidentums* (1897), p. 139, *note* 4.

[3] Gen. xxxv, 18.                           [4] See *supra*, p. 131.

[5] Among the Jews of South Russia it is still the custom to change the name of a child who is dangerously ill.  In the Talmud the changing of the name is a means of " destroying the evil fate of the person."  *Cf.* E. Samter, *Geburt, Hochzeit, und Tod* (1911), p. 106 f.

[6] Stade (p. 387, *note* 2) gives the pleasing example of the daughter of an Abyssinian Mohammedan, who was called Khemsa Kertsch (" Fifty Crowns ") because her father, on the day she was born, had had to pay a fine of fifty crown dollars.  Benzinger also gives an example (*Archäologie*, p. 116, *note* 2).

[7] Gen. xxx ; 1 Sam. iv, 21.

[8] Gen. iv, 1, xix, 37 f., xxix, 32.  Cf. *supra*, p. 116.

[9] Exod. ii, 22 ; 2 Sam. xii, 24 ; not to speak of the prophets, who gave their children symbolic names (Is. viii, 3 ; Hos. i, 4, 6, 9).

L

family name, and the father's name was added [1] only when it was necessary to distinguish two persons of the same name. There are also some examples of double names.[2]

In New Testament times [3] the naming and the circumcision of the child were performed at the same time. We have said in a former chapter [4] that circumcision was originally a rite connected with the attainment of the age of puberty. This explains why the rites were not performed together in ancient Israel. If it is permissible to infer an ancient practice from a later law,[5] circumcision was performed on the eighth day after the child's birth, whereas the child received its name immediately after birth. Tattooing also took place very early, and was, as has already been said,[6] likewise intended to ward off demonic influences.

Although we hear again and again of foster-mothers,[7] a child was, as a rule, nursed by its own mother, and nursing was continued a long time. Three years seems to have been the usual period.[8] The playground of the child was the street.[9]

The training and education of the child were carried on in the women's apartments. Girls, indeed, remained there till they were married. Here, again, we see the strong influence of the mother.[10] Where there were more wives than one, groups were easily formed in the harem ; these groups were little other than hostile camps. Each child naturally clung to its own mother, and, as a result, children of the same mother were bound together by specially close ties.[11] By and by the growing boy came under the discipline of his father, although people in exalted positions might have special attendants.[12] Solomon, for example, was put into the care of the prophet Nathan.[13] Apparently there were no schools. The decisive element in the education of the

---

[1] Micaiah, son of Imlah (1 Kings xxii, 8).

[2] Solomon-Jedidiah (2 Sam. xii, 24 f.).

[3] Luke ii, 21.    [4] *Supra*, p. 112.

[5] Gen. xvii, 12 ; Lev. xii, 3.    [6] *Supra*, p. 139.

[7] Gen. xxiv, 59 ; 2 Kings xi, 2 ; *cf*. Exod. ii, 9.

[8] 1 Sam. i, 23 (the bullock of three years spoken of in the original text was of the same age as little Samuel) ; *cf*. 2 Macc. vii, 27, and Josephus, *Antiquities*, II, ix, 6.    [9] Jer. vi, 11 ; Zech. viii, 5.

[10] *Supra*, pp. 116 f.    [11] 2 Sam. xiii, 32.

[12] Num. xi, 12 ; Is. xlix, 23.

[13] 2 Sam. xii, 25 ; *cf*. the guardians of the royal princes, 2 Kings x, 1, 5, and 1 Chron. xxvii, 32.

young was the tradition of the home.[1] The first lesson learned there was filial piety. The Book of Proverbs [2] contains numerous admonitions on this subject, meant for the ear of young people. But we need not come down so late—the Book of Proverbs is probably post-Exilic. The Book of the Covenant,[3] the most ancient collection of Hebrew laws, appointed death as the punishment of a son who should strike or curse father or mother ; and the Decalogue [4] places the duty of honouring parents on a level with duties that are purely religious. The training of the young in ancient Israel seems to have been harsh and strict. The law of Deuteronomy [5] ordains that when the community approves, the ill-bred and intractable son, the spendthrift and the drunkard, shall be put to death. Proverb-writers recommend parents and others not to spare the rod.[6] The family guarded with special care the good name of its daughters, and neglected nothing that might help to prove their innocence in case of an accusation against their chastity.[7] But the separation of the sexes, especially in country districts, was much less strict than one might imagine from a superficial knowledge of present-day life in the East.[8]

The precedence enjoyed by sons over daughters was shown in many ways, especially in the right of inheritance. It is only a very late law [9] that allows daughters any claim at all, and even that only on certain conditions. Among the sons the first-born had special privileges. According to Deuteronomic law [10] he inherited a double share. On the father's death the sons, along with the mother, seem to have acted as trustees for the sisters,[11] but even in this respect the first-born son had precedence over his brothers.[12]

## 3. THE SLAVES

The slaves formed part of the family, and this simple fact involves a revision of our current modern ideas regarding slavery.

---

[1] Deut. iv, 9, vi, 7, 20, xi, 19 ; Exod. xii, 24, xiii, 8.
[2] Prov. xx, 20, xxx, 17.
[3] Exod. xxi, 15, 17 ; cf. Lev. xx, 9 ; Deut. xxvii, 16.
[4] Exod. xx, 12 ; Deut. v, 16.
[5] Deut. xxi, 18–21.    [6] Prov. xxiii, 13.    [7] Deut. xxii, 13 ff.
[8] See Chapter III below.    [9] Num. xxxvi.    [10] Deut. xxi, 17.
[11] Song of Songs i, 6.    [12] Gen. xxiv, 50.

Our modern notions of liberty and equality cannot simply be carried back to ancient times : they would have been utterly unintelligible. The mere question of existence pointed in another direction. We must think ourselves back into conditions of life in which there was as yet no legal protection for the individual as such. He could find protection only as member of a sept, or community connected by blood, into which he had been born. What was to become of those whom misfortune had disinherited, or who were forced by circumstances to live elsewhere than among their own people ? In some cases war handed over the vanquished into the power of the victor ;[1] in other cases the natural course of economic conditions compelled an impoverished debtor, as the sole means of salvation, to sell himself or his children to his creditors.[2] To be sure, the slave lost his liberty, and he could be sold at the will of his owner ; but there was this compensation—his existence and livelihood were secured by the new connexion he had made. The slave was not compelled to go forth to earn his living—it was provided for him ; and this security was the bright side of his lot, as contrasted with that of the poor man who did not know beyond a day where his daily bread was to come from. The dark side of his lot was that he was delivered completely into the despotic power of his master. This is equivalent to saying that everything depended on the character of the master. There were, of course, bad masters, who cruelly ill-treated their slaves. But even the cruelty of such masters was limited by their own interests ; for a man who ill-treated his slaves was injuring his own property—after all, a slave represented a certain money value.[3] And if we to-day are naturally inclined to see in the mere fact that he was the property of another the deepest indignity of the slave's position, we should not forget that in ancient Israel the idea of property also included wife and children as well as slaves. The ancient law[4] treated the seduction of a maid as a case of injury to property. In this

[1] 1 Sam. xxx, 8 ; 1 Kings xx, 39 ; Deut. xx, 14.

[2] Exod. xxii, 3 ; Lev. xxv, 39 ; 2 Kings iv, 1 ; Is. l, 1 ; Neh. v, 5. It is not always clear whether the man sold himself or whether the matter was carried through by the courts.

[3] According to Exod. xxi, 32, he was valued at 30 shekels (about £3 10s. sterling).

[4] Exod. xxii, 16 f.

essential point, therefore, the slave's position was the same as that of his master's own family. And if by good fortune he had a good master his lot was certainly far from being a pitiable one. We only need to remember the slave of Abraham, who undertakes to find a wife for Isaac.[1] The fact that his master entrusted him with such a responsible and intimate errand testifies to a familiarity of intercourse which is very different from our ordinary conception of the slave-relation. Abraham even foresaw that his slave might possibly be his heir,[2] and this shows that if a master had no children, or even if his own sons were wastrels,[3] great prospects might open up for a slave.[4] To be sure, Abraham's slave was " born in his house "—that is, he was the son of slaves who were themselves in Abraham's service, and this perhaps helps to explain his devotion to his master and to his house. But we find similar intimacy with slaves where the circumstances were different. Abigail consults her slaves, almost as if they were friends, as to how she should meet David,[5] and when looking for the asses Kish's slave accompanies his master's son like a trusted tutor, who makes up by superior experience for the inequality of social position.[6] We even read that it was he who had the money.[7] Was it his own? A later law,[8] which envisages the possibility of a slave purchasing his own freedom, seems to imply that he could possess money of his own.

The legislators were never weary of emphasizing the rights of slaves. Even the Book of the Covenant,[9] the earliest collection of laws, says, " If a man smite his slave, male or female, with a rod, and he die under his hand, he shall be surely punished. . . . If a man smite the eye of his servant, that it perish, or if he smite out his servant's tooth, he shall let him go free "—as compensation. Deuteronomy protects the slave who has run away from his master,[10] and it also supports the law of the Sabbath by the plea that the slaves require rest.[11] In fact, the protection given by law was so great that we read of cases where

---

[1] Gen. xxiv.  [2] Gen. xv, 3.  [3] Prov. xvii, 2.
[4] I Chron. ii, 34 f. A descendant of Jerahme-El, who had no son, gives his daughter to an Egyptian slave, and thus continues the family line.
[5] I Sam. xxv, 14 ff.  [6] I Sam. ix.  [7] I Sam. ix, 8.
[8] Lev. xxv, 49.  [9] Exod. xxi, 20, 26.
[10] Deut. xxiii, 15 f. This provision seems to be unknown to the writer of I Kings ii, 39.  [11] Deut. v, 14; Exod. xxiii, 12.

the slave preferred his present lot even to freedom, in which he would have to take up the struggle for existence on his own account. By law the native slave (but not the slave of foreign birth) was to be set free in the seventh year,[1] but cases are mentioned where the slave refused to take advantage of this privilege. Prominence is given to a special reason which explains the slave's desire to remain—he has a wife (who is also, of course, a slave), and she has borne him children.[2] If he leaves his master he must leave his children behind, and his wife too if he had received her from his master and was not already married when he entered his master's service.[3] If he made up his mind to stay, his connexion with his master's house was expressed by a realistic ceremony,[4] which was known also to other nations besides Israel. His master led him to the household god, to the doorpost, and bored his ear with an awl, probably the right ear,[5] thus attaching the slave to the house itself. Even when the slave wished to leave the manumission was not carried through automatically. We read that when the danger of the Chaldæan attack was at its height in Jerusalem King Zedekiah arranged that liberty should be proclaimed to all slaves, irrespective of the length of their service.[6] The proclamation was made, but scarcely had the danger passed than the liberated slaves were retaken, and forced back into their former condition.[7] When personal profit thus loaded the scale we can imagine the difficulties with which humaner legislators had to contend.[8]

The dependent position of slaves affected them even in religious matters. They had to attach themselves to the religion of the family in which they served. Abraham's slave swears by the god of Abraham, his master.[9] On the other hand, the slaves were admitted to take part in all the religious exer-

---

[1] Exod. xxi, 2. The Deuteronomic legislation places male and female slaves on the same level in this respect, and directs the master to give his dismissed slaves a liberal gift " out of thy flock and out of thy floor, and out of thy wine-press" (Deut. xv, 12 ff.).

[2] Exod. xxi, 5.

[3] In this case the wife goes free, Exod. xxi, 3.

[4] Exod. xxi, 6.     [5] Lev. viii, 23, xiv, 14, 17.

[6] Hitzig was the first to notice this.     [7] Jer. xxxiv, 8 ff.

[8] The language of the law in Deut. xv, 18, shows this.

[9] Gen. xxiv, 12.

cises of the family,[1] and as circumcision was an indispensable preliminary to such admittance that rite was also performed.[2]

A further special circumstance marked the position of female slaves. Unless they were the private property of the wife,[3] the head of the house was entitled to dispose of them as concubines, either for himself or for his sons.[4] Naturally this also was bound to contribute to an amelioration of the lot of such slaves. As a matter of fact, the Book of the Covenant [5] contains ordinances on this very subject which are marked by great humaneness. The law for the female slave as contained in the Book of the Covenant, is here on the point of becoming identical with the law for the daughter of the house.[6]

## 4. THE DWELLING

Although expressions connected with tent-life long continued to be used,[7] tent-life itself came to an end when the Hebrews settled down in civilized territory. The invaders adopted the solid style of building which they found in Palestine,[8] and continued it without any essential change. All the same, their life was still passed mainly in the open air, in the fields and in the streets, so that their requirements in the way of housing were still very modest. There were not even separate quarters for human beings and animals,[9] and the portion used by the former was merely raised a little above the other, and contained, in addition to the family, all the stores.[10] The excavations have shown how small and confined the Hebrew houses were. In Gezer and Taanach the largest dimensions were 12 feet. In many cases the entire house consisted of one apartment; in others it contained two;[11] even in the house of the wealthy there were at most three, with a courtyard adjacent or enclosed.[12] The usual building material was clay brick, and the structures must

[1] Deut. xii, 18, xvi, 11.　　　[2] Gen. xvii, 12; Exod. xii, 44.
[3] *Supra*, p. 158.　　　[4] Exod. xxi, 8 ff.
[5] *Ibid.*; see also Deut. xxi, 10 ff.
[6] " After the manner [law] of daughters," Exod. xxi, 9.
[7] See *supra*, p. 127.
[8] See *supra*, p. 23, and see Thiersch in *AA* (1909), p. 386.
[9] 2 Sam. xii, 3.
[10] *Cf.* K. Jäger, *Das Bauernhaus in Palästina* (1912). Canaan, *Aberglaube und Volksmedizin im Lande der Bibel*, p. 3.
[11] Judges xv, 1; 2 Sam. xiii, 10.　　　[12] 2 Sam. xi, 2; Neh. viii, 16.

therefore in many cases have been wretched enough.[1] True, we find Isaiah [2] at a later period reproaching the people in Jerusalem for a snobbishness that sought to replace their fallen brick houses with structures of hewn stone ; and we read that it was the same in Samaria.[3] It was the same people who boasted that they would replace the common sycamore wood with cedar.[4] As a general rule very little timber was used in ordinary house-building in Israel. The frequent mention of whitewash [5] suggests that even in ancient times the Hebrew was fond of that dazzling white colour which strikes the visitor to the East, especially in its contrast with the deep blue of the sky ; but clay plaster was also in common use.[6]

The main purpose of the Hebrew house was to protect its inhabitants from the inclemency of the weather, but the chief trouble was not so much the winter rain as the summer sun. This explains why light was restricted as far as possible, and why houses were intentionally built to face the north.[7] The doors were low. " He that exalteth his gate seeketh destruction," said a proverb.[8] Windows were few, even although they also served to let the smoke escape,[9] and they were fitted with wooden shutters.[10] The houses were built very close together, and even then people kept close to the walls or doors [11] in order to get the benefit of the shade. Deuteronomy [12] recommends that the words of the law should be written on the doorposts. This seems to be a metaphorical reference to an ancient custom of attaching amulets to these posts [13] in order to ward off demonic influences, and that old custom was, as it were, revived when in course of time the Jews began to obey literally the counsel of the Deuteronomist.[14]

As a rule, the Hebrew house was of one story. Its chief feature, from the point of view of its influence on the life of the people, was the flat roof.[15] It was covered with smoothed

[1] Ezek. xii, 7, xiii, 11.  [2] Is. ix, 9 f.
[3] Amos v, 11.  [4] Is. ix, 10.
[5] Ezek. xiii, 10, 12, 14, xxii, 28.  [6] Lev. xiv, 41 f.
[7] Sellin and Watzinger, *Jericho*, p. 63.  [8] Prov. xvii, 19.
[9] Hos. xiii, 3.  [10] Judges v, 28 ; Prov. vii, 6.
[11] Ezek. xxxiii, 30.  [12] Deut. vi, 9.
[13] Is. lvii, 8. *Cf.* the smearing of the doorposts with blood, Exod. xii, 7.
[14] This is the so-called *mesusa*.
[15] This does not mean that the inside ceiling was not in some cases vaulted.

clay,[1] and a large part of the life of the occupants was passed there. It was to the roof that people hurried when anything of importance was happening in the city,[2] because the best view was to be had from there.[3] In the same way, anything that was meant to be done in public was done on the roof of the house.[4] To announce anything on the roof, to proclaim anything "from the house-top," [5] was to make it known to every one in the city, for roof adjoined roof,[6] and one was sure of an audience. Here, also, people walked about to take the air— the king himself did so [7]—just as they might do in a garden, and flowers were set there, although their blossom was short-lived.[8] Here booths of branches were erected,[9] and at times when sidereal worship was practised altars were erected on the roofs.[10] The roof was "nearer heaven," and was therefore a favourite place for prayer.[11] Certain kinds of work were also done on the roof—e.g., flax was dried.[12] Occasionally a special apartment was constructed on the roof, the "upper room" or attic, to which one retired when one did not wish to be disturbed.[13] It was also the "best room," and was the guest-room [14] because it had the advantage of better air and greater coolness.[15] In view of all this, it is not surprising to find the law [16] recommending that a balustrade should be affixed to the roof. The Old Testament also mentions the roof gutter-pipe—at least the dripping of it.[17] The courtyard contained the well or cistern,[18] and to have a well of one's own was a thing to be proud of.[19]

Perhaps the best description we have of the furniture of the house [20] is that contained in the words used by the rich woman of Shunem when she suggested to her husband that Elisha

---

[1] The stone cylinders used for smoothing the clay were left on the roof (Thomsen, *Kompendium*, p. 31).

[2] Is. xxii, 1.    [3] Judges xvi, 27.

[4] 2 Sam. xvi, 22. For lamentations over the dead see Is. xv, 3, Jer. xlviii, 38.    [5] Matt. x, 27.

[6] Escape could therefore be made "by the roofs" (Matt. xxiv, 17, and parallel passages).    [7] 2 Sam. xi, 2; Dan. iv, 29.

[8] 2 Kings xix, 26; Is. xxxvii, 27; Ps. cxxix, 6.

[9] Neh. viii, 16.    [10] Jer. xix, 13; Zeph. i, 5.

[11] Acts x, 9.    [12] Josh. ii, 6.    [13] 2 Sam. xix, 1; Dan. vi, 11.

[14] 1 Sam. ix, 25 (corrected text); 1 Kings xvii, 19; 2 Kings iv, 10.

[15] Judges iii, 20.    [16] Deut. xxii, 8.    [17] Prov. xix, 13, xxvii, 15.

[18] 2 Sam. xi, 2, xvii, 18.    [19] Prov. v, 15.

[20] For the furniture of a modern peasant's house in Palestine see Volz, *Die biblischen Altertümer*, p. 293.

might be lodged in their house.[1] " Let us make a little chamber on the wall, and let us set for him there a bed, and a table and a stool and a candlestick, and when he cometh to us, he shall turn in thither." A nail[2] driven into the wall probably replaced in most cases a press or cupboard. Even a bed was not indispensable, and the ordinary person merely wrapped himself in his cloak[3] and lay down on a carpet or straw mat. The bed used[4] was a kind of sofa raised at one end for the head[5]—at least, the same word is used for the couch on which a person sat or, at a later time, reclined at table.[6] The luxurious habits of the gourmands of Samaria drew the satire of Amos.[7] They vied with each other in the use of soft cushions and furniture inlaid with ivory.[8] Of course, all the refinements of coloured scented coverings and carpets were used by the light woman to allure her victims.[9] In the royal Court itself were gorgeous chairs, like those ordered by Solomon.[10] These, however, belong to the chapter on trade and industry.

A catalogue of kitchen articles could almost be constructed from the occasional mention of things so used. These comprise hand-mills and baking-troughs, baskets and water-skins, jars, pots, dishes, and bowls of all sizes, three-pronged forks for taking the meat out of the soup,[11] etc. The hearth or fireplace did not occupy anything like the place it does in the life of the Indo-Germanic peoples. For example, there is no mention among Semitic peoples of the marriage-rite,[12] common among Indo-Germanic peoples, in which the bride was chased round the fire ; and even more significant is the fact that the word which originally meant the fireplace is used in the Old Testament to denote the ' muck-heap.'[13]

---

[1] 2 Kings iv, 10.   [2] Is. xxii, 23, 25 ; Ezek. xv, 3.
[3] Exod. xxii, 27 ; Deut. xxiv, 13.
[4] 1 Sam. xix, 13, 15 ; 2 Sam. iv, 7 ; 1 Kings xvii, 19, xxi, 4.
[5] Gen. xlvii, 31.   [6] 1 Sam. xxviii, 23 ; Ezek. xxiii, 41.
[7] Amos iii, 12, vi, 4. In iii, 12, d<sup>e</sup>mesek should perhaps be dabbeset, ' camel's hump,' meaning any high cushion.
[8] Ivory bedsteads are mentioned by Sennacherib among the booty he took from Jerusalem. Cf. Ezek. xxiii, 41.
[9] Prov. vii, 16.   [10] 1 Kings x, 18–20.   [11] 1 Sam. ii, 13.
[12] Cf. Customs of the World (1913), edited by Walter Hutchinson, pp. 500 and 529. Hastings, RE, vol. viii, p. 471b.
[13] ashpôt. Cf. Robertson Smith, The Religion of the Semites (1899), and Wellhausen, Israelitische und jüdische Geschichte (1907), p. 86, note 3.

# FAMILY AND DOMESTIC LIFE

For protection against the cold of winter there was a stove, or at least a brazier.[1] Some of these were beautifully finished articles. One was found at Taanach, and was for a long time thought to be an altar. It is about 3 feet high, and is remarkable on account of its ornamentation—cherub heads and, on two sides, Babylonian and Cyprian subjects in relief.[2] We hear even of special winter houses of the rich,[3] but it is impossible to tell how these differed from the summer houses.[4]

Various other traces of the increasing love of luxury are found in the Old Testament. People were no longer content with a clay floor, and used a pavement of flags or tiles like those in Solomon's Castle at Megiddo, or even planks of cypress like those in the Temple at Jerusalem.[5] In some cases the walls were inlaid with ivory,[6] or empanelled with cedar, or painted with minium (oxide of lead) ;[7] and no doubt rich people here and there introduced into their own houses gilt ornamentation like that mentioned in connexion with Solomon's buildings.[8] Such ornamentation was usually done on doors and pillars.[9] Large windows were considered an extreme of luxury ;[10] indeed, spaciousness altogether was looked upon as the acme of indulgent living, for it presented the most striking contrast to the small dimensions of the average house.

## 5. CLOTHING

The primitive loincloth had long since developed into an under garment,[11] a sort of sleeved shirt reaching to the knees[12] or even lower.[13] It was made of wool or linen,[14] and was worn next to the skin. It was fastened by means of a girdle, usually of linen,[15] and could thus be tucked up in order

[1] Jer. xxxvi, 22.
[2] Sellin, *Tell Ta'annek*, vol. i, pp. 76, 109 ; Thiersch in *AA* (1909), p. 404.
[3] Amos iii, 15 ; Jer. xxxvi, 22.      [4] Amos iii, 15.
[5] 1 Kings vi, 15.      [6] 1 Kings xxii, 39 ; Amos iii, 15.
[7] Jer. xxii, 14.      [8] 1 Kings vi, 21.      [9] 2 Kings xviii, 16.
[10] Jer. xxii, 14.      [11] *Supra*, p. 127.
[12] Hence the possibility suggested in Gen. ix, 21, Exod. xx, 26, xxviii, 42, 2 Sam. vi, 20.
[13] On the reliefs from Sennacherib's palace at Kouyunjik [ancient Nineveh—TRANSLATOR] it reaches sometimes to the knees, sometimes to the ankles.
[14] The law in Deut. xxii, 11, and Lev. xix, 19, forbids clothes of the two materials woven together.
[15] Lev. xvi, 4 ; 1 Sam. xviii, 4 ; Jer. xiii, 1.

to secure greater freedom of movement.[1]  This was probably
the only garment worn by a person at work—at any rate, in
the fields ; [2] people worked, as we still do, " in their shirt-
sleeves." But—perhaps it was mere prudery—a person who
was dressed only in this garment was said to be " naked." [3]
When fully dressed one wore an upper garment.  If we may
judge from the dress of the modern fellaheen, this was a long
rectangular piece of woollen material, sewn up in primitive
fashion, leaving openings for the arms, and thrown round the
body after the manner of the Greek's *himation* or of the Roman's
toga.  All kinds of things could be carried in its folds and
corners,[4] so that people could speak of " recompensing it into
his bosom." [5]  This upper garment was more than a mere article
of clothing.  It could be used as a carpet,[6] and at night it could
serve as a blanket ; hence the provision in the law : [7] " If thou
take thy neighbour's raiment to pledge, thou shalt deliver it
unto him by that the sun goeth down ; for that is his only
covering : wherein else shall he sleep ? "

In essentials male and female clothing were the same, but
the prohibition against one sex wearing the clothes of the other
proves that they were not in all respects identical.[8]  Probably
the difference was that women wore clothing of richer or more
delicate material, and this supposition seems to be confirmed by
David's lamentation over the deaths of Saul and Jonathan :[9]

> Ye daughters of Israel, weep over Saul,
> Who clothed you in purple and other delights,
> And put ornaments of gold upon your apparel.

And it is possible that female love of fine dress and ornament is
also reflected in the words which the Song of Deborah [10] puts into
the mouth of Sisera's wives in explanation of his delayed return :

> Surely they found booty to be divided,
> Booty of coloured garments for Sisera,

---

[1] This is the meaning of "having the loins girded" in Exod. xii, 11,
and 2 Kings iv, 29, ix, 1.
[2] Matt. xxiv, 18. [3] Job xxii, 6, is specially clear.
[4] Exod. iv, 6, xii, 34 ; 2 Kings iv, 39 ; Hag. ii, 12.
[5] Is. lxv, 6 ; Ps. lxxix, 12.
[6] Judges viii, 25 ; 2 Kings ix, 13.
[7] Exod. xxii, 26 f. ; Deut. xxiv, 13.
[8] Deut. xxii, 5. [9] 2 Sam. i, 24. [10] Judges v, 30.

# FAMILY AND DOMESTIC LIFE

Booty of coloured embroidered garments,
Two embroidered coloured kerchiefs for the queen's neck.[1]

But these same words serve to show that men were as fond of finery as women, and there are other passages that point to the same conclusion. Love of luxury and finery in dress affected both sexes. It was a valuable cloak from Shinear [2] that tempted Achan to steal ; [3] and among the things that aroused the admiration of the Queen of Sheba were the clothes of Solomon's slaves ; [4] and even at a later period Zephaniah is found inveighing against the love of foreign fashions that prevailed in Court circles.[5]

Those who could afford it wore clothing of bright or light colours,[6] purple[7] or scarlet ;[8] they liked to have their upper garment embroidered with bright colours[9] or with gold.[10] They had, moreover, " changes of raiment," [11] " as numerous as layers of clay." [12] Clothes were therefore valuable presents.[13] In the case of the king and his nobles the upper garment developed into a splendid cloak,[14] although, probably in imitation of Babylonian and Assyrian models,[15] there were also cloaks which were worn above the upper garment.[16] Love of luxury extended even to the under garment. Jacob gave his favourite son an under garment with long sleeves,[17] similar, as it would appear, to what was worn by princesses.[18] And, moreover, especially among women, the under garment became so long that it trailed on the ground.[19] The trains of queens were borne by female slaves.[20] Luxurious women wore underneath the usual under garment a kind of chemise, for which only the finest

---

[1] Conjecturally restored ; perhaps the text was here also "for his [Sisera's] neck " ; cf. LXX in loc.  [2] See Ezek. xxvii, 24.
[3] Josh. vii, 21.  [4] 1 Kings x, 5.  [5] Zeph. i, 8.
[6] Eccles. ix, 8.  [7] Judges viii, 26 ; Prov. xxxi, 22.
[8] Jer. iv, 30 ; Lam. iv, 5.
[9] Ezek. xvi, 10, xxvi, 16 ; Ps. xlv, 13.  [10] Ps. xlv, 14.
[11] 2 Sam. xii, 20 ; Is. iii, 22 ; see 2 Kings x, 22, for the royal wardrobes, from which clothes were taken as required.  [12] Job xxvii, 16.
[13] Gen. xlv, 22 ; Judges xiv, 12 ; 2 Kings v, 5.
[14] 1 Sam. xviii, 4, xxiv, 5, 12 ; Ezek. xxvi, 16 ; Job i, 20, ii, 12. The cloak (m$^e$il) was also worn by prophets (1 Sam. xv, 27, xxviii, 14) and priests (Exod. xxxix, 22 ; 1 Sam. ii, 19).  [15] Josh. vii, 21 ; Jonah iii, 6.
[16] Mic. ii, 8.  [17] Gen. xxxvii, 3.  [18] 2 Sam. xiii, 18.
[19] Jer. xiii, 22, 26 ; Is. xlvii, 2 ; Nahum iii, 5 ; cf. Is. vi, 1.
[20] Esther iv, 4 ff. (apocryphal passage).

of linen or cotton material was fine enough.[1]  Much care was also expended on the girdle.[2]  It was frequently adorned with gold work,[3] and high officials, and even priests, were recognizable by the valuable girdles which they wore.[4]  Into this girdle the warrior put his sword,[5] and the scribe his writing materials.[6] Women attached to it a pocket or bag.[7]  In Israel, as elsewhere,[8] the girdle of the bride [9] had a special significance.

Amulets were worn attached to the four edges of the upper garment.  These were blue in colour, because blue was believed to have special efficacy against the evil eye.[10]  This may be inferred from the Jahvistic reinterpretation given to them by the law [11] when it enjoins the wearing of tassels with a cord of blue as tokens of remembrance of the Commandments.  That is the origin of the tassels that are still worn on the Jewish *tallith*, or prayer-cloth.

Hebrew women, at least in the earlier period,[12] do not seem to have worn veils.[13]  Veils were, however, worn by brides,[14] and also by loose women.[15]  A favourite article of women's apparel was a kind of shawl [16] or wrap,[17] which, judging from a later time, was frequently as " delicate as a spider's web." [18]

Great attention was given to the hair and to the dressing of

---

[1] It is impossible to say more exactly what the Hebrew *bad, bûz, shesh,* and *chûr* really were.  We do not know whether the *pᵉtigîl* in Is. iii, 24, was an upper or an under garment (as in LXX).  Shirts of the kind mentioned in the text were called *sᵉdinim*.  They were such as Samson gave to his guests (Judges xiv, 12) or such as the virtuous housewife sells (Prov. xxxi, 24 ; Is. iii, 23).  The name *satinnu* occurs in the Amarna letters.  The fellaheen to-day wear shirts (see Volz, *op. cit.*).

[2] Prov. xxxi, 24.

[3] Dan. x, 5.

[4] Is. xxii, 21 ; Exod. xxviii, 4.     [5] 2 Sam. xx, 8.

[6] Ezek. ix, 2.     [7] Is. iii, 22.

[8] See article " Girdle " in Hastings, *RE*, vol. vi, p. 229.

[9] Jer. ii, 32.     [10] *Supra*, p. 62.

[11] Num. xv, 38 ; Deut. xxii, 12.

[12] On the other hand, see Is. xlvii, 2, but perhaps this passage refers only to Babylonia.  All the same, the veil was included in the toilette of the Jerusalem women (Is. iii, 19, *rᵉalah*).

[13] Gen. xii, 12, xxvi, 7, xxix, 10.

[14] Gen. xxiv, 65 ; Song of Songs iv, 1, vi, 7.

[15] Gen. xxxviii, 14, 19.

[16] Ruth iii, 15 ; Is. iii, 22 (*mithpahat*) ; the *ma'ᵃtaphoth* here mentioned were also a sort of upper dress.

[17] Is. iii, 23 ; Song of Songs v, 7 (*rᵉdidim*).

[18] *Cf.* Philo, *De Somniis*, II, § 7.

it. A bald head called forth the mockery of young people,[1] and to be threatened with the loss of one's hair was a serious matter, especially for women.[2] Luxuriant hair was greatly admired, either in a young girl, whose hair was "like a flock of goats from Gilead,"[3] or in a young man like Absalom, whose hair grew so abundantly that he had to have it shorn once a year, the hair thus cut off weighing about 200 shekels, royal weight (about 6 lb.!).[4] This seems to imply that it was usual to let the hair grow to some length.[5] Paul's opinion that long hair is disgraceful in a man [6] seems not to have been shared by the ancient Hebrew. A man's hair must not be cut if he had taken upon him any kind of vow,[7] and this included the warrior.[8] On the other hand, a certain style of trimming the hair and beard was demanded by some non-Israelite forms of worship, especially in the worship of the dead,[9] and for this reason it was forbidden by later law.[10]

The care of the hair, in both sexes, consisted mainly in anointing it with oil. Even the Psalmist [11] knows no finer praise for brotherly love than to compare it to spiced ointment [12] on the head, flowing down the beard. Hence also the Preacher's wish that his head might never lack ointment.[13] To omit this anointing was the sign of deepest dejection and mourning,[14] and the usual failing was in the opposite direction—excessive use of it. Amos [15] upbraids the dissolute men of Samaria for using immense quantities of the best oil. The cost of this may be inferred from the proverb [16] "He that loveth oil shall not be rich."

The women were expert in all styles of dressing the hair,[17]

---

[1] 2 Kings ii, 23.   [2] Is. iii, 17, 24.

[3] Song of Songs iv, 1 ; see vii, 5—the words "a king is imprisoned in hair" are doubtful ; cf. Max Dauthendey, "Thy hair keeps me more securely than chains." [Moffatt renders, "Your hair is glossy as purple—its tresses hold captive your lord."—TRANSLATOR.]

[4] 2 Sam. xiv, 26. [The weight here given, "200 shekels after the king's weight," has been estimated by A. R. S. Kennedy, in Hastings' *Dictionary of the Bible* (vol. iv, p. 904), at 3⅝ lb. avoirdupois.—TRANSLATOR.]

[5] Ezek. xliv, 20.   [6] 1 Cor. xi, 14.

[7] Judges xiii, 5 ; 1 Sam. i, 11 ; Num. vi, 5.   [8] Judges v, 2.

[9] Is. xv, 2 ; Jer. vii, 29, xvi, 6, 7, xli, 5, xlviii, 37.

[10] Lev. xix, 27, xxi, 5.   [11] Ps. cxxxiii, 2.

[12] *tob* in this sense according to D. H. Müller.

[13] Eccles. ix, 8 ; Ps. xxiii, 5.   [14] 2 Sam. xiv, 2 ; Matt. vi, 17.

[15] Amos vi, 6.   [16] Prov. xxi, 17.   [17] 2 Kings ix, 30.

plaiting it and curling it.[1] But the men did not lag behind them in this respect either. They paid great attention to their beards,[2] and mention is made of Samson's " seven locks." [3] Josephus [4] declares that Solomon's postilions rubbed their hair daily with gold dust, so that their whole head gleamed like gold in the sunshine. In this he is probably transferring to olden times what was a late custom. The care and pains thus expended on the hair did not prevent other troubles connected with it. Even Samson [5] lays his head in Delilah's lap and she attends to it. Wellhausen [6] mentions that in ancient Arabia it was a common attention on the part of a female lover to comb her lover's hair in her lap and clear it of vermin.[7]

Under the burning rays of the Eastern sun [8] the head required a special covering in addition to the hair.[9] Judging from the practice of the present day, the head and hair were covered with a cloth, or at least a thick cord was wound round and round the head, and better-class people in cities, both men and women, never went out without the more or less elegant turban.[10]

Footwear seems to have been much more primitive, but, as time went on, to go barefoot came to be a sign of the utmost poverty.[11] It was also the mark of captives [12] or mourners.[13] The leather or wooden sandals which were used by almost everybody,[14] especially out of doors,[15] and the perishable [16] shoe latchets with which the sandals were fastened to the feet were

---

[1] Is. iii, 24 ; Song of Songs vii, 5. The original text of this verse was perhaps this : " The curls [in the Hebrew text *mikseh* must have fallen out after the similar word *dammasek*] of thy head are like crimson [read *kakkarmil* instead of *kakkarmel*], the plaits of thy hair like purple." [*Cf.* p. 175, *note* 3.—TRANSLATOR.]

[2] 2 Sam. x, 4, xx, 9 ; Is. vii, 20.       [3] Judges xvi, 13, 19.

[4] *Antiquities*, VIII, vii, 3.       [5] Judges xvi, 19.

[6] *GGN* (1893), p. 471, *note* 3.

[7] *Cf.* also Jer. xliii, 12, and von Gall in *ZatW*, vol. xxiv (1904), p. 105 ff.

[8] There are examples of sunstroke in 2 Kings iv, 19, and Ps. cxxi, 6. The latter also hints at a corresponding effect of the moon.

[9] Captive Jews are shown bareheaded on a picture from Kouyunjik.

[10] Is. iii, 20, 23, lxii, 3 ; Ezek. xliv, 18.

[11] *Cf.* Amos ii, 6, viii, 6.       [12] Is. xx, 2 ; Job xii, 17, 19.

[13] 2 Sam. xv, 30 ; Ezek. xxiv, 17, 23 ; Mic. i, 8.

[14] At the present day, while women almost always go barefoot, the peasant considers it a disgrace to be seen out of doors unshod. He at least carries his shoes in his hand. (Hans Schmidt, *Die grossen Propheten*, p. 88.)

[15] Song of Songs v, 3.       [16] Is. v, 27.

synonyms for anything of trifling value.[1]  But valuable specimens, such as sandals of badgers' skin,[2] were also included in
the wardrobe of the elegant ladies of Jerusalem.

One of the most essential items in the toilette of the Hebrew
woman was jewellery.  Armlets,[3] neck-chain,[4] nose-ring,[5] earrings,[6] and a beautiful crown on the head [7]—such is Ezekiel's
description [8] of the ornaments of the lady in whom he sees
Jerusalem herself.  The excess to which the love of such finery
was carried is shown by Isaiah's polemic [9] against the coquettish
women of Jerusalem, who sought to attract attention in the
street by the tinkling of their anklets.[10]  The subject was
attractive enough to tempt a later writer [11] to pour out with
evident delight all his knowledge of female dress and jewellery
in a catalogue which is still useful to the historian of civilization.
*Inter alia* he mentions their frontlets,[12] apparently of gold or
silver wire, their moons,[13] and finger rings,[14] and scent vials.[15]
Beads and corals seem to have been favourite ornaments.[16]
Mention is also made of a large number of precious and half-
precious stones, some of which are difficult to identify.[17]  A
dozen of them are named together in a later description of the
high priest's breastplate : [18] carnelian, topaz, emerald, ruby (?),
sapphire, jasper, hyacinth (?), agate, amethyst, chrysolite,
beryl (?), onyx (?).  Others are mentioned elsewhere,[19] including
the diamond, although this is mentioned not as a jewel, but as

---

[1] Amos ii, 6, viii, 6 ; Gen. xiv, 23.

[2] Ezek. xvi, 10 ; Song of Songs vii, 1.

[3] Gen. xxiv, 22 ; Is. iii, 19 ; Ezek. xxiii, 42.

[4] Prov. iii, 3, 22.                                   [5] Gen. xxiv, 22 ; Is. iii, 21.

[6] Gen. xxxv, 4 ; Exod. xxxii, 2 ; Is. iii, 19 ; ' earrings ' is literally ' small
drops '—*i.e.*, beads.  (See also Judges viii, 26.)

[7] Ezek. xxiii, 42.                            [8] Ezek. xvi, 12.

[9] Is. iii, 16 ; *cf.* also the Koran, Sure xxiv, 32.

[10] These were sometimes joined by ' hobble-chains '—*cf.* Is. iii, 20.

[11] Is. iii, 18–23.

[12] Verse 18, unless the word in question (*s͏ebîsîm*) means ' small suns.'

[13] Verse 18.  See *supra*, p. 61.

[14] Verse 21 ; see Exod. xxxv, 22, and Num. xxxi, 50.      [15] Is. iii, 20.

[16] It is uncertain whether the words *ra'môth* and *p͏eninim* mean either of
these.  Lam. iv, 7, suggests a red colour.  Peninna occurs as a female name
(1 Sam. i, 2, 4), and would correspond to Margaret.  Song of Songs i, 10, also
suggests strings of beads or corals.

[17] Nowack, *Hebräische Archäologie*, vol. i, p. 130.

[18] Exod. xxviii, 17–20, xxxix, 10–13 ; nine of them occur in Ezek. xxviii, 13.

[19] Is. liv, 12.

M

a generic name for a hard stone; it is therefore used as a symbol of the obstinacy of the nation,[1] the point being used as a stylus, like a " pen of iron." [2] Evidently a large number of precious stones were in use, and the fact that these came, or were supposed to come, from distant lands, from the wonderland of Ophir,[3] or even from the land of Havilah, compassed by one of the rivers of Paradise,[4] made them only more desirable. Of course they were included among the Queen of Sheba's gifts.[5] Ornament had not yet quite lost its original amuletic character,[6] and therefore even men continued to make lavish use of it,[7] not to speak of children.[8] For a man the seal ring was of special importance. He wore it on a string round his neck,[9] or, after the Egyptian manner,[10] on his finger.[11] In any case, he always had it on his person.[12] Further, he was never without his staff,[13] which could also be used as a weapon. Great stress was laid on ablutions, especially on the washing of the hands [14] and feet.[15] Even if it were not known from extra-Biblical sources, this would explain the great significance which these washings came to have in ceremonial worship.[16] In addition to washing, there was anointing, which included the whole body.[17] By and by common oil was not good enough for pampered tastes, and there arose a demand for foreign mixtures,[18] whose preparation grew to be a recognized art.[19] Women in particular showed special ingenuity in inventing materials for scenting the person ; and the city woman with her smelling-bottle [20] found a rival in the rustic beauty with her bundle of myrrh in her

---

[1] Ezek. iii, 9 ; Zech. vii, 12.       [2] Jer. xvii, 1.

[3] 1 Kings x, 1.  As to the situation of Ophir, see *infra*, Chapter II.

[4] Gen. ii, 12.

[5] 1 Kings x, 2.  In Ezek. xxvii, 22, Sheba appears as the land whence come diamonds to the market of Tyre.

[6] Cf. *supra*, p. 138, and note in Is. iii, 20, the name *lᵉchasim*, 'amulet,' as an article of female finery.  In Lam. iv, 1, the " holy stones " are probably precious stones.       [7] 2 Sam. i, 10 ; Job xlii, 11 ; Ezek. xxviii, 13.

[8] Exod. xxxii, 2.       [9] Gen. xxxviii, 18 ; Song of Songs viii, 6.

[10] Gen. xli, 42.  This practice goes back only to the new kingdom.

[11] Jer. xxii, 24 ; Song of Songs viii, 6.       [12] Hag. ii, 23.

[13] Gen. xxxviii, 18 ; Exod. xii, 11 ; 2 Kings iv, 29.

[14] Ps. xxvi, 6, lxxiii, 13 ; Job ix, 30.

[15] 1 Sam. xxv, 41 ; Song of Songs v, 3 ; Gen. xviii, 4, xix, 2.

[16] Exod. xxx, 19.       [17] 2 Sam. xii, 20 ; Ezek. xvi, 9.

[18] Prov. xxvii, 9 ; Song of Songs i, 12, iv, 13 f.

[19] See below, Chapter II.       [20] Is. iii, 20.

bosom.[1] Washing and anointing are mentioned together in the books of Ruth and Judith;[2] washing and cosmetics are similarly conjoined by Ezekiel.[3] One of Job's daughters was called Cassia, after a perfume,[4] and a sister bore the name of " Powder-box."[5] Galena[6] was used for a cosmetic, and was applied either in powder form or as ointment to eyebrows and eyelashes.[7]

All this beauty was, of course, not content to be seen of others : it also required to see itself. The mirrors[8] which served this purpose were made of polished bronze ; and it came to be the fashion with elegant ladies to carry a mirror about on the person.[9]

## 6. FOOD

In our first chapter we have already touched upon the question of the food of Israel in Palestine, and what was said about the nomad period is also applicable to a large extent to the period subsequent to the settlement. In the desert the chief food of the people had been milk ; and there could be no lack of milk, and of food prepared from it—including cheese[10]—in a country " flowing with milk."[11] As had always been the case, meat was eaten only on special occasions. Veal and beef were preferred to goat-flesh[12] or mutton,[13] and a " stalled ox " was a synonym for a sumptuous repast.[14] But the sheep provided other dainties that were highly valued—the fatty tail of the fatty-tailed sheep, which was offered to an honoured guest.[15] Roast meat was still preferred to boiled meat[16]—in fact, the latter method of cooking it was learned only after the

---

[1] Song of Songs i, 13.     [2] Ruth iii, 3 ; Judith x, 3.
[3] Ezek. xxiii, 40.     [4] Job xlii, 14.
[5] *Ibid.*
[6] [Sulphide of lead (PbS).—TRANSLATOR.]   Called *kohl* by the Arabs.
[7] 2 Kings ix, 30 ; Jer. iv, 30.
[8] Exod. xxxviii, 8 ; Job xxxvii, 18.
[9] Is. iii, 23, " the glasses," but the meaning is not quite certain.
[10] *Cf.* 1 Sam. xvii, 18 ; 2 Sam. xvii, 29 ; Job x, 10. Josephus (*Wars of the Jews*, V, iv, 1) speaks of the " Cheese-maker's Valley " at Jerusalem.
[11] See *supra*, p. 15, and *cf.* Deut. xxxii, 14, Is. vii, 22, Prov. xxvii, 27.
[12] Judges vi, 19 ; 1 Sam. xvi, 20.
[13] 1 Sam. xxv, 18.     [14] Prov. xv, 17.
[15] [*Ovis aries steatopyga.*—TRANSLATOR.]   1 Sam. ix, 24, according to corrected text.     [16] 1 Sam. ii, 15.

settlement in Palestine.[1]  Isaac's favourite dish was venison.[2]
The Deuteronomic law[3] permitted the eating of deer, doe,
ibex, gazelle, and antelope.  A historian of the Exodus[4] tells
that the Israelites recalled with longing the fish that they had
eaten in Egypt, so it is not surprising that in due time Jerusalem
had a fish-market of its own.[5]  The merchants from Tyre who
supplied that market[6] found ready customers, and, significantly
enough, a feature in Ezekiel's[7] ideal picture of the future of
the country was that the Dead Sea should once more contain
fish.  On the other hand, in a passage which reveals the daily
menu of the elegant Israelite lady the same prophet does not
mention fish at all.  He mentions fine flour, honey, and oil ; [8]
and another prophet names together wheat, barley, oil, and
honey as the precious food which is carefully concealed from the
enemy in critical days.[9]  The mention of honey raises once more
the question[10] whether this was bee-honey[11] or fruit-honey.[12]
It was possibly both, for both were highly valued.  The proverb
said, "My son, eat thou honey, because it is good ; and the
honeycomb, sweet to thy taste." [13]  The importance of oil was
shown by the amount of it supplied annually by Solomon to the
King of Tyre—20,000 *bath* (160,000 gallons) of best quality.[14]
Even the poorest widow had her cruse of oil.[15]  It supplied the
place of butter and of animal fat generally.  It was used to
make bannocks and cakes, the flour being mixed with oil ; or
the dough was smeared with oil, or cooked in oil.[16]  There were
numerous kinds and grades of flour, from the coarsest grain[17]
to the "finest of the wheat." [18]  Bread made from it is perhaps
the most distinctive food of people who have passed from
nomadic life to settled conditions.[19]  "To eat bread" was
practically synonymous with "taking food," [20] and one of

[1] Judges vi, 19 ; Exod. xxiii, 19 ; Ezek. xxiv, 3 ; Lev. vi, 21.
[2] Gen. xxvii, 3.          [3] Deut. xiv, 5.          [4] Num. xi, 5.
[5] The "fish gate," Zeph. i, 10, etc., seems to imply this.
[6] Neh. xiii, 16.          [7] Ezek. xlvii, 9.          [8] Ezek. xvi, 13.
[9] Jer. xli, 8.          [10] See *supra*, p. 15.
[11] Judges xiv, 8 ; 1 Sam. xiv, 27 ; 2 Sam. xvii, 29.
[12] Josephus, *Wars of the Jews*, IV, viii, 3.          [13] Prov. xxiv, 13.
[14] 1 Kings v, 25 (LXX, 3 Kings v, 11).          [15] 1 Kings xvii, 12.
[16] Exod. xxix, 2.          [17] Hebrew *'arîsā*.
[18] Hebrew *sôlet* ; common flour was called *kemach*.
[19] ZDPV, vol. xviii (1895), p. 93.
[20] Gen. xxxvii, 25 ; 1 Sam. xx, 24.

Gideon's men saw in a dream, as an image of the victory of the farmer over the nomad, a loaf of barley come rolling into the camp of the Midianites (typical nomads) and throw down the chief's tent.[1] The various names used show that the loaves were either of bannock or cake shape. As a rule they were leavened, but when the baking had to be done hastily—say, on the unexpected arrival of a guest,[2] or when, as at the feast of the beginning of harvest, cakes baked with the first of the new crop had to be offered as quickly as possible to the Deity [3]— the leavening was omitted. But at other times the dough was not only leavened; it was sweetened with honey.[4] On one occasion Ezekiel heard a command to mix wheat, barley, beans, lentils, millet, and fitches in a vessel and to bake them into bread;[5] he felt that this mixture would be nauseous, but the passage serves to show the materials the Hebrews had at their disposal. The simplest method of making the grain fit to eat was toasting it. Grain thus toasted was called *kâlî*, and formed the food of harvesters.[6] It was also a very convenient form of food to take with one on a journey or to war.[7]

With regard to vegetables, Esau's love of lentil pottage has become proverbial.[8] Beans,[9] gherkins, melons, onions, leeks, and garlic were so common that pity was felt for the desert wayfarer who could not procure them.[10] The small onions familiar to us under the name of shallots betray their origin by that name; they are the onions of Ascalon. The story [11] told of a prophet gives a picture of a memorable scene at a meal of cucumbers (gherkins). One of Elisha's young men had brought in from the field a large quantity of unfamiliar wild cucumbers, and had thrown them " into the pot." The food was served out to the company;[12] but no sooner had they tasted it than they cried out in terror: " Man of God, there is death

---

[1] Judges vii, 13.

[2] Gen. xix, 3; Judges vi, 19; 1 Sam. xxviii, 24.

[3] Hence the name Feast of Unleavened Bread or *Massôth*, Deut. xvi, 3.

[4] Exod. xvi, 31.

[5] Ezek. iv, 9.

[6] Ruth ii, 14. [A.V. " parched corn."—TRANSLATOR.]

[7] 1 Sam. xvii, 17, xxv, 18; 2 Sam. xvii, 28.

[8] Gen. xxv, 34.     [9] 2 Sam. xvii, 28.

[10] Num. xi, 5.     [11] 2 Kings iv, 39 ff.

[12] See, for serving out at table, Gen. xliii, 34, 1 Sam. i, 4, ix, 24. Usually the individual eats from the common dish (Prov. xix, 24, xxvi, 15).

in the pot." The prophet miraculously came to their rescue by adding flour to the food. Probably the young man had gathered the so-called colocynth, or coloquint [1] (squirting cucumber), which has a powerful emetic and purgative effect. Food was spiced by the addition of cummin,[2] dill,[3] coriander,[4] and also, although they are not actually mentioned till New Testament times, by mint [5] and mustard.[6] Salt was so important, and so much a matter of course,[7] that to eat anyone's salt [8] was a synonym for being maintained by him ; and people " between whom salt was " [9] were those who had entered into an indissoluble alliance.[10]

The fruits of the country were of great value. The pleasure provided by the early fig is reflected in the saying of Isaiah,[11] " which when he that looketh upon it seeth, while it is yet in his hand, he eateth it up." But figs were also preserved. They were dried and pressed into cakes,[12] just as was done with grapes.[13] There were also pomegranates,[14] mulberry-figs,[15] pistachio nuts,[16] almonds,[17] and nuts.[18] It is not certain whether the Hebrews were acquainted with the apple.[19] It is a late Latin tradition that the tree in Paradise whose fruit was forbidden was an apple-tree ; Greek tradition says it was a fig-tree, and that its leaves enabled Adam and Eve to cover their nakedness ; Jewish Rabbinical tradition speaks of it as a vine.[20]

The legend that tells how the ravens brought food to Elijah

---

[1] As ornament on building, 1 Kings vi, 18, vii, 24. [Squirting cucumber is *Ecballium officinale*.—TRANSLATOR.]

[2] Is. xxviii, 25, 27.  [3] *Ibid.*

[4] Exod. xvi, 31 ; Num. xi, 7.  [5] Matt. xxiii, 23 ; Luke xi, 42.

[6] Matt. xiii, 31, xvii, 20.  [7] Job vi, 6.

[8] Ezra iv, 14. [R.V.—TRANSLATOR.]

[9] So runs the Arabian expression.

[10] For a " covenant of salt " see Num. xviii, 19 ; 2 Chron. xiii, 5.

[11] Is. xxviii, 4.

[12] 1 Sam. xxx, 12 ; 2 Kings xx, 7. The Greeks learned this from the Semites. The name *palathe* is derived from the Hebrew *debelet*. Stade, *Geschichte des Volkes Israel*, vol. i, p. 371, *note* 1.

[13] 1 Sam. xxv, 18, xxx, 12.  [14] Deut. viii, 8 ; Song of Songs iv, 13.

[15] 1 Kings x, 27 ; Amos vii, 14.  [16] Gen. xliii, 11.

[17] *Loc. cit.* ; Jer. i, 11.  [18] Song of Songs vi, 11.

[19] The translation of *tappuach* by apple (tree) is uncertain ; it may mean apricot or orange (tree) (see Prov. xxv, 11).

[20] Enoch xxxii ; Greek Apocalypse of Baruch, iv ; Apocalypse of Abraham, xxiii. *Cf.* the commentaries of Tuch and Dillmann on Gen. iii, 6, and see Volz, *Jüdische Eschatologie von Daniel bis Akiba* (1903), p. 376.

morning and evening[1] probably reflects the ordinary custom of having two meals a day. The principal meal was that taken in the evening,[2] but no doubt it was the case even in ancient times, as can be seen to-day in any village or town, that the times at which meals were taken and the amount of food eaten were very irregular, and that then as now children ate the whole day long.[3]

Although the food of the ancient Hebrew was in the main of a simple kind, life at the royal Court, under a splendour-loving prince like Solomon, displayed a considerable degree of luxury. We are fortunate in possessing an account of the daily requirements of the Court at that time.[4] It amounted to 30,000 *kor* [5] of fine flour, 60,000 *kor* of ordinary flour, 10 stalled oxen, 20 oxen out of the pastures, and 100 sheep—besides game and fowl. The increase of national prosperity brought with it in certain circles, both in Samaria and in Jerusalem, a degree of luxury and fine living that aroused the wrath of the prophets. At a time when Isaiah was already seeing the approach of national destruction these revellers were spending their time amid " joy and gladness, slaying oxen and killing sheep, eating flesh and drinking wine," living out their motto, " Let us eat and drink, for to-morrow we shall die." [6] And Amos [7] hurls his invective against those who " lie upon beds of ivory "— in earlier, simpler days people had *sat* at meat [8]—and amid noisy music[9] " eat the lambs out of the flock and calves out of the stall." The wine flowed in bowls. In another passage Isaiah describes them as drinking from early morning till late at night.[10]

The drinking of wine as a beverage was universal, and not

---

[1] I Kings xvii, 6.

[2] Exod. xvi, 12 ; Eccles. v, 11 ; see also, however, Ruth ii, 14, I Kings xx, 16, and for Egypt Gen. xliii, 16.

[3] Canaan, *Aberglaube und Volksmedizin im Lande der Bibel*, p. 2.

[4] I Kings iv, 22.       [5] I *kor* = 80 gallons.

[6] Is. xxii, 13.       [7] Amos vi, 4.

[8] Gen. xxvii, 19 ; Judges xix, 6 ; I Sam. xx, 24.

[9] H. J. Elhorst's proposal is very attractive—to expand $k^e d\bar{a}wid$ into $kad\ w^e jad$: " they rattle to the sound of the harp : they have invented musical instruments out of jug and hand." Jug and hand, as the first things available, stand, of course, for all noise-making things (*ZatW*, vol. xxxv (1915), p. 63).

[10] Is. v, 11.

only the sweet juice of the grape,[1] but also the half-fermented must was used.[2] Actual wine was frequently diluted with water,[3] but it should be noted that those passages which speak of " mingling strong drink " [4] refer to the addition of spices in order to increase the potency of the liquor. Great care was taken to have it cleared of all dregs or lees.[5] It was treated carefully, because it was highly valued—it was looked upon simply as " wine which cheereth God and man." [6] Hence it was also used at ceremonial feasts, and the amount that was consumed on such occasions is revealed by Eli's suspicion with regard to Hannah at her prayers,[7] or by Isaiah's condemnation of the worshippers whose tables he found "full of vomit." [8] When so little restraint was shown in the public sanctuary we can imagine what occasionally went on in private houses. References to joyous banquets are frequently accompanied by the statement that drunkenness prevailed.[9] " His eyes shall be red with wine " is a commendatory statement about Judah with reference to the fertility of the vines.[10] This makes it easier for us to understand the protests represented by such sects as the Rechabites and Nazirites and their total abstinence from wine ;[11] at the same time, it would be a mistake to ascribe the rise of these sects to this cause. For the Nazirite abstained not only from wine, but also from grapes,[12] while the Rechabites would not even cultivate the vine. The fact is, the protest of both sects was directed against the culture of the vine in itself ; it was to them a typical symbol of the civilization of settled life, in which they, the protagonists of the purely nomadic life, saw the cause of declension from the simple faith of Jahveh that marked the desert period.

But wine in its various stages was not the only spirituous beverage that was known. It is not quite clear what exactly was meant by the frequent expression [13] *shēkhār*,[14] whether it was date-wine, or beer made from barley, or some other kind of

---

[1] Is. xlix, 26.　　　[2] Hos. ii, 8 f., 22, and often.　　　[3] Is. i, 22.
[4] Is. v, 22 ; Ps. lxxv, 8 ; Prov. ix, 2, 5 ; Song of Songs viii, 2.
[5] Is. xxv, 6.　　　[6] Judges ix, 13 ; Ps. civ, 15.　　　[7] 1 Sam. i, 13.
[8] Is. xxviii, 8.　　　[9] 1 Sam. xxv, 36.　　　[10] Gen. xlix, 12.
[11] See *supra*, p. 140.
[12] Judges xiii, 14 ; Num. vi, 3.　　　[13] 1 Sam. i, 15.
[14] *Cf.* Hrozny in *Anzeiger der Königlichen Akademie der Wissenschaften zu Wien* (1910), p. 172 ff.

liquor. Pomegranate-wine is also mentioned.[1] The favourite drink for field-workers was vinegar diluted with water.[2]

A chapter on food would be incomplete without a reference to the fact that eating and drinking meant far more to the ancients than it does to us in modern times. To them it was more than a mere external of life, and therefore it was by no means a matter of indifference *who* ate together. To eat and drink together meant to establish a kind of community of life, and those who ate of the same food and drank from the same cup were henceforth safe from evil at each other's hands.[3] *Vice versa*, eating and drinking together was indispensable to the making of a covenant which was meant to guarantee this immunity to the parties.[4] The sexes were not separated at meals.[5] In this respect Israel seems to have been less strict than other nations.[6] Again, it was not a matter of indifference *what* was eaten or drunk. Above all, nothing was permissible that had been offered to other gods. To partake of such food or drink made one ceremonially unclean. As we have already hinted,[7] this is the explanation of those Old Testament prohibitions against the eating of certain animals.[8] Hygienic considerations had little—if indeed they had anything—to do with the matter. Above all, blood was a prohibited food.[9] " In the blood is the soul."[10] And the custom of abstaining from eating the sciatic nerve was declared by an ætiological story to be due to the injury received by the tribal ancestor when he wrestled with the Deity.[11]

## 7. DOMESTIC EVENTS

Life itself decreed that the monotony of the daily round in the home should be interrupted by other notes, notes of joy and of sorrow.

[1] Song of Songs viii, 2.    [2] Ruth ii, 14.
[3] *Cf.* A. von Wrede, *Reise in Hadhramaut* (1870), p. 226.    [4] Josh. ix, 14.
[5] Deut. xvi, 11 ; 1 Sam. i, 8 ; Ruth ii, 14 ; Job i, 4.
[6] Gen. xliii, 32.
[7] *Supra*, pp. 40 and 112.    [8] Lev. xi ; Deut. xiv.
[9] Gen. ix, 4.
[10] Lev. xvii, 11 ; cf. *supra*, p. 116.
[11] Gen. xxxii, 33. For a corresponding custom among other peoples Gunkel in his *Genesis Kommentar* refers to Robertson Smith's *The Religion of the Semites*. See Sir J. G. Frazer in *Anthropological Essays presented to E. B. Tylor* (1907), pp. 136 ff., and in *The Golden Bough*, 2nd edn., vol. ii, p. 419.

The arrival of a guest would turn a working day into a holiday.[1] Hospitality, the glory of the nomad, had lost little of its value in the eyes of the Hebrew settled in Palestine. Job could boast [2] that his door had ever been open to the traveller, that he had never allowed a stranger to lodge in the street. As in other respects, so also in this, the Hebrew's ideal was embodied in Abraham, although he was still pictured as a tent-dweller.[3] No one could read or hear unmoved the story of how the patriarch, as soon as he saw strangers approaching, went forth to meet them, and begged them to stay and rest in his tent. They were offered water for their feet ; and while Abraham went to fetch a tender calf from the stall and milk, his wife in all haste prepared cakes of flour. The amount of flour so used should be noticed: three *sea*—*i.e.*, more than 8 gallons—for three men. To be thus lavish was the duty of courtesy. And the flour was of the finest quality. The older narrator, it is true, was content to call it ordinary flour, but the later narrative considers that only the best was worthy of Abraham, and interpolates the necessary word. Finally, it should be observed that Abraham waited upon the guests himself. In so doing (the narrative implies) he honoured himself. Who his guests were he did not as yet know ; but a guest was a guest, and even an unknown guest was made welcome. To take another example : the priest of Midian scolded his daughters for not bringing home with them the fugitive Egyptian, Moses, who had met them in the fields.[4] Even a slave travelling on his master's affairs was sure of a courteous reception.[5] As for the hospitality offered to the recognized prophet, whose presence was fraught with promise of blessing, a special room, with all appurtenances, was offered him as his permanent quarters.[6]

Among the peoples of North Africa the custom prevails that if a stranger has no protector to look after him and his belongings, he betakes himself to the market or the principal square. There he is immediately invited by an inhabitant to enter his house and find protection there ; after that, the dictates of hospitality

---

[1] Journeys were made if possible on Sabbaths and at new moons, because on these days the beasts used for riding were not needed in the fields (2 Kings iv, 23).

[2] Job xxxi, 32.      [3] Gen. xviii, 1.

[4] Exod. ii, 20.      [5] Gen. xxiv.      [6] 2 Kings iv, 8–10.

make it the duty of this inhabitant to protect him.[1] An analogous custom prevailed in Israel. The stranger Levite who entered the city of Gibea[2] waited in the market to see if anyone would thus receive him. The fact that no invitation was extended to him only proved the utter degradation of the people. The sole exception was an old man, returning from his field-work, who was himself a resident foreigner. One striking feature in the protection offered to the Levite by this old man shows more clearly than any other how seriously the duties of hospitality were taken. When the men of the city came and surrounded his dwelling, demanding that the stranger should be handed over to them for their own base purposes, the host declared himself ready to surrender instead the honour of his own daughter.[3] Even such a price was to be paid for a guest's safety! A similar story is told of Lot.[4] The custom of thus offering hospitality was perhaps made necessary by the fact that there was no other way of making a stranger's life tolerable. Public inns, in our sense, were unknown ; the caravanserais, of which we hear repeatedly, were entirely different,[5] being little more than sheds where homeless people might take shelter.

Just as the arrival of a guest brought a pleasant excitement, so a departure was accompanied by suitable ceremonies, especially where the loss of the person departing was likely to be deeply felt. Laban upbraided Jacob for having departed secretly, and said that had he known of his intention to leave he would have sped him on his way with song and drum and harp.[6]

Festivities were also held in connexion with the building of a new house, the laying of a foundation-stone,[7] the placing of a gable-stone,[8] and the dedication of a house.[9]

Special joy reigned in the house when the news was brought to a father, "A man child is born to thee."[10] Such an announce-

---

[1] Post, *Grundriss der ethnologischen Jurisprudenz*, vol. i, p. 449, *note* 2.

[2] Judges xix, 15.

[3] Judges xix, 24. The mention of the stranger's concubine is due to a gloss.     [4] Gen. xix, 8.

[5] Gen. xlii, 27, xliii, 21 ; Exod. iv, 24; Jer. xli, 17. [The need of shelter led very early to the erection of rude and simple buildings of varying size, known as *khans*, which offered the wayfarer the protection of walls and a roof, and water, but little more.—TRANSLATOR.]

[6] Gen. xxxi, 27.          [7] Job xxxviii, 6 ; Ezra iii, 10.

[8] Zech. iv, 7.       [9] Ezra vi, 16.       [10] Jer. xx, 15.

ment implies that the father was not personally present at the birth, and his absence was not accidental. Among many peoples the father's presence at the birth of a child is—of course for superstitious reasons—expressly forbidden.[1] There was also a superstitious basis for the custom that the mother should kneel on the ground to give birth to the child.[2] This probably represented originally an attempt to bring the child at once into touch with Mother Earth, in order to receive from her its soul.[3]

The weaning of the child also gave occasion for family rejoicing. It was celebrated by a great feast.[4] Although the story of Joseph mentions a birthday feast of the King of Egypt,[5] we do not know whether birthdays were similarly marked in Israel.

Events that concerned the animals belonging to the household were also matters of family importance—*e.g.*, the sheep-shearing time was always one of high festival in the family.[6]

Another event that filled the house with special joy was the marriage of a son or daughter.[7] Marriage, apparently, was constituted by a pledge taken under oath,[8] and was accompanied by a ceremony in which the husband spread the skirt of his cloak over his wife-to-be.[9] This was a form of 'nostrification,'[10] and in the Koran[11] Mohammed, who went through this ceremony with the captive Jewess Khadija, expresses the relation between spouses by calling the wife the garment of the man and the husband the garment of the wife.[12] The climax of the marriage ceremony was reached when the bridegroom, after having been crowned by his mother,[13] went, accompanied by armed friends,[14] amid strains of music,[15] to bring his bride from her parents'

---

[1] Hastings, *RE*, vol. ii, p. 636 f.
[2] 1 Sam. iv, 19; Job xxxix, 3. Whether the Hebrew woman used a chair for this purpose is uncertain. The word in Exod. i, 16, sometimes taken to mean this is doubtful.     [3] *Cf.* A. Dieterich, *Mutter Erde* (1905, 1913).
[4] Gen. xxi, 8.     [5] Gen. xl, 20.
[6] 1 Sam. xxv, 4; 2 Sam. xiii, 23.
[7] Jer. vii, 34, xvi, 9, xxv, 10, xxxiii, 11.
[8] Ezek. xvi, 8. *Cf.* Pedersen, *Der Eid bei den Semiten*, p. 56.
[9] *Ibid.* Ruth iii, 9; *cf.* 1 Kings xix, 19.
[10] Wellhausen, *AR*, vol. vii (1904), p. 40.     [11] Sure ii, 183.
[12] Mal. ii, 16, where perhaps the word translated ' dress ' does mean ' wife.'
[13] Song of Songs iii, 11 ; Is. lxi, 10.
[14] 1 Macc. ix, 39. [*Cf.* Judges xiv, 11 ; Matt. ix, 15; John iii, 29.—TRANSLATOR.]     [15] *Ibid.*

house to his own—that is, in most cases, to the house of his parents.[1] There was a special significance in the presence of these weapons at the peaceful feast. They might be supposed to be a survival from the days of marriage by capture, but a passage in the Song of Songs points in another direction.[2] Describing the marriage procession, that passage portrays the approach of Solomon's litter, in which the bride is seated amid the fragrance of balsam and incense, surrounded by sixty men of Israel's host, all girt with swords, experienced in war, each with his sword at his side, " because of fear in the night." This seems to mean that these warriors were present to meet not only human foes, but supernatural demons lying in wait for the bride; and ethnological parallels make this practically certain. For example, in Algeria all the way to the house of the bridegroom one of the invited guests holds his sword-point pressed against the inside of the litter in order to keep the demons at a distance. In their eagerness to possess the bride these demons mean to steal her. In order to protect her the sword is kept for a week in the bridal chamber.[3] In the Tobit narrative [4] the evil spirit Asmodi kills the seven husbands of Sarah in the marriage-night. This makes it abundantly clear that conceptions of this kind were current among the Jews.[5] Further, the large amount of ornament worn by the bride,[6] and the fact that she was veiled,[7] and remained so—as we gather from the case of Jacob and Leah [8] —till the moment when she entered the marriage-chamber with her husband,[9] are explicable only as having been originally defensive measures against harmful influences on the part of evil spirits. And the use of torches and lamps, which prevailed in Israel long before New Testament times,[10] probably served

---

[1] The case is, of course, different in Gen. xxix, 22, Judges xiv, 10.

[2] Song of Songs iii, 7–10. *Cf.* Is. lxi, 10.

[3] Gaudefroy-Demombynes, *Les Cérémonies du Mariage chez les Indigènes de l'Algérie* (Paris, 1901), p. 37. Other examples are to be found in E. Samter, *Geburt, Hochzeit, und Tod* (1911), p. 41.    [4] Tobit vi, 14.

[5] A superstition of this kind probably lies behind Gen. xxxviii, 11, also.

[6] Ps. xlv, 10, 14 ; Is. lxi, 10.

[7] Gen. xxiv, 65.    [8] Gen. xxix, 25.

[9] Professor Socin would explain the use of ' to know ' in the sexual sense by the fact that " the husband then saw his wife's face for the first time." The verb ' to know ' occurs also in this sense in Hammurabi's law (§§ 154–156).

[10] Matt. xxv, 1 ff. ; Luke. xii, 35.

this same purpose,[1] because evil spirits were understood to fear the light. Among the Jews of the Sahara oasis Mzab the head of the bride is still wrapped in a silken cloth into the folds of which lighted candles are stuck.[2] It is abundantly clear that the candles are not placed there to give light.

A remarkable passage in the Song of Songs,[3] in which the bridegroom calls upon the bride to flee with him into the mountains, contains perhaps a reminiscence of the custom, still found among various peoples, of the hiding of the bride.[4] This is usually looked upon as a survival of the ancient marriage by capture. The flight of the bride into the mountains, where girl-friends who know her hiding-place supply her with food till the bridegroom finds her—and this is soon or late according to the state of her affections toward him—was, J. L. Burckhardt tells us,[5] still practised in his day by certain Bedouin tribes.

The marriage-feast usually took place in the house of the bridegroom [6] or of his parents—very rarely in the house of the bride's parents.[7] The whole village took part in it,[8] and the festivities usually lasted seven days.[9] They were brightened by dancing,[10] exchange of gifts,[11] and all kinds of games and jokes—like Samson's riddle.[12] Occasionally also, as is the case still, there were horse-races.[13] The bridal couple played the parts of king and queen. To this day the Arabs in Palestine call the bride *malaki*, or 'queen.'[14] The best man was the vizier of the Royal Highnesses. A special throne was constructed for them, and, if the ancient custom was at all like that which Wetzstein, consul at Damascus,[15] tells us still prevails in Syria, the beautiful

---

[1] Samter, *op. cit.*, p. 73.    [2] Sartori, *Sitte und Brauch*, vol. i, p. 83.

[3] Song of Songs iv, 8.

[4] Sartori, *op. cit.*, p. 90. I have given a different explanation of this passage in the supplement to *ZatW*, vol. xxxiii, pp. 47–53.

[5] *Notes on the Bedouins* (1830), vol. i, p. 269.

[6] Even in Samson's case (Judges xiv, 10), although Samson has gone to his bride's village.    [7] Gen. xxix, 22 ; Tobit vii, 13.    [8] Gen. xxix, 22.

[9] Gen. xxix, 27 ; Judges xiv, 12. It was two weeks in the case of Tobit (viii, 18).

[10] Song of Songs vii, 1. See Budde's commentary, *Das hohe Lied* (1898), *in loc.* Songs of the kind sung to-day are given by Gustav Dalman in his *Palästinensischer Diwan* (1901), p. 254.

[11] Judges xiv, 12, 19.    [12] Judges xiv, 14.

[13] Jer. xii, 5.    [14] *ZDPV*, vol. vi (1883), p. 100.

[15] See *ZE*, vol. v (1873), p. 270, under the title "Die syrische Dreschtafel." It forms the "throne" mentioned in the text.

# FAMILY AND DOMESTIC LIFE

illusion lasted till the end of the week, when one of the young husband's friends threw cow-dung in his face to remind him that he was once more a peasant. All this has led most scholars to-day to explain the Song of Songs as a collection of independent marriage-songs, such as were sung during the marriage-week. " King Solomon " is merely the name of any and every bride-groom, and " the Shulamite " [1] is merely the name given to any pretty maid.[2] The widespread custom of solemnly proving that the bride entered the marriage-chamber a virgin is also reflected in the Old Testament legal enactments.[3]

The entrance of death into a house laid on the relatives of the deceased many duties which to us seem very strange. The first thing done was to close the eyes of the dead [4] and to kiss him.[5] The mourners rent their clothes,[6] dressed themselves in sackcloth [7] (a coarse, hairy material), undid their turbans,[8] strewed dust and ashes upon their heads [9]—covering them,[10] or at least the upper lip.[11] They shaved off hair [12] and beard,[13] took off their sandals,[14] and sat down on the ground.[15] They beat their breast and sides,[16] and even cut themselves.[17] They raised the dirge for the dead.[18] The funeral feast was held,[19] but with that exception they fasted.[20] The mourning period lasted

---

[1] After Abishag of Shunem, specially famous for her beauty (1 Kings i, 3).

[2] This view of the book has been greatly forwarded by Budde's commentary, *Das hohe Lied*, in the " Kurzer Hand-Commentar zum Alten Testament " (1898).

[3] Deut. xxii, 13. *Cf.* J. D. Michaelis, *Mosaisches Recht*, pp. 1776 ff., § 92 ; Niebuhr, *Beschreibung von Arabien* (1772), p. 35, and *ZE*, vol. v (1873), p. 291.

[4] Gen. xlvi, 4.  [5] Gen. l, 1.

[6] 2 Sam. i, 11 ; 2 Kings ii, 12.  [7] 2 Sam. iii, 31 ; Amos viii, 10.

[8] An exception in Ezek. xxiv, 17, 23.

[9] 2 Sam. i, 2 ; Ezek. xxvii, 30.

[10] 2 Sam. xv, 30 ; Jer. xiv, 3 ; Esther vi, 12.  [11] Ezek. xxiv, 17.

[12] Is. xxii, 12 ; Jer. xvi, 6. The Arab curse on a woman, " May her hair be shaved off "—*i.e.*, may she lose children and relatives—is quoted by Wellhausen (*Reste arabischen Heidentums*, p. 181).

[13] Is. xv, 2 ; Jer. xli, 5, xlviii, 37 ; Mic. i, 16.

[14] Ezek. xxiv, 17.  [15] Ezek. xxvi, 16.

[16] Is. xxxii, 12 ; Jer. xxxi, 19. The Semitic word for ' to wail ' originally meant ' to beat.'

[17] Jer. xvi, 6, xli, 5, xlvii, 5, xlviii, 37.

[18] 1 Kings xiii, 30 ; Jer. xxii, 18 ; Amos v, 16 ; Zech. xii, 11.

[19] Jer. xvi, 7 ; Ezek. xxiv, 17 ; Hos. ix, 4. Connected with this was the practice of laying food on the grave (Deut. xxvi, 14 ; Tobit iv, 17 ; Ecclus. xxx, 18).

[20] 1 Sam. xxxi, 13 ; 2 Sam. iii, 35.

seven [1] days, or, in the wider sense, thirty [2] days. The meaning of all these practices cannot be explained here. [3] Some of them have already been dealt with in the chapter on the early ancestor-worship practised by Israel's forefathers, [4] but it would be an error in method to derive them all indiscriminately from a root connected with cultus. In matters with which reason has so little to do the most varied conceptions intermingle. Some of these customs no doubt arose from a desire to be protected against taboo, and others were intended to render the mourners unrecognizable by the dreaded spirit of the dead.

The usual method of disposing of the dead was burial. Cremation, [5] like intentional neglect of burial, [6] was either a form of punishment or a sign of barbarism ; [7] for to fail to lay the dead in the resting-place of the grave meant that the soul would wander about haunting people. Soon after death the corpse, uncoffined, [8] but clothed, was laid in the grave. It was conceived as wearing in the underworld the clothes worn in life. [9] Food was placed in the grave. The excavations have proved this, even although only the empty clay vessels were found. But, in comparison with former times, there was far less care devoted to the dead. The jars and dishes were of less careful manufacture, and were carelessly placed in a corner at a distance from the corpse. Over the graves of well-to-do people fragrant spices were burnt, [10] and the ashes which mourners poured upon their heads were originally the residue of these burnt-offerings.

The grave was originally the family grave. "To be gathered to one's fathers" [11] is one of the expressions that are to be taken quite literally. The grave was situated in the immediate neighbourhood of the living family. [12] The excavations in Jericho

---

[1] Gen. l, 10 ; 1 Sam. xxxi, 13.  [2] Num. xx, 29 ; Deut. xxxiv, 8.

[3] I have done this in my book *Die israelitischen Vorstellungen vom Zustand nach dem Tode* (1914).  [4] See *supra*, p. 132.

[5] Lev. xx, 14, xxi, 9 ; Josh. vii, 25. The text of 1 Sam. xxxi, 12, and Amos vi, 10, is corrupt.

[6] 2 Kings ix, 10 ; Jer. xvi, 4 ; Ezek. xxix, 5.

[7] On the other hand, to inter the unburied is a charitable duty (Tobit i, 18, ii, 8).

[8] Different, of course, in Gen. l, 26.

[9] 1 Sam. xxviii, 14 ; Ezek. xxxii, 27.

[10] Jer. xxxiv, 5 ; 2 Chron. xvi, 14, xxi, 19.

[11] 2 Sam. xxi, 14 ; 1 Kings xiii, 22.

[12] 1 Sam. xxv, 1 ; 1 Kings ii, 34 ; Ezek. xliii, 7.

are still furnishing evidence that the dead were occasionally interred in the court of the house or under its floor.[1] But the course of development tended in the direction of removing the graves from the dwellings of the living. Being no longer necessarily tied to one dwelling, people selected for their dead places that were as quiet and secure as possible. The natural caves [2] were the first places that offered themselves. Where these were not available they were imitated by art. The grave was dug in the rock,[3] perpendicularly or horizontally, as wide and deep as possible, to meet the ancient desire that all the members of the family should be buried beside each other. Necessarily, perhaps, less trouble was taken with poorer people,[4] and occasionally human bones were mingled with those of animals—"with the burial of an ass."[5] In all such matters the Israelites simply followed the customs of the earlier inhabitants of the country. Discoveries in Megiddo prove that the practice of burying children in urns and jars was still followed, but any extension of the ancient customs, in the way of embellishing or improving upon them, met with strong opposition in the religion of Jahveh and its strong protest against everything that might encourage worship of the dead. Indeed, this in itself explains to some extent the increasing lack of care in the choice of offerings for the dead.

[1] Sellin and Watzinger, *Jericho*, p. 71.     [2] Gen. xxiii, 9.
[3] Is. xxii, 16; 2 Kings xxiii, 16.
[4] 2 Kings xxiii, 6; Jer. xxvi, 23; Is. liii, 9.     [5] Jer. xxii, 19.

# CHAPTER II

## TRADES AND CALLINGS

WE must lay aside our modern conceptions of trades and callings when we try to understand what these meant to the ancient Hebrew. It is significant that the story of Paradise was written under the impression that the divine curse rested on all human toil. Man toils " in the sweat of his brow," and the ground brings forth thorns ! In spite of all the passages lauding the excellence of the land, the fact that its stony ground yielded a harvest only in return for great toil schooled the Hebrew to take the view that all work meant toil, and he would not have been an Oriental had he not done his best to keep all toil as far away from him as he could. All work that a man could possibly hand over to a woman the woman had to do, both indoors and outside, and nothing of the nature of ' gallant ' consideration for the female sex need be looked for among an Eastern peasant population.[1]

The typical symbol of everyday household work was the sound of the hand-mill in which the corn was ground.[2] This task, like that of pounding the corn in a mortar,[3] was the regular work of the Hebrew woman. It was so laborious that it was left, wherever possible, to the lowest female slave.[4] The wife was also responsible for the baking of bread and cakes,[5] and expert knowledge was necessary to detect the right moment for turning the cakes in the hot ashes.[6] After her husband had killed an animal [7] the preparation of the meat fell to the wife.[8] It was also the woman's task to fetch water from the well [9] and to spin the flax and wool,[10] and we repeatedly hear of women in the fields filling the part of shepherdesses.[11]

---

[1] But see Gen. xxix, 10 ; Exod. ii, 17.

[2] Jer. xxv, 10. The LXX is different. The hand-mill was so indispensable that it could not be taken in pledge (Deut. xxiv, 6).          [3] Num. xi, 8.

[4] Exod. xi, 5 ; cf. Is. xlvii, 2. The work was given to prisoners (Judges xvi, 21 ; Lam. v, 13).

[5] Gen. xviii, 6 ; 1 Sam. viii, 13.          [6] Hos. vii, 8.

[7] Gen. xviii, 7.          [8] Gen. xxvii, 14.          [9] 1 Sam. ix, 11.

[10] Josh. ii, 6 ; Prov. xxxi, 13.          [11] Gen. xxix, 6 ; Exod. ii, 16.

# TRADES AND CALLINGS

Many familiar metaphors [1] make it plain that the shepherd's calling was one of the main occupations of Hebrew men. It had, however, little of the idyllic character which we have been taught to ascribe to it by many beautiful figures of speech. [2] Taken as a whole, the work was rough and exhausting. Listen to Jacob, the typical Hebrew shepherd, [3] describing the twenty years he had spent in the service of Laban : " These twenty years have I been with thee, and not one ram of thy flock have I eaten. That which was torn by beasts, I bare the loss of it : thou didst require it at my hand, whether stolen by day, or stolen by night. In the day the drought consumed me, and the frost by night ; and my sleep departed from mine eyes." [4] Besides being exposed to the inclement weather, the shepherd had to be continually on the watch against living enemies. David tells of lions and bears carrying off his sheep, [5] and in the prophetic writings we read of shepherds being summoned together to drive away a wild beast, [6] and succeeding only in rescuing from him " two legs, or a piece of an ear." [7] Incidents of this kind were frequent enough to necessitate legal enactments anent the shepherd's responsibilities, [8] and it is interesting to find that these questions were decided in exactly the same manner as was done in the code of Hammurabi. That code enacted : [9] " If in a fold a stroke of God has taken place, or a lion has killed, the shepherd is to clear himself by oath before God, and the owner must bear the loss. But if a sheep has been lost through the shepherd's carelessness, he must make the loss good to the owner of the beast."

The Hebrew version is as follows (Exod. xxii, 10–13) : " If a man deliver unto his neighbour an ass, or an ox, or a sheep, or any beast to be looked after ; and it die or be hurt or driven away, no man seeing it ; then shall an oath by Jahveh be between them both, that he hath not put his hand unto his neighbour's goods ; and the owner must accept the loss and the other need not make it good. If it be stolen from him, he shall

---

[1] Jer. xxiii ; Ezek. xxxiv ; Is. lxiii, 11 ; Ps. xxiii, 1.
[2] Judges v, 16, " the bleatings of the flocks." [Moffatt renders, " with only an ear for pastoral notes."—TRANSLATOR.]
[3] Gen. xlvii, 3.                           [4] Gen. xxxi, 38.
[5] 1 Sam. xvii, 34.                  [6] Is. xxxi, 4, v, 29 ; Jer. xlix, 19.
[7] Amos iii, 12.          [8] Exod. xxii, 9 ff.          [9] § 266 et seq.

make it good to the owner. But if it be torn by a wild beast, let him produce evidence, and he shall not need to make good that which was torn."

Of course, in order to know if any loss had occurred it was necessary to know exactly the number of sheep entrusted to the shepherd's care. For this purpose, when the shepherd brought them to the fold in the evening,[1] or led them forth in the morning, he made them pass under his shepherd's staff.[2] There were also special watch-towers [3] from the top of which a wide view could be obtained, and the shepherd had live coadjutors in his dogs.[4] Besides his staff, his weapon—it is the same to-day [5]— was a sling, stones for which he carried in his scrip or pouch.[6] Not the least dangerous of the enemies he had to meet were men. Disputes readily arose over the ownership or use of wells.[7] But the shepherds had also to guard their flocks against robber bands, and they were grateful when they found armed help at hand, men who were " as a wall unto them both by night and by day." [8] In addition to members of the family, there were also hired men who aided in this shepherd work. Their wages were paid either in money [9] or in kind [10]—i.e., they received a share of the increase of their flock ; [11] and of course an astute man could find various ways and means of making things turn to his own advantage.[12] There were also other subsidiary occupations by which the shepherd could eke out his living. Amos was at once shepherd and dresser of sycamore-trees.[13] Yet despite all the difficulties and hardships that attended the shepherd's calling many of the descriptions of the various phases of his work—seeking the lost and bringing back the strayed, bandaging the wounded and tending the sick, carrying the lambs and gently leading the ewes that were suckling their young [14]—are eloquent of the affection and zeal with which the conscientious shepherd fulfilled the duties of his calling.

---

[1] Num. xxxii, 16 ; 1 Sam. xxiv, 3 ; Mic. ii, 12.
[2] Lev. xxvii, 32 ; Jer. xxxiii, 13 ; metaphorically in Ezek. xx, 37.
[3] Gen. xxxv, 21 ; 2 Kings xvii, 9, xviii, 8 ; Mic. iv, 8.
[4] Job xxx, 1 ; Is. lvi, 10.
[5] A. Musil, *Arabia Petræa* (1908), vol. iii, p. 284.   [6] 1 Sam. xvii, 40.
[7] Gen. xxi, 25, xxvi, 20.   [8] 1 Sam. xxv, 16.   [9] Zech. xi, 12.
[10] Ezek. xxxiv, 3.   [11] Gen. xxx, 32.   [12] Gen. xxx, 37.
[13] Amos vii, 14 ; read *nôkēd* after LXX and Amos i, 1.
[14] Gen. xxxiii, 13 ; Is. xl, 11 ; Ezek. xxxiv, 16.

We obtain some idea of the size of the flocks from what we read of the possessions of the Calebite Nabal. In the south of Judah, which, next to the land east of Jordan, was the chief sheep district, Nabal owned 1000 goats and 3000 sheep.[1] Job had finally 14,000 sheep ;[2] he began with 7000.[3] A man who, like Job, had plenty of pasture-ground[4] kept cattle as well as sheep and goats. Job was credited with a holding of 3000 camels, 500 yoke of oxen, and 500 she-asses ;[5] and after the restoration of his fortunes these numbers were doubled.[6] A man's wealth was estimated by his property in cattle, so that one and the same word was used to denote cattle and wealth.[7] The ass was the usual riding animal and beast of burden, and it was so popular[8] that the introduction of horses, which took place in Solomon's reign, aroused strong resentment.[9] The breeding of mules also, which must have been extensively carried on at one time,[10] was interdicted by a later law which forbade all inter-breeding between different species.[11] Altogether, this wide-spread occupation with animals produced and maintained in Israel a real love for animals. Of this we have several fine examples in the legislation. Apart from express enactments in favour of the lower animals, which have no doubt a superstitious background,[12] it is an eloquent testimony to the sentiment that prevailed on this subject when we find that this love for animals so overbore the ruthlessness that usually marked the treatment of an enemy that the law required a man to hasten to the aid of any beast, even if it belonged to an enemy, that was sinking under its load.[13] It is a characteristic sign of a very much later age that it had lost all understanding of the law which forbade the muzzling of " the ox when he treadeth out the corn."[14] In his allegorical interpretation of this ancient passage Paul asks scornfully if anyone could imagine that God cares for the oxen.[15]

---

[1] 1 Sam. xxv, 2.  [2] Job xlii, 12.  [3] Job i, 3.
[4] Bashan was specially noted for its pastures (Ezek. xxxix, 18 ; Mic. vii, 14 ; Amos iv, 1).  [5] Job i, 3.  [6] Job xlii, 12.
[7] Hebrew *mikneh*. [Cf. Latin *pecus*, German *Vieh*, English *fee*.—Translator.]
[8] Gen. xlix, 11, 14 ; Judges v, 10, x, 4, xii, 14.
[9] Deut. xvii, 16 ; Is. ii, 7 ; cf. Zech. ix, 9.
[10] 2 Sam. xiii, 29 ; xviii, 9.  [11] Lev. xix, 19.
[12] Exod. xxxiv, 26 ; Lev. xxii, 28.  [13] Exod. xxiii, 5 ; Deut. xxii, 4.
[14] Deut. xxv, 4.  [15] 1 Cor. ix, 9.

To the ancient legislator that was as axiomatic as it is to the Arabian or Syrian peasant of to-day, who allows his oxen to eat without stint of the corn that is being threshed. The repeated mention of a certain mash or fodder points to special care in the preparation of suitable indoor feeding. The ingredients included salt or saltwort.[1]

The breeding of fowls seems to have been limited to the breeding of pigeons or doves, but this must have been carried on very extensively.[2]

Next to cattle-breeding the chief occupation of the Hebrew was agriculture.[3] The method of tillage had advanced from hoeing to ploughing. As the soil of Palestine requires to be only lightly turned over the plough used was much lighter than ours.[4] But, simple as it was, the ploughshare was nevertheless made of iron.[5] It was drawn by oxen or asses,[6] probably also (though a later law forbade this [7]) by both together. It was so much the custom to work the animals in pairs that field-measurements came to be stated in terms of yokes of oxen.[8] The ploughman urged on his animals with his staff,[9] the pointed end of which is familiar to us from the expression " to kick against the pricks." [10] The ground had to be ploughed at least three times. The plough was followed by the harrow.[11] The care used in putting in the seed is evident from the parable of Isaiah,[12] according to which the seeds of barley and wheat were not scattered broadcast, but " laid " in the ground. Apparently manure was liberally applied.[13] In all these matters the Hebrews simply followed in the footsteps of the Canaanites, but to satisfy

---

[1] Is. xxx, 24 ; Job vi, 5. According to the Arabian proverb, sweet fodder is the camel's bread, salt fodder its confectionery.

[2] Cf. the significance of the dove in ritual offering, and its use in the language of simile and metaphor.

[3] For agriculture in Palestine see Bertholet, " Landbau und Altes Testament," in the Schweizer Archiv für Volkskunde, vol. xx (1916), pp. 29–37.

[4] Volz, Die biblischen Altertümer (1914), p. 369.

[5] 1 Sam. xiii, 20.          [6] Is. xxx, 24.          [7] Deut. xxii, 10.

[8] Is. v, 10 [10 acres, literally 10 yoke—TRANSLATOR] ; 1 Sam. xiv, 14. [Cf. the Scottish phrase which indicates the size of a farm by saying, " It has six pair o' horse."—TRANSLATOR.] In Lev. xxvii, 16, the estimate is based on the amount of seed required.

[9] Judges iii, 31.

[10] Deut. xxxii, 15 ; 1 Sam. ii, 29 ; Acts xxvi, 14.

[11] Hos. x, 11.          [12] Is. xxviii, 25.

[13] 2 Kings ix, 37 ; Jer. viii, 2 ; Is. xxv, 10.

their religious faith they expressed it in another way. The occupation of Canaan by Israel was, to their faith, equivalent to Jahveh taking the land, and it was *He* who thus became the real instructor of the Hebrew farmer. Therefore—this is the teaching of the Isaianic parable just mentioned [1]—it was Jahveh who instructed the husbandman how to level the soil, how to sow dill and cummin, how to place barley and fitches at the edge of the field—in short, how to deal suitably with all kinds of grain and how to do everything in the due season. How thoroughly they understood the importance of accurate observance of the course of the agricultural year is seen from an agricultural calendar which was discovered at Gezer. It dates from about the sixth century B.C.,[2] and is as follows : two months, garnering the fruits ; two months, seed-time ; two months, late seed-time ; one month, pulling the flax ; [3] one month, barley harvest ; one month, harvesting other crops ; two months, gathering the grapes ; one month, fruit harvest.

According to this calendar the cereal harvest began with the cutting of barley. It began in April, and should,[4] so it was thought, always begin on a Sunday—a remarkable example of belief in a " lucky day." The barley harvest was followed, two or three weeks later, by the wheat harvest. The date for beginning varied, of course, in different districts. Between the beginning and the end of harvest lay, roughly, seven weeks.[5] That was a merry season—the joy of harvest was proverbial [6]— and the fusion of these agricultural climaxes with the religious element did not detract from their festive character ; it rather suffused the religious service with their joyousness. Numerous details of harvest operations have been preserved in many figures of speech. We see the mower grasping the corn-stalks with one hand and cutting them with the sickle held in the other. He is followed by the sheaf-binder, who gathers the ears in the voluminous bosom-folds of his garment.[7] When only a small

---

[1] Is. xxviii, 24.    [2] *Cf.* Marti in *ZatW*, vol. xxix (1909), p. 222.

[3] For flax-cultivation see Josh. ii, 6, Hos. ii, 5, 9.

[4] Lev. xxiii, 10 f. See my commentary on this passage in *Leviticus* in the " Kurzer Hand-Commentar zum Alten Testament " (1901).

[5] Hence the Feast of Weeks, the feast that marked the close of harvest, seven weeks after the Feast of *Massôth*, " when the sickle is put into the corn " (Deut. xvi, 9).

[6] Is. ix, 2 ; Ps. cxxvi, 6.    [7] Is. xvii, 5 ; Ps. cxxix, 7.

quantity of grain was to be threshed, or when it was of extra fine quality, or where it was desired to do the work so as to attract as little attention as possible, the threshing was done simply with the flail.[1] The usual method was to drive oxen, or asses and horses, round and round upon the corn.[2] Others used a threshing-cart [3]—*i.e.*, a small cart-body with sharp studs —or a threshing-sledge [4]—*i.e.*, large weighted boards with hard pointed stones affixed to the underside. A winnowing-shovel or fork [5] was used to separate the wheat from the chaff, and as the evening was the favourite time for this work the evening wind carried the chaff away.[6] The last and most delicate part of the threshing process was done with the sieve.[7] The resultant crop was gathered into barns,[8] or, in critical times, buried in holes in the ground.[9] It varied greatly in amount according to the district, but it was perhaps on the whole greater than it is to-day. But even in ancient as well as modern days it must have been a rare exception to have a return of a hundredfold, such as is mentioned both in the New Testament [10] and in the Old.[11] The New Testament parable also mentions sixtyfold and thirtyfold ; and even this last figure, although it comes nearest to the average crop, must be taken as a round number, especially when we remember how often mention is made of failure of crops.[12] Great loss was caused by the thorns and thistles that are so often referred to.[13] Every seven years the land was allowed to rest,[14] but this fallow year did not affect each field simultaneously. It was already carrying the idea of rest too far, and betraying the love of the legal mind for artificial symmetry, when legislation enacted a special Sabbatic year in order to secure a universal fallow year,[15] but this was actually carried through, though with great difficulty.[16] On the other

---

[1] Judges vi, 11 ; Ruth ii, 17 ; Is. xxviii, 27.

[2] Deut. xxv, 4 ; Hos. x, 11 ; Jer. l, 11. *Cf.* the graphic relief from the grave of Ti in Saccara, representing scenes from Egyptian peasant-life, in Hunger and Lamer, *Altorientalische Kultur im Bilde* (1912), No. 76, p. 28. The artist depicts ox and ass greedily devouring a few stalks. Cf. *supra*, p. 197.

[3] Is. xxviii, 27, xli, 15.  [4] 2 Sam. xxiv, 22.

[5] Is. xxx, 24 ; Jer. xv, 7.  [6] Ps. i, 4.  [7] Amos ix, 9.

[8] Deut. xxviii, 8.  [9] Jer. xli, 8.  [10] Matt. xiii, 8.

[11] Gen. xxvi, 12. Cf. *supra*, p. 142, *note* 8.  [12] See *supra*, p. 19.

[13] Gen. iii, 18, and frequently.

[14] Exod. xxiii, 10 f.  [15] Lev. xxv, 2.  [16] 1 Macc. vi, 49, 53.

hand, the general year of jubilee, which was appointed to be celebrated every fiftieth year, and which was intended by a later [1] lawgiver even to outdo the demand of the Sabbatic year, remained an ideal, unattained and unattainable. To keep it would have meant that for two successive years, the forty-ninth and the fiftieth, the husbandman should renounce or give up all produce of his fields !

Of vegetables the gherkin (cucumber) and the pumpkin (gourd) deserve special mention as the only plants that grow in the open fields in Palestine before the summer sun has parched the soil.[2] In the centre of the field the watchman hangs up his hammock.[3]

Of far greater importance was the culture of the vine, the olive, and the fig. To " sit in safety under his own vine and fig-tree " [4] was the true ideal of the husbandman in Palestine. The culture of the vine demanded more attention and labour than the others. First of all, the stony slopes, whose thin covering of *humus* was easily washed away by winter rains, required to be built in terrace fashion, and the amount of careful work necessary in a vineyard may be gathered from Isaiah's song about a friend's vineyard : [5]

> He dug it and removed the stones,
> And planted it with noble vine ;
> He built a tower in the midst of it,
> A wine-press too he hewed therein.

Other passages speak of a " cottage " or " booth " in the vineyard instead of a " tower." [6] The purpose of both was to aid the keeper in guarding the vineyard against all foes. Among these were the " little foxes " [7] and the wild pig.[8] The smallest enemy of all, the " worm," tasked the best efforts of the most careful keeper.[9] Sometimes the vines were trained to grow tall ; [10] sometimes they were trained along the ground.[11] The

[1] Lev. xxv, 11.
[2] Robertson Smith, *The Religion of the Semites.*
[3] Is. i, 8. Comparison with Is. xxiv, 20, shows that the word elsewhere called 'cottage' means something that was movable.
[4] 1 Kings iv, 25 ; Mic. iv, 4.     [5] Is. v, 2.
[6] Is. i, 8 ; Job xxvii, 18.
[7] Song of Songs ii, 15.     [8] Ps. lxxx, 14.     [9] Deut. xxviii, 39.
[10] Ps. lxxx, 11 ; *cf.* also the expression to sit " under the vine."
[11] Ezek. xvii, 6.

familiar expression " the blood of the grape "[1] implies that, contrary to modern practice,[2] it was chiefly red grapes that were grown.[3] The size of the grapes thus grown can be guessed from the story of the spies,[4] with suitable discount in view of its legendary character. The noisy joy of the vintage was such as to repay in full all the trouble expended on the vineyard throughout the year.[5]

The olive-tree called for much less attention.[6] The tree grown was the wild olive, improved and cultivated.[7] On the average it yielded a full crop, gathered in the autumn, only every second year. It yielded various kinds of oil. The common oil was obtained by treading the olives in the oil-press,[8] just as grapes were trodden in the wine-press. The finer oil was produced by pounding in a vessel olives taken from the tree before they were fully ripe.[9] Figs were also extensively cultivated, and trade was also done with the cheaper fruit of the sycamore, the so-called mulberry-fig.[10] In order to give it a better flavour the harsh-tasting juice was allowed to escape by pinching the fruit or making incisions in it.

In districts like that round Jericho[11] where palms and balsams grew luxuriantly the Hebrews devoted themselves to their cultivation; and occasionally, especially in later writings, we read of actual horticulture, meaning by that the culture not only of vegetables[12] and fruit,[13] but also of pleasure-gardens.[14] Bee-keeping, too, deserves to be mentioned in this connexion. Isaiah refers to it when he compares Jahveh to the " father hissing for the bees."[15]

Leading a life of this kind, the Hebrew came to love life on the land, and the pride and the loyalty with which the Hebrew

---

[1] Gen. xlix, 11 ; Deut. xxxii, 14.

[2] ZDPV, vol. xi (1888), p. 160.

[3] Prov. xxiii, 31.                                          [4] Num. xiii, 23 f.

[5] Is. xvi, 10 ; Jer. xxv, 30.

[6] F. Goldmann, Der Ölbau in Palästina (1907).         [7] Rom. xi, 17.

[8] Mic. vi, 15. Gethsemane means " Oil-press." A splendid specimen belonging to Israel's time was found in Gezer (Palestine Exploration Fund, Quarterly Statement (1909), p. 92).

[9] Exod. xxvii, 20.

[10] Amos vii, 14, and supra, p. 196.                   [11] Supra, p. 14.

[12] Deut. xi, 10 ; 1 Kings xxi, 2 ; supra, p. 182.

[13] Song of Songs iv, 13, vi, 11 ; Eccles. ii, 5.      [14] Eccles. ii, 6.

[15] Is. vii, 18. [Cf. Ps. cxviii, 12.—TRANSLATOR.]

husbandman clung to his ancestral property finds splendid expression in Naboth's words to Ahab : " The Lord forbid it me, that I should give the inheritance of my fathers to thee." [1] It was also a fine feature that even a wealthy man—at least in the ancient period—did not consider it beneath him to take a personal share in the work. Saul, although he was already anointed king, is seen returning from his day at the plough,[2] and we find Elisha working one of his father's twelve yoke of oxen.[3] A wealthy man like Boaz [4] and the rich farmer of Shunem [5] are found in the fields among the reapers. In this respect, of course, things slowly changed as time went on.[6] Speaking generally, the nature of the country was such that farming was carried on more largely in the north and stock-breeding in the south ; therefore it is not fortuitous that Saul was called to the throne from the plough, while David was a shepherd-boy.[7]

After settling down in Palestine the Hebrew seems to have lost all fondness for the chase. The typical hunter is sketched for us in Esau, hairy and rough, contrasted with the smooth, gentle Jacob.[8] And while Israel's neighbour-kings followed the chase, none of the Hebrew kings was a " mighty hunter before Jahveh." [9] We have to come down to the days of Herod the Great [10] to find a king of that kind in Palestine, and his love of hunting was only an additional reason for the dislike with which the Jews regarded him. All the same, many stories were in circulation regarding brave deeds done by great hunters,[11] and a liking for venison[12] prevented the hunter from disappearing entirely.[13] The hunter's life supplied the language with many figures of speech, and from these we hear of pits for the lions,[14] nets or enclosures for antelopes,[15] slings and traps for birds.[16] Even the art of taming wild animals must have been known.[17] The art of fishing was well understood, and we read again and

---

[1] I Kings xxi, 3.  [2] I Sam. xi, 5.  [3] I Kings xix, 19.
[4] Ruth ii, 4.  [5] 2 Kings iv, 18.
[6] See below, Chapter III.
[7] Cf. Löhr, *Israels Kulturentwickelung* (1911), p. 40.
[8] Gen. xxv, 27, xxvii, 11.  [9] Gen. x, 9.
[10] Josephus, *Wars of the Jews*, I, xxi, 13.
[11] Judges xiv, 6 ; I Sam. xvii, 34 ; 2 Sam. xxiii, 20.
[12] *Supra*, p. 180.  [13] Jer. xvi, 16.  [14] Ezek. xix, 8.
[15] Is. li, 20.  [16] Amos iii, 5.  [17] Ezek. xix, 4 ; Ps. iii, 7.

again of both net [1] and fishing-rod.[2] It is perhaps merely accidental that we seldom read of actual fishermen in the Old Testament.[3]

Abandoning nomad life and settling down in " cities which they had not built," [4] the Hebrews found themselves faced with the new task of learning and developing a building trade among themselves. Here, if anywhere, they followed the methods of the Canaanites, and built, as these latter had built, in accordance with their needs from day to day, making the best of the conditions presented to them. For example, a favourite device was to build a clay house against a rock.[5] The measuring-line, the plumb-line, and the builder's level became familiar expressions.[6] Where the requirements went beyond the simplest efforts they had to call in outside help, and in this way foreign styles of building were introduced. David sent to King Hiram of Tyre for carpenters and masons [7] to build his palace ; and to an even greater extent his son Solomon, knowing that there was no one in Israel " that had skill to hew timber " like the Phœnicians,[8] employed Phœnician help in the construction of his spacious buildings.[9] He concluded an agreement with Hiram that Hiram's men should bring cedar and cypress timber from Lebanon to the coast, and from thence it was brought south in the form of rafts and transported by Solomon's men to Jerusalem. Working with timber was evidently well understood in Phœnicia, and from that country experts followed the timber to Jerusalem.[10]

We have a first-hand account of the building operations that went on in Jerusalem under Solomon.[11] It supplies, however, merely ground-plans, so that in attempting to reproduce the buildings we have to fall back to a large extent on our imagination. This explains why engravings from the sixteenth century exhibit Solomon's Temple as a building in Renaissance style, while those from the seventeenth century, with equal justification, present it as a specimen of rococo ! As a matter of fact,

---

[1] Ezek. xlvii, 10 ; Hab. i, 16.
[2] Amos iv, 2 ; Hab. i, 15.
[3] Jer. xvi, 16 ; Ezek. xlvii, 10.      [4] Cf. Deut. vi, 10.
[5] Cf. Guthe, ZDPV, vol. v (1882), p. 339, vol. viii (1885), p. 42.
[6] Is. xxviii, 17 ; Amos vii, 7 ; 2 Kings xxi, 13.
[7] 2 Sam. v, 11.                        [8] 1 Kings v, 6.
[9] 1 Kings v, 32.      [10] See supra, p. 26.      [11] 1 Kings vi, f.

the æsthetic impression which it might have been expected to produce must have been considerably affected by the method of its construction. On three sides the main Temple build-ing was screened from view up to more than half its height [1] by an outbuilding, three stories high, containing low rooms [2] with small windows. The entire building formed a massive rectangle, whose mere size doubtless produced a striking effect : to the Semitic mind at all times " large " and " beautiful " were synonymous terms.[3] In front, on the east side, a stair led up to the " porch," 10 yards long and 20 wide, which stood in front of the Temple proper.[4] Leading into the Temple itself was a door with posts of olive-wood and two leaves of cypress-wood.[5] The Temple was divided into two parts, a larger outer court, 40 cubits long, 20 wide, and 60 in height,[6] with windows [7] (although, owing to the already-mentioned buildings round the walls these could be inserted only in the topmost third of the walls), and, divided from this by a thin wall of cedar-wood and a pentagonal door with leaves of olive-wood,[8] a completely dark [9] rear portion, cube-shaped, 20 cubits each way,[10] in which the Ark of Jahveh was placed underneath the outspread wings of two cherubs.[11] This was conceived to be the actual dwelling-place of Jahveh.[12] The court next to it was, so to speak, His audience-chamber. Compared with Christian churches, even this court was not large.[13] It was not meant to hold a congrega-

---

[1] The main building was 30 cubits high (1 Kings vi, 2), and each of the three stories of the " chambers against the house " 5 cubits (verse 10). The cubit is roughly 19 inches.

[2] In the visionary temple of Ezekiel there were thirty-three on each story (Ezek. xli, 6).

[3] *Cf.* Bäthgen's *Die Psalmen* in the " Hand-Kommentar zum Alten Testa-ment " (1912), Ps. xciii, 4.

[4] The two pillars, Jachin and Boaz (1 Kings vii, 21), cannot have been merely architectonic. The fact that they had names proves this. No doubt they were an echo of the ancient *massebas* (*supra*, p. 103 f.)—if, indeed, they had not a cosmological significance (Gunkel, *Schöpfung und Chaos*, p. 153). *Cf.* the two pillars which recur in connexion with other temples—in Paphos, Hierapolis, and Tyre.                                        [5] 1 Kings vi, 33 f.

[6] 1 Kings vi, 2, 17. The measurements refer to inner width.

[7] They were also latticed, so the light they admitted must have been scanty.

[8] Verse 31.          [9] 1 Kings viii, 12.          [10] 1 Kings vi, 20.

[11] For the cherubs see below, p. 211, *note* 3.

[12] 1 Kings viii, 13.

[13] The nave of Ulm Cathedral would hold the Holy of Holies of Solomon's Temple four or five times over.

tion—the outer court was there for that purpose. The roof was of cedar beams, but it is not clear how they were laid.[1] Inside the Temple the walls, from the floor to the beams of the roof, were panelled with planks of cedar, so that the masonry of the walls was invisible; the floor was laid with planks of cypress-wood.[2] In the outer court stood the altar, made of cedar, and meant to hold the shewbread.[3]

The Temple when viewed in connexion with the other buildings of Solomon was merely what we should call a royal chapel; the site on which it stood was divided from the palace site only by a wall on the south side.[4] We have practically no information about the palace and the harem. The buildings to the south of them were these: a throne-room, which served as a court of law, panelled with cedar from floor to ceiling;[5] immediately connected with this, forming, in fact, the front part of it, was a pillar-hall, 50 cubits long and 30 wide;[6] and finally, still farther to the south, the Lebanon forest-house, used as an armoury,[7] which owes its name to the forty-five pillars of cedar of Lebanon, standing in three rows, and carrying an upper story. It was 100 cubits long, 50 wide, and 30 high.[8]

This whole range of buildings was surrounded by an enclosing wall consisting of three rounds of hewn stone and a top layer of cedar beams. That was the so-called Great Wall,[9] which formed a rectangle running approximately from north to south. Inside this wall, as has been indicated, the palace area and the Temple area were again enclosed by special walls, so that we read of an " inner court " [10] and of " another court." [11]

A piece of masonry in a greater style was the circumvallation of Jerusalem—also a work of Solomon.[12] It enclosed apparently only the west side of the city, having the Ephraim Gate and the Corner Gate in the north and the Valley Gate and the Dung

[1] I Kings vi, 9.
[2] Verses 15, 18. The statement that the whole Temple was covered with gold inside (verse 21) is a later exaggeration added to the original account.
[3] Verse 20. The golden altar (vii, 48) is also a later addition.
[4] This did not please Ezekiel (xliii, 7). He holds the sanctity of the Temple so high that the city must be entirely removed from its vicinity.
[5] I Kings vii, 7.
[6] I Kings vii, 6.
[7] I Kings x, 16 f.; Is. xxii, 8, xxxix, 2.
[8] I Kings vii, 2–5.      [9] I Kings vii, 12.      [10] *Ibid.*
[11] I Kings vii, 8, 12.      [12] I Kings ix, 15.

Gate in the south.[1] To Solomon's reign also belongs in all likelihood the connexion with the fortifications of the south-eastern hill, which barred off the valley of the Tyropœon. Here was situated the "gate between the two walls," [2] also called the Spring or Well Gate. To bring the east hill as a whole within the surrounding wall was the task of later kings. Uzziah,[3] Jotham,[4] Hezekiah,[5] and Manasseh [6] are all expressly said to have built walls. To this extent, therefore, building operations continued after Solomon's time, and, besides, buildings like the Temple were always calling for repair.[7]

But Jerusalem was not the only city that was provided with new fortifications by Solomon. Among others Hazor, Gezer, and Megiddo [8]—perhaps also Taanach—were thus fortified. Still others were fortified by Rehoboam,[9] and his grandson Asa, after defeating Baasha, monarch of the northern kingdom, had the stones and beams with which Baasha had fortified the frontier city of Ramah removed and employed in the fortification of Geba and Mispah.[10] All knowledge of the ancient Canaanite technique of fortification, which had delighted in brick structures, had been lost in Israel,[11] and all building was done exclusively in stone. Some stones were partly hewn and dressed, but buttresses were built only along the top ledge of the upper rows of foundation-stones. Larger blocks formed the corners, binding-stones being mostly laid transversely through the wall, whole layers of them in unbroken series as far as the large corner blocks. These were laid longitudinally. The joints were frequently trimmed off with dressed small stones.[12] In Gezer more than thirty towers, built with carefully dressed ashlar stones, were constructed to strengthen the city-wall.[13]

This new art of building came to the Israelites from the Phœnicians, who were also expert workmen in hewn stone.[14]

---

[1] See Josephus, *Wars of the Jews*, V, iv, 2 ; Benzinger, *Hebräische Archäologie*, p. 35.

[2] Jer. xxxix, 4.  [3] 2 Chron. xxvi, 9.  [4] 2 Chron. xxvii, 3.

[5] 2 Chron. xxxii, 5 ; Is. xxii, 8–11.  [6] 2 Chron. xxxiii, 14.

[7] 2 Kings xii, 5, xv, 35, xxii, 5.  [8] 1 Kings ix, 15.

[9] 2 Chron. xi, 5. Cf. *AA* (1908), pp. 34, 365.

[10] 1 Kings xv, 22 (Geba = Gibea of Benjamin, the modern Geba).

[11] Thomsen, *Palästina*, p. 67.  [12] Thiersch, *AA* (1907), p. 334.

[13] *Gezer*, vol. i, p. 244 ; Thomsen, *Kompendium*, p. 38.

[14] 1 Kings v, 18.

The Phœnicians had in their turn learned it from others. Peculiar mason's marks have enabled scholars to trace the art back to Crete.[1] In Jericho, on the other hand, the Syrian-Hittite traditions were followed, and a mighty work was carried out there according to a symmetrical plan. The ancient Canaanite fortress was completely covered by a gigantic covering of earth with steep sides. This artificial mountain of rubbish was kept in place by several walls running radially and by walls of boulders running in concentric curves and edging the mound at the foot. All round ran a mighty enclosing wall with smoothed escarpment, and this wall was connected with the city on the top of the mound by a staircase of stone.[2]

The new architecture which arose under Phœnician influence also led to a great deal of castle-building. An example is found in the palace at Megiddo, which is believed to go back to Solomon's time.[3] Here the rickety medley of wall-layers consisting of small stones and boulders held together merely by masses of earth mortar, which was characteristic of the preceding stages of civilization, suddenly changes into an intelligent arrangement of large dressed stones with smoothed bases and fronts, fitted and jointed perpendicularly and horizontally. The edging is carefully finished, and in some cases a kind of bastion edge is found.[4] Not less noteworthy is the technique exhibited in the palace in Samaria, built by King Omri and continued by Ahab, with its well-known ashlar-work and rectilinear joints. The foundation-stones were carefully fitted [5] into the rock base, which had been specially cut out for this purpose.

A structure of a different type was the Siloam tunnel of Hezekiah.[6] It was meant to solve the problem of excluding an enemy besieging Jerusalem from the water of the Gihon, the present-day Well of the Virgin, and to make that water available for Jerusalem itself. A former arrangement, by which the water was brought round the rock [7] in the open, had proved

---

[1] Thomsen, *Kompendium*, p. 37 ; Thiersch, *AA* (1907), p. 296.
[2] Thiersch, *ZDPV*, vol. xxxvii (1914), p. 84. *Cf.* Sellin and Watzinger, *Jericho*, p. 61.　　　　　[3] Schumacher, *Tell el-Mutesellim*, vol. i, p. 91.
[4] Thomsen, *Palästina* (1909), p. 63.
[5] Volz, *Die biblischen Altertümer* (1914), p. 456.
[6] 2 Kings xx, 20 ; 2 Chron. xxxii, 30 ; Ecclus. xlviii, 17.
[7] Is. viii, 6, probably refers to this.

useless in time of war. The task of making a tunnel was under-taken, and the chisel marks on its sides prove that the work was begun from both ends at once. Measured in a straight line from end to end, the distance was 372 yards; the actual length of the tunnel is 594 yards. That means, of course, that the tunnel follows a winding direction. This was not due to any lack of skill.[1] The workmen followed to some extent natural clefts in the rock, and this also explains the variations in the height of the tunnel (1½ feet to 14 feet).[2] It is a tribute to the skill employed that the difference of level at the point of meeting was only one foot. Apart from its great importance for Hebrew epigraphy, the inscription on one of the tunnel-walls is of great interest. It recounts the progress of the operation, and is as follows:[3] ". . . the tunnel. This was the history of the opera-tion. While an excavator was still lifting up his pick toward his neighbour, and while yet there were 3 cubits to be pierced, there was heard the voice of a man calling to his neighbour; for there was a cleft in the rock on the right side. And on the day when the break-through occurred, the workers struck pick against pick, and the water flowed from the spring into the pool, for a distance of 1200 cubits, and the height of the rock over the heads of the diggers was 100 cubits."

Efforts to provide cities with water, which, in a waterless land like Palestine, could not but be a matter of great interest to its kings, led to the construction of large reservoirs, some hewn in the rock, others artificially enclosed; so that we hear frequently of "pools," in Jerusalem[4] and elsewhere.[5] If there is a trust-worthy tradition behind the name of the largest of these, the so-called Solomon's Pool, which lies four miles south of Jerusalem, Solomon must have given a new impetus to this kind of building also.[6]

From what has been said it is clear that the Hebrews were

---

[1] Abandoned galleries do show that the direction was corrected more than once. [2] The average width is about 24–32 inches.
[3] Details in Lidzbarski, *Handbuch der nordsemitischen Epigraphik*, vol. i, p. 439, vol. ii, Plate 21. Also Guthe, *ZDMG*, vol. xxxvi (1882), pp. 725–750.
[4] 2 Kings xx, 20.
[5] 2 Sam. ii, 13 (Gibeon); 2 Sam. iv, 12 (Hebron); 1 Kings xxii, 38 (Samaria); Song of Songs vii, 4 (Heshbon).
[6] The age of Solomon's Pool is uncertain: the water-course is partly Roman (Josephus, *Antiquities*, XVIII, iii, 2).

o

greatly indebted to foreign aid in their building. To an even greater extent this was the case with regard to finer work in stone. A convoluted capital from the fortification wall of the temple-castle in Megiddo, which belongs to the Hebrew period, and which Puchstein declared to be " among the ancestors of the Ionian capital," represents a type that is well known in Cyprus and Phœnicia.[1] Here also, therefore, we come upon foreign influence. The same is true of the ram's horn capitals at Lachish, which probably belonged to the temple of Hathor, the city-sanctuary of the time.[2] Special interest attaches to the incense-holder found at Megiddo. It is of limestone, and its chief beauty is the painting on it, which is in a marvellous state of preservation.[3] But the characteristically Syrian leaf overfall beneath the scooped-out bowl again betrays foreign origin, or at least foreign models.[4] Of foreign (this time Egyptian) origin also is a grave stele and two male grave figures from Gezer [5] and the statuette of polished granite from Taanach (of about the seventh century).[6]

But it was not only in architecture that Phœnician aid in timber work was borrowed by the Hebrews. They made use of it also in ship-building. It was only along the northern coast that the ancient Hebrews interested themselves in shipping.[7] Solomon had ships built at Ezeon-Geber, the seaport on the Bay of Eloth,[8] and his example was followed by Jehosaphat,[9] but the latter's enterprise came to an unfortunate end. The proud name of these ships seemed a mockery. They had been called, after the Phœnician trading colony of Tartessus in Spain, the distant goal of Phœnician mariners, " ships of Tarshish," [10] much as we should speak to-day of " East India liners." When Ezekiel [11] spoke of Tyre as a noble vessel with planks of cypress from Hermon, a mast of cedar of Lebanon, oars of Bashan oak, and a deck of boxwood or pine of Cyprus,[12] inlaid with ivory,

---

[1] Schumacher, *Tell el-Mutesellim*, vol. i, p. 119, and Fig. 178 on p. 118.

[2] Thiersch, *AA* (1908), p. 21.   [3] *Tell el-Mutesellim*, vol. i, p. 126.

[4] Thiersch, *AA* (1907), p. 299.   [5] *Gezer*, vol. ii, p. 308.

[6] Thomsen, *Palästina* (1909), p. 72.

[7] Gen. xlix, 13 ; Deut. xxxiii, 18.

[8] I Kings ix, 26.   [9] I Kings xxii, 49.

[10] I Kings x, 22, xxii, 49.   [11] Ezek. xxvii.

[12] Translation uncertain. See my commentary *Das Buch Hesekiel* on this passage.

he was showing an accurate knowledge of the sources from which the Hebrew drew his knowledge of shipbuilding.

The fact that the imitation of all living forms [1] was forbidden in Israel was an obstacle to the development of any independent skill in wood-carving ; and even apart from this prohibition the Hebrews seem to have possessed little skill in that direction. It is probable, therefore, that even the two cherubs carved in olive-wood in the Holy of Holies were the work of a foreign artist. Unfortunately, we have no information about them other than their dimensions.[2] They were 10 cubits high, and as each of the outspread wings measured 5 cubits across they must have filled the whole width of the room, which was 20 cubits. The inner wings, which were held probably at a dependent angle, formed the protective covering of the Ark of Jahveh.[3]

A later passage [4] gives us a glance into the workshop of a wood-carver. To a faithful Jew all that came from such a workshop could be only an abomination. " The carpenter stretcheth out his rule; he marketh it out with a line; he fitteth it with planes, and he marketh it out with the compass, and maketh it after the figure of a man, according to the beauty of a man ; that it may inhabit a house." Less offence was given by the commissions which wealthy people, with a growing desire for increased comfort in their homes, gave to wood-carvers for imitations of the panelling on the Temple-walls,[5] and no doubt native talent was equal to carrying out requirements of that kind.

The Palestine smithy produced far more than the nomad workshop had ever been able to supply, and its output was of another kind—weapons and all sorts of tools. Tools were now usually made of iron.[6] Even in the days before the monarchy the importance of the Hebrew smiths had grown to such an extent that the Philistines, when they had Israel at their feet, considered it wise, as the Babylonians did at a later time, to

---

[1] Exod. xx, 4.     [2] 1 Kings vi, 23–27.
[3] To the cherubs, originally personifications of the thunderclouds, is assigned in the Old Testament the duty of guarding the divine dwelling-place (Gen. iii, 24), whereas the cloud conceals the dwelling-place (Exod. xxiv, 15 ; Job xxii, 14 ; Lam. iii, 44). They are also mentioned as bearers of deity in 2 Sam. xxii, 11 ; Ps. xviii, 10 ; Ezek. i, x.
[4] Is. xliv, 13 ; Jer. x, 3.
[5] See *supra*, p. 171.
[6] Deut. xix, 5, xxvii, 5 ; 2 Kings vi, 5 ; Jer. xvii, 1. Cf. *supra*, p. 90.

deport them from the country altogether.[1] No doubt this industry flourished all the more after the Philistines had been subdued, because David's victories in the north brought abundance of ore into the country.[2]

In close connexion with the smiths mention is also made of locksmiths.[3] The ancient locks [4] probably resembled the modern Syrian and Arabian ones. The locking arrangement consisted of a bolt with iron studs attached, and when these were down they were raised by corresponding nails in the key. The complicated nature of the process necessitated keys of such a size that they were usually carried on the shoulder.[5]

It presaged a brilliant period for metal work when Solomon proceeded to furnish the Temple with artistic articles made of cast bronze. Among these were the two pillars at the entrance of the Temple-porch.[6] With a girth of 10 cubits, they were hollow, the walls being four fingers in thickness. They were 18 cubits high, and the capital crowning them was 5 cubits high. This capital displayed some kind of lily work, surrounded by network ornamentation, with two rows of pomegranates, a hundred pomegranates in each row. Our text [7] does not give a very clear idea of them. The multiplicity of details conveys the impression of a certain hypertrophy of artistic conception. The altar of burnt-offering which Solomon erected in the outer court was also of bronze. We know only its dimensions—20 cubits long, 20 cubits broad, 10 cubits high.[8] Later it was replaced by another, which Ahaz had made after a Damascus model.[9] Great admiration was called forth by the Brazen Sea [10]—a gigantic basin, 5 cubits high, with a circumference of 30 cubits. The walls were a hand's-breadth in thickness, the rim being shaped like the calyx of a lily, with two rows of knops (colocynths) just beneath it. The basin stood on twelve oxen of bronze, three looking toward the north, three to the west, three to the south, and three to the east. It cannot have been of any practical use: if used as a wash-basin, as has been suggested,[11]

---

[1] 1 Sam. xiii, 19 ; 2 Kings xxiv, 14.
[2] 2 Sam. viii, 8.        [3] 2 Kings xxiv, 14, 16.
[4] Eccles. xii, 4, presupposes that houses could be locked on the street side.
[5] Is. xxii, 22.        [6] See *supra*, p. 205, *note* 4.
[7] 1 Kings vii, 15–22 ; 2 Kings xxv, 16.    [8] 2 Chron. iv, 1.
[9] 2 Kings xvi, 10.     [10] 1 Kings vii, 23–26.
[11] 2 Chron. iv, 6.

it must have been extremely inconvenient. More probably it had a symbolic meaning, and was an imitation of a Babylonian model of the world-sea or of the ocean of heaven.[1] There were also ten lavers,[2] 4 cubits in diameter, for which a practical use can be more easily imagined.[3] These lavers were round, fitted into four-cornered stands of bronze provided with bronze wheels ;[4] the framework and ledges were ornamented with lions, oxen, and pendant tracery.[5] Similar, but smaller, cauldron-carriers have been found in Larnaca and Encomi in Cyprus,[6] and it is possible that Western influences were here at work. These lavers were provided by the Phœnicians, for, as native art was incapable of producing articles worthy of the sanctuary, Solomon sent for a Tyrian artist to cast them in bronze,[7] and he had to make everything, down to " the pots and the shovels and the basins." [8] These foreign models no doubt helped native talent. There was plenty of clay in Palestine suitable for making the moulds,[9] and a tradition, contained in the Greek Bible, ascribing to Solomon the opening of mines in Lebanon is in itself not incredible.[10]

The working of the precious metals also owed much to Solomon's initiative. " All King Solomon's drinking vessels were of gold, and all the vessels of the house of the forest of Lebanon were of pure gold." [11] He also ordered to be set up 200 large shields, each containing 600 shekels [12] of beaten gold, and 300 targets, each containing three *minas* of gold.[13] His large

---

[1] See Gunkel, *Schöpfung und Chaos*, pp. 153, 164. The twelve oxen would thus have a reference to the signs of the Zodiac.

[2] 1 Kings vii, 27–39.

[3] A mythological reference has also been suggested here, a representation of the clouds as movable water-carriers, just as the cherubs which form the ornament on the ledges were originally personifications of the thundercloud (see p. 211, *note* 3).

[4] They were about 27 inches in height (verse 32).

[5] The translation is uncertain.

[6] See Furtwängler's article " Über ein auf Zypern gefundenes Bronzegerät " in the *Sitzungsberichte der philosophisch-philologischen und der historischen Klasse der bayrischen Akademie der Wissenschaften zu München* (1899), vol. ii, No. 3.

[7] 1 Kings vii, 13.       [8] 1 Kings vii, 45.

[9] Especially Adama in the Jordan plain (1 Kings vii, 46, corrected text).

[10] See Benzinger's *Die Bücher der Könige*, in the " Kurzer Hand-Commentar zum Alten Testament " Series, on 1 Kings ix, 19.

[11] 1 Kings x, 21.

[12] 1 shekel = a little over $\frac{1}{2}$ lb.       [13] 1 Kings x, 16 f. 1 *mina* = nearly 3 lb.

ivory throne, with its six steps,[1] was overlaid with the best gold. His successor in the northern kingdom, Jeroboam I, ordered two golden calves for the sanctuaries of Dan and Beth-El.[2] With orders of such magnitude the art of the goldsmith must have made great progress, and a later passage,[3] which is striking on account of the various technical names of the specialists concerned, proves that this was the case. The passage suggests that it was this very manufacture of images for worship—although these were of subordinate importance otherwise—that contributed to the development of the technique of metal-work. It takes us into the workshop : " They helped every one his neighbour and every one said to his brother, On with the work ! The carpenter encouraged the goldsmith, and he that smootheth with the hammer him that smote the anvil, saying of the casting, It has turned out well." The increasing familiarity of others with the processes of metal-working is shown by the prophets' frequent use of metaphors from smelting,[4] and a later age imagined that the entire interior of the Temple at Jerusalem, including all the utensils used in it, was overlaid with gold.[5] But the Hebrews did not stop at the manufacture of gold foil : we also hear of gold thread ; " they cut it into thread," we read in the description of the priest's dress, " to work it in the blue and in the purple and in the scarlet, and in the fine linen, with cunning work." [6]

How far fine carving of ivory, which was used to inlay furniture,[7] seal-cutting, and the working of precious stones [8] were undertaken by native workmen we do not know. Thanks to the excavations, there is no lack of articles of this kind, and some of them are specially interesting on account of the inscriptions which they bear. Among them is a jasper seal, found in Megiddo, with the label, " To Shema, servant of Jeroboam." [9] The lion which is represented on it with wide-open jaws and uplifted tail resembles so closely the figures found in Mesopotamia that we are compelled to conclude, either that

---

[1] 1 Kings x, 18.  [2] 1 Kings xii, 28.  [3] Is. xli, 6 f.
[4] Is. i, 25 ; Jer. vi, 29, ix, 7 ; Ezek. xxii, 20, 22 ; Mal. iii, 2.
[5] 1 Kings vi, 20 ff. ; Exod. xxv, 11, 24. See *supra*, p. 206, *note* 2.
[6] Exod. xxxix, 3.
[7] 1 Kings x, 18 ; Amos vi, 4 ; Song of Songs v, 14.  [8] Exod. xxviii, 9.
[9] This must refer to Jeroboam II (783–743 B.C.). " Servant " might in Hebrew mean a high official, or minister, or high military officer.

it was made in Babylon, or that it is the work of a Babylonian artist.[1] Scarcely less noteworthy is a Phœnician scarab found close beside it, made of lapis lazuli, with the royal symbol consisting of lions and falcons. It bears also hieroglyphics in a sort of royal cartouche, and in the segment below, in ancient Semitic letters, the owner's name, Asaph.[2] The fact that these things were found so close together strongly suggests once more how Babylonian and Egyptian, and now also Phœnician, influences intermingled in Palestine.

The potter's art was undoubtedly widespread. It was a favourite source for metaphors used by the prophets, God Himself being the potter and men the vessels formed by His hand.[3] The potter when at work used hands and feet. He used his feet not only to knead the clay,[4] but also to drive his wheel [5]—the word used for wheel is a dual form and denotes two wheels, one above the other—while he shaped the clay with his hands.[6] Another description shows us the potter attending to the furnace, and anxious to secure a perfect enamel.[7] The Hebrews could hardly be expected to attain the skill of their Canaanite teachers in the finer technique of this art, and the excavations have decisively proved that they did not. " The material gets coarser, the shapes more ungainly." [8] The inferiority of the native manufacture was also shown by its inability to compete with the imported Greek, or rather Cyprian, wares ; these, which came in increasingly from the ninth or eighth century onward, are unmistakable, with their yellow-brown enamel, and the dark concentric rings and circles painted over it. The way for this importation, which was carried on by Phœnicians, was prepared, as it were, by the penetration of the coast district of South Palestine by early Hellenic goods.[9] Among the things found in Jericho a number of beautifully made vases, with an overlay of thick whitish yellow, almost like an enamel, rouse special interest, as they betray plainly the influence of metal patterns. Their discoverer

---

[1] Thomsen, *Kompendium*, p. 65.

[2] Schumacher, *Tell el-Mutesellim*, vol. i, p. 100 ; Thiersch, *AA* (1907), p. 297.

[3] Is. xxix, 16, xlv, 9, lxiv, 8. The metaphor was also current in Egypt.

[4] Is. xli, 25.  [5] Ecclus. xxxviii, 29.

[6] Jer. xviii, 4.  [7] Ecclus. xxxviii, 30.

[8] Thomsen, *Palästina*, p. 75.  [9] Thiersch, *AA* (1908), p. 383.

assigns them to a Syrian factory, which cannot be more definitely located, and which seems to have continued the Cretan metal industry in the late Mycenæan period.[1]

The Hebrews may at first have been unwilling to imitate these foreign imports,[2] but after a time they certainly set themselves to do so. The stamps on the jug-handles found in excavations in the south of Palestine—the first words are " to the king," followed by the names of the places where they were made, Hebron, Ziph, Socho, or Memshath—show that, in addition to numerous private workshops,[3] there were royal factories. These were probably situated in those places where there were close potter organizations in post-Exilic times.[4] The stamps themselves of course again reveal foreign influence. They are either scarabs, after the Egyptian practice, or winged sun disks, in imitation of Assyrio-Persian models. The brick kilns also, which provided the material commonly used in house-building, seem to have developed into something like royal factories.[5]

Among the terracotta figures there are a number of heads that call for special mention. In Megiddo there are six, one of which shows a unique type, with sharply bent Semitic nose, prominent cheek-bones, very large eyes and ears, and hair parted perpendicularly. Two of the others are of a distinct Egyptian type.[6] In Jericho were found a few youthful male heads of red-brown clay. The low forehead, the receding mouth, the angular shape of the face, the prominent but flat eyes—like a head from Tell ed-Judejide—resemble in style the archaic Greek heads from the beginning of the sixth century B.C.[7] In Tell es-Safi the chief interest lies in the excellent head of a Scythian with a tall Phrygian flapped cap and pointed beard, in which we have perhaps a reminiscence of the destructive Scythian invasion of Palestine in the second half of the seventh century.[8]

[1] Sellin and Watzinger, *Jericho*, p. 131.
[2] Thomsen, *Palästina*, p. 75.
[3] In Tell ed-Judejide we meet the names Hosea, Sebanja, Azariah, Nahum, Sebna, Menahem, Michaiah, and Shomer *AA* (1908), p. 387.
[4] 1 Chron. iv, 23. The stamps are in no case older than the seventh century.
[5] See 2 Sam. xii, 31, but the meaning of the passage is disputed. [See *infra*, p. 264, *note* 7.—TRANSLATOR.]
[6] Schumacher, *Tell el-Mutesellim*, vol. i, p. 106.
[7] Sellin and Watzinger, *Jericho*, p. 149.
[8] Thiersch, *AA* (1908), p. 374, *note* 23.

# TRADES AND CALLINGS

In the primitive life of the desert weaving and spinning were the tasks of the housewife, but with the growing requirements of a settled population cloth-making came to be a separate occupation ; at least, the later literature speaks of weavers and workers in coloured thread.[1]  Of course, this did not exclude foreign importations ; [2] still less did it exclude the ancient female industry in the home.[3]  It was in this home industry that the primitive forms of the loom were longest retained.  We have little information about them, but the repeated mention of the weaver's beam [4] suggests an upright loom.  The threads were hung on the loom and kept in place with weights, like those found in the excavations.  It is difficult to decide whether it is only by chance that the weaver's shuttle is not mentioned till a late period.[5]  The law [6] forbade the interweaving of linen and wool.  There was a background of superstition behind this prohibition ; in fact, it was in the practice of magic that mixtures of this kind were used.[7]

A field outside of Jerusalem was called after the fullers.[8]  It lay not far from the Upper Pool, and this was a natural arrangement, for the fuller needed water for his work.  Lye, boron, and soda, which were used in the operation, are also mentioned.[9]  The dyes used were obtained chiefly from the purple-fish and the cochineal insect.  It is probably a mere accident that we hear nothing of leather-workers, for leather articles were known.[10]  The more elegant requirements of the toilet were supplied by barbers [11] and makers of ointment.[12]  In view of the importance attached to the anointing of the body, it is easy to understand that the ointment-makers, both male and female,[13] were kept busy.  We hear occasionally of the ingredients of a good salve : myrrh,[14] cinnamon, calamus, cassia ; [15] or, again, stacte, onycha,

---

[1] Exod. xxvi, 1, 36, xxvii, 16, xxviii, 6, 15, 39.
[2] Ezek. xxvii, 7, 16.
[3] 1 Sam. ii, 19 ; Prov. xxxi, 19, 22, 24.
[4] 1 Sam. xvii, 7 ; 2 Sam. xxi, 19 ; Judges xvi, 14.
[5] Job vii, 6.                         [6] Deut. xxii, 11 ; Lev. xix, 19.
[7] See *supra*, p. 71, *note* 6.
[8] 2 Kings xviii, 17 ; Is. vii, 3.
[9] Mal. iii, 2 ; Jer. ii, 22 ; Prov. xxv, 20.
[10] Exod. xxv, 5.                      [11] Ezek. v, 1.
[12] Exod. xxx, 25, 35 ; Neh. iii, 8.      [13] 1 Sam. viii, 13.
[14] Clothes (Ps. xlv, 8) and couches (Prov. vii, 17) were also sprinkled with it.
[15] Exod. xxx, 23.

galbanum, incense.[1] The mixture was boiled in "a seething pot."[2] Food requirements were met by the bakers[3] and, in the houses of the wealthy, by private cooks.[4]

Those who followed the same calling apparently lived, as far as possible, together. Thus, there was a Bakers' Street in Jerusalem,[5] a Fullers' Field outside the city,[6] and a Carpenters' Valley in Benjamin.[7] No doubt, this was because a trade was originally a clan affair,[8] and was hereditary in it. Thus a child taken by an artisan to be trained and taught his trade was not allowed by the law of Hammurabi to return to his parents' house.[9]

The increased estimation in which handicrafts were held in civilized territory, in comparison with that which prevailed under desert conditions, is apparent from the numerous illustrations which the prophets took from them. They were far more in sympathy with trades than with commerce, whereas the nomads had naturally a greater regard for the latter. The fact that the merchant had originally no settled domicile appears in the names which the Hebrew applied to him. The usual name for him was "the roamer." This conception was taken from the caravans which from times of old had traversed the land, their camels laden with the goods in which they dealt. The Ishmaelites who came across from Gilead brought tragacanth, balsam, and spicery to Egypt.[10] Spices and condiments were especially popular articles of commerce.[11] A typical street figure, then as now, was the water-seller. The cry with which he sought to attract the attention of those passing by, "Ho! every one that thirsteth, come ye to the waters," finds an echo in a well-known prophetic passage.[12] Dealers and merchants were, of course, to be found wherever people were assembled for a religious celebration, just as fairs and religious feasts occur together in heathen Arabia.[13]

---

[1] Exod. xxx, 34.  [2] Job xli, 20.  [3] Hos. vii, 4.
[4] I Sam. viii, 13, ix, 23.  [5] Jer. xxxvii, 21.  [6] Is. vii, 3.
[7] I Chron. iv, 14 ; according to Neh. xi, 35, iii, 32, the goldsmiths also lived together. See also Josephus, *Wars of the Jews*, V, viii, 1.
[8] Gen. iv, 20.  [9] § 188 f.  [10] Gen. xxxvii, 25.
[11] Gen. xliii, 11 ; Song of Songs iii, 6.
[12] Is. lv, 1. *Cf.* Littmann, "Der Cairiner Strassenhandel in seinen Ausrufen," in the *Archiv für Wirtschaftsforschung im Orient* (1917), p. 125 ff.
[13] Deut. xxxiii, 19.

# TRADES AND CALLINGS

All the same, the spirit of commerce took some time to capture Israel. It speaks volumes that even in the oldest legislation, the Book of the Covenant,[1] the theft of money was punished by a fine only half of that imposed in a case of cattle-theft. For a time commerce was left in the hands of the Canaanite, who to a trained sense of the requirements of civilized life united a real commercial spirit ; so that for many a day Canaanite and trader were synonymous names.[2] The rise of the native Hebrew trades dates from the establishment of the monarchy. A bronze weight found at Gezer bears the legend *lmlk*, " To the king." [3] It was one of Solomon's merits that he was discerning enough to exploit the unique geographical position of Palestine and lay tribute on trade in favour of the infant state. He was the originator of the policy of customs, and it helped to fill his treasury. The import and transport trade of horses and chariots was ascribed to him.[4] Unfortunately, the state of the text does not enable us to say with certainty whence they came and whither they went.[5] Further, Solomon was the instigator of considerable enterprises by sea. From the seaport of Eloth, which he conquered, his ships sailed to Ophir (a country which has been long searched for, and which cannot yet be definitely identified; we must look for it in Arabia, or, more accurately, South Arabia, rather than in Africa or India), from which they returned bringing gold, silver, ivory, monkeys, and peacocks (?).[6] Solomon also seems to have encouraged the settlement of foreign colonists in Jerusalem. The temples to foreign deities which he is said to have built for his wives [7] were probably built by him rather with a view to meet the needs of foreign merchants who had settled in the city.[8] As was also the case elsewhere,[9] these merchants lived together in their own districts, and they had, perhaps standing on earth brought from their native

---

[1] Exod. xxi, 37, xxii, 6.

[2] Is. xxiii, 8 ; Zeph. i, 11 ; Zech. xiv, 21 ; Prov. xxxi, 24 ; Job xli, 6.

[3] Palestine Exploration Fund, *Quarterly Statement* (1909), p. 189.

[4] 1 Kings x, 28.

[5] Alt, *Israel und Ägypten* (1909), p. 23.

[6] 1 Kings x, 11, 22. The last word is uncertain. The view, based on 2 Chron. ix, 21, that Solomon took part in Hiram's voyages on the Mediterranean is doubtful. See Guthe's *Geschichte des Volkes Israel* (1914), p. 140.

[7] 1 Kings xi, 8 ; 2 Kings xxiii, 13.

[8] *Cf.* my book *Die Stellung der Israeliten und der Juden zu den Fremden* (1896), p. 75.      [9] *Op. cit.*, pp. 75, 368.

country,[1] altars of their own. We have an example also of how success in war was exploited in favour of new trade-relations. When Ahab had defeated the Aramæan king he acquired from him the right to open in Damascus a Hebrew street of bazaars like that which the father of the conquered king had possessed in Samaria.[2] It goes without saying that under such circumstances Hebrew trade was bound to expand, and confirmation is found in the fact that in the excavation layers of the Hebrew period trade weights are more numerous. The prophets, who opposed with all their might the evils that dogged the steps of this trading, bear involuntary but eloquent testimony to the great impetus it had received.[3]

Of course, when political troubles befell the land, when, for example, the seaport at Eloth was lost, Judah lost, temporarily or permanently, important trade connexions. But something far more important remained, the knowledge of and the love for commerce as such, and this form of activity suited the Jewish national character too well for it ever again to be completely given up. A new impetus came with the Exile. After all, that meant the transplanting of the people to a commercial empire whose commerce was at that time at its zenith. Babylon had come to be a centre of the world's trade, and that trade was so far from being restricted to one class that even slaves frequently possessed businesses of their own.[4] It is not surprising that the Jews profited from this fact, and entered successfully into trade. In the year 519 we read of exiles who were able to send gold and silver to Jerusalem,[5] and we can understand how, twenty years previously, when the Jews in Babylon received permission to return to their ancient home, not all of them availed themselves of the permission thus given. This explains why numerous Jewish names appear in the business archives of the firm of Murashu in Nippur in the time of Artaxerxes I (465–424).[6]

In the Babylonian and Persian periods we find Hebrew and Jewish traders in the markets of Tyre dealing in wheat, honey,

---

[1] 2 Kings v, 17.  [2] 1 Kings xx, 34.
[3] Amos viii, 5; Hos. xii, 8; Is. ii, 7, 16.
[4] Köhler and Peiser, *Aus dem babylonischen Rechtsleben*, vol. i, p. 1 ff.
[5] Zech. vi, 10 f.
[6] Landersdorfer, *Die Kultur der Babylonier und Assyrer* (1913), p. 75.

oil, and balm.[1] The author of Ps. cvii draws a vivid picture of the dangerous voyages of Jewish merchants.[2] In Jerusalem itself about the middle of the fifth century traders were already organized into guilds,[3] and the writer of Proverbs shows the connexion between trade and religion in his significant statement, " Just weights and balances are the Lord's; all weights are His concern." [4]

It is only from an occasional chance reference that we are able to see how business practices and methods kept pace with the development of trade. In the eighth century we have clear evidence of the combination of barter and the use of money in business transactions.[5] That was probably also the case in the time before the Exile. A post-Exilic passage [6] speaks of silver shekels as regular currency. How far back these go we do not know, but silver shekels had long been a unit of payment,[7] and we even hear of a quarter-shekel as a current coin.[8] In the absence of State control, however, the pieces had to be weighed at each transaction.[9] The honesty of the Hebrew trader was far from being above suspicion.[10] At an early time temples took over the *rôle* of banks, at least to the extent of receiving money for safe deposit.[11] On the other hand, there is absolutely no trace in the Old Testament of anything like capitalist finance. As every one knows, the taking of interest was forbidden.[12] The reason was that lending of every kind fell, or was supposed to fall, not into the category of business, but merely into that of benevolence.

Other occupations arose naturally to meet the requirements

---

[1] Ezek. xxvii, 17. The passage is probably later than Ezekiel (see my commentary *Das Buch Hesekiel*). The passage mentions another product, but the name is unintelligible to us. For wheat and oil *cf.* 1 Kings v, 25, and Hos. xii, 1.

[2] Ps. cvii, 23 ; Prov. xxxi, 14, vii, 19.      [3] Neh. iii, 31.

[4] Prov. xvi, 11. How different the sentiment expressed in Ecclus. xxvi, 29 ff. !      [5] Hos. iii, 2 ; Gen. xx, 14, 16 (see Gunkel on the passage).

[6] Gen. xxiii, 16.

[7] Gen. xx, 16, xxxvii, 28 ; Exod. xxi, 32 ; Judges xvii, 10 ; 2 Sam. xviii, 11 ; 2 Kings vii, 1 ; Jer. xxxii, 9.

[8] 1 Sam. ix, 8.      [9] Cf., *e.g.*, Exod. xxii, 16.

[10] Amos viii, 5 ; Mic. vi, 10 ; Deut. xxv, 14 ; Prov. xx, 10.

[11] Judges ix, 4 ; *cf.* 2 Macc. iii, 10.

[12] Exod. xxii, 25 (text enlarged) ; Lev. xxv, 36 ; Deut. xxiii, 20. In ancient Babylon the rate of interest was $33\frac{1}{3}$ and 40 per cent., in the later Babylonian empire 20 per cent.

of family life, as those of nurses,[1] midwives,[2] watchmen, male and female,[3] door-keepers, male and female,[4] day labourers.[5] Others, such as those of gate-keepers [6] and night-watchmen,[7] were called into being by the needs of public order. Others which were created by the needs of political, intellectual, and religious life will be best dealt with in connexion with the discussion of these aspects of the national life.

[1] Gen. xxiv, 59, xxxv, 8 ; 2 Kings xi, 2.
[2] Gen. xxxv, 17, xxxviii, 28 ; Exod. i, 15 ; cf. *supra*, p. 160, *note* 9.
[3] Num. xi, 12 ; Is. xlix, 23 ; 2 Sam. iv, 4.
[4] 2 Sam. iv, 6.
[5] Deut. xxiv, 14 ; Lev. xix, 13 ; Is. xvi, 14, suggests a year's engagement. In Babylonia the engagement varied from a few days to two years (Jastrow, *The Civilization of Babylonia and Assyria*, p. 353).
[6] 2 Sam. xviii, 24 ; 2 Kings vii, 11, ix, 17.
[7] Song of Songs iii, 3, v, 7.

# CHAPTER III

## SOCIAL LIFE

WHEN we speak here of social life we are using the phrase in the sense of social intercourse, and this chapter will deal with the forms of it. We have already discussed family and domestic life ; we now leave the threshold of the home and step into the public street.

In the village, and to an even greater extent in the city, the streets were as narrow as they could possibly be. People who looked to their houses mainly for protection from the burning sun attached little importance to good light in them ; and in the case of a city the fact that it was surrounded by a wall necessitated all possible economy of space. In order to escape the burning rays of the sun people in the street kept as close as possible to the houses.[1] A further reason for doing so was the desire to avoid the dirt of the street—street dirt was proverbial.[2] It could hardly be otherwise, for the only scavengers were the dogs.[3] Those who were too dignified to walk rode upon an ass,[4] or were carried in a litter.[5] To keep horses was the privilege of royal princes, and gave rise to criticism.[6]

The meeting of acquaintances out of doors was the occasion of much ceremony. Our busy age and our Western haste reduce the forms of courtesy to a minimum. Ancient times and the customs of the East attached greater importance to them, and this found expression in ceremonious formality. This is the meaning of Elisha's admonition to Gehazi : " If thou meet any man, salute him not ; and if any salute thee, answer him not again " ; [7] and we find an echo of these words in Jesus' instructions to the Seventy when He sent them forth

---

[1] Ezek. xxxiii, 30.　　　　　　　　[2] See *supra*, p. 34, *note* 2.

[3] Exod. xxii, 31 ; Ps. lix, 7, 15. Dogs were considered to be all the more " unclean " on this account.

[4] 2 Sam. xix, 27. It is only in later times, when the horse was more highly esteemed, that we find the ass used by poor people (see Zech. ix, 9).

[5] Song of Songs iii, 9. The word used here is of Greek origin, so that perhaps the litter itself was also later.

[6] 2 Sam. xv, 1.　　　　　　　　[7] 2 Kings iv, 29.

to preach.[1] In both cases the implication is that greeting takes up time, a great deal of it. It required a profusion of words, and their formal reiteration led to a waste of time which no man on urgent business could afford. To be sure, the Oriental has always plenty of leisure—this strikes the Western visitor still [2]—and the East is so conservative that it has preserved all the formalities of courtesy down to the present day. This is the case to such an extent that we can hardly err if we take the present-day forms of greeting as a guide to the customs of ancient times. The sameness extends even to the words used. The Moslem expression, " Peace be to thee," has its exact equivalent in the Old Testament.[3] The greeting is in form a blessing,[4] and it is felt to be so in Palestine to this day. The Mohammedans do not bestow this greeting on Christians, because they are not considered to be " children of peace." And when Moslems mistake the identity of the person they have greeted they in all seriousness request the return of the greeting because of its important content.[5] What adds to the ceremoniousness of the greeting is that it involves not only mutual inquiries regarding the welfare of the parties and their male relatives,[6] but an endeavour by each to outdo the other in the expressions used. Mohammed says : " If ye are greeted, greet the person with a better greeting." [7] Kissing was usual also, both at meeting [8] and at parting.[9] A remarkable gesture when men kissed was that each seized the other by the beard with the right hand.[10] The underlying conception was that if you thus seized a person by the beard you had him in your power. It was for this reason that Alexander the Great ordered his soldiers to remove their beards, in order that the enemy might not thus take advantage of them. And when Selim I (A.D. 1512–20) was taken to task because he was the first caliph to go beardless he said he had removed his beard that his vizier might have nothing by which to seize him.[11] The extreme of servility

[1] Luke x, 4.       [2] Cf. the Turkish proverb, " Haste is of the devil."
[3] Judges xix, 20.     [4] Judges vi, 12 ; Ruth ii, 4 ; Ps. cxxix, 8.
[5] L. Bauer, Volksleben im Lande der Bibel, p. 168.
[6] Gen. xliii, 27 ; 1 Sam. xxv, 6 ; 2 Kings iv, 26.
[7] See Bauer, op. cit., p. 169.
[8] Gen. xxix, 11, xxxiii, 4, xlv, 14.
[9] Gen. xxxi, 28 ; Ruth i, 14.
[10] 2 Sam. xx, 9.       [11] Hastings, RE, vol. ii, p. 442.

toward anyone was expressed by kissing his feet.[1] In the presence of a superior a man bowed himself till his face touched the ground.[2] This was done thrice,[3] or even seven times.[4] A person riding or driving dismounted in presence of a superior,[5] as, also, did a woman in presence of a man.[6]

Not less striking was the way in which servility was expressed in speech. " Thy servant," " thy handmaid," was the regular way one spoke of oneself, and that, too, not merely in the presence of a superior.[7] In that case, indeed, it was not sufficient, and expressions like " dog " and " flea " were used.[8] Of course, this self-depreciation was not meant to be taken too literally—it was merely good manners. When Samuel suggested to Saul that he was to be king Saul scouted the idea, basing his rejection of the proposal on the ground that his clan was the least of all the clans of Benjamin, which was the smallest of the tribes.[9] But that can hardly have been the case. Various things combine to suggest that Saul's father was actually a wealthy man.[10] This excessive modesty is, and was, simply the Oriental way. Similarly, Gideon's entire history [11] contradicts his own words [12] that his clan was the weakest in Manasseh and that he was the least important member of his family. No Hebrew reader expected him to speak of himself in any other way. In fact, exaggeration of this kind was habitual.

The same was the case with the opposite tendency, and boasting and bragging were similarly habitual.[13] The "boasting oneself " of which the Old Testament speaks so often is mostly used in a religious sense. But the language employed in this religious meaning was simply transferred from the speech of ordinary life ; and a passage in Jeremiah [14] almost shows us the transference being made : " Let not the wise man glory in his wisdom, neither let the mighty man glory in his might, let not the rich man glory in his riches ; but let him that glorieth glory in this, that he understandeth and knoweth Me." Psalmists faithfully followed this admonition of Jeremiah, and the

---

[1] 2 Kings iv, 27 ; Ps. ii, 12. Cf. *ZatW*, vol. xxviii (1908), pp. 58, 193.
[2] 2 Sam. ix, 6.   [3] 1 Sam. xx, 41.   [4] Gen. xxxiii, 3.
[5] 2 Kings v, 21.   [6] Gen. xxiv, 64 ; Josh. xv, 18 ; 1 Sam. xxv, 23.
[7] Gen. xviii, 3 (Abraham is unaware of the identity of his visitors).
[8] 1 Sam. xxiv, 14 ; 2 Kings viii, 13.   [9] 1 Sam. ix, 21.
[10] 1 Sam. ix, 1, 3, xi, 5.   [11] Judges vi, 25, viii, 18.
[12] Judges vi, 15.   [13] Gen. iv, 23.   [14] Jer. ix, 23.

P

Pharisees pursued the same line, till their boasting stank in men's nostrils.  But the origin of this feature of Hebrew life lay in ancient social custom, and its ultimate root lay in the mentality of the Hebrew race.  Not that it was exclusively Hebrew.  Inordinate thirst for glory is an essential feature of Oriental mentality, just as lust of dominion was inherent in the Roman character.[1]  The words that are put into the mouth of the Philistine Goliath,[2] of the Aramæan Ben-Hadad,[3] of the Assyrian Sennacherib,[4] and of the Babylonian Nebuchadnezzar [5] all point in the same direction.

Further examples of the same feature are found in the fondness for exaggerating the numbers of an army, especially of that of a conquered enemy.  Such figures cannot be taken at their face value—they stand simply for a very large number, but are grossly exaggerated.  The same tendency to hyperbole was carried into the words of the Deity : Jahveh promises to make Abraham's posterity as numerous as the dust of the earth,[6] as the sand on the seashore,[7] as the stars of heaven.[7]  It is not to be wondered at that a society with tendencies of this kind was not content to let its yea be yea, and its nay nay.  The oath had a great vogue.[8]  Even the Deity confirmed His assertions by an oath.  Again, gestures were used to heighten the force of the words : shaking the head,[9] clapping the hands [10]— Deutero-Isaiah even uses this expression of the trees of the field [11]—stamping the foot,[12] tearing the hair,[13] rending the garments.[14]  A further development of the same tendency is found in certain symbolical actions of the prophets which do not commend themselves to modern taste.[15]  But this love of exaggeration found other methods of expression in action.  The portions which were served to guests were excessive,[16] as were also the gifts to the man whose good-will it was desired to gain.  When Hazael came to inquire of the prophet Elisha regarding the outcome of the King of Syria's illness he brought with

---

[1] See Birt, *Zur Kulturgeschichte Roms* (1917), p. 17.
[2] 1 Sam. xvii, 8.  [3] 1 Kings xx, 10, 18.  [4] 2 Kings xix, 23.
[5] Dan. iv, 27.  [6] Gen. xiii, 16.  [7] Gen. xxii, 17.
[8] *Cf.* J. Pedersen, *Der Eid bei den Semiten* (1914).
[9] Jer. xviii, 16.  [10] Ezek. vi, 11, xxii, 13, xxv, 6.
[11] Is. lv, 12 ; Ps. xcviii, 8.  [12] Ezek. xxv, 6.
[13] Ezra ix, 3.  [14] *Ibid.*, and 2 Kings xxii, 11.
[15] 1 Kings xxii, 11.  [16] *Cf.* Gen. xliii, 34, and *supra*, p. 186.

him forty camel-loads of valuables from Damascus.[1] It is not necessary to imagine that these camels were heavily laden—the longer the cavalcade the more impressive it was. The entire round of social life was marked by love of ceremony and pompousness.

Life in the country districts was, no doubt, much simpler and more natural. On the way to fetch water,[2] or at the well-head itself,[3] young girls could be met, and from Old Testament examples we know how frankly they entered into conversation with any man who passed that way. His readiness to help them more than made up for the injustice which they may occasionally have experienced at the hands of rude male fellow-workers.

In the city the natural centre of life was the gate. It was here that meetings were held, bargains made, and news of the day discussed. The gate was for the city what the flat roof was for the house. In most cases it was men of standing in the city who took the leading part in such discussions. In magnificent lines Job depicts such a scene : [4]

> " When I went to the city council,
>     and sat down in the market-place,[5]
> the youths fell back before me,
>     seniors rose to their feet,
> the nobles ceased to talk
>     and held their peace,
> the magnates became mute
>     and were struck dumb. . . .
> Men listened to me carefully,
>     and silently waited my advice.
> My words fell fresh on them like showers ;
>     they waited for me as for rain,
>     like the dry clods in spring for rain,
>     and when I spoke, no one would speak again."

Anyone who was anxious to bring himself forward in the public eye was sure to find his way to the gate. The law was administered there,[6] and therefore it was that Absalom took up a

---

[1] 2 Kings viii, 9.   [2] 1 Sam. ix, 11.

[3] Gen. xxiv, 15, xxix, 9 ; Exod. ii, 16.

[4] Job xxix, 7–10, 21–23. [Moffatt's translation, slightly altered.—TRANSLATOR.]

[5] The market was in the square inside the gate. That was the place for public gatherings (see Neh. viii, 1, 3).

[6] Amos v, 10 ; Ps. cxxvii, 5 ; Deut. xxv, 7.

position at the gate when he tried to arrogate to himself the privilege of giving judgment.[1] The gate, indeed, was the centre of the entire life of the city. All important business transactions were carried through there, especially those that required to be legally attested. A vivid description of such a scene is given in the Book of Ruth.[2] The question at issue was, Who was to take possession of the ancestral property of Elimelech and marry his widowed daughter-in-law, Ruth? Was it to be the next-of-kin or the next to him—viz., Boaz? Boaz was anxious to meet the next-of-kin. The story shows us Boaz sitting at the gate, with citizens and others all round him. He waits for him to come—he is bound to come to the gate some time or other. When he does appear Boaz calls upon him to sit down beside him, and summons ten of the bystanders—men of standing—to sit down also, probably in a circle, with the two chief actors in the centre. The question is opened; the two discuss it eagerly, emphasizing their words by gestures, until ultimately the other takes off his shoe in token of renunciation.[3] Then Boaz calls on those present to witness, and the ten men answer solemnly, " We are witnesses "; and finally the whole audience, who have been watching the entire scene with interest, add their confirmation by repeating the same formula.

There is a similar scene in the history of Abraham.[4] At the city-gate of Hebron sits the sheik, with all the signs of mourning upon him. He implores the people of the place—the Hittites of Hebron—to make over to him a place of sepulture where he may lay Sarah to rest. The people around him declare their willingness, and assure him that he may bury his dead "in the choice of their sepulchres." [5] None of them will withhold his sepulchre. Then Abraham rises and bows himself to the people of the land. He knows exactly the place he desires; he asks for the cave of Machpelah, the property of a man named Ephron, and is prepared to pay the full price. Ephron, who has heard his words, raises his voice that all may hear : " Nay, my lord, hear me. I give it thee for nothing." But the reader

---

[1] 2 Sam. xv, 2.     [2] Chapter iv.

[3] See my commentary on Ruth iv, 7, in *Die fünf Megillot* in the " Kurzer Hand-Commentar zum Alten Testament " (1898) ; also Pedersen, *Der Eid bei den Semiten* (1914), p. 53.

[4] Gen. xxiii.     [5] [Gen. xxiii, 6.—TRANSLATOR.]

must not misunderstand this. Buhl[1] recalls a fine analogy
from a tale in *The Arabian Nights*. A vizier of the Sultan is
buying a female slave for his master. " If she is for the Sultan,"
says the slave-dealer, " I must make him a present of her."
Thereupon the vizier immediately sent for the money and paid
him the price. Similarly, the Palestinian seller of to-day is
wont to begin his bargaining with the words, " Take it for
nothing : I give it to thee." After some haggling he names
an excessive price, adding coolly enough, " But what is that
between me and thee ? "[2] " Four hundred shekels of silver.[3]
What is that between me and thee ? " says Ephron likewise,
and immediately the scales are brought to weigh out the price.
And thus " the field of Ephron, which was in Machpelah, which
was before Mamre, the field and the cave which was therein,
and all the trees that were in the field, were made over unto
Abraham for a possession in the presence of the children of
Heth, before all that went in at the gate of the city."[4] The
special mention of the trees should be noticed ; it is of set
purpose. To this day when a piece of land planted with trees
is bought the contract of sale records also the purchase of the
trees ; otherwise the buyer would run the risk of seeing the
seller one day come to lay a legal claim to the fruit of the trees.[5]
In Babylonian contracts of sale it is expressly mentioned that
the trees are included in the sale, and the Jewish-Aramæan
deeds of sale found in Egypt give a very careful and exact
description of the property in question. The concluding words
of the Abraham story are so clearly documentary in style that
it is practically certain that in the fifth century—the time when
the story was written down—oral negotiations concluded with
the drawing up of a written deed of sale. Scribes will have
been in attendance at the gathering at the gate, ready to put
in written form the arrangement reached.

Purchase-deeds are mentioned in Babylonia as early as the
law of Hammurabi. The requirements are remarkable for their
strictness. " If anyone buys silver or gold or a male or female
slave or an ox or an ass or anything else from the son or slave of

---

[1] *Die sozialen Verhältnisse der Israeliten*, p. 94, *note*.
[2] L. Bauer, *Volksleben im Lande der Bibel*, p. 166.
[3] About £50, clearly a very high price.
[4] Gen. xxiii, 17.　　　　　　　　　　[5] L. Bauer, *op. cit.*, p. 166.

anyone without assessor and written deed, he shall be treated as a thief and be put to death." [1]  Two such deeds, belonging to the years 649 and 651, were found in Gezer.  They are—after the Babylonian style—clay tablets with cuneiform inscriptions in the Assyrian language.  As cuneiform writing cannot possibly have been used in Gezer at that time this discovery proves that the use of such deeds in Palestine must be very much older, although the Old Testament contains no example of them previous to Jeremiah's time.  When Jeremiah bought from his cousin a piece of ground in his native town of Anathoth he wrote, as he himself tells us,[2] the deed of sale on a sheet, sealed it, and took witnesses.  Their names would, of course, appear on the deed itself.[3]  Previous to the introduction of this method of attesting transactions by written deed other tangible proof was needed to make such transactions valid.  Abraham, for example, set seven ewe lambs of the flock by themselves in order to attest his claim, as against the Philistine king, to the well of Beer-sheba, which he had digged.[4]  The number seven was selected in view of the fact that Beer-sheba signified "the Seven Wells." [5] By a naïve transference of human customs to natural phenomena God was represented as having set the rainbow in the sky in token of a covenant obligation that He would never again bring a flood upon the earth.[6]  The Hebrew word for covenant was *b<sup>e</sup>rîth*.  Every one knows the significance this word (German, *Bund*, English, covenant) has acquired in the history of theology. This makes it all the more necessary to keep in view the fact that the Hebrew associated with *b<sup>e</sup>rîth* other ideas than those which are suggested to us by the word ' covenant.'  We usually assume that the contracting parties are equals ; but, in the Hebrew view, one of the parties was superior to the other, and it was usually he who *imposed* the covenant on the other.[7]

---

[1] § 7.     [2] Jer. xxxii, 10.

[3] The text distinguishes between a part that is sealed and one that is open (verse 11).  *Cf.* the Babylonian tablets, which were put into an outer case. The sealed part would correspond to the tablet enclosed ; the open part to the cover.     [4] Gen. xxi, 28.

[5] See *supra*, p. 65, *note* 1.     [6] Gen. ix, 12.

[7] Hos. xii, 1, is only an apparent contradiction.  Israel presumes to enter upon a world-policy by making a covenant with Assyria.  It is noteworthy that in 2 Chron. xxiii, 3, the post-Exilic author puts the community above the king.

# SOCIAL LIFE

The Hebrew phrase "to cut a covenant" perhaps contains a hint of the method by which a covenant was made. In Israel's historical period the primitive custom according to which the contracting parties made incisions in their flesh and drank each other's blood [1] had, no doubt, been left behind. But in that period the animals sacrificed at the making of a covenant were still divided into two parts ; and the contracting parties walked between them,[2] entering thus into a mysterious, mystical union, cemented, as it were, by one blood. This may have been conjoined with an expressed or tacit vow that if the covenant were broken the guilty party should share the fate of the animal that had been divided.[3] There is also evidence that a covenant could be confirmed by the parties shaking hands.[4]

In the mind of the Hebrews there was another conception that fell into the category of a covenant thus understood—viz., friendship. Friendship thus rested on a formal agreement. This is a characteristic example of that feeling of the Oriental for formality which dominated even purely human affairs. The Deity was also brought into the making of any covenant of friendship. Thus we read [5] that it was " because of the oath before Jahveh that was between David and Jonathan " that David spared Jonathan's son when he delivered over the survivors of Saul's house to the blood-vengeance of the Gibeonites. The ceremony by which the friendship of David and Jonathan was constituted included, as in other lands, an exchange of clothing. We read of Jonathan taking off his mantle and giving it to David, also his coat of mail and his sword, his bow and his girdle.[6] This reminds us of the similar behaviour of Glaucus and Diomede in the *Iliad* : " Let us make exchange of arms between us, that these [others] also may know how we avow ourselves to be guest-friends by lineage." [7] Such exchange of armour was also common among the Celts. This story of the

---

[1] See *supra*, p. 119.      [2] Gen. xv, 17 ; Jer. xxxiv, 18.
[3] See 1 Sam. xi, 7. The present text is perhaps only a weaker form of an original threat affecting not the cattle, but the owners themselves. An (Assyrian) treaty between Assurnirari (*c.* 755–745) and Mati'ilu runs : " If Mati'ilu infringes these obligations, his head shall be cut off, just as the head of this goat is cut off." *Cf.* Pedersen, *Der Eid bei den Semiten*, p. 110.
[4] See Ezek. xvii, 18, and Ezra x, 19, compared with x, 3.
[5] 2 Sam. xxi, 7.
[6] 1 Sam. xviii, 3.      [7] *Iliad*, VI, 230.

friendship of David and Jonathan—an immortal page of glory for Old Testament ethics—makes up for the striking fact that there is scarcely any other mention of friendship in the ancient Hebrew period. It is rarely spoken of till the late Jewish period. The writer of Proverbs, though aware that true friendship was a rarity,[1] boasts that in many cases a friend sticks closer than a brother;[2] and Jesus, son of Sirach, is never weary of praising the priceless value of a true friend.[3] It would appear, indeed, that his own experiences of friendship had not always been happy. At least, it is he who gives the knowing counsel, "Beware of thy friends."[4] How many are friends only when the sky is fair, and are sought for in vain in days of stress![5] Admit to thy intimacy only one out of a thousand.[6] In post-Exilic days there must have been a pronounced development of clannishness, small circles banded together against others. Actual cliques arose, which became the breeding-grounds of endless evil-speaking and wicked gossip. They were occupied with talk about their neighbours and about things that did not concern them. The tongue must have been the cause of an incredible amount of harm; on the one side intrigues and slanders, tale-bearing and falsehood, and on the other cringing flattery and obsequiousness, seem to have been universal.[7] There was no privacy; tale-bearing and scandal-mongering were rampant.[8] A proverb current in Palestine still says, "What two people discuss together is soon known to two thousand." There is hardly a page of post-Exilic literature in which we do not hear of "the dreadful tongue," and the malice of it makes itself felt even in the pages of Holy Scripture. There we find the "pious" saying all manner of evil things against the "wicked," and calling down evil upon them. It is difficult to say how far this is to be put to the account of the exclusive party piety that marked post-Exilic days, or how far back it goes into the time before the Exile. But, all the same, even pre-Exilic law[9] found it necessary to restrain the evil talk that besmirched the honour

---

[1] Prov. xx, 6.  [2] Prov. xviii, 24.
[3] Ecclus. vi, 14–17, vii, 12, 18.  [4] Ecclus. vi, 13.
[5] Ecclus. vi, 8–12, xii, 8, xxxvii, 1–6, xl, 23.  [6] Ecclus. vi, 6.
[7] See p. 92 of my book *Die jüdische Religion von der Zeit Esras bis zum Zeitalter Christi*, which is vol. ii of Stade's *Biblische Theologie des Alten Testaments*.
[8] Prov. xxvi, 20.  [9] Deut. xxii, 13.

of matron and maid. No doubt talk of this kind abounded at those wine feasts where people discussed everything except the serious outlook of the times. But Amos, who denounces these gatherings,[1] also declares that in the idle and luxurious life that had taken hold of Samaria women not only took part, but were even the ring-leaders.[2]

A picture worthy to be put alongside that of Amos is drawn for us by Isaiah.[3] He shows us the streets of Jerusalem, the decked-out ladies tripping along with heads held high, making the chains of their anklets jingle in order to attract the notice of the passers-by. The Old Testament also speaks of professional loose women. They sat at the city-gate or near it, at the doors of their houses, calling to the men passing that way ; [4] or they strolled through the city, singing and playing.[5] They were known by their mode of dress ; their heads were hidden from sight.[6] The reward they asked was, say, a kid [7]—which also seems to have been the sacrificial animal of the Greek *hetæræ*.[8] A woman of this class gained fame in the history of Israel— Rahab, who treated the spies so well that she and hers were spared when Jericho was taken.[9] The fact that her house— probably a known house of ill-fame [10]—was close to the city-wall was no doubt connected with her vocation. Josephus says she was an inn-keeper ; [11] probably she was. The metaphor in the Apocalypse [12] of the wine of the wrath of whoredom is based no doubt on the fact that houses of ill-fame existed in the form of inns, and in the law of Hammurabi the regulations for the mistress of such an inn and those for public women are found close together.[13]

The transition from nomadic conditions to settled life was marked by the rise of a social distinction between the rich and the poor. Concerning the nomad, Benzinger [14] justly writes : " Wealth means neither influence nor power. At the most, it means the privilege of practising hospitality on a great scale.

[1] Amos vi, 4.   [2] Amos iv, 1.   [3] Is. iii, 16.
[4] Gen. xxxviii, 14, 21 ; Prov. ix, 14.   [5] Is. xxiii, 16.
[6] Gen. xxxviii, 15.   [7] Gen. xxxviii, 17; *cf.* Judges xv, 1.
[8] Lucian, *Dialogi meretricii*, VII, 1.
[9] Josh. ii, vi, 17.
[10] *Cf.* 1 Kings iii, 17, for an example of these women living together.
[11] *Antiquities*, V, i, 2.   [12] Rev. xiv, 8, xviii, 3.
[13] § 108 *et seq.*   [14] *Hebräische Archäologie*, p. 133.

The life of the wealthiest sheik differs in no way from that of the poorest man. They eat the same simple fare : they wear the same humble clothing. Their daily work is identical—it is robbery. Their pleasures are the same, to ride a swift horse, to put jewels on wife and children. There is a very sufficient reason why wealth cannot mean power—among the Bedouins the saying holds good, ' Lightly come, lightly go.' In one night, an enemy attack may reduce the richest to beggary, and there are few who have not gone through this experience once or even oftener. Of course, one single bold stroke may just as quickly make up for what was lost." In contrast to this condition, the higher the civilization of the country where a people has settled down, the more quickly will social differentiations be likely to set in. At first, of course, there may be causes that arrest this development—the common conflict against a common foe, the uncertain hold of the newly gained prize, which its former owners still seek to regain. These tend to keep people together. While a nation is engaged in war or in the colonization of new territory there is not much opportunity for the emergence of social inequalities. There are evidences that the newly conquered country continued for a time to be held in common—that is to say, it was divided by lot among all the members of the community. Again and again down to a late period there are references [1] that seem to indicate that this had been the case, and these references are accompanied by all kinds of efforts to maintain this system of land-holding.[2] To this day, indeed, a portion of the territory of Palestine belongs to the State and is farmed by the entire village—of course, in this case the members of the community are replaced by the inhabitants of the district —while the other portions, those which are situated close to the village, are private property, which is heritable and can be given away.[3]

It is no longer possible to make out the process by which in ancient Israel the transition from communal possession to private

---

[1] Mic. ii, 5 ; Jer. xxxvii, 12 ; Ps. xvi, 5 ; *cf.* the Hebrew expressions to give some one " a portion in the land " (Josh. xiv, 4) and " to have a portion with " some one (Deut. xii, 12).

[2] Jer. xxxii, 7 ; Ruth iv, 3 ff. ; Lev. xxv, 25 ff.

[3] See Buhl, *Die sozialen Verhältnisse der Israeliten*, p. 57. It is also possible that the arrangement of the Sabbatic year is a relic of this communal land-holding (Wellhausen, *Prolegomena zur Geschichte Israels* (1905), p. 113).

property was made.   It is only occasionally that a step in the process can be seen.   Although legend has greatly exaggerated it, there must have been some basis for the tradition of Solomon's great wealth.   That king maintained a Court of a brilliance that had never before been known in Israel.   The people got a near view of luxurious living, and took pleasure in copying it. Anyone who had the faculty of making money had the oppor- tunity of doing so.   A class of rich people began to be formed, and unfortunately landed property came to be accumulated in the hands of the rich at the expense of the common peasant and small-holder.   It was an additional disadvantage to the latter class that, as was the case in Greece and Rome, the right of citizenship was restricted to those who held property in land. Micah [1] describes the insatiable greed of those who " covet fields and take them by force ; and houses, and take them away, who oppress a man and his house, a man and his heritage."   And Isaiah [2] denounces those who " join house to house and lay field to field."   The result of all this must have been a piling up of wealth and prosperity in the hands of a few.[3]   Isaiah declares that the country was " full of silver and gold, neither is there any end of their treasures." [4]

The worst of it was—and the conditions were the same in both kingdoms, Israel and Judah—that these " new rich," giving up all work on field and farm, and leaving all the trouble con- nected with it to paid officials,[5] spent their wealth in luxurious living, in gluttony and debauchery.   Luxury appeared in their houses, which became palaces.   They anointed their bodies with the finest oil.   They reclined on soft cushions on couches inlaid

---

[1] Mic. ii, 2.     [2] Is. v, 8.

[3] It is not easy to estimate the value of money at the time.   Some fixed points may be found as follows.   A slave was valued at 30 silver shekels (see *supra*, p. 164, *note* 3), a daughter at 50 (see *supra*, p. 156).   A silver shekel was worth about half a crown.   The threshing-floor of Araunah cost 50 (2 Sam. xxiv, 24), the hill of Samaria 6000 (1 Kings xvi, 24 = two talents), the cave of Machpelah 400 (Gen. xxiii, 15).   The price of provisions seems to have been comparatively cheaper : 1 shekel for 1 *sea* (2⅔ pecks) of fine flour or for 2 *sea* of barley (2 Kings vii, 1).   1 shekel for a vine (Is. vii, 23) presupposes a prosperous condition.   It is interesting to see that a later estimate (1 Chron. xxi, 25) gives the price of Araunah's floor as 600 gold shekels (each £2 5s.).   This seems to indicate a rise in the value of land. See Buhl, *loc. cit.*, p. 96.

[4] Is. ii, 7 ; *cf.* for northern kingdom Hos. xii, 11.

[5] 2 Sam. ix, 10.

with ivory, and feasted on roast meat and revelled in wine, with garlands of flowers round their heads.[1] The music that was played to them could hardly be heard above their own noisy singing.[2] Besides, their methods of obtaining the money for this gay life were ruthless and unscrupulous ; they harried and tormented the poor, and sold up helpless widows,[3] and when these widows sought justice in the law-courts their oppressors, sitting as judges, made further gain by accepting bribes to give judgment against them.[4] Even kings down to the latest times before the Exile were guilty of this wicked abuse of power.[5]

This rampant illegality and injustice not only called forth the loud protests of the prophets, but also aroused the opposition of people like the Rechabites and Nazirites. These sects held civilization itself responsible for all this wickedness, and maintained that the true national ideal could be reached only by renouncing it and returning to the nomadic life.[6] The prophets, although they heartily condemned certain results of civilization,[7] by no means agreed with this one-sided view, Hosea least of them all. According to Hosea, Jahveh owns the civilized land of Palestine—it is " His house " [8]—and the gifts of the land, its corn and wine and oil, nay, even its silver and gold, are all gifts of Jahveh to his spouse Israel.[9] This is sufficient to show that caution is necessary in accepting the view, widely held to-day, that the prophets were social reformers. All idea of a social question as such was far from their minds. What roused their indignation when they looked at certain social wrongs were things of a purely inward, moral, and religious kind—the contempt for justice and righteousness,[10] callousness and infidelity,[11] false trust in external possessions,[12] the entire turning away from God that marked the life of the time.[13] Therefore they did not set before themselves the task of changing the outward social conditions of their day, but they did demand that justice and righteousness should flow down as a mighty stream,[14] that the people should return to God in love and loyalty and

[1] Is. xxviii, 1.    [2] Amos vi, 4 ; cf. *supra*, p. 183.
[3] 2 Kings iv, 1.    [4] Amos v, 11 f. ; Is. v, 23 ; Zeph. iii, 3.
[5] 1 Kings xxi ; Jer. xxii, 17 ; Ezek. xlvi, 18 ; differently in Jer. xxii, 16.
[6] See *supra*, p. 140.    [7] Is. ii.    [8] Hos. viii, 1, ix, 15.
[9] Hos. ii, 8.    [10] Amos and Micah *passim*.
[11] Hosea.    [12] Isaiah.
[13] Jeremiah.    [14] Amos v, 24.

practise kindness,[1] that they should seek the springs of power in faith in Him alone,[2] and " circumcise their hearts." [3] Their whole attitude meant simply a reduction of all the social problems of their day to social ethics.[4] If in this campaign they specially assisted the poor and the oppressed that could hardly have been otherwise.

Such powerful exhortation to have regard to the poor could not long remain without result. The better instincts of the Hebrew nation responded to the prophetic preaching, and the result was a system of laws for the protection of the poor. Even the Book of the Covenant, which in its original form goes back to pre-prophetic times, contains ordinances of various kinds in their interests. For example, the poor man is not to be treated harshly or usuriously in connexion with a loan of money.[5] Legal proceedings against him are to be carried out with the utmost possible generosity.[6] Further, the year when the land lies fallow—every seventh year [7]—is to be turned to his benefit, and all the yield of that year is to be left to him.[8] Ordinances of this kind were adopted by Deuteronomy, and carried a stage further.[9] The poor man is to be allowed to eat as many grapes as he likes in the vineyard, but he must not carry any away with him ; [10] or he may pluck ears of corn in the field, but he must not " move a sickle unto the standing corn." [11] If at harvest-time a sheaf was left in the field the owner was forbidden to return to fetch it ; and when the grapes and olives were gathered no gleaning was allowed. In both cases what was left belonged to the poor.[12] Again, the tenth part of the yield of every third year was to be kept for the use of the poor—*i.e.*, of the Levites (those priests who had lost their occupation by the abolition of all the sanctuaries outside Jerusalem), of strangers, widows, and orphans.[13] The day labourer was to be paid at the end of each day's work,[14] and when a man who had been enslaved for

---

[1] Hos. vi, 1, xii, 6 ; Mic. vi, 8.    [2] Is. xxx, 15.    [3] Jer. iv, 4.
[4] P. Kleinert, *Die Profeten Israels* (1905) ; J. Herrmann, *Die soziale Predigt der Propheten* (1911).    [5] Exod. xxii, 24.
[6] Exod. xxii, 25 ; cf. *supra*, p. 172.    [7] See *supra*, p. 200.
[8] Exod. xxiii, 11.    [9] Deut. xv, 7 ff.
[10] Deut. xxiii, 25. There is a similar provision in German law. See H. Fischer, *Grundzüge der deutschen Altertumskunde*, p. 92.
[11] Deut. xxiii, 25.    [12] Deut. xxiv, 19.
[13] Deut. xiv, 28.    [14] Deut. xxiv, 14.

debt was set free his master was to give him a sum of money to help him over the first days of his freedom.[1] The law showed a special interest in legal procedure as affecting the poor,[2] and tempered the rigours of the law of lien or pledge.[3] Finally, it interested itself in the unfortunate, not only in regard to the daily concerns of their life, but also in regard to their religious interests—the poor were to be admitted to the sacrificial feasts in order that they also might " rejoice before God." [4]

This strongly marked humane tendency, which is characteristic of Deuteronomy, was not allowed to fall into desuetude. Later legislation re-enacted some of the provisions just mentioned, and even went farther in the same direction. For example, the custom,[5] superstitious in origin, of leaving a corner of a field unreaped became an express grant to the poor,[6] and the enhancement of the Sabbatic year to be a year of jubilee [7] was intended to abolish all poverty ; the law in question required that all property which had been pledged owing to poverty should then be restored, and that all those who had become slaves on account of debt were then to be set at liberty.[8] It is very evident, however, that the Priests' Code here goes beyond all that is either historically true [9] or even possible. The Deuteronomic legislators held the soberer and truer opinion that " the poor shall never cease out of the land." [10] The actual estimate of poverty and the popular attitude toward the poor varied. At times people treated them with open contempt, and did so with all the better conscience as the prevalent opinion of society was that men's lot was in exact accordance with their deserts.[11] But there was also another way of looking at things. Was it not the case (people asked) that poverty was a part of the divine government of the world ? [12] Nay, had not God a special interest in the poor,[13] so that a special nimbus seemed to shine round them as the favourites of God ? To be interested in the poor

---

[1] Deut. xv, 13.  
[2] Deut. xxiv, 17.  
[3] Deut. xxiv, 6, 10–13, 17.  
[4] Deut. xvi, 11.  
[5] *Supra*, p. 71.  
[6] Lev. xix, 9, xxiii, 22.  
[7] *Supra*, p. 201.  
[8] Lev. xxv, 25–28, 39–41, 54.  
[9] Neh. v.  
[10] Deut. xv, 11. Verse 4 expresses a different opinion—there will be no poor in Israel ; but the passage is not in accordance with the original context ; it refers to a time when Israel was spread over the world, and was a power because of its wealth.  
[11] Prov. xiii, 13, 18.  
[12] Prov. xxii, 2, xxix, 13.  
[13] Prov. xxii, 25.

seemed thus to be doing just what God did.[1]  Proverb-writers even went so far as to say that to have mercy on the poor was equivalent to lending to God,[2] while on the other hand to mock the poor was to be guilty of blasphemy against God.[3]  And, finally, linguistic usage in Hebrew teaches that the sum and substance of right conduct was alms-giving.[4]  In proportion as the lot of the post-Exilic community became less comfortable this view gained ground, especially in pious circles.  " Poor," " lowly," " wretched " became titles of honour.  People took pleasure in applying them to themselves,[5] although their main purpose in doing so was to lay claim to the help and deliverance that God vouchsafes to the poor.

There was a similar fluctuation in the estimate of wealth.  Men did not find it easy to give up the thought of all the desirable and attractive things that wealth could bestow,[6] and they saw in it, if not something that was simply natural,[7] at least the special blessing by which God distinguished His own.[8]  But experience gave a bitter contradiction to this theory.  The methods by which the wealth of many people had been acquired were so detestable,[9] the ruthlessness and the harshness,[10] the greed,[11] the arrogance, and the conceit [12] of rich men caused suffering so widespread, that people could not fail to see that the possession of wealth had another side.  Further, the times, with the catastrophes they were bringing upon land and people, could not fail to bring vividly before men's minds the instability [13] and the worthlessness [14] of riches.  And so voices still continued to be heard warning men of the dangers of wealth, and as time went on these voices gained the day.

[1] Prov. xiv, 31.  This thought found frequent expression by Egyptians of the new empire (Erman, *Die ägyptische Religion*, p. 85).

[2] Prov. xix, 17.  [3] Prov. xvii, 5.

[4] The word referred to is s⁽e⁾dākāh, ' righteousness ' ; later it meant ' alms.'

[5] Is. xiv, 30, 32, and often in the Psalms.

[6] Prov. x, 15, xiv, 20, xviii, 11, xix, 4.

[7] The usual Hebrew word for inheritance (*nachalah*) also meant property or possessions in general, as if men had a natural right to property and possessions.

[8] 1 Kings iii, 13 ; Prov. iii, 10, 16, xiii, 18, xxii, 4 ; Ps. cxii, 3.

[9] Jer. v, 27 ; Ps. lxii, 11 ; Prov. xxviii, 8.

[10] Prov. xviii, 23.  [11] Prov. xi, 26.

[12] Jer. ix, 22 ; Ps. xlix, 7, lii, 9 ; Prov. xxviii, 11.

[13] Jer. xvii, 11 ; Prov. xxiii, 5, 8 ; Eccles. v, 9 ff.

[14] Ps. xlix, 17 ; Prov. xi, 4.

# CHAPTER IV

## POLITICAL LIFE

WE have seen that the main bond of union between individuals in the nomadic period was that which was based on community of blood—*i.e.*, it was based on membership in a clan or tribe. From the moment when settled life began that bond gave place to one founded on local contiguity. Those belonged together who dwelt together, and the community of interests that connected those who were neighbours could even become stronger than that of those who were connected by blood-relationship. After all, their main interest now was the protection of the territory that was their common home and the conjoint cultivation of the land that provided their common sustenance. Under such circumstances people were drawn together by the cares and dangers in which they all alike shared, and these were more powerful bonds than common descent or lineage. How under such circumstances this new community of interests can sometimes overshadow the old is clearly seen from the exhortation of the Caliph Omar to his Arabs : " Hold fast to your ancestral connexions, and be not like the peasants of Irak, who when asked ' Whence come ye ? ' answer ' From such and such a village.' " [1] All the same, the way in which the conquest of Canaan was carried through prevented the ancient forms of tribal and clan constitution from losing their meaning all at once. Speaking generally, the tribes went their separate ways, and their individual peculiarities lay too deep to be easily eradicated. We have evidence of this in the characterizations of the separate tribes given in the so-called " blessings " of Jacob [2] and Moses.[3] At first the tribal organization was still so strong that it needed special circumstances [4] to bring the tribes together in joint action. We must not allow ourselves to be misled by the account given in the Book of Judges. It shows throughout a tendency to represent as

[1] *ZDMG*, vol. xl (1886), p. 183.
[2] Gen. xlix.       [3] Deut. xxxiii ; *cf*. Is. ix, 21.
[4] See *supra*, p. 144, and Judges viii, 1, xii, 1.

general undertakings enterprises that were merely local. The more we succeed in separating the kernel of the ancient stories from the subsequent wrappings, the more evident it becomes that many a deed attributed to the various " judges " was really carried out by the tribe to which they severally belonged, or even by only a portion of it.

It was just detached incidents of this kind, in which the inspiring energy of one man brought deliverance to his clan or tribe by a brilliant victory, that gradually undermined that democratic feeling which, as we have seen, dominated the ancient tribal organization of the nomadic period.[1]  A man who had led his people to victory in war easily became their leader in time of peace.  Besides, the Hebrew invaders could not fail to be impressed by the Canaanite type of organization which they still saw in practice.  From the Tell Amarna letters we know that Canaan was governed by separate district chieftains and city-princes, who were fond of styling themselves kings.[2] These separate spheres of dominion, varying in size, having a city as political centre in the middle of a number of smaller localities dependent upon it, continued to exist even after they had passed under Hebrew rule.  Hence the Old Testament phrase which speaks of a city and its " daughter " cities.[3]  We are perhaps inclined to withhold from the Hebrew chieftains of ancient times the title of king because we are accustomed to connect the thought of Hebrew kingship with the national monarchy that came into being when Saul ascended the throne. But it is *a priori* probable that this national monarchy was preceded by various experiments in the form of tribal or district or city monarchies, even if they were no more than attempts on the part of the victorious Hebrew invaders to copy the Canaanite example just mentioned.  As a matter of fact, the rule of a man like Gideon[4] or Abimelech[5] was little other than a monarchy, although Gideon's authority did not extend far beyond the borders of his own tribe Manasseh,[6] and his only real support

---

[1] See *supra*, p. 122 f.  [2] See *supra*, p. 114.

[3] Josh. xvii, 11 ; Judges xi, 26.  These Hebrew cities were not very large. According to Jer. lii, 29, Jerusalem, to modern ideas, was a small town. See Duhm's *Das Buch Jeremia*, in the " Kurzer Hand-Commentar zum Alten Testament," *in loc.*

[4] Note his harem, and the claims of his seventy sons (Judges ix, 2).

[5] Judges ix.  [6] Judges vi, 35.

Q

was his own clan Abiezer, and Abimelech's authority was restricted to the region of Shechem, where his support was derived from his mother's clan. We have, indeed, a proof of the great strength and the long continuance of the political power of the clan in those continual revolutions that took place in the northern kingdom and in the alternations of policy—now leaning toward Assyria and now toward Egypt—that marked its history. These alternations of policy were due to the rivalries that existed between separate clans, just as was the case in Babylon, where her various enemies each found supporters in the clans of that city.[1] This also explains the lasting influence of the " elders " and " nobles " of Judah, in whom even Isaiah recognized the actual responsible political leaders of the time.[2]

The rise of a kingdom—i.e., of a sphere of monarchical rule extending beyond the limits of a tribe or district and embracing a whole nation—was the outcome of external pressure, which urgently called for a closer concentration of the national forces. It was Samuel's merit that he saw this need clearly, and in order to relieve that pressure suggested to the man best qualified for the task the idea of seizing the moment and putting himself at the head of the nation. The words that are put into Samuel's mouth at his interview with Saul,[3] " Thou shalt rule over Jahveh's inheritance and save them from the hands of their foes round about," express correctly what the people of the time expected from the establishment of a monarchy ; and there is no doubt whatever that, from that point of view, it was felt by the people to be a great gain. As a matter of fact, according to the account we have the thought of setting up a king was suggested to Samuel by God Himself, who had graciously looked upon the misery of His people.[4] We must not allow ourselves to be disturbed by the fact that our present text is interwoven with a second account which ascribes the establishment of the monarchy to a popular desire that was displeasing to God, and which looks upon it as an invasion of the exclusive governing rights of God. It is easy to see that this second account reflects ideas of a later time which was completely dominated by theocratic conceptions.

---

[1] Buhl, *Die sozialen Verhältnisse der Israeliten*, p. 39.
[2] Is. iii, 12, 14.      [3] 1 Sam. x, 1 (Greek text).
[4] 1 Sam. ix, 16 (correct text).

Even the choice of David as king was the unanimous act of "all the elders of Israel." [1] And when the kingdom was split into two—and this also was decided by a national gathering—the question at issue was merely who should succeed to the throne, not whether the monarchy as such should be continued. [2] This does not imply that there was no opposition, even in ancient times, to the idea of a monarchy. We have direct evidence of such opposition in the so-called "parable of Jotham." [3] The trees desired to anoint a king to reign over them, but none of the nobler trees would agree, neither the olive, nor the vine, nor the fig, but only the thorn. There was, that is to say, little that was attractive or dignified in the monarchical idea. This view re-echoes the democratic ideas that had prevailed in the nomadic period. [4]

With such views still powerfully at work, we can understand that it took some time for the authority of the monarch to become effective, and that there could not fail to be a trial of strength between opposing influences before his authority became supreme. But the opposition to it was not based on spiritual ideas, although the second account mentioned above suggests that this was its origin. The opposition was natural. It was the opposition that always and everywhere arises between centralized power and centres of power that were originally independent. This opposition made itself felt as late as David's reign. When Sheba the Benjamite stirred the hearts of the people with the cry, [5]

> " No part have we in David,
> No inheritance in Jesse's son.
> Each to his tent, O Israel,"

his words were a faithful expression of the ancient centrifugal tribal consciousness; and the real meaning of Solomon's division of the land into twelve districts [6] is seen in its true light only when we realize that he deliberately drew the boundaries of these divisions so as to cut through the ancient tribal boundaries, and thus broke down the independence of the earlier tribal authority. It was in this way that he became the real founder of the Hebrew State; but it was also a sign that the ancient

---

[1] 2 Sam. v, 3.  [2] 1 Kings xii, 1, 20.  [3] Judges ix, 7-15.
[4] See *supra*, p. 122 f.  [5] 2 Sam. xx, 1.  [6] 1 Kings iv, 7.

tribal influence was not yet extinct when, immediately after his death, the kingdom split asunder.

But there was something else that helped to ensure the victory of the monarchical idea. The East knows no monarchy other than one " by the grace of God," and to God's will man must needs submit. The outward expression of the divine character of the chosen king was his anointing—an inheritance from the Canaanite period.[1] This surrounded the king—at least in the minds of all right-thinking people—with a peculiar sanctity which made him inviolable.[2] But, with all their awe of the king, this attitude never went in Israel, as it did in Egypt, the length of deifying him. To the Hebrew mind the line of division between divine and human was too sharply drawn for that. The wise woman of Tekoa, eager to obtain a boon from King David, might carry her flattery so far as to speak of his angelic wisdom and goodness;[3] and others, using the language of poetry, might call the king " the breath of life " of his people,[4] " the adopted of God," or even God's " son ";[5] but it would be reading too much into these expressions to imagine that they have any metaphysical background whatever. They are merely the religious reflex of the despotic conception of an Oriental monarchy and echoes of the extravagant adulation with which in solemn moments the king was surrounded—as, for example, on the day when he ascended the throne, and at the sound of the trumpets all the people clapped their hands with joy, and broke forth into the cry, " God save the king," so that the earth seemed to tremble at the noise.[6]

The first embodiment of royal absolutism was Solomon. In Saul and David it was still in its early stages. Saul did, indeed, order the priests at Nob, eighty-five in number, to be put to death for having helped David, and no protest was raised by any of those present; but his authority was not yet sufficient to compel his myrmidons to carry out his command. They refused to lay hands on the consecrated persons of the priests, and the King had to entrust the order to the hands of a sycophant foreigner.[7] Another act of violence on the part of the same king

---

[1] See *supra*, p. 114.  [2] 1 Sam. xxiv, 7, xxvi, 9; *cf.* Exod. xxii, 28.
[3] 2 Sam. xiv, 17, 20.  [4] Lam. iv, 20.  [5] Ps. ii, 7, lxxxix, 27.
[6] 1 Kings i, 34, 39; 2 Kings xi, 12; 2 Sam. xv, 10; Ps. xlvii, 2.
[7] 1 Sam. xxii, 17.

—his violence to the Gibeonites—had to be atoned for by his posterity with their lives.[1] Altogether, the picture of Saul's Court and Court-life shows a patriarchal, almost idyllic, simplicity which is hardly in keeping with despotic rule. Under a sacred tree at Gibea was the only dwelling-place provided for himself and the officials around him.[2] We read of a minstrel being brought to his Court [3] to dispel his melancholy moods, but there is no word of any other form of amusement. And even if the tale that makes David this minstrel is no more than a tale, it is valuable in this respect, that it implies the possibility that a simple minstrel might marry the King's daughter.[4] Or, again, take the picture given us of the royal table. Only four places were laid ; the King's seat was at the back wall, his son Jonathan's opposite him, and on either hand sat David, his son-in-law, and Abner, his cousin and " captain of the host." [5] The fact that this captain was the King's own cousin—we have a similar condition of things in the reign of David, in the persons of Joab and Amasa—shows that these early kings were still compelled to find their main support in members of their own clan. Nor must we overlook the significance of the fact that the members of the tribunal held under the tamarisk at Gibea were addressed by Saul as Benjamites [6]—his following was still limited to his own tribe. His place of residence was this same Gibea, his native town, outside whose gates he was ploughing with his oxen when the messengers brought the news that roused him to the decisive act of his life.[7] With such an *entourage*, the ceremonial side of his Court must have been very simple, altogether different from what came, under his second successor, Solomon, to be considered suitable.[8] The sole insignia of royalty seem to have been the javelin [9] and the bracelet.[10] Probably David was the first monarch to wear the crown.[11]

When we come to David's reign we find conditions that

---

[1] 2 Sam. xxi.  [2] 1 Sam. xxii, 6, xiv, 2.  [3] 1 Sam. xvi, 14.
[4] 1 Sam. xviii, 17.  [5] 1 Sam. xx, 25.  [6] 1 Sam. xxii, 7.
[7] 1 Sam. xi, 4.
[8] *Cf.* 1 Kings ii, 19. This passage deals with the ceremonial at the reception of the queen-mother, who played a special part at Court (see 1 Kings xv, 13 ; 2 Kings x, 13).  [9] 1 Sam. xxii, 6.
[10] 2 Sam. i, 10 ; 2 Kings xi, 12 (corrected text). Both passages mention the diadem (*cf.* Ps. lxxxix, 40, cxxxii, 18) ; 2 Sam. i, 10, is perhaps not in all points really historical.  [11] 2 Sam. xii, 30.

already reveal development. It was in itself a forward step when, with great political sagacity, he selected a residence situated as Jerusalem was. With regard to personal matters, David invited to his table anyone who pleased him.[1] His harem was larger than Saul's, although it was still modest in comparison with Solomon's.[2] Besides Michal, Saul's daughter, another wife of David was a king's daughter—viz., Maacha— but her father, king of the petty Aramæan kingdom of Geshur, could not be compared with Solomon's father-in-law, the King of Egypt.[3] Then we hear also of David's concubines.[4] The increased number of these rival mistresses meant, of course, an increase in the number of royal princes to grudge each other the succession to the throne. (An hereditary kingship was already an understood thing.) Intrigues, and things worse than intrigues, were introduced into the royal Court. David's eldest son Amnon fell by Absalom's hand, perhaps for other reasons than that Absalom had his sister's dishonour to avenge.[5] Absalom's own desire to succeed to the throne was clearly shown by his revolt. After his death Adonijah and Solomon contended for the succession. David's intervention, and his decision in favour of Solomon,[6] although Adonijah, as the older, had a better claim, revealed unmistakably a leaning toward despotism. The strong protest aroused by this step is shown by the fact that Adonijah's supporters included some of David's most loyal adherents, such as Joab and the priest Abiathar.[7] It was perhaps another proof of the growing despotic power of the throne that the royal princes now began to have a rank different from that of ordinary citizens. They had incomes for their own use, and were able to keep horses and carriages.[8] They could even have a private celebration of the Feast of the Sheep-shearing, and invite to it such guests as they pleased.[9] Further, the king now began to dispose according to his sovereign will of the property of his subjects and to grant at his pleasure freedom from taxation to certain families.[10] When Meribaal joined Absalom's revolt David gave his property to Meribaal's steward, Ziba; and when, after David's return, Meribaal again

---

[1] 2 Sam. ix, 7.  [2] See *supra*, p. 149.  [3] 2 Sam. iii, 3.
[4] 2 Sam. xvi, 21.  [5] 2 Sam. xiii, 22.  [6] 1 Kings i, 17, 28.
[7] 1 Kings i, 7.  [8] 2 Sam. xv, 1; 1 Kings i, 5.
[9] 2 Sam. xiii, 23.  [10] 1 Sam. xvii, 25 (Saul).

submitted the property was divided between the two.[1] We need only pursue this line to reach one of the objections which those who were opposed to the monarchy urged against its institution—viz., that the king would take the best fields and vineyards and olive-groves and bestow them upon his officials.[2] There must have been some ground for this objection, for even Ezekiel, in his ideal constitution, awards to the monarch a large private estate, so that he might not in the future oppress his people, but leave them their land.[3] It was a significant question that fell from Saul's lips when he was accusing his followers of conspiring against him : " Will the son of Jesse give every one of you fields and vineyards ? "[4]

While the number of Saul's officials was modest, the number under David's *régime* was much larger. There were his military leaders, first and foremost the redoubtable Joab, and later, when Joab had fallen for the time into disfavour, Amasa ; also Joab's brother Abishai—all of them cousins of David. Also he surrounded himself with a foreign bodyguard ; for the " Cherethites and the Pelethites " were not, as was formerly supposed, " executioners and runners," but " Cretans and Philistines," who had been adherents of David since his free-booting days in Philistia ; the Philistines had migrated from Crete.[5] The captain of this bodyguard was an influential person—so much is clear from the part played by Benaiah.[6] The person styled the " king's servant "[7] (*ebed* means ' servant,' perhaps ' adjutant ') seems to have held a military post. The heads of the political administration were the Maskir and the Sopher : the latter was the scribe—*i.e.*, the Secretary of State—who looked after the political correspondence ;[8] the former

[1] 2 Sam. xvi, 4, xix, 30.  [2] I Sam. viii, 14.
[3] Ezek. xlvi, 18, xlviii, 21.  [4] I Sam. xxii, 7.
[5] Cf. *supra*, p. 90, *note* 2. These Cretans and Philistines are not to be confused with the six hundred Gathites with Ithai at their head (2 Sam. xv, 18, and see my book, *Die Stellung der Israeliten und der Juden zu den Fremden*, p. 39). In 2 Sam. xx, 23, Carian is a clerical error for Cretan. Whether 2 Kings xi, 4, 19, really implies Carian soldiers is uncertain.

[6] I Kings i, 8, ii, 34.

[7] 2 Kings xxii, 12 ; *cf.* the seals " Sch^e^ma's, the servant of Jeroboam," (II) and " Obadiah's, the servant of the king." See *supra*, p. 82, *note* 3.

[8] Under Solomon there were two of them (I Kings iv, 3) ; later there was only one again (2 Kings xii, 11, xix, 2, xxii, 3). His place of work is mentioned (Jer. xxxvi, 12, 20).

(literally, "He who brings to Remembrance") was not, as was long thought, the royal historiographer, but the vizier, who reminded the king orally of the business that required attention.[1] In addition to these the king had his counsellors, men mostly of mature years,[2] known for their subtlety, like the famous Ahithophel. "A counsel, which Ahithophel had counselled, was in those days as if a man had inquired of the oracle of God."[3] Was it a special distinction among these counsellors to have the title "the king's friend"?[4] The title was also known at the Egyptian Court.[5] Under Solomon other offices were added, among them a minister of the royal household,[6] and the holders of this office came frequently into prominence in subsequent times.[7] It is noteworthy also that the priests were included in the category of royal officials. The after-history of the Hebrew priesthood proves that this was the case. They were the blind tools of the kings, compelled to obey their master's command, even in connexion with things like the erection of a new style of altar,[8] and to conserve the royal interests whenever the throne seemed to be in danger.[9] Naturally, therefore, the fall of a royal dynasty meant the fall of the priesthood—they were an integral part of the *régime*.[10] David appointed, among others, two of his own sons as priests,[11] and in addition he personally performed priestly duties in connexion with a matter of such importance as the bringing of the Ark to Zion. Clad in the linen ephod which was part of the priests' uniform, he performed a ceremonial dance before the Ark, offered sacrifice, and blessed the people.[12] Similarly, at the consecration of the Temple at Jerusalem Solomon gave from the altar the priestly blessing.[13] It is a question whether the kings

[1] In Egypt "the recorder."

[2] David had one of his uncles among them (1 Chron. xxvii, 32), and Rehoboam was blamed because he took the advice, not of the older men, but of the youths who had grown up with him (1 Kings xii, 6, 8).

[3] 2 Sam. xvi, 23.

[4] This seems to be the meaning of the mention of both in 1 Chron. xxvii, 33. The title is also given in 2 Sam. xv, 32, and 1 Kings iv, 5. Like many other expressions, this was taken over into religious speech, "the friend of God."

[5] Erman, *Die ägyptische Religion*, p. 110.

[6] 1 Kings iv, 6

[7] 2 Kings xv, 5; Is. xxii, 15, xxxvi, 3, 22.

[8] 2 Kings xvi, 10.

[9] Amos vii, 10.

[10] *Cf.* 2 Kings x, 11.

[11] 2 Sam. viii, 18.

[12] 2 Sam. vi, 14, 18.

[13] 1 Kings viii, 34.

derived this privilege from their anointing; the oil used for that purpose was taken from the sanctuary.[1] And later the priests (at first only the high priest,[2] but ultimately all of them [3]) were anointed. In ancient times, of course, any person was entitled to perform sacrifice, even although he did not belong to the tribe of Levi.

The task of raising the money for the maintenance of the Court and the State revenue fell on "the master of the tribute," [4] who corresponded to the Minister of Finance in modern governments. This money was collected partly by voluntary gift, partly by compulsion. But the voluntary element was so fixed by custom and tradition that it was to all intents and purposes compulsory. One and the same word was used to denote a voluntary donation and a compulsory contribution. This of itself gives us an idea of what was meant by "gifts to the king." The fact that some people brought no gift to Saul on his election to the kingship was sufficient to stamp them as worthless people; [5] and it was not advisable, when one had a favour to ask of the king, to come into his presence with empty hands. This principle was at a very early period carried over into matters connected with the cultus.[6] Such gifts at times were of touching simplicity. David brought to Saul ten loaves of bread, a skin of wine, and a kid.[7] When a king paid a visit he took with him suitable gifts, vessels of gold, silver, and brass, clothing, armour; [8] and the gifts brought by a visitor like the Queen of Sheba to Solomon seem to have been of a value almost fabulous.[9] The most fruitful source of income for the king was, of course, a successful campaign.[10] It was in this way that all manner of treasures poured into the country.[11] As a result of his victories over the Aramæans David gained possession of abundant ore, silver and gold,[12] and the Aramæans themselves became tributary. To collect this tribute officials were installed in the conquered country,[13] a practice which the Hebrews themselves had learned by personal experience in the difficult days before

[1] I Kings i, 39.      [2] Lev. iv, 16, vi, 15.
[3] Exod. xxviii, 41, xxx, 30.     [4] 2 Sam. xx, 24.
[5] I Sam. x, 27.      [6] Exod. xxxiv, 20.      [7] I Sam. xvi, 20.
[8] 2 Sam. viii, 10 ; I Kings x, 25.      [9] I Kings x, 10.
[10] 2 Sam. xii, 30.      [11] 2 Sam. i, 24.
[12] 2 Sam. viii, 8, 11.      [13] 2 Sam. viii, 6.

the monarchy.[1] In Solomon's time the number of tribute-paying nations was greatly increased, in keeping with the expansion of the kingdom.[2]

Such tribute was paid chiefly in natural produce. At a later time King Mesha of Moab is said to have paid the King of Israel with 100,000 lambs and the wool of as many rams.[3] The king claimed also at least a part of the war-booty taken by independent roving bands, who, like David himself in Philistia, had thus purchased royal protection.[4] But the king's government could never have been carried on merely with what was thus voluntarily given or with what came from abroad. In the nature of things these sources of revenue failed at times, and efforts had to be made to obtain a steady supply. This seems to have been David's purpose in instituting the "numbering of the people," which was probably meant to be a basis for regular taxation. The attempt failed at first,[5] but Solomon achieved it by his expedient of dividing the Hebrew territory into twelve districts.[6] Each of these had to support the royal Court for one month with the necessaries of life— and this may have been the germ from which developed afterward the "tithe" of the produce of the land and of sheep and goats [7]—either by gifts in kind or, if distance made this form of tribute impossible, by sending money to Jerusalem.[8] A bailiff in each district was held responsible for the due fulfilment of these requirements. Judah, being the king's tribal territory, seems to have been exempted from this payment,[9] and we have already seen that certain individuals also enjoyed this immunity.[10] Solomon's talent for organization was also shown in the comprehensive measures he took to encourage commerce and State revenue.[11]

Solomon's talent for exploiting all possible methods in the

---

[1] 1 Sam. x, 5, xiii, 3 f. [The translation in the Authorized Version is "garrisons."—TRANSLATOR.]  [2] 1 Kings iv, 21.
[3] 2 Kings iii, 4.  [4] 1 Sam. xxvii, 8.
[5] 2 Sam. xxiv.  [6] 1 Kings iv, 7.
[7] 1 Sam. viii, 15. The word ' tithe ' often means tax in general, without reference to the rate per cent. (Buhl, *Die sozialen Verhältnisse der Israeliten*, p. 117).
[8] There is something similar to this in the tithes mentioned in Deut. xiv, 22.
[9] *Cf.* A. Alt, *Israels Gaue unter Salomo* (1913), p. 18 f.
[10] See *supra*, p. 246.  [11] See *supra*, p. 219.

interests of his state appears more patently and also more ruthlessly in the methods by which he sought to bring the personal labour of his people into the public service. He levied from Israel 30,000 forced labourers, and sent them in turn to Lebanon, 10,000 per month, so that they were one month in Lebanon and two months at home.[1] Later reporters could not reconcile themselves to the thought that Solomon had employed his own people for this forced labour, for which they thought foreigners would have been good enough ; and they say expressly that he conscripted for this purpose only the descendants of the conquered former inhabitants of the country, and that he employed no Hebrews for this work ; he employed his soldiers and officials only, his chief charioteers and his captains ![2] But this is simply adapting history to suit their theories. It is a sufficient refutation to say that stories are never invented that record the humiliation of the inventor's own countrymen. As a matter of fact, the people felt Solomon's demands to be a heavy yoke,[3] and they seized the opportunity given by his death to point out to his successor how they really regarded it.[4] It is no mere accident that we hear of a national assembly in connexion with this very matter. The higher the claims of despotism rose, the louder was the expression of the ancient democratic instincts that lay deep in the hearts of the once nomadic people ; [5] and we find these instincts emerging again and again. The resistance of a man like Naboth to the avaricious desires of King Ahab [6] expressed exactly the general feeling of the average Hebrew citizen. Occasionally we see even how the king had to take into account a feeling of this kind in order not to imperil a measure called for by the need of the time. This explains why King Zedekiah, at the beginning of the siege of Jerusalem, did not simply by his own *fiat* order the liberation of all male and female Hebrew slaves, but ensured the consent of those concerned by giving it the form of a religious covenant.[7] That this procedure was exceptional is clear from the words which were subsequently put into the mouth of Samuel, protesting against the setting up

---

[1] 1 Kings v, 14.  [2] 1 Kings ix, 22.  [3] 1 Kings xii, 4, 11.
[4] 1 Kings xii, 3.  [5] See *supra*, p. 122.  [6] 1 Kings xxi.
[7] Jer. xxxiv, 8. See Cornill's commentary on Jeremiah, *in loc*. The introduction of the Deuteronomic law was carried through in a national assembly (2 Kings xxiii, 3).

of a king on the score of the ruthlessness of his demands.[1] But worse than all the extravagant claims of a native despotism was what the nation had by and by to bear in order to meet the demands of foreign rulers,[2] and long afterwards we hear echoes of the dread inspired by the " receivers," or collectors who had to count the money and weigh the bars of gold and silver.[3]

How the individual citizen was affected by the royal taxation, whether it took the form of a poll-tax or of a tax on property, we have no means of knowing. Hebrew history provides an example of both kinds, although both are exceptional cases— i.e., they are examples of the payment of tribute to foreign rulers, and are therefore no criteria for the usual practice. In the one case, when Menahem of Israel bought off the Assyrian king, Tiglath Pileser, with one thousand talents of silver, he imposed on each man liable for military service a payment of 50 shekels of silver.[4] In the other case, when Jehoiakim paid to Pharaoh Necho, whose vassal and creature he had become, a huge sum of money he numbered the people, and each citizen gave him silver and gold.[5] We can well believe that such extra taxation greatly increased the popular discontent, and the fact that at such times the king did as he liked even with the Temple treasure was hardly likely to allay it.[6] And there were still other royal ways of raising money which were felt to be oppressive. One of these was that the Crown arrogated to itself the right to appropriate confiscated property.[7] Another, mentioned by Amos, was " the king's mowings."[8] He had apparently the right to the first cutting of forage, in order to provide for the horses and mules of the army food which in dry summers was otherwise difficult to procure.[9] This right implies the possession of extensive royal domains. The chronicler[10] speaks of special officials, who, he states, were appointed to look after these as early as David's time.

At this point, indeed, we can see how greatly the progress of

---

[1] 1 Sam. viii, 11.  [2] 2 Kings xii, 19, xv, 19, xviii, 14, xxiii, 35.
[3] Is. xxxiii, 18 ; Zech. ix, 8 [" oppressor "—margin has " exactor." The cognate Hebrew verb is used in 2 Kings xxiii, 35—see previous note—TRANSLATOR].
[4] 2 Kings xv, 19.  [5] 2 Kings xxiii, 35.
[6] 2 Kings xii, 18, xvi, 8, xviii, 15.  [7] 1 Kings xxi, 15.
[8] Amos vii, 1.  Gressmann considers the text corrupt.
[9] 1 Kings xviii, 5.  [10] 1 Chron. xxvii, 25.

252

civilization was promoted by the active help of sensible kings. They seem to have carried on agriculture and cattle-breeding on a considerable scale. In particular, the Book of Chronicles says of Uzziah : [1] " He built towers in the desert, and digged many wells : for he had much cattle, both in the low country and in the plains ; husbandmen also and vine-dressers in the mountains and in Carmel : for he loved husbandry." This reminds us of the boast of the Aramæan king Kalamu, a hundred years earlier, about what he had done to promote stock-raising in his dominions : " Men who never before had seen the face of a sheep, I have made the owners of flocks, and men who had never before seen an ox, I have made the owners of cattle and of silver and gold." [2] Sheep and goats and shepherds are also mentioned by King Mesha of Moab (c. 850) in his inscription,[3] an inscription which bears brilliant testimony to his work on behalf of civilization. We have already seen that the kings of Israel were interested not only in stock-farming and in agriculture, but also in industry and commerce.[4] We have also spoken of their interest in building. It is sufficient here to recall the fact that King Omri founded the city of Samaria.[5] A late tradition asserts that Solomon paved with black stones all the roads leading to Jerusalem.[6] Some may doubt this, although it is not out of keeping with his efforts to make Jerusalem the metropolis of his empire. We shall see later what the kings did to encourage the rise of a Hebrew literature.

But the chief part played by the kings was that twofold one which fell to them as leaders in time of war and judges in time of peace. Military successes had always been the rungs of the ladder by which the first kings had reached the throne ; and the fact that the royal title was paraphrased by the name *shôfēt*, ' judge,'[7] shows that judicial duties were looked upon as a main *rôle* of the head of the people. (*Cf.* the name *suffetes* given to the heads of the Carthaginian State.)

Let us take first the part they played in war.[8] We have seen

---

[1] 2 Chron. xxvi, 10.
[2] I owe this translation to a letter from Professor Littmann.
[3] Line 30.     [4] See *supra*, p. 219.     [5] I Kings xvi, 24.
[6] Josephus, *Antiquities*, VIII, vii, 4.
[7] Amos ii, 3 ; Hos. vii, 7.
[8] See my book, *Altes Testament und Kriegsfrömmigkeit* (1917).

in an earlier chapter [1] that the traditional opinion that Israel gained possession of Canaan by a uniformly successful military advance must be given up. But it remains true, all the same, that it was to their military prowess that Israel owed their victory over the earlier inhabitants of the country. They came from the desert keen for war. War was a sacred thing. Jahveh Himself was the supreme war-lord, and " a man of war " indeed. [2] A day of battle was a " day of Jahveh," [3] and, therefore, so glorious that even the sun and the moon, when duly invoked, stood still to prolong its duration. [4] This is probably the original meaning of Jahveh's full name, Jahveh-zebaoth—" Jahveh of the War-hosts." [5] The nation's enemies were Jahveh's enemies, [6] and when Israel marched forth against them they felt that they were doing God's work and coming to His aid. [7] " For Jahveh " was the battle-cry, or at least a portion of it. [8] The ideal personality was embodied in heroes like Gideon and Samson. [9] And what a splendid picture is given us ! Saul, returning from his work in the fields, is filled with holy rage by the news of the humiliation that has been put upon the town of Jabesh. He seizes a yoke of oxen, cuts them into pieces, and sends the pieces throughout the country—" whosoever cometh not forth after Saul, so shall it be done unto his oxen." [10]

And not only did Israel fight for Jahveh—Jahveh Himself fought with them. He sent the sudden " terror of God " ; [11] He threw the horse and his rider into the sea ; [12] He hurled from heaven great stones upon the fleeing foe. [13] And when we find that an ancient collection of lays, comprising songs of war and of victory, bore the name of *The Book of the Wars of Jahveh* [14] the name must be understood in its full meaning. Clad in the terrors of the thunderstorm, Jahveh came in person from Sinai [15] to fight against His foes. He Himself marched at the head of the army, [16] and even the Deuteronomic legislator speaks of

---

[1] See *supra*, p. 143.    [2] Exod. xv, 3.    [3] Zeph. i, 16.    [4] Josh. x, 12.
[5] See *supra*, p. 129 f. Of course, angels and stars and all cosmic phenomena were viewed under the figure of an army of Jahveh (Josh. v, 13 ; Is. xl, 26), and later generations may have understood the name in this sense, so that it became for them the name of God as the Almighty (*cf.* LXX).
[6] Judges v, 31 ; 1 Sam. xxx, 26.    [7] Judges v, 23.
[8] Judges vii, 18, 20.    [9] Judges xv, 16.    [10] 1 Sam. xi, 7.
[11] Gen. xxxv, 5 ; Exod. xxiii, 27 ; etc.    [12] Exod. xv, 1, 21.
[13] Josh. x, 11.    [14] Num. xxi, 14.    [15] Judges v, 4.    [16] 2 Sam. v, 24.

Jahveh's literal presence in the camp, and exhorts the army to keep it clean from all impurity.[1]  Or, again, the Deity was carried in one of His forms of manifestation, or in one of His places of abode, into battle.  When things were going sorely against them the Israelites fetched the Ark of Jahveh,[2] and it is one of the things that impress us to see how unquestionably they felt that, with this Ark in their midst, they had the presence of God Himself.[3]  On other occasions an ephod, an image of the Deity, accompanied the Hebrew army,[4] and in the same war the Philistines took the field accompanied by their " gods." [5]  A priest also accompanied the army to serve the ephod, and with the aid of it he gave an oracle as to when and where the attack should be made, and whether it would meet with success.[6]  It was a further token of God's interest in the fight that He did not leave His people without a token of His presence.  By the rustling in the leaves of the mulberry-trees David knew the moment when Jahveh was advancing and calling upon him to follow.[7]  By omens of all kinds,[8] dreams,[9] and revelation through His prophets [10] He made Himself heard.  Sometimes, even, He was induced by a magical incantation to declare His will—as often as the King of Israel at the bidding of the prophet strikes the earth with his arrows so often shall he defeat his Aramæan foe.[11]  In this way primitive magical ideas survived unopposed under the cloak of the faith of Jahveh.  The miraculous power of Moses' rod was also attributed to Jahveh's direct influence—when held aloft it brought defeat on the enemy.[12]  And many a Hebrew warrior, like those Midianites who fought against Gideon,[13] and even like the Jewish soldiers who followed Judas Maccabæus [14] centuries afterward, looked upon an amulet as a direct guarantee of divine aid.

Seeing that war was in so pronounced a fashion the cause of

---

[1] Deut. xxiii, 10 ; Num. v, 3.    [2] 1 Sam. iv, 4.    [3] 1 Sam. iv, 7.

[4] 1 Sam. xiv, 3, xxiii, 6. It is possible that even Israel's banners (Exod. xvii, 16) had their origin in such war idols (Schwally, *Semitische Kriegsaltertümer*, vol. i (1901), p. 16 f.).    [5] 2 Sam. v, 21.

[6] 1 Sam. xiv, 37, xxiii, 2, 9, xxx, 7 f. ; Ezek. xxi, 26.

[7] 2 Sam. v, 24 ; see *supra*, p. 110.

[8] Judges vi, 36 ; 1 Sam. xiv, 10.

[9] Judges vii, 13.    [10] 1 Kings xxii, 13.

[11] 2 Kings xiii, 17.  Analogies are given by Schwally, *op. cit.*, p. 22.

[12] Exod. xvii, 9 ; *cf.* Josh. viii, 18, 26.

[13] Judges viii, 26.

[14] 2 Macc. xii, 40.

God, every one who took part in it had to consecrate himself—
*i.e.*, he passed out of the sphere of secular life into the condition
of sanctity.[1] Sometimes the overwhelming power of the
" Spirit " of itself called forth the warrior and consecrated him
for his new calling ; [2] otherwise careful preparation was required.
The warrior abstained from sexual intercourse ; [3] he fasted,[4]
anointed his weapons,[5] and offered sacrifice.[6] In one instance
the sacrifice seems to have taken the form of a libation of water,[7]
and this raises the question whether the drinking of water was
not a symbolic representation of the warrior's obligation to
abstain from wine.[8] In that case, they shared this obligation
with the so-called Nazirites ; [9] and there was a second point of
resemblance between them—the warriors allowed their hair to
grow during a campaign.[10] Something like a sacred vow seemed
to be upon them while they were in the field. The prohibition
against sexual intercourse held good as long as the war lasted.
This is the explanation of the refusal of the upright Uriah to
visit his wife Bath-sheba, much as David desired him to do so.[11]
This same prohibition may also explain why in the Hebrew
accounts of military operations no mention is made of the viola-
tion of women, although they are not silent regarding other
horrors.[12] Such prohibitions were no mere dead forms. The
consciousness that they were fighting in the name of Jahveh and
along with Him fanned into flame their sacred enthusiasm, and
the feeling that each victory was a fresh proof of Jahveh's aid [13]
kept it at full strength. Songs were sung over the tens of
thousands that David slew,[14] and even in Isaiah's picture of the
future strikingly martial notes are heard when the prophet calls
to mind the " day of Midian," [15] when Gideon defeated the
Midianite invaders, or when he speaks of the " joy of dividing
the spoil." [16] The warlike people of Assyria he paints in

---

[1] Is. xiii, 3 ; Joel iii, 9.  [2] Judges iii, 10 ; 1 Sam. xi, 6.

[3] 1 Sam. xxi, 5.  [4] Judges xx, 26 ; 1 Sam. vii, 6.

[5] Is. xxi, 5. The anointing of the shield (2 Sam. i, 21) seems to have had
a different purpose.

[6] Judges xx, 26 ; 1 Sam. xiii, 9, xiv, 32.  [7] 1 Sam. vii, 6.

[8] Schwally, *op. cit.*, p. 58.  [9] See *supra*, pp. 140, 184.

[10] Judges v, 2 (a probable translation), xiii, 5. *Cf.* " the long-haired
Achæans " [*Iliad* II, 11, 28, and Ps. lxviii, 21—Translator].

[11] 2 Sam. xi, 8 ff.  [12] 2 Kings xv, 16.

[13] The Hebrew for ' aid ' often means ' victory.'

[14] 1 Sam. xviii, 7, xxi, 12.  [15] Is. ix, 3.  [16] Is ix, 2.

brilliant colours, as if he himself delighted in them.[1]   And an ancient writer thought such prowess in war so desirable that he explained the presence of Canaanite remnants in Israel by saying that God had left them in the land to train in the arts of war those Hebrew clans who had known nothing of the earlier struggles.[2]   How well the art of war had been learned in Israel is evident from the fact that Israel was able to send a surplus of men keen for war as auxiliaries to Egypt.[3]

Gradually, however, a love for the peaceful tasks of husbandry began to undermine these warlike instincts, and the ideal condition came to be that in which swords would be beaten into ploughshares and spears into pruning-hooks,[4] in which every man would sit in safety under his own vine and fig-tree,[5] and the people have rest from all their enemies round about.[6] According to later theological thinking, that was the essential preliminary to the erection of a temple that would please God and to the inauguration of the one legitimate form of worship.[7] This breach with the ancient war-religion of Israel was helped on by the prophets, with their message—subverting what had been the faith of the people till now—that Jahveh was in the camp of the enemy.[8]   That meant that His cause was no longer the nation's cause, and that the nation's enemies were no longer His enemies.   And did it not seem as if events themselves, by bringing about the downfall of the State both north and south, mocked the ancient conception of the solidarity in war of Israel and Jahveh?   Their defensive strength had failed, and they passed into exile, a broken people.   Among those thus deported special mention is made of the smiths.[9]   These were the men who were experts at making weapons.   Besides, what further use was there for weapons?   Who can tell how many had changed their minds like Ezekiel, who declared that the nation could do nothing better with the weapons which the defeat of Gog had brought into its possession than to burn them with fire through years?[10]

---

[1] Is. v, 26–29.          [2] Judges iii, 2.

[3] Deut. xvii, 16, and Eduard Meyer, *Der Papyrusfund von Elephantine* (1912), p. 32 ff.          [4] Is. ii, 4 ; Mic. iv, 3.

[5] 1 Kings v, 5 ; 2 Kings xviii, 31 ; Mic. iv, 4 ; Zech. iii, 10.

[6] 1 Kings viii, 56.          [7] Deut. xii, 9 ff. ; 1 Chron. xxii, 9 f.

[8] See Gunkel in *Die Internationale Monatsschrift*, vol. ix (1915), p. 746.

[9] 2 Kings xxiv, 14 ; cf. *supra*, p. 211.          [10] Ezek. xxxix, 9.

R

From the Exile some returned, but not as they had gone away. Their life now was that of a religious community, gathered round their sanctuary and the interests of their cultus. It is instructive to observe how, under the altered conditions, the ancient stock phrases of war were increasingly converted into religious technical terms.[1] The word for war-service itself took on the meaning of holy service, *militia sacra*; the ancient war-cry became the call to worship; the war-trumpet, at whose sound the nation gathered ready for battle, became the instrument of peace, blown by the priest as a call to worship. It was as if that later age knew war only at a distance. However many foreign armies might traverse the land, they were allowed to pursue their work of war; the nation waited for the intervention of God which the need of the time required. With an exclusiveness that was splendidly complacent, the divine aid was conceived so one-sidedly that the people persuaded themselves and each other that there was nothing for them to do but look on as spectators of the great doings of God; [2] at most they could raise the war-cry and blow the trumpets, and under their magical spell even the stoutest walls must fall.[3] But it was chiefly spiritual forces, like prayer and sacrifice, that were the infallible means to prevail with God, who gave victory to His people without further assistance from them.[4] One has only to read the astoundingly inaccurate accounts of battles of this later time—the incredible numbers mentioned [5] are eloquent—and compare them with the ancient Song of Deborah [6] to be convinced that times have changed.

But, for all that, vengeance and hate of the foe, which had steeled for war the arm of the young and lusty nation, did not disappear. They now guided the pens of busy writers, like the author of the Book of Esther and others, and intoxicated their minds with imaginary pictures of bloodshed. Writings continued to appear that seemed to breathe the very spirit of war. The ancient promise of peace was reversed, " Beat your ploughshares into swords and your pruning-hooks into spears," [7] and a curse was invoked upon him that " kept back his sword from

---

[1] *Cf.* Wellhausen, *Israelitische und jüdische Geschichte* (1904), p. 184.
[2] 2 Chron. xx.      [3] Josh. vi.      [4] 2 Chron. xiv, 9 ff.
[5] 1 Chron. v, 21 ; 2 Chron. xiii, 17.
[6] Judges v.      [7] Joel iii, 10.

blood." [1] Nor did they stop at words. Lagarde said with justice that every nation can show more than one blossoming of its characteristic qualities. Thus, when oppression came the latent strength of the enslaved Jews found elemental expression in the heroism of the Maccabees and again in a glorious defence against Rome. But the final victory which ensured the continuance of Judaism was gained not by men of the sword, but by men of the pen and of intellect.

Returning to the ancient period, the expressions of frank joy in martial success must not mislead us as to the imperfections that marked the waging of war and the cruelty that stained it. In comparison with the strategy of the Canaanites, who with their bronze and iron war-chariots and sledges long continued to maintain their superiority in the plains, the Israelites were mere beginners ; but they were ready learners, and by and by they not only captured the fortresses of the Canaanites, but built others of their own. [2] The equipment of the individual soldier was either the sling of the simple herdsman [3] or the club, [4] bow, and arrows (and poetical metaphors prove that they were also acquainted with the practice of poisoning the arrows [5]) ; by and by came sword and javelin [6] as weapons of attack, with shield and coat of mail [7] and helmet [8] as defensive armour. The shields used seem to have varied greatly in size—at least, Solomon had his shields of gold made of very various weights. [9] Probably they were usually made of wood, for they could be burned. [10] The introduction of war-chariots and of war-horses was traced back to Solomon, [11] whereas David knew so little what to do with the horses captured from the Syrians that he ordered them to be houghed—*i.e.*, the sinews of their feet were severed. [12] The name "three men" [13] applied to those who fought in the chariots

---

[1] Jer. xlviii, 10. The favourite saying of Gregory VII !

[2] See *supra*, p. 207.

[3] 1 Sam. xvii, 40, reproduced as a metaphor in xxv, 29.

[4] Jer. li, 20 ; Prov. xxv, 18.

[5] Job vi, 4.

[6] 131 javelin-points were found in one grave.

[7] 1 Sam. xvii, 38 ; 1 Kings xxii, 34 (a Hebrew coat of mail was found in Tell Sakarije. Its dainty iron scales had been attached with bronze wire to a leathern doublet (*AA*, 1908, p. 357)).

[8] Is. lix, 17 ; 2 Chron. xxvi, 14.

[9] *Supra*, p. 213.      [10] Ezek. xxxix, 9.

[11] 1 Kings x, 26.      [12] 2 Sam. viii, 4.      [13] Hebrew *shalîsh*.

seems to imply that the Hebrew war-chariots [1] required three men. But Solomon's innovation, although it was pushed with great energy—his chariots were said to number 1400 and his horsemen 12,000 [2]—met with opposition. [3] A passage in the law [4] contains a late protest against their use. Opinion only began to change about the middle period of the monarchy. Isaiah's words [5] reveal how completely the political leaders of his day were intoxicated with the thought that their alliance with Egypt would enable them to ride on horses and in chariots. Now, as before, the decision of a battle depended to a large extent on the bravery of the individual soldier ; the actual contest was hand to hand, fought out by individuals. Occasionally a battle was preceded by a sanguinary contest between champions, [6] the outcome of which was read as an omen. Naturally, also, when the equipment for war was far from sufficient, recourse was had to stratagem. Night attacks, ambuscades, and various wiles to deceive the enemy were frequently practised. [7]

Originally every fit man was liable to be called for war-service —the Priests' Code says [8] " from twenty years of age and upward." This obligation, however, was to begin with only a moral one. No other compulsion than that of honour and custom was known to antiquity. The condemnation in the Song of Deborah of the conduct of some tribes in absenting themselves from the fight against Sisera is entirely of this kind—these tribes were held up to scorn and cursed. [9] And when Saul imperiously called upon Israel to follow him to rescue the hard-pressed city of Jabesh [10] he depended only on his power to arouse the national spirit. Certain regulations concerning exemption from service were made by the Deuteronomic law. [11] Whoever had built a new house and had not yet consecrated it ; whoever had planted a vineyard and had not yet begun to enjoy the fruit of it ; whoever had married a wife and had not yet taken her to his house ; nay, whoever was faint of heart was to return home. [12] These regulations—at least, the first three—are nowadays ascribed to an

---

[1] Eduard Meyer, *Reich und Kultur der Chetiter*, p. 13.
[2] 1 Kings x, 26.     [3] See *supra*, p. 197.     [4] Deut. xvii, 16.
[5] Is. xxx, 16, xxxi, 1 ; *cf.* Hos. xiv, 3 ; Mic. v, 8 f.     [6] 2 Sam. ii, 14.
[7] Josh. viii, 4 ff. ; Judges vii, 15 ff.     [8] Num. i, 3.
[9] Judges v, 16, 23.     [10] See *supra*, p. 254.     [11] Deut. xx, 5 ff.
[12] Among the Amazulu the newly married man does not go to war (Schwally, *op. cit.*, p. 78).

increase of humane feeling in the law-giver's day ; but this is not the true explanation of the motives that underlay the legislation. These motives are rather to be sought in the region of faith and of superstition. War was sacred to Jahveh ; therefore only he could take part in it who had not been drawn under the ban of a cult originally alien to Jahveh. But it was a primitive conception that whoever had begun to build a house, or had planted a vineyard,[1] or betrothed himself to a wife had thereby entered into quite definite relations with demons ; and these watched jealously lest they should be cheated of any claim they had upon a man, and took dreadful vengeance if they were thus deprived of their due. That Protesilaus was the first Greek to fall before Troy was ascribed to the wrath of a *jinn*, who thus took vengeance on him because he had left his house at home unfinished.[2] And the dread of such demonic intervention was all the greater because it was believed that those in the vicinity of the guilty man might be involved in his doom. The fact that the law above mentioned puts the timid man on a level with the others shows that fear was looked upon as a result of demonic influence, and this view finds its best parallel in the Greek conception of ' panic ' terror.

Speaking generally, little importance can be attached to the figures given as representing the strength of armies.[3] Their trustworthiness increases in inverse ratio to their size. For example, the statement that Gideon in his fight against the Midianites had only 300 men at his disposal [4] makes a good impression. But it is in connexion with this story that we can see with great clearness the tendency to overstate numbers originally small. To a later historian it seemed impossible that only 300 men should have gathered round Gideon, and he proceeds to show his like-minded reader that this number, 300, which was the number actually given in the ancient source, was reached by the reduction of a number which was originally much higher—32,000. That in so doing he makes 22,000 faint-hearted men withdraw is again a proof of the degree to which the ancient military ideals had faded in the later time.[5]

---

[1] See *supra*, p. 72.　　　　　[2] *Iliad*, II, 698 ff.
[3] See *supra*, p. 226.　　　　　[4] Judges vii, 16.
[5] For the method by which the sifting of the remaining 10,000 was carried out see Mez in *ZatW*, vol. xxi (1901), p. 198.

In the days before the monarchy the leadership belonged to the man who was conscious of possessing special gifts of courage and initiative (according to the Old Testament idea this consciousness was the result of a special measure of the divine spirit) ; after the institution of the monarchy the *rôle* of leadership naturally fell to the king as such. A standing force of armed men was part of the king's *entourage*. Of Saul we are told [1] that whenever he saw any strong man or any valiant man he took him unto him. We have already spoken of David's Cherethites and Pelethites. It is clear that the formation of a strong royal bodyguard was another step in the direction of restricting the influence of the ancient clans, although landowners [2] were still required to provide a militia. But the leaders of bodies of troops, both great and small—not only the commander and his " scribe,"[3] but the " officers over 1000, over 100, and over 50 "—were selected by the king directly, and he had means and methods of disposing of them at his pleasure.[4] When once war had been resolved upon express messengers carried the news throughout the country.[5] Everywhere was heard the sound of the trumpet ; [6] the standard was lifted up so as to be visible from afar,[7] and it perhaps indicated the direction in which the enemy lay.[8] It was the main mustering-place, and from the country men gathered to the nearest city for joint action.[9] Apparently each city sent its men as a separate unit.[10] Here once more we find that territorial arrangements had displaced the older clan associations. The local connexion of the men was still kept up by the manner in which the feeding of the army was carried out. Either the men going to war set up a service of their own so as to get provisions from home,[11] or the relatives left at home sent food after them into the field so far as that was possible.[12]

There was a season for taking the field.[13] " The time when

---

[1] I Sam. xiv, 52.

[2] Hence their name *ish chajil* = " the armed man " = the " capable " or " rich man."

[3] 2 Kings xxv, 19, and Jer. lii, 25, in the better reading.

[4] I Sam. viii, 12, xviii, 13 ; 2 Sam. xviii, 1.

[5] I Sam. xi, 7.

[6] I Sam. xiii, 3 ; Ezek! vii, 14.

[7] Is. v, 26, xi, 12.

[8] Jer. iv, 6, li, 12.

[9] Jer. iv, 5.

[10] Amos v, 3.

[11] Judges xx, 10.

[12] I Sam. xvii, 17.

[13] Eccles. iii, 8, in the special sense!

kings go forth to battle "[1] was the spring-time ; in winter war was usually suspended. Seeing that war was a sacred thing, to return from it meant a return to ordinary life. It was analogous to the termination of a vow. The taboo was raised, and sacrifice was offered.[2] Later theological views demanded in addition to this, or in place of it, a thorough purification from all "uncleanness" which might have been contracted by contact with the slain,[3] and this demand was not confined to the person of the warrior, but extended to his clothing and all parts of his equipment.[4]

The lot of the vanquished was a hard one. The idea that war was sacred to Jahveh entered also into the method of waging it. All booty, including living beings, was forfeit to Jahveh. That was the custom of the so-called 'ban.'[5] Its sacrificial character cannot be disputed. Like any other sacrificial offering, it could be devoted to the Deity ;[6] and whoever took for his own use any portion of it was guilty of sacrilege.[7] This same custom is met with among Israel's neighbours and among Israel's kindred peoples, and in all cases it has this unmistakable sacrificial character. Mesha, King of Moab, tells us on his inscription that he devoted the inhabitants of the cities Nebo and Ataroth to his god Chemosh—*i.e.*, he put them to death in honour of that deity.[8] And Al-Harith ibn 'Amr, Prince of the Ghassanides, called on his gods when he was burning his enemies in their name.[9] The Hebrew ban passed through many changes. The strictest form of it was that practised in the ancient days.[10] At that period every human being was put to death, either with the sword or with the rope ;[11] even the animals were killed, and all inanimate booty was committed to the fire, except what was brought into the sanctuary as a votive offering.[12] Saul's attitude toward Agag, King of the Amalekites,[13] indicates already a tendency toward a modification of the cruel practice. He spared

---

[1] 2 Sam. xi, 1.
[2] Num. vi, 13.
[3] Num. xxxi, 19, xix, 13.
[4] Num. xxxi, 20.
[5] Hebrew *herem* ; cf. *supra*, p. 144.
[6] Num. xxi, 2.
[7] Josh. vii, 11.
[8] Lines 11 and 16.
[9] Schwally, *op. cit.*, p. 35.
[10] Deut. xiii, 16, xx, 16.
[11] Josh. viii, 29, x, 26. *Cf.* 1 Kings xx, 32, where captured troops of Ben-Hadad appear before Ahab with ropes round their necks.
[12] Num. xxxi, 50 ; Josh. vi, 19 ; 1 Sam. xxi, 10, xxxi, 10 ; 2 Sam. viii, 11.
[13] 1 Sam. xv, 9.

the King's life, and left to the people the best of the sheep and oxen, as well as the most valuable articles among the booty. In that case, it is true, Samuel at once intervened as the strict zealot, to save for his god that which was his by ancient law, and with his own hand he hewed Agag in pieces.[1] But Samuel was not able to stop the process which was leading to the gradual restriction of the practice. It was carried out only on human beings, while the cattle and all that was without life fell as spoil to the victors.[2] It should also be taken into account that a share in the booty took the place of pay for soldiers of all ranks.[3] Another step was taken when only the men [4] (including, however, male children and violated women [5]) were killed. But by and by even of the men some were spared. For example, David ordered the conquered Moabites to be laid on the ground and measured with a line. Those comprised within two lengths of the line were put to death ; those within the third length were spared.[6] To be sure, in another case, that of the Ammonites, he even augmented the horror of death.[7] We hear also of prisoners.[8] At that time to be taken prisoner meant slavery. Of course, a female slave might have the good fortune to marry her master.[9] But in spite of all the influences that were tending in the direction of more humane behaviour we find down till quite a late time, even in civil war, certain widespread horrors, such as the cutting open of pregnant women and the dashing to pieces of children.[10] Yet in view of what was done by other peoples Israel could take credit, and not unjustly, for its merciful treatment of defeated foes.[11] An Assyrian king [12] wrote : " Many prisoners I burned to death, many I buried alive; I cut off the hands and arms of some, the noses and ears of others, and I gouged out the eyes of many."

The treatment dealt out to conquered towns was likewise

---

[1] 1 Sam. xv, 33.  
[2] Deut. ii, 34 ; Josh. viii, 2, 27, xi, 14.  
[3] 1 Sam. xxx, 24.  
[4] Num. xxxi, 7 ; Deut. xx, 13.  
[5] Num. xxxi, 17 ; Judges xxi, 11.  
[6] 2 Sam. viii, 2.  
[7] [2 Sam. xii, 31.—TRANSLATOR.] One translation reads : " He sawed them asunder, laid on them iron picks and axes, and burnt them in brick kilns." Another translation is : " He compelled them to work at the saws and iron picks and axes, and made them labour with the brick moulds.' See *supra*, p. 216, *note* 5.  
[8] 2 Sam. viii, 4.  
[9] Deut. xxi, 10 f.  
[10] 2 Kings xv, 16; *cf.* 2 Kings viii, 12, Is. xiii, 16, Amos i, 13, Hos. x, 14.  
[11] 1 Kings xx, 31.  
[12] Assurnazirpal.

determined by the conception of the ban. They were razed to the ground, and the site sown with salt [1]—a practice which was also known in Assyria.[2] Doubtless this ceremony expressed in some way the dedication of the place to the Deity,[3] for the " covenant of salt " was synonymous with an obligation that could not be broken.[4] Perhaps it was also connected with the idea that the salt, or, as the case might be, sulphur,[5] indicated the permanent desolation of the conquered territory.[6] Indeed, at times resort was also had to a solemn curse to call down lasting desolation upon it. Of this nature was the curse pronounced by Joshua over Jericho : [7]

> Cursed before Jahveh be the man
> Who starts to rebuild this town of Jericho.
> At the cost of his eldest son shall he lay its foundations,
> And at the cost of his youngest shall he erect its gates.

The absolute ruthlessness that marked the treatment of the enemy's country was shown by the not unusual practices of covering good soil with stones, of choking up wells, and of cutting down fruit-trees.[8] This destruction of fruit-trees so offended the Deuteronomic legislator that he felt compelled to protest against it,[9] but in this protest we hear the humaner spirit of a new age.

Passing from war to peace, the most important feature of public life was the administration of justice. It plays a significant part in the Old Testament, and occupies a place large enough to show that we are dealing with a quarrelsome society, with a people fond of disputes. It is not a mere accident that tradition carries back the connexion between law and religion to the time when the religion itself was founded and makes Moses himself the originator of the Hebrew law code.[10] From early morning till late evening, we are told, the people came to Moses, seeking justice, till his father-in-law, Jethro, the high priest of the Midianites, intervened, and advised him to institute a regular organization and so relieve himself of a part of the

---

[1] Judges ix, 45.
[2] As Tiglath Pileser did to Chanusa and Assurbanipal to Shushan.
[3] Schwally, *op. cit.*, p. 32 ; but see *supra*, p. 160, *note* 13.
[4] *Supra*, p. 182.      [5] Job xviii, 15.      [6] Deut. xxix, 22.
[7] Josh. vi, 26. [After Moffatt.—TRANSLATOR.]      [8] 2 Kings iii, 25.
[9] Deut. xx, 19 f.      [10] Exod. xviii ; cf. *supra*, p. 136.

burden. " Provide out of all the people able men, such as fear God, men of truth, hating covetousness, and place such over the people, to be rulers of thousands and rulers of hundreds, rulers of fifties, and rulers of tens : and let them judge the people at all seasons ; every great matter they shall bring unto thee ; but every small matter they themselves shall judge." The advice, we are told, was taken. No doubt this narrative reflects the conditions existing at the time when it was itself composed— that is, about the ninth century. What it does show is that secular and sacred law were administered together. The secular administration already existed in the nomadic period. We have already seen the part played at that time by certain men of moral weight, to whom people were wont to come for counsel [1] and for settlement of disputes. If these men were originally elders of the clan, then possibly the transition to settled life was accompanied here too by a transition from a clan association to a territorial one, and the place held by elders of the clan was naturally taken by the elders of the city or community.[2] Their number no doubt grew till it reached the average number of seventy, or even more.[3] But whereas under the unfettered conditions of nomad life the influential men who pronounced judicial decisions had no power to enforce them, under the changed conditions of settled life, when people lived in closer and more constant touch with each other, it was essential that the penalty which had been pronounced should be actually carried out against individuals who injured the common weal. Even then, however, the lodging of a complaint continued to be the affair of the individual. Public opinion had as yet no organized authority which could lodge a complaint in its name. The public character of the tribunal was secured only by the publicity of its proceedings, whether these took place at the sanctuary, or at the city-gate, or in the chamber of justice built by Solomon.[4]

When compared with the secular administration of justice, that of the priests, like that of inspired prophetic persons such as Deborah [5] or Samuel,[6] had an essential advantage—it was done in the name of God, the Deity Himself being judge. The person judged guilty naturally submitted more readily to the

---

[1] See *supra*, p. 122.  [2] I Kings xxi, 8 ff.
[3] Judges viii, 14, ix, 2 ; *cf.* Num. xi, 16.
[4] I Kings vii, 7.  [5] Judges iv, 4.  [6] I Sam. vii, 16.

decision given because he feared that contumacy would be visited by divine judgment. The priestly tribunal bore the divine name Elohim ; [1] when it was a question of discovering, say, an unknown thief the common phrase ran, " The matter comes before Elohim." [2]

It goes without saying that, as time went on, opposition arose between the secular and the priestly judges, and the situation became still more complicated when, with the rise of the monarchy, a new authority was created, which claimed the sphere of jurisprudence as its own.[3] It is next to impossible to disentangle the threads, and to say exactly what relations existed between the various judicial authorities. It is natural to suppose that the royal tribunal became a kind of supreme court, to which appeal could be made in cases where the decisions of the ordinary secular judges were not considered satisfactory. There is, indeed, actual proof of this in the story of the wise woman of Tekoa.[4] One of her two sons had killed his brother, and had been condemned to death by her clan. But the unhappy mother thereupon appealed to the king, " lest they quench my coal, which is left " ; and the king dismissed her with the comforting promise that he would look after her. It is clear from this that jurisdiction was still in the hands of the clan, but that any member of the clan who considered himself aggrieved by its verdict had the right of appeal to the king. There must also have been cases when the king's judgment was asked without the intervention of other authorities. This is the explanation of Absalom's behaviour. He went to the gate and tried to persuade all litigants who had come to seek judgment from the king that, were he judge, he would be far juster than his father.[5] The well-known story of the judgment of Solomon, in which the litigants were two harlots,[6] shows that

[1] 1 Sam. ii, 25.    [2] Exod. xxii, 7 f. [See Revised Version.—TRANSLATOR.]
[3] *Cf.* even Ps. cxxii, 5.    [4] 2 Sam. xiv, 4.    [5] 2 Sam. xv, 2 ff.
[6] 1 Kings iii, 16 ff. The story is not confined to Israel. Gressmann has collected twenty-two parallels. The narrative probably arose in India, for in the story as there current the two litigant women were not harlots, but wives of the same husband, jealous of each other, and anxious to have the child because its possessor would be mistress in the household and inherit the whole estate. The point of all versions is the same—the real mother is known by her lack of selfishness. According to the Indian, Chinese, and Tibetan versions the child was to be tugged at by the women, and belong to the one who tore it from the other.

this right of approach to the king had few restrictions. The word ' Hosannah' as an appeal for the royal help may have had its origin among weak people seeking justice.[1]

If we can trust the evidence of the chronicler on this subject [2] Josiah seems of all the kings to have done most to strengthen the administration of justice. He not only appointed judges, but impressed strongly upon them the responsible nature of their duties. In any case, his reign was a turning-point in the history of Hebrew jurisprudence. The introduction of the Deuteronomic law, which took place in his time, abolished at one stroke all the sanctuaries outside of Jerusalem. The administration of sacred justice, therefore, could henceforth take place only in the Temple at Jerusalem. The Deuteronomic legislator is quite alive to the importance of this change. He states [3] that in places outside of Jerusalem the administration of justice was in the hands of secular officials, probably the elders of the places concerned,[4] and tries to ensure the supremacy of the priestly tribunal of the central sanctuary by the enactment that all difficult cases requiring special decisions were to be reserved for its consideration. It reveals the actual conditions that prevailed when we find that in the present form of the text this perfectly clear meaning of the law has been obscured by a process of redaction,[5] by which the legal privileges of the priests at Jerusalem are nullified. Along with them mention is made of " the judge that shall be in those days " [5]—an expression which in all probability means the king. The monarchy was evidently very unwilling to allow its privileges to be usurped by the priesthood at Jerusalem. In actual practice compromises must have been frequent, and in the end, of course, the monarchy succumbed. When with the loss of national independence the monarchy itself came to an end the priests entered into their inheritance.[6] To be sure, secular judges are met with in the post-Exilic period [7]—they were simply the continuation of the old arrangement of tribunals composed of the elders of city and village. If we may accept the evidence of post-Biblical sources these tribunals gradually strengthened their position and the

---

[1] Cf. Wellhausen, Israelitische und jüdische Geschichte (1904), p. 95.
[2] 2 Chron. xix, 5 ff.     [3] Deut. xvi, 18, xvii, 8–13.
[4] Cf. Deut. xxi, 19, xxii, 15.     [5] Deut. xvii, 9, 12.
[6] Ezek. xliv, 24.     [7] Ezra vii, 25, x, 8, 14.

number of such judges increased, but we are completely ignorant of the conditions under which they worked.

The civil court held at the city-gate seems to have met every morning.[1] Probably in early times the whole proceedings were oral.[2] The plaintiff was the injured man in person. He stood on the right hand [3] of the judges. The accused, probably in mourning garb,[4] stood on their left. The judges were seated.[5] The onus of proof was on the accused. He was fortunate if he had influential men to speak on his behalf.[6] There could be no case without witnesses.[7] At least two were necessary; at all events, no one could be condemned to death on the statement of one witness.[8] Everything possible was done to impress upon the witnesses a sense of responsibility. If their evidence led to the condemnation of the accused they had to be the first to lay hands on him.[9] If their evidence was proved to be false they were liable to the punishment they had hoped to bring upon the accused man.[10] The oath seems to have been an important part of the court procedure.[11] It was chiefly used, of course, in cases where there were no witnesses. If, for example, a man had entrusted an animal to the care of another, and the animal perished, or was hurt or stolen, without anyone having seen it, an oath "before Jahveh" decided the question.[12] The oath was usually part of the procedure at a sanctuary—it is the same to this day.[13] A person taking the oath did so with hands raised to heaven,[14] where the Deity was conceived to dwell.

For certain cases there was still another method employed to get at the truth—the judgment of God. The typical example of this is the method of procedure adopted in the case of a woman suspected of adultery.[15] The priest summoned her to appear before Jahveh. Then he poured holy water into an earthen vessel, and put into it some earth from the floor of the sanctuary. If the woman were innocent the water would do her no harm.

---

[1] Jer. xxi, 12.    [2] Prov. xviii, 17.    [3] Zech. iii, 1.    [4] Zech. iii, 3.
[5] Ps. xciv, 20 ; Dan. vii, 9.    [6] Gen. xliii, 9 ; Jer. xxvi, 17.
[7] An exception in Deut. xxi, 18 ff.
[8] Deut. xvii, 6 ; Num. xxxv, 30.
[9] Deut. xvii, 7 ; cf. Lev. xxiv, 14.
[10] Deut. xix, 19.    [11] See supra, p. 226.
[12] Exod. xxii, 9 ; Lev. v, 22 ; 1 Kings viii, 31.
[13] Palästinajahrbuch (1911), p. 102.
[14] Gen. xiv, 22 ; Deut. xxxii, 40.    [15] Num. v, 11 ff.

If she were guilty it would cause her abdomen to swell and her thigh to rot. This curse, which the woman expressly accepted, was written by the priest on a sheet, and wiped off into the water ; the water was then given to the woman to drink. All this is on a par with many ancient customs current among superstitious peoples in all ages.[1] The judicial decision was conceived as being delivered by the Deity Himself. The same conception underlay the use of the holy lot. The Old Testament contains two examples of it, the case of Achan [2] and that of Jonathan.[3] In the case of Achan tribe after tribe came forward. Each tribe had its own lot, probably an arrow [4] bearing its name. The quiver containing the arrows was shaken, and the arrow that fell out indicated the tribe to which the guilty man belonged. Then this tribe came forward, clan by clan. As before, each clan had its own lot, and the procedure was repeated. The clan which was thus indicated came forward by families. There was a lot for each family, and that which fell out indicated the guilty one. This family came forward individually, and again the lot fell on some one. In the case of Jonathan only two lots were employed, the well-known Urim and Thummim.[5] Saul and Jonathan stepped to one side and the people to the other. If the guilt were on the former Urim was to appear ; if on the people then Thummim.[5] After Saul and Jonathan had been indicated the lot was cast as between these two ; and it decided against Jonathan. Possibly Urim and Thummim were of different colours ; in that case Urim was probably the light colour.[6] The later proverb,[7] " The lot causeth contentions to cease," seems to indicate that the lot continued to be used till a late period. As was most natural and convenient in this form of procedure, the decision was given orally, but occasionally, in cases where the accusation was made in writing,[8] the judgment also was given in written form.[9]

As soon as the decision had been given the sentence was carried out. The usual form of corporal punishment was beating. In the presence of the judge who had condemned him the guilty

---

[1] *Cf.* Hammurabi, § 132, and Robertson Smith, *The Religion of the Semites*, p. 138.    [2] Josh. vii, 16.    [3] I Sam. xiv, 40.    [4] *Cf.* Ezek. xxi, 21.
[5] I Sam. xiv, 41 (LXX).    [6] *ôr* means ' the light.'    [7] Prov. xviii, 18.
[8] Job xxxi, 35. See the fragment of a written charge in the Assuan papyri (Sachau, No. 27).    [9] Is. x, 1 ; Job xiii, 26.

man was laid down and received the stripes—not more than forty, " lest, if he should receive more stripes than these, he be degraded in thine eyes." [1]  Evidently the punishment began to be considered degrading at the point when the beaten man was reduced to such a condition that he lost his outward dignity. The humane character of the Deuteronomic legislation is shown by this attempt to protect the man from this loss, as well as by the provision that the officials should do their office under the eyes of the judge.  It is not quite clear whether the law meant forty strokes to be given in each case, or whether forty was the maximum.  At a later period, in their fear of overstepping the legal number, the Jews appointed forty strokes less one. [2]  It is possible, however, that the number thirty-nine was fixed upon for the purely practical reason that a scourge with three thongs was used at that time, and thirteen strokes were given with it. [3] In the earlier period a rod was used. [4]  But, judging from Rehoboam's answer to the Israelites that, outdoing his father, he would chastise them with scorpions (*i.e.*, whips with hooks or something of that kind), [5] there were worse weapons of chastisement than rods.  Punishments involving the loss of personal liberty were always rare, and they gradually disappeared ; [6] but the stocks and the pillory were by no means unknown. [7]

In the infliction of the death-penalty, except in those cases where the avenger of blood had a claim, [8] the whole community took part.  The guilty person was stoned to death. [9]  If this were not considered a sufficient vindication his dead body was hung up [10] or burnt to ashes. [11]  Among a people to whom cremation was unknown [12] this burning was felt to be a special mark of dishonour. [13]  It was the regular form of death-penalty

---

[1] Deut. xxv, 3.                                    [2] *Cf.* 2 Cor. xi, 24.
[3] The 'unlucky' character of the number thirteen is older than Christianity : the thirteenth month which was inserted into the Babylonian calendar was looked upon as unlucky, and stood in the constellation of the Raven (R. Winckler, *Die babylonische Kultur* (1902), p. 27).
[4] Prov. x, 13.                            [5] 1 Kings xii, 11, 14.
[6] 1 Kings xxii, 27 ; Ezra vii, 26 ; Lev. xxiv, 12 ; Num. xv, 34.
[7] Jer. xx, 2, xxix, 26 ; Job xiii, 27, xxxiii, 11.
[8] 2 Sam. xiv, 7.                                [9] Deut. xvii, 5, xxi, 21.
[10] Josh. x, 26 ; 1 Sam. xxxi, 10 ; 2 Sam. iv, 12 ; *cf.* Num. xxv, 4 ; 2 Sam. xxi, 6, 9.          [11] Josh. vii, 25.          [12] See *supra*, p. 73.
[13] 1 Sam. xxxi, 12, does not disprove this.  The text is corrupt ; *cf.* 1 Chron. x, 12.

in certain cases of unchastity.[1]  To what extent other methods
of inflicting it were practised [2] we do not know.  Joseph's
prophecy that Pharaoh's baker would be beheaded [3] may
perhaps be an intentional touch of foreign colour on the part of
the narrator.[4]

If the guilty man could not be found a solemn curse was
pronounced upon him in his absence.[5]  This gave him over to
the direct punishment of God.  Whoever heard this pronounced
and, knowing the guilty one, failed to give information became
equally culpable,[6] and could be freed only by a sin-offering—
such, at least, was the enactment of the later law.[7]

Some significant glimpses into the actual conditions that
prevailed in connexion with the administration of justice are
afforded us both by the prophets and the proverb-writers, with
their ceaseless charges of unfairness and venality against the
judges.[8]  This can surprise no one who has any acquaintance
with Oriental courts of the present day.  Why should it have
been otherwise in Israel ?  But it is deeply significant that we
read thus early in the pages of many of the Old Testament
writers the unfailing testimony of the nation's better self.

By the year 722 B.C. the northern kingdom of Israel had
played out its part, and the year 586 B.C. saw the end of the
kingdom of Judah.  In the northern kingdom, in Samaria, this
meant the close of long struggles in which time and again one
dynasty had displaced another.  In the southern kingdom, in
Jerusalem, the last occupant of the throne was still a descendant
of the royal house of David.  It was to the house of David that
the people looked for the king that was to be.  What actually
arose, notwithstanding the return from the Exile and the
resettlement of Jerusalem and its immediate neighbourhood—
the recovered territory did not extend beyond these limits [9]—
was less than a kingdom—or some would say it was more.  It
fulfilled the ideals of those circles that were theocratically

---

[1] Lev. xx, 14, xxi, 9 ;  cf. Gen. xxxviii, 24.     [2] Cf. Exod. xix, 13.
[3] Gen. xl, 19 ;  besides, the translation has been questioned.
[4] But see Jer. xxvi, 23.                                   [5] Prov. xxix, 24.
[6] Ibid. ;  cf. Deut. xiii, 9.                              [7] Lev. v, 1 ff.
[8] E.g., Is. i, 23, v, 23 ;  Mic. iii, 11 ;  Prov. xvii, 23.
[9] This is proved by Neh. iii, xii, 27 ff. ;  cf. Ezra x, 8.

inclined,[1] inasmuch as it brought to the leading place in the community the high priests, who felt themselves to be the representatives of God on earth. The anointing which had made the kings sacrosanct passed over to them ; they wore the royal purple and the diadem. Of course, they did not attain to all this power and authority in a day. In the years that followed the Exile a political governor held the supreme place in the State. But gradually his glory faded before the rising star of the spiritual princes, especially in the minds of the Jews themselves. Outwardly, in the eyes of the foreigners under whose domination post-Exilic Judaism lay, the governor (occasionally a Persian[2]) might be the first person in the State, even although the Persian king, by ratifying the Priests' Code of Ezra,[3] had also thereby ratified the lofty position which that code gave to the high priest. Probably the Jews became most conscious of the existence of a political supreme head alongside of their high priest when he began to impose taxes.[4] But Persian policy was wise enough to grant the conquered people a far-reaching measure of self-government. This took the form of a revival of the ancient democratic constitution with elders at the head,[5] a constitution which had naturally returned to favour during the Exile.[6] In particular, the elders had the administration of the secular jurisprudence.[7] The elders of Jerusalem, mainly the heads of the clans, held their sittings in the capital ; [8] in the provincial towns there were once more native " elders and judges." [9] We see here the germ of what was later called the Sanhedrin, with local authorities in addition functioning throughout the country. When the representatives of these rural Jewish communities had official business in the capital they were guests at the governor's table, just like the authorities of the capital themselves.[10] Indeed, this was the form in which they received from the State their pay, or, rather, their sustenance

---

[1] See *supra*, p. 242.

[2] *E.g.*, Bagohi, to whom the petition of the Jewish community of Elephantine is addressed.

[3] Ezra vii, 14.

[4] Ezra iv, 13, 20 ; Neh. v, 4. Ecclesiastics enjoyed exemption from taxation (Ezra vii, 24).　　　　　[5] Ezra v, 9 ff., vi, 7.

[6] Jer. xxix, 1 ; Ezek. viii, 1, xiv, 1, xx, 1.

[7] See *supra*, p. 268.　　　　　[8] Neh. ii, 16, iv, 8.

[9] Ezra x, 14 ; *cf.* vii, 25.　　　　　[10] Neh. v, 17.

S

in lieu of pay.[1]  In return the governors indemnified themselves for this outlay by taxing the people.  The taxation demanded amounted, we are told,[2] to 40 shekels (£5) a day for bread and wine.

In view of the modest proportions of the post-Exilic community, a more extensive application of the democratic principle was possible in some cases.  We read repeatedly of public assemblies.[3]  That meant now merely a transference of ecclesiastical customs to the secular sphere ; for the whole community was already in the habit of assembling together for the more important religious ceremonials, and the political community and the religious community were now identical.

[1] See Eduard Meyer, *Die Entstehung des Judentums* (1896), p. 133.
[2] Neh. v, 15 ; also *cf*. Mal. i, 8.
[3] Ezra x, 7 ; Neh. viii ff.

# CHAPTER V

## INTELLECTUAL LIFE

OUR study of Israel's domestic, industrial, social, and political life has already disclosed a large part of its intellectual life. This chapter will deal with its intellectual culture in the narrower sense, and in order to supplement what has just been said about the administration of justice we shall begin with jurisprudence.

## 1. JURISPRUDENCE

As long as the opinion prevailed that the Mosaic law was a unique phenomenon there was very little danger of underestimating Israel's talent for jurisprudence and the work it accomplished in that sphere. The discovery of the law of Hammurabi has perhaps tended to arouse the contrary impression. We must be careful not to rush to either extreme. One result at least has followed from the famous discovery of the law at Shushan—no one can henceforth discuss Israel's conceptions of law without trying to show their connexion with ancient Oriental law in general. We have already indicated the channels that connected Hebrew jurisprudence with that of Babylon.[1] That the Hebrews were the borrowers is patent, for the code is adapted throughout to the conditions of settled life in a civilized country.

But this does not mean that Israel, settling in a new home, simply adopted a code of law that was equally new. They brought with them from their nomadic life a great deal of law, and they held to it tenaciously. In the desert the supreme law had been that of blood-vengeance,[2] and it is instructive to see that the nascent Hebrew State, in contrast to the more highly developed Babylonian State,[3] was unable to conquer or suppress the principle of blood-vengeance. When a brother kills his brother the clan demands the surrender of the murderer, that

---

[1] See *supra*, pp. 52, 92.　　　　[2] See *supra*, p. 121.
[3] There is no mention of blood-vengeance in the code of Hammurabi.

he may atone with his life for the life he has destroyed.[1] The requirement of the Book of the Covenant,[2] that the slayer " shall be surely put to death," means that he is to be delivered up to the avenger of blood. As a matter of fact, the idea of blood-vengeance retained its force in Israel even after that people had settled in Palestine, and historical tradition has preserved a whole series of examples in which it was carried into effect.[3]

Blood-vengeance was one application of the legal principle of retaliation—*lex talionis*—a principle that was common to all Semitic peoples, and, indeed, to all mankind. The Book of the Covenant [4] lays down the principle with unmistakable clearness : " If any mischief follow, then thou shalt give life for life, eye for eye, tooth for tooth, hand for hand, foot for foot, burning for burning, wound for wound, stripe for stripe." This enumeration embodies the principle that atonement is to be made with that member of the body with which the injury had been done.[5] But the principle of retaliation is never so rigid as to exclude suitable intensifications or mitigations ; for example, stolen property was to be restored in multiple. The Book of the Covenant lays down [6] that for a sheep four were to be repaid, for an ox five oxen, if the stolen animal was not found alive in the possession of the thief. (Earlier custom had gone the length of requiring that a stolen sheep be repaid sevenfold.[7]) A payment in money, which appears early,[8] is to be interpreted as a relaxation of the originally strict principle of retaliation. In connexion with it there is an unmistakable advance from an arbitrary to a strictly fixed amount of indemnification. We can still see in Hebrew law the stages of this advance. If, as the result of a quarrel, a married woman has been so injured that her unborn child has been lost the culprit is liable to such payment as the woman's husband may impose.[9] But from the

---

[1] 2 Sam. xiv, 7.  [2] Exod. xxi, 12.
[3] Judges viii, 18 ff. ; 2 Sam. iii, 27, xxi, 1 ff.
[4] Exod. xxi, 23–25 ; *cf.* Lev. xxiv, 19 ; Deut. xix, 21 ; Job ii, 4. " Skin for skin " in Hammurabi, §§ 196 f., 200.
[5] Deut. xxv, 11 f.  [6] Exod. xxii, 1.
[7] 2 Sam. xii, 6. The Hebrew text speaks only of a fourfold repayment, but that is a subsequent assimilation to the letter of the provision of the law.
[8] See *supra*, p. 122.
[9] Hammurabi (§ 209) mentions 10 shekels of silver.

very beginning limits were set to the caprice of the injured person's demand [1]—the sum to be paid was decided by arbitrators. And when a husband brought against his wife an unfounded charge that she had not come to him a *virgo intacta* the fine was fixed at 100 shekels of silver, to be paid to the woman's father. [2] Even the death-penalty could be redeemed by a money payment, [3] unless it had been decreed as a punishment for murder, in which case, as we have seen, the deep-rooted law of blood-vengeance had to be satisfied. [4]

In connexion with this very point another mitigation gradually came into force. A distinction was drawn between intentional and unintentional slaying, and for the man who had unintentionally caused the death of another [5] there was the right of asylum in a city of refuge, which provided an efficient protection against the wrath of the avenger of blood. [6] In exceptional cases this might be replaced by the temporary banishment of the murderer. [7] But what was of far greater influence in gradually relaxing the strictness of blood-vengeance was the gradual weakening of the idea of solidarity. Thus the Deuteronomist, perhaps taking advantage of a new practice that had already been gathering strength, [8] lays down the principle that fathers are not to be put to death for their children, nor children for their fathers, but that each is to be punished only for his own offences. [9]

This, however, reveals a new conception of justice, according to which the individual as such is the responsible subject, and the negative portion of the formula in which this principle is laid down still shows plainly the ancient contrary conception. This ancient conception, an inheritance from the life of the desert, was based wholly on the idea of solidarity. The classical example is that of Achan, [10] whose crime of theft was expiated by his whole family, including their animals ! The limits within which this solidarity was valid were not always constant ; but although they

---

[1] Exod. xxi, 22.

[2] Deut. xxii, 19 ; *cf.* Gen. xx, 16.     [3] Exod. xxi, 29 f.

[4] Deut. xix, 11 f. ; Num. xxxv, 19–21.

[5] Deut. xix, 5, supposes the case that while a man is cutting timber his axe-head flies off and kills his fellow-workman.

[6] Exod. xxi, 13.

[7] 2 Sam. xiii, 37.     [8] 2 Kings xiv, 6.

[9] Deut. xxiv, 16.     [10] Josh. vii, 24.

were originally determined by consanguinity,[1] as the nation grew accustomed to settled life the tendency revealed itself here also to replace the ancient clan connexion by territorial association. This liability of the local community comes out very clearly in the story of Sodom, whose inhabitants (excepting, of course, Lot and his dependants) were punished indiscriminately for wickedness of which in reality only individuals could have been guilty.[2]

An outstanding feature of the Hebrew conception of penal law is the emphasis laid on the objective character of the crime or offence—that is to say, only the deed done is taken into consideration, without regard to the motives lying behind it. For example, Jonathan was adjudged worthy of death because, contrary to his father's command, he had eaten food while pursuing the Philistines.[3] That he knew nothing and could have known nothing of the prohibition was not accounted a mitigating circumstance. A similar view is ascribed to God Himself. He threatens the Philistine king Abimelech with death for having treated Sarah as Abraham's sister, not as his wife. And yet, as the Deity expressly testifies, Abimelech had done this "in the integrity of his heart," because both Abraham and Sarah had declared to him that they were brother and sister.[4] The subjective attitude of the person, therefore, had little to do with the case. This explains why, in the Old Testament code of law, the ideas of intent, of complicity, of participation are never developed.[5] It is quite clear that under such circumstances punishment does not aim at the reform of the evildoer. The agent is altogether of secondary importance : whether he be human or not, the evil deed as such must be atoned for. Therefore it is that an animal can be liable to punishment as well as a man. Not only was it provided that if a man had sexual intercourse with an animal

---

[1] And not only, as in the case of Achan or of Korah (Num. xvi, 32), in "transverse section" of family relationship, but also in "longitudinal section" (Exod. xx, 5, xxxiv, 7 ; Num. xiv, 18).

[2] Gen. xix. In the story of Gibea, imitated from the Sodom story, the conception of the local community intermingles with that of tribal relationship. Gibea's deed is atoned for by the tribe Benjamin. For another example of solidarity founded on local connexion see Deut. xxi, 1 ff.

[3] 1 Sam. xiv.      [4] Gen. xx, 1 ff.

[5] Cf. G. Förster, Das mosaische Strafrecht in seiner geschichtlichen Entwickelung (1900), p. 49.

both should be put to death ;[1] but an animal alone might be condemned to die—for example, an ox that had gored a person to death.[2] That this was not merely a question of getting rid of a dangerous animal, but that the intention was to punish it, is proved by the manner in which the death-penalty was inflicted —it was stoned to death. But death by stoning was the death for criminals,[3] and arose from the conception that the heavy covering of stones would prevent his dreaded spirit from roaming about.[4] In fact, the killing of the offending animal was so little due to utilitarian motives that the eating of its flesh was expressly forbidden.[5] The serpent in Paradise received an independent punishment,[6] and the so-called covenant with Noah enacted that the shedding of human blood by animals was to be avenged upon them.[7] All this becomes more intelligible to us if we remember that in antiquity man, and above all others the husbandman, did not draw so sharply as we now do the lines of cleavage between man and animal.[8]

The objective view of guilt which finds expression in all these ways has its ultimate roots in the primitive conception that evil is a kind of contagious entity, which necessitates the destruction of every person or thing in which it is known to inhere. This is why the punishment of Achan included the burning of everything that was his. The same idea found further expression in the conception that the land as such was rendered unclean by an evil deed, and called for purification, such as could best be secured by blood.[9] Hence the real purpose of punishment was the eradication of the evil thing, not the reform of the evildoer, and this was for long the prevailing conception.[10] There was also probably alongside of this an intention to deter men from evil-doing.[11]

---

[1] Lev. xx, 15.  [2] Exod. xxi, 28.  [3] See *supra*, p. 271.

[4] There are other traces of superstitious belief in the penal code. The enactment that the body of a criminal should not be allowed to hang overnight on the tree (Deut. xxi, 22 f.) had behind it originally (though the legislator may not have known it) this fear of the roaming spirit.

[5] Exod. xxi, 28. Here we have religious motives penetrating into the law.

[6] Gen. iii, 14.  [7] Gen. ix, 5.

[8] Note in this regard the tender care of the Book of the Covenant for ox, ass, sheep, and goat. (Horse and camel are, significantly, not mentioned.)

[9] Deut. xxi, 1 f. ; Num. xxxv, 33 ; 2 Sam. xxi.

[10] Deut. xiii, 6, and often ; Lev. xviii, 24 ff, and elsewhere. *Cf.* Nowack, *Lehrbuch der hebräischen Archäologie*, vol. i, p. 335.

[11] Deut. xiii, 12, xvii, 13, etc.

Of course, the principles of Hebrew jurisprudence are at all points in perfect keeping with the social conditions in the midst of which they arose and were enacted ; and the social differences between Israel and Babylon, the Babylon of Hammurabi, whose people had already outgrown primitive conditions and had become a commercial people,[1] explains the differences between the two legislations. The social conditions presupposed by the Book of the Covenant, the most ancient Hebrew law code, going back to the ninth or tenth century, are of the utmost rural simplicity. There is no trace whatever of anything that could be called town life. Evidently it deals with life in the northern territory. The use of money was just beginning. Commerce did not exist ; debit and credit were present only in germ. A strong feeling of unity pervaded all members of the nation. Custom was still powerful ; " it is not done in Israel "[2] expresses the standpoint from which right and wrong were judged. Custom was still specially effective in preserving family discipline and family honour. The authority of father and mother was still held in high esteem. Severe punishment fell upon an offence against filial piety and upon incest in any of its forms. One is struck with the predominantly legal view taken of all offences against chastity. The Book of the Covenant deals with the seduction of a maid in the section that treats of injuries to property.[3] And that is quite intelligible. Whoever injures a girl injures her father's property. Similarly, whoever has intercourse with a married woman is guilty of an offence against the property of her husband.[4] All forms of property, movable and immovable, were guarded by special regulations. Hebrew law resembles that of many ancient peoples in this, that the only sections that deal with civil law refer to the constitution of the family and the protection of property.[5] With regard to the latter, the already-mentioned intensifying of the principle of retribution in the case of stolen property is instructive. It might seem at first sight a laxity in the treatment of offences against property that robbery and theft only rendered the criminal liable

---

[1] See *supra*, p. 51.
[2] 2 Sam. xiii, 12.
[3] Exod. xxii, 16 ; *cf.* Küchler, *Hebräische Volkskunde* (1906), p. 34.
[4] See *supra*, p. 154.
[5] *Cf.* Dareste, *Études d'histoire du droit* (1889), p. 37.

to civil claims on the part of the injured person.[1] Evidently
that is an echo from the desert period, when offences of that kind
were almost necessarily everyday occurrences,[2] and it cannot be
denied that in this respect the Hebrew idea of law is more closely
akin to nomadic conditions than the law of Hammurabi, which
punishes robbery in practically every case [3] with death, and
inflicts the same penalty on theft in a large number of cases,[4]
the only alternative being restitution ten or even thirtyfold.[5]
Hammurabi was thus much stricter in his treatment of theft
than Hebrew law was.[6]  At the same time, although the intensifications of the Hebrew law of retaliation [7] are more moderate,
there is perceptible increase in the protection given to property,
and, as the story of Achan shows,[8] a sense of the criminal guilt
of the thief also becomes effective.

Another advance is revealed in the already-mentioned distinction between intentional and unintentional killing,[9] which opens
the door for a consideration of the motives of the person concerned, and paves the way for a subjective conception of guilt
instead of an objective one.  For instance, an offence against a
betrothed woman is treated differently according as it took place
in the city or away from an inhabited locality.  In the former
case, it is assumed, the woman had an opportunity of escaping
from her assailant by calling for help, whereas in the latter case
she had none.  Accordingly, in the first case she is punished
along with the aggressor, while in the second case she goes free.[10]
*Pari passu* with this regard for the subjective element there goes
also an increasing appreciation of human responsibility.  If an
ox gores a person to death inquiry must be made as to whether
its owner was aware that the animal was inclined to be dangerous,
and, if so, whether he took the necessary precautions.  Neglect

---

[1] The absence of a real differentiation between criminal and civil law is
also shown by the enactment that if a slave does not immediately succumb
to his master's blows, but dies one or two days later, his master shall escape
punishment, because the slave was property purchased with money (Exod. xxi,
21 ; see Holzinger, *Exodus*, in the " Kurzer Hand-Commentar zum Alten
Testament ").      [2] *Cf.* Küchler, *op. cit.*

[3] § 22.          [4] §§ 6–10, 34.                    [5] § 8.

[6] *Cf.* Benzinger, *Hebräische Archäologie*, p. 294.      [7] See *supra*, p. 276.

[8] It must not, of course, be overlooked that the goods taken by Achan
were part of the booty that was dedicated to the Deity by the ban.

[9] Exod. xxi, 12 ff ; Deut. xix, 1–13 ; Num. xxxv, 16–29.

[10] Deut. xxii, 23 ff.

of these rendered him liable to death, or, if the person killed were a slave, to a money payment, whereas if he were not guilty of neglect he only lost his beast.[1]  These enactments again bring clearly before us resemblances to the law of Hammurabi, although there are differences in the penalties awarded.[2]

But the real element common to the Book of the Covenant and to the law of Hammurabi is the whole style.  In both there is an increasing casuistry and differentiation in the enactments. Cases are carefully and minutely distinguished.  For example, a man who slays in self-defence—at least in the night-time—is guiltless ;[3] the case is different if the sun has already risen.[4] One can actually see the legal maxims growing out of actual experience with all the varieties of individual cases ; and this case-law finds expression in the form of the enactments.  When men fight together, and this or the other result follows, then this or that shall be done.[5]  From this it is only a step to the systematic classification of the separate but kindred cases, until an exact classification is reached, with sub-sections under main heads.  The very beginning of the Book of the Covenant is of this kind.[6]  " If thou buy a Hebrew slave . . . in the seventh year he shall go out free.  [a] If he were unmarried when he came, he shall go out by himself.  [b] If he were married, his wife shall go out with him.  [c] If his master have given him a wife and she have borne him children, [aa] he shall go out alone, if he care to make use of his right ; [bb] he shall be his master's slave for ever, if he prefer to remain out of love for his master or wife or child."

It is, however, only a portion of Hebrew law that is determined by specific enactment, and we get the impression that, on the whole, very wide liberty was allowed for the good sense of the judge.  The more the written law left open, the more depended on the personality of the judge.  It was not without reason that

---

[1] Exod. xxi, 28 f., 32.

[2] §§ 250–252 : " If an ox gores a man on the street and kills him, no claim can be made.  If the ox of anyone is given to goring, and the owner has been made aware of the vice, and has not blunted its horns or shut it up, if it gores a freeman to death, he must pay half a *mina* of silver.  If the ox kills anyone's slave, its owner must pay one-third *mina* of silver."

[3] *Cf.* Hammurabi, § 21.                    [4] Exod. xxii, 1 f.

[5] Exod. xxi, 18 f. ; there is an exact parallel in Hammurabi, § 206.

[6] Exod. xxi, 2 ff.

the prophets and the law itself did their utmost to awaken in judges a sense of responsibility in discharging the duties of their office.[1]

For the rest, a spirit of mercy and humanity pervades the Hebrew legal system. It can be felt even in the Book of the Covenant.[2] Still more does it distinguish the Deuteronomic legislation, which is unwearying in its efforts to protect widows, orphans, and all in need.[3] In subject-matter, to be sure, the Deuteronomic legislation belongs more to religion than to jurisprudence. The chief interest of the legislator was the completion of the centralization of worship at Jerusalem, but this had results that were purely legal. For example, the abolition of all sanctuaries outside of Jerusalem—they had also been places of sanctuary for criminals—called for a new arrangement in the matter of such refuges. The legislator settled this question by enacting that three easily accessible cities should be " cities of refuge."[4] Subsequently the number was increased to six.[5]

The lauded humanity of Hebrew legislation had, however, its limits. It would be a mistake to read into its provisions a feeling of universal humaneness. Deuteronomy itself, by coupling together a difference of nationality and a difference of religion, did its part toward making more acute the contrast between Israel and non-Israel.[6] To this was also due the different legal treatment of Hebrew and foreigner—a matter in regard to which there is an essential difference between Hebrew law and that of a code like Hammurabi's.[7]

To a certain extent the so-called Priests' Code (middle of the fifth century) marks the end of the evolution of Hebrew jurisprudence. On the one hand, conceiving the Jewish community to be of divine constitution, it completely shut off Israel from non-Israel, thus widening the gulf between the two. At the same time, however, it constructed a bridge across which non-Hebrews, at least those residing among Israel, might be admitted to re-

---

[1] Exod. xxiii, 2 f., 7 f. ; Lev. xix, 15, 35 ; Is. i, 17, etc.

[2] Exod. xxi, 22 (protection of pregnant women)—*cf.* Hammurabi, § 209 ; Exod. xxiii, 4 (protection of an enemy's beasts).

[3] Deut. xiv, 28, xvi, 11, 14, xxiv, 17, xxvi, 11, xxvii, 19.

[4] Deut. xix, 2.                      [5] Num. xxxv, 13.

[6] Deut. iv, 8, xxvi, 19.

[7] Deut. xxiii, 20. This is elaborated in my book *Die Stellung der Israeliten und der Juden zu den Fremden* (1896).

ligious, though not to complete civil equality.[1] The sole condition was the adoption of the law, including, if possible, circumcision.

It is this union of law and religion that constitutes the specific peculiarity of the development of Hebrew jurisprudence.[2] While we do not forget that Hammurabi also claimed to have received his code from the hands of his god, it must still be said that the connexion of law and religion in the two codes is far from being identical, inasmuch as Jahveh was a God of law and morality in quite a different sense from the Babylonian Shamash. But the deeper knowledge and recognition of Jahveh's legal and moral character was the growth of time, and though it would be an error to place the highest interpenetration of law and religion at the beginning of the process of development, it is undoubtedly true that in the Priests' Code (which was practically its ultimate phase) the process of development did not altogether escape the danger which only too often accompanies an increased legalizing of religion. That danger is that when men conceive themselves in their conduct to be related to God exclusively by a definite external law the differences between great things and small things in the law inevitably disappear. " Whoso keepeth the whole law and is guilty in one point, the same is guilty of all." [3] It is significant that, intensifying an earlier commandment,[4] the law ultimately decreed that intercourse with a menstruous woman should be punished by the death of both parties,[5] as if their offence were on a level with murder or any other crime adjudged worthy of death. The most perfect interpenetration of law and religion is found in the great prophets, beginning with Amos. But what they preached on this subject was less a reflection of the life they saw around them than a protest *against* what they thus saw, and their message was, and continued to be, a demand for the Ideal.

## 2. WHAT ISRAEL KNEW

It is but little that can be said about Israel's knowledge ; not so much because we have insufficient information on the subject,

---

[1] According to the law (Lev. xxv, 23–31) the *ger*—*i.e.*, the stranger resident among Israel—can only own a house in an unwalled city. See the work mentioned in the previous note, p. 166 f.

[2] Hence the close intermixture in the Book of the Covenant of *jus* and *fas*.

[3] James ii, 10 ; *cf.* Matt. v, 19.     [4] Lev. xv, 24.     [5] Lev. xx, 18.

as because knowledge—theoretical knowledge—hardly existed. Wherever we find the verb which is usually translated by 'know' the things known do not form part of theoretical or scientific knowledge. Even when used with the name of God the word means always and only practical knowledge of God. If there be a kind of knowledge which implies an actual penetration into things and their mysterious connexion, such knowledge is too high for man and is reserved for God alone. This is the meaning of the great divine speech to Job ; it was meant to bring the hearer to a modest opinion of his powers, and it ultimately caused him to " lay his hand upon his mouth." [1]

And the man who boasts of his wisdom [2] is not boasting that he can speak with expert botanical knowledge of trees, from the cedar of Lebanon to the hyssop that grows out of the wall,[3] but of their symbolical importance for human life. Wisdom, knowledge, is purely practical in its nature, and even the detailed descriptions of the ostrich,[4] crocodile,[5] and hippopotamus [6] are meant only to illustrate the glory of God.

Some have even tried [7] to ascribe to Israel, as to other Eastern peoples, a knowledge of an astral science which, it is said, began in Babylon and drew under its spell the entire Near East, if not even a wider realm. The misleading element in this is the use of the word ' science ' to denote what deals mainly with imaginative concepts, the outcome of very naïve fancies. This play of imagination begins, of course, with isolated phenomena. Whence, for example, comes the rain ? Evidently from heavenly containers which ordinarily are closed. These containers are naturally conceived after the fashion of those which are familiar to men on earth. But men keep water in skins ; hence also God (it is of course always assumed that personal powers are at work) must keep it in skins. When He reverses them it rains.[8] There is nothing marvellous about it. The marvel is that these skins do not rend.[9] Or perhaps the rain-clouds are such rent skins shedding their contents.[10] But there may be another explanation

---

[1] Job xxxviii–xlii, 6 ; *cf.* xxviii.  [2] Jer. ix, 23.  [3] 1 Kings iv, 33.
[4] Job xxxix, 13–18.  [5] Job xl, 25–xli.
[6] Job xl, 15–24.  [7] Cf. *supra*, p. 129.
[8] Job xxxviii, 37 ; *cf.* Duhm's comment on Ps. civ, 13, in *Die Psalmen* in the " Kurzer Hand-Commentar zum Alten Testament."  [9] Job xxvi, 8.
[10] *Cf.* the Arabic *wahâ*, meaning both the tearing of the skin bottle and the rainstorm (Jacob, *Altarabisches Beduinenleben* (1897), p. 5).

altogether : behind and above the visible firmament there are great masses of water,[1] and God requires only to make a way for this water, a sort of heavenly waterpipe [2] through the firmament, or to open a window in the sky,[3] and then the rain pours down upon the earth. Either way, the firmament is clearly composed of solid material ; the only question is, What material is it? According to a passage [4] which, though late, perhaps reflects ancient ideas, the men who built the Tower of Babel meant to pierce the sky with a gimlet, in order to see whether it was made of clay or brass or iron.[5] Of course, it might conceivably be made of some material like tent-cloth [6] or of some finer gauze [7] stuff.[8] How, in that case, it could support large quantities of water is beyond human ken. It is characteristic of these cosmological conceptions that they commingle with each other, no attempt being made to reach a uniform agreement between the separate parts. Thus the various atmospheric conditions, snow and hail,[9] storm and winds,[10] the rose of dawn,[11] etc., have each their separate chambers, from which they are released by God according to His will ; but no attempt is made to locate more exactly these different storehouses,[12] or to understand their relation to each other. At times, too, those chambers which contain the heavenly manna pour forth their contents.[13] The dew also falls from heaven upon the earth,[14] and men spoke of its life-giving powers.[15] Altogether, a far-reaching influence upon the earth was ascribed to the heavenly bodies, especially upon its fertility, both vegetable and animal. The parturition of the animals was affected by the moon.[16] Indeed, heaven and earth

[1] Ps. xxix, 3, xxxiii, 7.

[2] Job xxxviii, 25, uses the expression which is found in Is. vii, 3, and elsewhere as the name of a Jerusalem waterpipe.

[3] Gen. vii, 11, in the story of the flood.

[4] The Greek Apocalypse of Baruch, iii.

[5] In Job xxxvii, 18, the sky is compared to a metal mirror. The Persian *Bundehesh* (xxx, 5) conceived it as of steel.

[6] Ps. civ, 2 ; *cf.* the " stretching out like a tent " (Is. xliv, 24 ; Job ix, 8).

[7] Is. xl, 22. [8] Hence the sky can be rolled up like a book (Is. xxxiv, 4).

[9] Job xxxviii, 22.

[10] Ps. cxxxv, 7 ; Job xxxvii, 9 ; Jer. x, 13, li, 16.

[11] Job xxxviii, 12.

[12] What the " chambers of the south " (Job ix, 9) means we do not know.

[13] Ps. lxxviii, 23 f.

[14] There are special dew-clouds (Is. xviii, 4). [15] Is. xxvi, 19.

[16] Deut. xxxiii, 14, in the present text ; but it is probably not the original.

are not so very distant from each other. The birds fly along the vault of heaven,[1] and when God looks down from heaven upon earth He sees men " as grasshoppers."[2] In view of all that it has to contain heaven must consist of several layers or there must be a plurality of heavens.[3]

We need feel no surprise that the author of the Creation story on the first page of the Bible says that light existed before the creation of sun and moon. He imagines light to be independent of the sun, a fine material which, like the corresponding material of which darkness is composed, issues [4] from its special dwelling-place and envelops sun and moon as well as the earth. Occasionally the sun and moon are conceived as more personal—the sun being a young hero coming forth every morning from his chamber and rejoicing to run his race ; [5] or, with reminiscences of myths, the sun spends the night in the company of the sea-monster, until with break of day it escapes while the monster is still asleep.[6] The rising dawn has wings ; [7] mention of its eyelids [8] suggests a human-like being—a youth, from the gender of the word in Hebrew. The moon also has its own dwelling-place,[9] and what is said about the stars shows clearly how vague is the differentiation between the actual visible objects and the star-spirits that inhabit them. The morning stars sang while creation was going on.[10] God issues orders to the stars as a prince does to his troops. Organized as an army, they fight from their orbits.[11] God knows each by name, and when He summons them not one fails to come.[12] Men too knew the names of some of them,[13] the Great Bear, Orion, the Pleiades ; but this did not mean any gain " scientifically." The names cannot even be certainly identified, and what we read of the bands and cords [14]

---

[1] Hence the standing expression " the birds of heaven."

[2] Is. xl, 22.    [3] Deut. x, 14 ; 1 Kings viii, 27 ; Ps. cxlviii, 4.

[4] Job xxxviii, 19, xxvi, 10.    [5] Ps. xix, 6.

[6] Job iii, 8. Whoever awakens the monster retards the rising of the sun (Schmidt, *Jona* (1907), p. 90).

[7] Ps. cxxxix, 9.    [8] Job iii, 9.    [9] Hab. iii, 11.

[10] Job xxxviii, 7. Here, therefore, they are older than in Gen. i, 14 ff.

[11] Judges v, 20.    [12] Is. xl, 26 ; Ps. cxlvii, 4.

[13] *Cf.* Schiaparelli, *Die Astronomie im Alten Testament* (1904). In these matters the Bedouin is perhaps more at home than the settled dweller. When asked how he knew so much about the stars he answered : " Who does not know the pillars of his house ? " *Cf.* Jacob, *Altarabisches Beduinenleben*, p. 207.

[14] Job xxxviii, 31.

of some star or other only shows that what was known of them lay more in the region of sagas or myths than in that of sober knowledge.

Mythological elements also intermingled with the prevalent conceptions about the processes of storm. The thunder is the voice of Jahveh,[1] his roar like that of a lion.[2] The lightning flashes are the arrows of his bow.[3] When the storm is past He lays back His bow in the clouds, and it is visible to all as the rainbow.[4] The marvel about lightning is that, though it follows a zigzag line, it does not miss its target : [5] evidently it has its appointed paths.[6]

The vault of heaven rests on the earth.[7] It needs supports, and these are the mountains which on the far horizon bear the heavens.[8] What gives the needed strength to these " pillars of heaven " is the depth of their foundations.[9] These foundations cannot be in the earth—the earth itself is not solid enough for that. It is enough for God to look at the earth to cause it to tremble.[10] (Earthquakes were familiar enough in Palestine,[11] and when men were rocked as in a ship it was easy for them to entertain such conceptions.) Indeed, the earth seemed to be floating on the vast world-ocean ; if you went to where the land ceased you looked out upon the boundless sea that girdled the world. There was another reason for thinking that there must be water beneath the earth—one came upon water when digging down.[12] And, besides, where otherwise did the streams and springs have their source ? They need only break through and the earth would be flooded.[13] But if the world-ocean thus bore up the earth,[14] whence did the earth derive its solidity and strength ? For, notwithstanding all their other thoughts, men retained an impression of the comparative strength of the earth.[15] The answer was, the pillars that bore up the heavens also upheld

---

[1] Job xxxvii, 2, 4, and often.　　　[2] Amos i, 2, iii, 8.
[3] Hab. iii, 11 ; Ps. xviii, 15, lxxvii, 18.　　　[4] Gen. ix, 13.
[5] Job xxxvii, 12.　　　[6] Job xxviii, 26, xxxviii, 25.
[7] Job xxvi, 10. According to this passage beyond the dividing line is darkness.　　　[8] Job xxvi, 11.
[9] Job xviii, 4, ix, 5. Hence a faith that moves mountains is a proverbial expression for strong faith (Matt. xvii, 20 ; 1 Cor. xiii, 2).
[10] Ps. civ, 32.　　　[11] See *supra*, p. 21.
[12] Num. xxi, 17. [The Song of the Well.—TRANSLATOR.]
[13] Gen. vii, 11 ; Is. xxiv, 18.　　　[14] Ps. xxiv, 2, cxxxvi, 6.
[15] Ps. xxiv, 2, xciii, 1, civ, 5 ; Prov. viii, 29.

the earth.[1]  Therefore the foundations of these pillars must reach down to the bottom of the ocean that was underneath the earth.[2]  And, again intermingling their thoughts with half-mythical conceptions, Israel sometimes conceived this ocean as a rebellious being, whose keenest desire was to swallow up the earth and scale the heavens.  Therefore from of old God had confined its violence behind strong bars, and appointed for it bounds, at which its proud waves are stayed.[3]  This was done in the days when all things were made.[4]

All this gives us a picture of a tripartite world—the heavens above, the earth beneath, and the waters under the earth [5]—an image which was common to both Hebrews and Babylonians.[6]  The earth occupies the centre.  The lowest place of all is the bottom of the primeval ocean.[7]  But (and this again shows the absence of any attempt to correlate or reconcile his conceptions) the Hebrew knew something lying still deeper.[8]  " Under the waters and the inhabitants thereof " [9] is the underworld with its shades.  That would mean that this underworld is lower even than the primeval ocean.  But that is inconsistent with the idea that the earth has only to open its mouth to let evildoers go down to Sheol (the underworld),[10] and that deceased persons have only to rise out of the earth to be seen of men.[11]  Such inconsistencies show how little attempt was made to reach a comprehensive idea of the universe.  In fact, there is no word in Hebrew for ' world.'  When people mean to speak of it they speak of " earth and heaven," [12] or later " heaven and earth," [13] and metaphorical forms of expressions were never abandoned.  For example, the author of the great Old Testament Psalm of Nature [14] conceives of the world as a finely constructed house.

For the geographical and ethnological knowledge of the Hebrews we naturally turn in the first instance to the famous list of the nations in Genesis.[15]  It is not a unity.  It has been

---

[1] 1 Sam. ii, 8 ; Ps. lxxv, 4 ; Job ix, 6.  The thought of Job xxvi, 7, is exceptional—the world is suspended over nothingness.
[2] Ps. xlvi, 3.    [3] Job xxxviii, 8, 10 ; Prov. viii, 29.
[4] *Cf.* Gunkel, *Schöpfung und Chaos* (1895).    [5] Exod. xx, 4.
[6] Jensen, *Die Kosmologie der Babylonier* (1890).
[7] Ps. xviii, 16 ; Job xxxviii, 16.    [8] Job xi, 8.
[9] Job xxvi, 5, xxxviii, 16.    [10] Num. xvi, 32.
[11] 1 Sam. xxviii, 13.    [12] So the Jahvist, Gen. ii, 4b.
[13] So the Priests' Code, Gen. i, 1, ii, 4a.    [14] Ps. civ.    [15] Gen. x.

T

put together from two sources, one belonging to the ninth century and the other to the fifth. Both authors, the Jahvist and the writer of the Priests' Code, had the same purpose in view, to include all mankind in one genealogical scheme.[1] The horizon of the later writer is of course wider than that of the earlier, but both have their limitations. The list is practically confined to the region east of the Mediterranean Sea. In the north it extends as far as Armenia, in the east to the Elamites, in the south to the Ethiopians and South Arabians. As for the west, if by Tartessus [2] is meant Tarshish in Spain, the Hebrews probably knew of this city as a Phœnician colony with which the mother-country kept up vigorous commercial relations.[3]

The transmutation of ethnology into genealogy, as if each people, each city, had arisen through the growth of one family, is extremely naïve. It is the outcome of that mythological way of thinking that seeks to explain all that exists, social connexions as well as external objects, as being due to physical procreation.[4] But with all the childish immaturity of this endeavour we cannot miss the great thought that mankind is ultimately one ; and the very attempt to investigate the origin of the various peoples might well be considered the first stirrings of a scientific impulse. But the scientific inadequacy of the results reached, even in details, must simply be admitted. For example, it is now known that the Elamites and Lydians do not belong to Shem,[5] nor do the Canaanites belong to Ham rather than to Shem.[6] In this last instance, the wish was probably father to the thought—the Hebrews simply did not wish to have the same ancestor as the accursed Canaanite ! With regard to the people of Cush (Ethiopians), the close connexion with Arabian tribes assigned to them is striking.[7] It would seem as if they assumed a direct geographical connexion of Arabia with Ethiopia. That is to say, they had extremely vague ideas of the boundaries of Asia and Africa, and yet these countries lay

---

[1] Some peoples who must have been known to the authors, Edomites, Moabites, Ammonites, etc., are not mentioned, but this is probably because, in the opinion of the authors, they did not come into existence till a time later than that chosen by them as the date of their list.

[2] Gen. x, 4.    [3] *Cf.* Ezek. xxvii, 12, 25, and *supra*, p. 210.

[4] Eduard Meyer, *Geschichte des Altertums*, vol. i, Part I, p. 35. Cf. *supra*, p. 119.    [5] Gen. x, 22.    [6] Verse 6.    [7] Verse 7.

comparatively near their own. Again, the author of the story of Paradise makes the river Gihon, which he traces to the same source as the Euphrates and the Tigris, encircle the whole land of Cush,[1] as if the Nile—later tradition identifies the Nile and the Gihon [2]—rose in Asia. This same fantastic geography locates in the far north the Mount of God which occupied so much of their thoughts.[3] This location was probably part of an inheritance which they shared with the races inhabiting Central Asia south of the great mountains.[4] Naturally, to the Hebrews their own land was the centre of the world, " the navel of the world," [5] and in this respect Jerusalem was to the Hebrews what Delphi was to the Greeks.[6] The points of the compass were named with Palestine as the centre. The sea (Mediterranean) became the word for the west; the Negeb—*i.e.,* the parched, dry land [7]—for the south. All " orientation," as its name implies, means facing the Orient, so that " in front " means east; " behind " means west; " on the right " means south; " on the left " means north.

Israel's historical knowledge was not a whit more scientific than their geography. It deals mainly with separate events, and makes no endeavour to connect them. Above all, it is attuned to their own impressive national experience, and is entirely derived from it. But in this sphere Israel accomplished something great. They lived through their experiences conscious that these were history, conscious that they were the actors and the witnesses of it, and this was a main element in their own training, religious as well as other. For in what was taking place they saw the doings of their own God, Who was the living Creator of national and of human history, and it is this that constitutes the peculiarity of Old Testament religion.[8] A prophet like Hosea deliberately and knowingly draws history into the

---

[1] Gen. ii, 13.     [2] Josephus, *Antiquities*, I, i, 3. *Cf.* Jer. ii, 18 (LXX).

[3] Is. xiv, 13; Ezek. xxviii, 14; Ps. xlviii, 3. [See A. F. Kirkpatrick's rendering in *The Book of Psalms* (" Cambridge Bible for Schools and Colleges "). —TRANSLATOR.]

[4] See Duhm's comment on Is. xiv, 13, in *Das Buch Jesaias* in the " Kurzer Hand-Commentar zum Alten Testament."

[5] Ezek. xxxviii, 12.

[6] Ezek. v, 5. In the same way the Book of Jubilees makes Sinai the centre of the desert.     [7] See *supra,* p. 13.

[8] See my little work *Die Eigenart der alttestamentlichen Religion* (1913).

circle of his religious thinking, in order to deduce from it proofs of how Jahveh out of His own love chose Israel for His own, how He had brought them up and guided them, and how Israel had disloyally turned from Him. In using national history for this purpose Hosea showed others the way. The Deuteronomic legislator, and the " Deuteronomist" writers who carried on his work, were his faithful followers ; Jeremiah also, with his characteristic words : [1] " Stand ye in the ways and see and ask for the old paths. Which is the good way, that ye may walk therein and find rest for your souls ? " This recollection of past history was to be stirred up and fed by the questions of children to their parents.[2] This was the living tradition on which their historical knowledge rested.[3] This conception of Jahveh as the maker of history [4] means that it was His superior will and purpose that was being accomplished, and that all history therefore served a higher purpose and moved toward a divine goal. This conception of the teleology of history is the great achievement of the Hebrew mind. Even the Jahvist makes his historical narrative subserve this idea by means of his ever-recurring theme that Israel needs must, in spite of all obstacles, become masters of Canaan.[5] But he is surpassed by Isaiah, who in all the world-wide struggles of the nations sees only the trial of strength between the principle of the flesh and of the spirit, and is convinced that ultimately victory will be to the spiritual, which for him is summed up in the personality of Jahveh.[6] And, in his turn, Deutero-Isaiah lets us see how Jahveh takes nature up into the historical process, in order to co-ordinate it with, or subordinate it to, His purposes in history, to restore Israel from exile to His land. Alongside of this there runs another thought no less significant : in proportion as Jahveh transcends His own people, foreign nations become the instruments to carry out His will, and finally this thought soars to the magnificent conception of the unity of mankind, which we have already tried to trace in the list of nations.

These two thoughts, the unity of mankind and its steady

---

[1] Jer. vi, 16.      [2] Deut. iv, 32, xxxii, 7 ; Job viii, 8.

[3] Joel i, 3 ; Ps. lxxviii, 3 f.      [4] See *supra*, p. 136.

[5] This is worked out in my little book just referred to, in *note* 8 on the previous page.

[6] See Duhm on Is. xxxi, 3.

progress to a destined goal, contain the germs of the conception of a universal history.[1] For its realization it needed only the technical means of a uniform chronology. This also is supplied by the Old Testament, in attempts which we have still to discuss ; and it was reserved for a later age to make the framework of a chronology with Daniel's scheme of the four world-empires, into which even Christian historians as late as the eighteenth century thought they could fit the course of history.[2]

Compared with these great contributions which Israel made to later conceptions of history, small importance is to be attached to separate, isolated references to history, to history of civilization and to antiquities, such as those about Egypt contained in the story of Joseph, or to long narratives like that about the market of Tyre.[3] The historical value of each of these has to be tested by itself, but taken together they give a certain, if incomplete, idea of what Israel knew about the nations whose history lay outside their own. There is also a series of sagas, which were adopted by Israel when they settled in their new country.[4] They deal *inter alia* with the origin and history of human callings—Noah, the first wine-grower,[5] Cain, the first founder of cities,[6] etc.

A knowledge of the calendar was of great importance, because on it depended the due celebration of the holy seasons. The author of the story of Paradise [7] claims that this was the purpose of the stars. They were not only to be signs according to which coming events could be read in the sky, sometimes with fear and terror,[8] but they were also to fix the times by which the whole of life, especially the religious assemblies, was to be regulated. We cannot explain here in detail how that was done.[9] Speaking generally, the course of development reveals a contest between two tendencies—the tendency to adopt foreign ways and the inclination to oppose these. The changes in the manner of

---

[1] *Cf.* A. Merx's article on " Der Einfluss des Alten Testamentes auf die Bildung und Entwickelung der Universalgeschichte " in *Die Verhandlungen des dreizehnten Orientalistenkongresses (zu Hamburg)* (1904), p. 195 f.

[2] *Cf.* my article " Danielbuch " *RGG*, vol. i (1909), p. 1966.

[3] Ezek. xxvii.

[4] Guthe, *Geschichte des Volkes Israel* (1914), p. 179.

[5] Gen. ix, 20.        [6] Gen. iv, 17.

[7] Gen. i, 14 ; Ps. civ, 19.       [8] Jer. x, 2.

[9] For details see the manuals of archæology ; *KAT*, pp. 325-332.

naming the months [1] and the changing methods of fixing when the year and the day began were probably due to this. The various ways of determining the beginning of the year have left a remarkable trace in the fact that New Year's Day could fall on the tenth day either of the first [2] or of the seventh [3] month. It was ultimately fixed by law for the seventh month, and on the first day of that month. [4]

There is one mention of the use of the sundial as a chronometer. [5] As it was called after Ahaz, it is natural to suppose that it was an innovation on the part of that king. He may have introduced it from abroad, probably from Damascus. We know that he was so impressed by an altar he had seen there that he ordered one like it to be made in Jerusalem. [6] How his sundial was constructed we do not know. We are only told about the steps up to it. Perhaps it was an actual indicator of the sun's position, in the form of a column on a height, with steps leading up to it. In that case, we may perhaps assume that the column cast the shadow of its summit on the top step at midday, and on the lowest steps in the morning and in the evening. [7] The ordinary method of indicating the time of day was by names connected with something else. The division into twelve hours was perhaps post-Exilic. [8] The time was reckoned by sunrise or sunset, by the heat of noonday, [9] or the cool of evening, [10] by the time of the offering of the evening sacrifice, [11] by the evening hour, when the women went out to draw water, [12] by the three watches of the night, [13] and so on.

A similar method was followed for the reckoning of the years : two years before the earthquake, [14] in the year the Tartan came unto Ashdod, [15] in the fifth year of King Jehoiakin's captivity, [16] in the second year of their coming unto the house of God at

[1] Sometimes by name, sometimes by number. Note also the change of the Hebrew word for month (Nowack, *Lehrbuch der hebräischen Archäologie*, vol. i, p. 216). [2] Ezek. xl, 1. [3] Lev. xxv, 9.
[4] Lev. xxiii, 23 ff. ; Num. xxix, 1 ff.
[5] 2 Kings xx, 9–11 ; also Is. xxxviii, 8. [6] See *supra*, p. 212.
[7] See Kittel's commentary on Is. xxxviii, 8.
[8] Only in Aramaic (Dan. iii, 6, etc.) is there a word in the Old Testament for 'hour.'
[9] Gen. xviii, 1 ; 1 Sam. xi, 11. [10] Gen. iii, 8 ; Song of Songs ii, 17.
[11] 1 Kings xviii, 29, 36 ; Ezra ix, 4 ; Dan. ix, 21. [12] Gen. xxiv, 11.
[13] Exod. xiv, 24 ; Judges vii, 19 ; 1 Sam. xi, 11.
[14] Amos i, 1. [15] Is. xx, 1. [16] Ezek. i, 2.

Jerusalem,[1] and so on. A very popular method was to reckon by the years of the monarchs, or occasionally by the year in which a king died.[2] But this method left it uncertain whether the year of a king's death was also reckoned as the first year of his successor,[3] or whether the new king's first year was the year following the death of his predecessor.[4] The possible sources of error due to this uncertainty were increased when the fashion arose of drawing up synchronizing tables such as we have in our Books of Kings. *E.g.*, "Now Jehoram, the son of Ahab, began to reign over Israel in the eighteenth year of Jehosaphat, king of Judah."[5] However, there was gradually evolved a system of chronology for which we should have been more grateful to the redactor of the Books of Kings if the value of his statements were not affected by the introduction of an artificial scheme. The period from the building of Solomon's Temple to the end of the Exile was supposed to be exactly 480 years, to correspond with the 480 years which were said to have intervened between the Exodus from Egypt and the building of the Temple.[6] This number 480 was tempting, because it could be factorized as twelve times forty. In the period from the Exodus to the building of the Temple twelve generations, averaging forty years each, can be made out almost completely from data supplied by the Old Testament.[7] During the 480 years that followed there were, according to the Chronicler,[8] twelve generations of high priests. To the eleven high priests from Azariah, who was the first to officiate in the Temple, down to Jehosadak, who went into exile, we have only to add one generation of high priests for the period of the Exile. "But this casts a strange light on the fact that 240 years—*i.e.*, half the period of 480 years—fall to the series of northern Israel."[9] This by itself

---

[1] Ezra iii, 8.     [2] Is. vi, 1.     [3] Thus 1 Kings xv, 25, 33.
[4] Thus 1 Kings xv, 1, compared with xiv, 21.
[5] 2 Kings iii, 1. This contradicts 2 Kings i, 17. The latter passage says Jehoram ascended the throne of Israel in the second year of Jehoram of Judah. But this is incorrect if Jehoram's predecessor on the throne of Israel, Ahaziah, became king in the seventeenth year of Jehosaphat and reigned two years (1 Kings xxii, 51) and if Jehosaphat reigned twenty-five years (1 Kings xxii, 42).     [6] 1 Kings vi, 1.
[7] 1 Chron. vi, 4–10, also reckons twelve high priests from Aaron to the first Temple. The note in verse 10*b* should follow 9*a*.     [8] 1 Chron. vi, 11–15.
[9] From Jeroboam I to Jehoram were 98 years; from Jehu to Hosea 144 years; but the first 98 correspond to the 96 years of the kingdom of Judah

betrays something of the artificiality that dominates Old Testament chronology, and the impression is confirmed and strengthened if we look at what follows. From Adam to the Exodus the figures [1] given us bring out a period of 2666 years— *i.e.*, 26⅔ centuries. Is it merely an accident that it was the twenty-seventh generation that took part in the Exodus? [2] To this, as a generation still living, are added two-thirds of the century required to make up a whole generation. When so much artificiality dominates the whole we need not be surprised to find it in the details.[3] To arrive at such results requires a certain deftness in the handling of the simplest arithmetical operations. This skill must be conceded to these chronologists, and if we occasionally come upon a mistake in the addition of three items [4] it is better to hold the transmission of the text responsible for the error [5] than to think that the chronologists were so poor at figures. In fact, they attempted far more complicated calculations than these, if the Assyriologist Oppert [6] is correct in thinking that he has discovered that the chronology of the Priests' Code is simply the chronology of the Babylonian primeval history reduced according to a definite system. Oppert makes out that while the Chaldæans reckoned for the first ten men up to the flood 432,000 years, Genesis [7] allows only 1656 years. By this ratio, a Jewish week would correspond exactly to a Babylonian *lustrum* of five years.[8]

In addition to the drawing up of this chronology, there were

from Rehoboam to Ahaziah, who was contemporary with Jehoram ; thus, 96 + 144 = 240. See Wellhausen, *Die Composition des Hexateuchs*, p. 299 ; also for a demonstration of artificiality in the details.

[1] According to the Massoretic text, Gen. v, xi, 10 ff., xxi, 5, xxv, 26, xlvii, 9, Exod. xii, 41.

[2] The generation of Eleazar, the great-great-grandson of Levi (Exod. vi, 16). Levi's father, Jacob, according to the passages in the previous note, belongs to the twenty-second generation.

[3] 100 is made up of 70 + 30, or 65 + 35, 300 treated as 130 + 105 + 65, 500 as 90 + 162 + 187 + 32 + 29.

[4] According to Num. iii, 22, 28, 34, 39, the items are 7500 + 8600 + 6200 ; the sum is given as 22,000 instead of 22,300.

[5] In verse 28 read instead of *ses*, ' six,' *selos*, ' three.'

[6] *GGA* (1877), pp. 201–223.　　　　　[7] *Cf.* Gen. vii, 6.

[8] 432,000 : 1656 = 6000 : 23 (divisor 72). 6000 years = 1200 *lustra* ; 23 years = 23 × 52 = 1196 weeks. As a year contains 52 weeks + 1¼ days, we must add 23 × 1¼ days, which equals in round numbers 4 weeks. That is, together, 1200 Jewish weeks, which correspond to the 1200 Babylonian *lustra*.

regular duties which gave the priests occasion for various forms of calculation. These included the calculations of the amounts of poll-tax,[1] those for the redemption of the first-born,[2] tributes on war-booty,[3] the weight of votive offerings,[4] etc.

Among the Hebrews both the decimal and the sexagesimal systems were in use. Proof of the use of the decimal system is found in the fact that the tens are expressed by the plural form of the numbers from three to ten. 10, 50, 100, and 1000 were the units for tribunal and military purposes.[5] Actual decimation of soldiers is mentioned by Amos in one of his threatening passages.[6] Other applications of the decimal system were the tenths, or tithes, as imposts and the extensive use of measures based on ten,[7] and, not the least important one, the Decalogue.[8] Evidently it was preferred to have the laws grouped together as ten, because they could then be counted on the fingers, and the ten fingers are the natural starting-point of the whole system. The sexagesimal system was taken over from Babylonia. Sixty and its factors, 5 and 12, were the standard numbers in the system.[9] Every one knows the place occupied by the number 12 in the Old Testament: 12 tribes, 12 pillars,[10] 12 precious stones,[11] 12 oxen for the Brazen Sea,[12] 12 cakes of shewbread,[13] 12 gates in the New Jerusalem,[14] the 12 words—a dodecalogue as well as the decalogues[15]—not to speak of the 12 months. The number 60 and its multiples were mainly used in the systems of weights and of money : one talent = 60 *mina* = 3600 shekels. But it is clear that in this connexion the decimal system gradually

---

[1] Exod. xxxviii, 25 f., a half-shekel per head ; that is, with a population of 603,550 men 301,775 shekels = 100 talents (at 3000 shekels) + 1775 shekels.

[2] Num. iii, 46, 50, for 273 at 5 shekels each = 1365 shekels.

[3] Num. xxxi, 32. 2 per cent. of the soldiers' booty to the priests, 2 per cent. from the share of the community to the Levites.

[4] Num. vii, 13, 85 : 12 × (130 + 70) shekels = 2400 shekels.

[5] Exod. xviii, 21 ; Deut. i, 15 ; 1 Sam. xxii, 7.

[6] Amos v, 3 ; *cf.* Is. v, 10, vi, 13.

[7] The *epha*, the most frequently named dry measure, is $\frac{1}{10}$ *homer* ; and the *bath*, a liquid measure of the same capacity, is $\frac{1}{10}$ *kor* ; the *omer* = $\frac{1}{10}$ *epha*. See Exod. xxix, 40 ; Lev. xiv, 10 ; Num. xv, 4.

[8] There are two decalogues (Goethe had already noticed it), one in Exod. xx and Deut. v, and the other in Exod. xxxiv.

[9] See H. Winckler, *Die babylonische Kultur* (1902), p. 21 ff.

[10] Exod. xxiv, 4 ; Josh. iv, 3, 8 ; 1 Kings xviii, 31.

[11] Exod. xxviii, 21.    [12] 1 Kings vii, 25.    [13] Lev. xxiv, 5.

[14] Ezek. xlviii, 30.    [15] Deut. xxvii, 15–26.

displaced the sexagesimal.[1] Every one is familiar with the significance of the numbers 7 and 40 in the Old Testament. It is not so easy to say how they came to have that significance. The number 7 finds a natural explanation as the number of the planets, and of the days of the phases of the moon, and the number 40 is explained as the number of the days on which the Pleiades were below the horizon.[2] But this last explanation is extremely doubtful. In considering the prominence of these and other 'sacred' numbers (*e.g.*, 70) we come again and again upon an element of irrationality in Hebrew arithmetic. Even from the purely technical standpoint that arithmetic had its limitations. It is said [3] that the Brazen Sea in the Temple held 2000 *bath*, or 1620 gallons, but calculation shows that a hemisphere or cylinder with the perimeter and height of the dimensions given for the Brazen Sea could have held only from half to a third as much.[4] And the Chronicler [5] makes the error worse by raising the 2000 to 3000.

The high esteem in which the medical art was held is indicated in the fact that God was so frequently spoken of as " the Healer." A closer examination of such passages shows that in the majority of cases the writers had the surgeon in their minds. God " maketh sore and bindeth up ; he woundeth and his hands make whole." [6] The word usually translated ' heal ' originally meant ' mend ' or ' patch.' This seems to indicate that the healing art among the Hebrews consisted mainly of a knowledge of the treatment of wounds. For example, Isaiah describes a body in which from the soles of the feet to the crown of the head there is no soundness—" nothing but bruises and gashes and raw, bleeding wounds, unsqueezed, unbandaged, unsoftened with oil." [7] This shows what the treatment was. And Jeremiah [8] mentions the balm of Gilead, whose healing effect he expects to

[1] On it is based the above-mentioned (p. 297, *note* 1) calculation of the talent as 3000 shekels. The number five had no importance among the Hebrews. But see Benzinger, *Hebräische Archäologie*, p. 166, on the pentagram.

[2] Böklen in *AR*, vol. vi (1903), p. 56, gives a different explanation.

[3] 1 Kings vii, 26.

[4] See Benzinger, *loc. cit.*, p. 217.

[5] 2 Chron. iv, 5. With a perimeter of 30 cubits and a diameter of 10 (verse 2).          [6] Job v, 18 ; *cf.* Hos. vi, 1.

[7] Is. i, 6. [Moffatt's translation.—TRANSLATOR.]

[8] Jer. viii, 22.

find in a new layer of flesh over the wound.[1]   To soften tumours
fig poultices were used,[2] just as is regularly done in the East
to-day.   Each individual did what he could in such matters as
occasion offered—Bedouin women were born doctors [3]—but as
time went on a special profession arose, who took payment for
their services.   This is the meaning of the enactment in the
Book of the Covenant [4] that if men strive together, and one is
laid up in bed as the result of the injuries he has received, his
assailant is responsible for the expenses of medical treatment.
In this connexion we cannot help glancing again into the code
of Hammurabi.   It contains [5] a similar enactment that the
assailant must pay the doctor.   But in other respects that code
was very hard upon the surgeon.   " If a doctor has severely hurt
a person with his bronze operating-knife and caused his death,
or if he opens a person's lachrymal fistula with his operating-
knife and thereby destroys his sight, his hand shall be cut off." [6]
In all likelihood the Hebrew surgeon could also have been found
with his bronze operating-knife in his hand.

From a passage in Job [7] we learn the conceptions current
regarding the physiological origin of man.   As milk curdles into
cheese, the male seed coagulates in the mother's womb to form
the embryo, which God then clothes with skin and flesh, inter-
lacing it with bones and sinews,[8] much as a hedge is interlaced
with thorns.

The name, ' stroke,' usually employed to denote ailments
indicates how sickness was regarded.   The dealer of the stroke
was, to very ancient thinking, a demonic being, but in course
of time either Jahveh takes his place,[9] or the demon has become
Jahveh's servant—i.e., His angel—and carries out His will.
Among these servants of Jahveh are the Angel of Death [10] and
the Satan, who " smote Job with sore boils from the sole of his
foot unto his crown." [11]   The treatment of ailments of course
corresponds to this conception of their nature.   It was for the

---

[1] Cf. Jer. xlvi, 11, xxx, 13, 17, xxxiii, 6 ; Is. lviii, 8.     [2] 2 Kings xx, 7.
[3] Wellhausen, Reste arabischen Heidentums, p. 160, note 4.
[4] Exod. xxi, 19.                    [5] § 206.              [6] § 218.
[7] Job x, 10.   See Duhm's Das Buch Hiob in the " Kurzer Hand-Commentar zum Alten Testament."
[8] Ezek. xxxvii, 6, 8.
[9] Supra, p. 72, and cf. Exod. xi, 4, Is. xxxvii, 36.
[10] 2 Sam. xxiv, 16.                   [11] Job ii, 7.

most part suggestive—an exorcism, frequently accompanied, however, by the use of some form of magic or enchantment.[1] Probably also it was a common practice to act upon the faith of the sufferer by some miraculous sign.[2] The person professionally equipped for this work was the " man of God," [3] at a lower stage the magician,[4] usually the priest.[5] There can be no question that men of this class, with their abundant opportunities for studying ailments, would gather a certain amount of medical knowledge. One only needs to read the subtle powers of diagnosis which the law [6] expected from the priest in his examination of persons suspected of leprosy. Such men must have been skilled in the diagnosis and differentiation of skin diseases.[7] Further, they seem to have been aware of the connexion between plague and rats or mice as the carriers of its germs. At least, that seems to be the best explanation (although many scholars do not accept it) of the ancient story of the golden mice which the Philistines sent as a propitiatory offering to stay the plague sent to punish them for having carried off the Ark of Jahveh.[8] Evidently the offering belongs to the category of sympathetic magic. Plague and mice appear together in another case. According to the Old Testament narrative the army of Sennacherib suddenly marched off because the Angel of the Lord smote them with plague.[9] According to Herodotus[10] the sudden departure was caused by mice having gnawed their weapons and rendered them useless. The different versions of the story

---

[1] 2 Kings v, 11. Is. xvii, 11, refers to expectations of salvation from the gardens of Adonis.

[2] 2 Kings xx, 8. The $m^e kashsheph$ here mentioned (' sorcerer ') seems to have originally meant a person who brews magic potions or shreds herbs.

[3] 2 Kings v.                    [4] Exod. xxii, 18 ; Deut. xviii, 10 f.
[5] Deut. xxiv, 8.                [6] Lev. xiii.

[7] Details in Nowack, *Lehrbuch der hebräischen Archäologie*, p. 53 ; G. N. Münch, *Die Zaraath [Lepers] der hebräischen Bibel* (1893) ; *ZDPV*, vol. xvi (1893), pp. 247–255, vol. xviii (1895), pp. 34–40, 41–44. The author of the Book of Job reveals profound knowledge of the characteristic features in his description of the leper in Job vii, 5, 15, xix, 17, etc.

[8] 1 Sam. vi, 4. Examination shows that the original narrative mentioned only mice. Subsequently golden emerods were added in explanation, and thereafter it was supposed there had been a double plague, pestilence *and* mice. The tradition appears in the Greek Bible.

[9] 2 Kings xix, 35 ; Is. xxxvii, 36.

[10] II, 141. [" Mice devoured their quivers and bowstrings and ate the thongs by which they managed their shields."—TRANSLATOR.]

may be due to the original view that mice (or rats) brought the plague. Other ailments mentioned in the Old Testament are consumption,[1] fever,[2] affections of the sexual organs,[3] diseases of the intestines,[4] and foot troubles [5] (gout?), but exact identifications are hardly possible. Blindness is so often mentioned [6] that eye troubles must have been very common.[7] Apoplexy was also known, and of a person so stricken it was said " his heart died within him, and he became as a stone." [8] Death was explained as the departure of the soul from the body;[9] it might either depart with the last breath [10] or flow away with the streaming blood.[11] In any case, a person was alive as long as the soul remained in the body.[12] This also supplied a belated explanation for another method of treatment, which sought to retain the soul in the body or even to bring it back by a spell.[13] This was probably the purpose of the magical bandages made by certain prophetesses, the bandages being tied round the wrists.[14] Judging from the well-known narrative of Elisha restoring a boy to life,[15] the soul was thought to return through the nostrils, just as the author of the Creation narrative makes God breathe the breath of life into man's nostrils.[16]

The idea that illness was caused by God or by some spirit was thought even more applicable in cases of mental ailment. It was an evil spirit from Jahveh that caused Saul's attacks of melancholia,[17] and the idea that sufferers were possessed by a spirit or spirits was destined to become universal at a later time in Palestine. Owing to this opinion nobody dared to lay hands on madmen.[18] In Saul's case the means of cure employed

---

[1] Is. x, 16, 18.

[2] Lev. xxvi, 16; Deut. xxviii, 22. Actual ague or intermittent fever is mentioned by Josephus, *Antiquities*, XIII, xv, 5.

[3] Lev. xv.  [4] 2 Chron. xxi, 15, 18.  [5] 2 Chron. xvi, 12.

[6] Lev. xix, 14; Deut. xxvii, 18.

[7] It is so still; *cf.* Canaan, *Aberglaube und Volksmedizin im Lande der Bibel*, p. 4.

[8] I Sam. xxv, 37.

[9] Gen. xxxv, 18; Hab. ii, 19; Jon. iv, 3. See articles " Tod " and " Mensch " in *RGG*.

[10] Jer. xv, 9; Job xi, 20.  [11] *Supra*, p. 116.  [12] 2 Sam. i, 9.

[13] " To restore the soul " is equivalent to " refresh " (Ps. xix, 8; Ruth iv, 15).

[14] Ezek. xiii, 18. *Cf.* A. Lods, *La croyance à la vie future*, vol. i, p. 46.

[15] 2 Kings iv, 35; *cf.* I Kings xvii, 21.  [16] Gen. ii, 7.

[17] I Sam. xvi, 14.  [18] I Sam. xxi, 13 ff.

was music.[1]   The conviction that it had this healing power was universal in antiquity.[2]

In post-Exilic times the healing art among the Jews could not fail to be unfavourably influenced by the opinion, made familiar by the Book of Job, that sickness was a divine punishment for open or secret sins.   This belief made the sufferer an object of suspicion, and encouraged an attitude of uncharitableness toward him.   In the same period the Chronicler, for a different reason, had a poor opinion of the physician.[3]   When he upbraids King Asa for seeking help of physicians rather than of Jahveh we can read between the lines his fear lest human skill should do aught to injure the divine honour.   But common sense overcame this prejudice, and Jesus, son of Sirach, exhorts his readers to " honour the physician with the honours due to him." [4]

Some may see the rudiments of botanical knowledge in the classification of the vegetable world into herbs and trees given in the Creation narrative,[5] the ground of distinction being that herbs bear their seed in themselves, openly, while in the trees the seed is contained in the fruit.

The nature of the linguistic knowledge of the Hebrews is shown by the large number of popular etymologies, which have, of course, no scientific value whatever.[6]   The fact that divers languages existed was sufficiently explained by the well-known story of the confusion of tongues at Babel.[7]   Before that took place there was only one language ; and for the Israelite, of course, that one language was Hebrew.   At the Creation God gave to things their names in Hebrew, and in His converse with Adam in Paradise it was Hebrew that He spoke.   Hebrew, indeed, was the only language worthy of the name—the speech of the other nations was a mere ' babble.' [8]   As time went on, however, close contact with other nations compelled the Hebrews to learn some of these babbling words.   According to the Joseph saga, the hero spoke Egyptian, and used an interpreter when speaking with his brethren.[9]   By the eighth century at least the political

---

[1] 1 Sam. xvi, 15 ff.      [2] Cf. E. Rohde, Psyche (1910), vol. ii, p. 48 f.
[3] 2 Chron. xvi, 12.      [4] Ecclus. xxxviii, 1 ff.      [5] Gen. i, 12, 29.
[6] Gen. v, 29, xvii, 5 ; 1 Sam. i, 20.      [7] Gen. xi, 1.
[8] Is. xxviii, 11.   Every ancient people was equally arrogant in this matter. Gunkel, Das Buch Genesis, p. 106.
[9] Gen. xlii, 23.

# INTELLECTUAL LIFE

leaders in Jerusalem knew Aramaic,[1] and 'Aramaisms' were already making their way into Hebrew before the Exile.[2] During the Exile individuals assumed Babylonian [3] or Persian [4] names, and no doubt they understood their meaning. A man of education like Deutero-Isaiah [5] must have been able to use the Babylonian Court style from his own knowledge of the language. So many of those who returned from the Exile married women of the surrounding peoples that Nehemiah found Jews in Jerusalem whose children could speak the language of Ashdod or the language of their mothers, but had forgotten the Jewish tongue.[6] In the interval Aramaic influence had made great advance in Palestine, as well as throughout the Near East and in Egypt. In the Persian period Aramaic was the official language of diplomacy and commerce, and the papyrus discoveries at Assuan and Elephantine show how familiar the Jews there had become with it. It was the same in the homeland. Aramaic even found its way into the text of the Bible, sometimes as a learned gloss,[7] sometimes as a popular formula of exorcism,[8] and specially in the form of official documents,[9] set in a frame of historical narrative which itself is Aramaic.[10] As the Chronicler himself at times uses Aramaic to form a suitable transition to the material which he takes from his Aramaic sources,[11] its use must have been natural and easy to the Jews of his time (c. 300 B.C.). A century and a half later its use had become so universal [12] that a large portion of the Book of Daniel, which was obviously meant for popular reading, was written in Aramaic.[13] The author of that book, however, is at fault in thinking that Aramaic was the speech of the wise men of Babylon in the time of Nebuchadnezzar.[14] In this sphere his knowledge

---

[1] Is. xxxvi, 11. Another view is given by Schulthess in *Das Problem der Sprache Jesu* (1917), p. 18.

[2] Kautzsch, *Die Aramaismen im Alten Testament* (1902).

[3] *E.g.*, Zerubbabel.   [4] Bigvai (Ezra ii, 2).

[5] Kittel, *ZatW*, vol. xviii (1898), p. 161.

[6] Neh. xiii, 24.   [7] Gen. xxxi, 47.

[8] Jer. x, 11. [This verse is in Aramaic and is a gloss.—TRANSLATOR.]

[9] Ezra iv, 8–23, v, 6, to vi, 12, vii, 12–26.

[10] Ezra iv, 24, v, 3–5, vi, 13–15.   [11] Ezra v, 1 f., vi, 16–18.

[12] The Aramaic form *pascha* (= *passah*) with which the then translators of the law rendered the Hebrew *pesach* shows that Aramaic had already gained the mastery in Judaism in the 3rd century.

[13] Dan. ii, 4b, to vii, 28.   [14] Dan. ii, 4.

303

is just as defective as it is with regard to the whole history and external conditions of the Babylonian and Persian periods.[1] Notwithstanding all this, Hebrew continued to be the language of official worship and of the educated classes.

One would scarcely look for anything like speculative science in ancient Israel; the Hebrew was far too much of a realist, incapable of abstract thinking, and unable to get away from the sensuous. We have only to look at the words he uses for 'thinking.' The commonest word [2] means originally 'to murmur' or 'mumble,' and is also the word used to denote both the cooing of a pigeon [3] and the growling of a lion.[4] The word next in favour was the one which usually meant to 'speak.'[5] To the Hebrew mind the connexion between thinking and its vocal utterance was thus axiomatic.

And just as, in his thinking, he was unable to dispense with the medium of the senses, so his attempts to render abstract ideas exhibit the same characteristic feature. For example, for transitoriness, a conception so significant to the Indian mind, Hebrew has no word,[6] although, of course, the idea finds touching expression in the familiar metaphors of "breath"[7] or "the grass which in the morning groweth up and in the evening withereth."[8] And, again, the idea of the divine omnipresence the Hebrew could express only by a variety of metaphorical paraphrases:

> I climb to heaven? but thou art there;
> I nestle in the nether-world? and there thou art;
> If I darted swift to the dawn,
> To the verge of the ocean afar,
> Thy hand even there would fall on me,
> Thy right hand would reach me.[9]

We frequently meet the word for 'eternity,' but linguistic usage shows how great a mistake it would be to take it in an abstract, not to say a metaphysical, sense. There are passages in which eternity means merely the duration of life,[10] and ever

---

[1] See my *Daniel und die griechische Gefahr*, p. 38 ff.  [2] *hagah.*
[3] Is. xxxviii, 14, lix, 11.     [4] Is. xxxi, 4.     [5] *'amar.*
[6] *hādēl* in Ps. xxxix, 5, is not a contradiction of this.
[7] Job vii, 16.
[8] Ps. xc, 5; Is. xl, 6.
[9] Ps. cxxxix, 8–10. [Moffatt's translation.—TRANSLATOR.]
[10] Exod. xxi, 6; I Sam. i, 22.

and anon the Hebrew finds it necessary to measure it by sensuous standards and to objectify it by concrete description. "A thousand years are in Thy sight but as yesterday, or as a watch in the night." [1]

The mind of the Hebrew was not directed to the universal. We have already spoken of his inability to form a comprehensive view of the universe and of the lack of a word for the 'world.' This is characteristic of his whole mentality. His whole tendency is to emphasize striking details. Accordingly, Hebrew diction is always most graphic when it can restrict itself to what is characteristic.[2] It has often been said both of Hebrew and of Semite that they lack imagination. It is true if by imagination is meant the power of combining mental presentations. Image is placed loosely beside image, without any organic connexion between them, and without even an attempt being made to combine them. A verbal similarity is enough to cause a change of image.[3] The Hebrew must have possessed a very nimble mind, and this must be kept in view. Literary criticism often overshoots the mark, especially in the prophetic writings, when it straightway declares a passage "not genuine" or "an interpolation" because it finds an abrupt transition from one image or figure to another. What unites the disparate elements is their connexion in the personality of the man who is considering them. Some scholars have even gone the length of saying that subjectivity is a fundamental feature of the Semitic mind, and this is often adduced as explaining why lyric poetry is so predominant in Hebrew poetry, and why the more objective types, epic and drama, are to all intents and purposes absent.[4] This being so, the more the writer's presuppositions determine his estimate of the world and of all things, all the more, in view of the strong religious tendency of Hebrew thought, does this estimate take on a religious colour; and seeing that to the Hebrew religion is an entirely practical matter this estimate is made from standpoints that are mostly if not exclusively practical. This confirms the impression with which we started,

---

[1] Ps. xc, 4.
[2] Köberle, *Natur und Geist nach der Auffassung des Alten Testamentes* (1901), p. 66. [3] Is. xxx, 13 f.
[4] Thus Lassen, *Indische Altertumskunde*, p. 414; Renan; Köberle, *loc. cit.*, p. 50, and also in *Die geistige Kultur der semitischen Völker* (1901), p. 14 f.

that Hebrew knowledge is entirely different from all that we mean when we speak of theoretical knowledge.

In the Hellenistic period Greek philosophy made its way into Hebrew minds, but it was only the practical aspects of it that aroused any interest. Indeed, its entry was not made without friction and opposition. We can see this from the Book of Ecclesiastes, which may be looked upon as the attempt of a philosophic Jew to come to terms with the Greek spirit. He has not given his ear to the new wisdom with impunity. It enticed him with the lust of life, and drove him to adopt toward his inherited faith an attitude of scepticism in which he could not really enjoy the offered delights. But in this mingling of the Jewish spirit with the Greek spirit we come on signs of a new era which lies beyond the limits of our subject.

## 3. PLASTIC ART, MUSIC, AND LITERATURE

On the subject of plastic art there is little to be added to what has already been said in the chapter on artistic industry [1] about work in stone, wood, and metal. The prohibition, " Thou shalt not make unto thee any graven image, nor any likeness of anything that is in heaven above, or in the earth beneath, or in the waters under the earth," [2] was a bar to all progress in this direction, and as a central commandment of Hebrew religion it is only conceivable among a people whose sense for plastic art was undeveloped. Even if it is only partially true that of all the arts painting was the least developed among the Hebrews,[3] it is easy to imagine what this implies for the other arts. It speaks volumes that the Hebrews had one and the same word for to ' paint ' and to ' smear,' or to ' anoint.' [4] We hear of houses panelled with cedar-wood and painted with vermilion.[5] Vermilion was also used to give a red colour to incised designs. Ezekiel [6] speaks of pictorial representations of Chaldæan warriors which had been brought from Babylon, and which had, as he thought, roused in the Jews a desire to have sexual intercourse

---

[1] *Supra*, p. 209 ff.　　　　[2] Exod. xx, 4.
[3] Benzinger, *Archäologie*, p. 233.
[4] *māshach*; cf. *supra*, p. 113, *note* 4.
[5] Jer. xxii, 14. [Vermilion or minium, red oxide of lead.—TRANSLATOR.]
[6] Ezek. xxiii, 14 ; *cf.* Kraetzschmar's *Das Buch Hesekiel, in loc.*

with the men so depicted.   He also [1] mentions having seen on
the walls of a room in the Temple drawings of " every form of
creeping things and abominable beasts," to whom smoke-offer-
ings were made.   Both, it is clear, were foreign importations.
The Hebrew sense of colour was no doubt in itself strong enough,
but how little it could differentiate [2] is evident from the language,
which has but one word for green and yellow, and one for red and
brown.   Hence also the common practice of denoting colours by
sensuous objects.   Thus the " tents of Kedar " [3] means black
tents (from the colour of the black goats from whose hair the
people of Kedar wove their tent-cloth) ;  the " blood of the
grape " [4] means red wine ; and so on.

We should be inclined to expect far more from the music [5] of
the Hebrews than from their plastic art when we remember how
highly music was esteemed in nomadic life, [6] and how frequently
it is referred to in subsequent periods.   Unfortunately, these
expectations are very imperfectly fulfilled.   An unlucky star
seems to have presided over their selection of the various technical musical terms, which are fairly abundant in the Old Testament,
especially in the Psalter and Chronicles.   We can make practically nothing of them. [7]   One passage [8] has been taken to mean
that a soprano melody played on the harp was accompanied on
the zither in the octave.   That would mean that the Hebrews
were already acquainted with the seven notes.   We cannot be
certain about it.   It is possible that voice and accompaniment
were in unison. [9]   There can certainly be no talk of harmony
(concerted music) in Hebrew melody.   On the other hand, judging
from the large use made of percussion instruments, rhythm seems
to have been well marked, and the music of the Hebrews may
have owed this rhythm [10] to its close connexion on the one hand
with work and on the other hand with dancing.   We shall deal

---

[1] Ezek. viii, 10.
[2] This lack is practically universal in the ancient world.
[3] Song of Songs i, 5 ; cf. *supra*, p. 126.        [4] *Supra*, p. 202.
[5] *Cf.* Gressmann, *Musik und Musikinstrumente im Alten Testament* (1903) ;
also Cornill, *Music in the Old Testament* (Chicago, 1909).
[6] Cf. *supra*, p. 129.
[7] This is also the case with the " Selah " of the Psalms.
[8] 1 Chron. xv, 20.
[9] 2 Chron. v, 13.
[10] It was also helped by hand-clapping and beating time with the feet ;
*cf.* Ezek. vi, 11.

with the songs of work in connexion with literature : in their case, of course, we know that they were actually sung. Apart from these, it was on the multifarious ceremonial occasions of life, joyous and sad, private and communal, that music found its place. At the banquet,[1] at the wedding,[2] at leave-taking,[3] and at the death-ceremony [4] there was music ; at the home-coming of victorious armies there was music, and it is in con-nexion with this last that we hear of the dancing of women to the accompaniment of tambourine and cymbals.[5] We hear, too, of music as the soother of troubled minds [6] and still again as the means of arousing passion and ecstasy.[7] It was efficacious even with demons—that is, in the last resort, the meaning of the ordinance [8] that the high priest entering the sanctuary should wear golden bells on his garment. These bells were meant to inform the spirits of the threshold of his approach.[9]

Music must have occupied a special place in religious cere-monial, especially in later days.[10] This is evident both from the Psalter and from Chronicles. The author of Chronicles betrays such an interest in the Temple choristers that it has been sug-gested that he himself must have been one. And he found a disciple in a later writer, who, in a number of additions to the work of the Chronicler,[11] shows special interest in the Temple music, particularly in the instruments. To the Chronicler David was the ideal " cantor and liturgist." To this later age David was no longer the king and hero at the head of his comrades-in-arms, but the pious singer, who " could not help putting his muse at the service of religious worship and composing psalms along with Asaph, Heman, and Jeduthun, the Levite minstrel clans." [12]

Vocal music must have been in a flourishing state in Israel.

[1] Amos vi, 5 ; Is. v, 12 ; Ps. lxix, 13 ; Job xxi, 12.
[2] Jer. vii, 34, xvi, 9, xxv, 10, xxxiii, 11.
[3] Gen. xxxi, 27.          [4] Amos viii, 3 ; Jer. xlviii, 36.
[5] Exod. xv, 20 ; Judges xi, 34 ; 1 Sam. xviii, 6 ; Jer. xxxi, 4.
[6] 1 Sam. xvi, 16.          [7] 1 Sam. x, 5 ; 2 Kings iii, 15.
[8] Exod. xxviii, 33 ff.
[9] Cf. Sir J. G. Frazer, *Belief in Immortality*, vol. i (1913), p. 100, and Sir J. Lubbock, *The Origin of Civilization* (1877), p. 155.
[10] For the earlier time, Amos v, 23, Is. xxx, 29.
[11] 1 Chron. xv, 19–24a, 28 ; 2 Chron. v, 11b–13a, etc. Cf. *RGG*, vol. i, p. 1801.
[12] Wellhausen, *Prolegomena zur Geschichte Israels* (1895), p. 181.

Hebrew kings maintained singers, both male and female.[1] Part of the tribute which Hezekiah had to hand over to the victorious Sennacherib was his Court orchestra.[2] A separate class of songsters sang love-ditties to popular audiences.[3] The beauty of the songs of Israel must have impressed other nations, for the exiles were called upon to " sing some of the songs of Zion."[4] Not the least attractive feature, appealing to the heart and mind of Orientals, is that tremor of the voice which is still characteristic of their vocal music. That this practice goes far back is proved by a picture of a company of musicians, in which one of the female singers is holding her hand under her chin and compressing her throat in order to impart to her notes the tremor of which we have spoken.[5] The ordinary type of song sung is suggested by the proverb, " Like vinegar upon nitre, so is a song to a heavy heart." [6]

I cannot quite agree with the assertion frequently made that instrumental music was only used as an accompaniment to vocal singing. I cannot believe that the music which preceded the bands of ecstatics [7] was anything other than instrumental music. The Hebrews had string, wind, percussion, and jingling instruments. The string instruments were the *nebel* and the *kinnôr*, *nebel* being the word already[8] mentioned as the name of a skin bottle or jar. The name thus seems to indicate a bellied sounding-board. The only question is whether the strings were stretched lengthwise, as in the lyre, or were more or less perpendicular to it, as in the harp. The evidence of the Church Fathers, who speak of a wooden body forming a sort of roof for the strings, is decisively in favour of the second alternative—so the *nebel* must have been a sort of harp.[9] It cannot have been very large, as the performer could walk while playing it.[10] According to the Old Testament, it had ten strings;[11] it had twelve according to Josephus,[12] who also mentions that it " was played upon by the

---

[1] 2 Sam. xix, 36 ; Eccles. ii, 8.
[2] *TBAT*, vol. i, p. 121.
[3] Ezek. xxxiii, 32 ; *cf*. Is. v, 1.
[4] Ps. cxxxvii, 3.
[5] See Benzinger, *op. cit.*, p. 246.
[6] Prov. xxv, 20.
[7] 1 Sam. x, 5.
[8] *Supra*, p. 126, *note* 4.
[9] According to Jerome shaped like a reversed *delta*.
[10] 1 Sam. x, 5.
[11] Ps. xxxiii, 2, xcii, 4, cxliv, 9. Of course, a " harp [*nebel*] with ten strings " might be in contrast to one with a different number of strings.
[12] *Antiquities*, VII, xii, 3.

fingers." The *kinnôr*, on the other hand, was, he says, struck with a plectrum, and had ten strings. The name *kinnôr* is derived from the name of the wood of which it was (originally) made—viz., the lotus.[1] According to the tradition of the Church Fathers, which is no doubt correct, the strings ran along the sounding-board. Egyptian and Assyrian pictures of it show that it resembled the lyre. As it had no fret-board each string produced merely its own note. Thus the *kinnôr* resembled less the zither, with which it is usually compared, than the harp, which Luther evidently had in mind when he translated the word. It was the *kinnôr* that David played to Saul,[2] and the loose woman used it also as she went singing through the streets.[3] Altogether, it was suggestive to people's minds of gladsome, merry music.[4]

On the other hand, the *halîl*,[5] the flute, had elegiac associations.[6] This does not imply that it could not be used on joyous occasions, both secular and religious.[7] The sound of the *'ûgāb*[8] suggested more sensuous ideas—at least, its name indicates that it was the instrument used to accompany love-songs.[9] Again, this pipe or flute[10] was the typical shepherd's instrument. The Song of Deborah[11] upbraids the tribe of Reuben for having preferred piping among the flocks to taking a share in the fight for freedom.

The more powerful wind instruments were the *shôfār* and the *hazôzerāh*. From the name, which means literally 'ram's horn,'[12] the former was curved, whereas the latter, originally a 'short'[13] instrument of metal, occasionally of silver,[14] was straight. We may perhaps think of the trumpets from the Jewish Temple

---

[1] According to 1 Kings x, 12, *nebel* and *kinnôr* were made of sandalwood. In Greek *lōtos* means 'pipe' or 'flute,' but 1 Sam. xvi, 23, proves that the Hebrew *kinnôr* was a stringed instrument. It is difficult to say what connexion there is between *kinnôr* and the name of the Lake of Gennesareth (in Hebrew *Kinarôth*). The lake may have derived its name from the town of the same name.          [2] 1 Sam. xvi, 23. [Luther's word is *Harfe*.—Tr:]

[3] Is. xxiii, 16.          [4] Gen. xxxi, 27; Is. xxiv, 8; Ps. cxxxvii, 2; Job xxi, 12.

[5] The name means simply 'perforated.'          [6] Jer. xlviii, 36.

[7] 1 Kings i, 40; Is. v, 12; 1 Sam. x, 5; Is. xxx, 29.

[8] Gen. iv, 21; Ps. cl, 4; Job xxi, 12, xxx, 31.

[9] *'agab* means 'to be eager,' 'to love.'

[10] *mashrôkîth* (Dan. iii, 5), 'pipe,' is from *sharak*, 'to whistle' or 'pipe.'

[11] Judges v, 16.

[12] Hence also the connexion of *shôfār* and *jôbēl*, 'ram' (Josh. vi, 4, 6, 8, 13); and the same is true of *jôbēl* alone (Exod. xix, 13) or *keren jôbēl* (Josh. vi, 5).

[13] A possible etymology.          [14] Num. x, 2; 2 Kings xii, 14.

depicted on the Arch of Titus. Both the *shôfâr* and the *hazôzerāh* were used as bugles both in secular and religious ceremonies. We have already [1] referred to the significant change that took place when the trumpet of war became the instrument used in worship. Descriptions of the coming "day of judgment" still recall the thrill of terror which the instrument formerly inspired.[2] From the musical point of view neither the *shôfâr* nor the *hazôzerāh* can be rated highly; they evidently gave but one note, the only distinction being between a long and a short note.[3]

The chief percussion instrument was the *tōph*, meaning the tambourine. It was the instrument used by women,[4] especially dancers. We find them also using another instrument which, from its name,[5] may best be compared to the triangle. We know nothing about the size of the cymbals,[6] which are frequently spoken of in connexion with the Temple music. They seem to have been of various kinds.[7] The name perhaps also includes castanets, used by dancing women. The jingling instrument mentioned in the Old Testament [8] was perhaps a modification of the sistrum-like rattles which we have already [9] spoken of as among the excavation finds of the Canaanite period.

The Hellenistic period brought new instruments into the country. Their names [10] betray them—the *kîtharôs* (Greek *kitharis*), an instrument resembling the lyre, something like the *kinnôr*; *pesanterîn* (Greek *psalterion* [11]), a string instrument like the cymbal or dulcimer, said to have had twenty strings; *sumponia* (Greek *symphonia* [12]), the favourite instrument of Antiochus Epiphanes; [13] the bagpipe, *sabka* (Greek *sambyke*), made of elder-wood.[14] The Greek form of the latter was a

---

[1] *Supra*, p. 258.  [2] Zeph. i, 16; Matt. xxiv, 31.

[3] Hence probably also the different verbs *māsak*, ' to elongate ' (Exod. xix, 15, and Josh. vi, 5, connected in both passages with *jôbêl* or *keren jôbêl*), and *taka*, meaning ' to push.'

[4] By men in 1 Sam. x, 5, and a few passages in the Psalms.

[5] *shālîsh*, 1 Sam. xviii, 6. According to Athenæus, Book IV, xxiii, 175, the triangle was a Syrian instrument.

[6] The name *selselim*, or *mesiltaim*, is onomatopœic. 1 Cor. xiii, 1, shows they were of metal.

[7] Ps. cl, 5.  [8] 2 Sam. vi, 5, *mena'ane'im*.  [9] *Supra*, p. 100.

[10] Dan. iii, 5, 7, 10, 15.  [11] The modern *santir* of the Arabs.

[12] The name is still found in the Italian *zampogna*.

[13] Polybius xxvi, p. 1151, ed. Hultzsch.

[14] Cf. *sambucus* (or *sabucus*), ' elder-bush.'

triangular stringed instrument, producing the highest notes, but was considered undignified.[1]

Here, therefore, as in all other spheres, we have evidence of the great adaptability of the Jews, their great gift for assimilating the culture of other peoples.

The literary treasures which the Hebrews brought with them from the desert still continued to circulate among them in oral form,[2] and there is no reason to suppose that the transition to settled life stopped the springs of oral production. It is well known that peoples who do not possess the art of writing have highly developed powers of memory. These demand material to work upon, and the people take pride in their achievements. It is perhaps not irrelevant to point out how frequently the word ' remember ' and its various derivatives occur in the Old Testament. The Hebrew memory contained rich stores of literary treasures.[3]

As we have already seen,[4] the art of writing was well known in the country to which Israel came. It goes without saying that, while assimilating the rest of the new civilization, the Hebrews adopted this art also.[5] But we must be on our guard against the false inference (which we are all too ready to draw in an age so much in love with scribbling as ours) that reading and writing were widespread among the people. Although oil- and wine-jars, dating from about 900 B.C., have been found bearing clay labels with information about the origin and ownership of their contents ;[6] although a source of approximately the same age tells us that some youth wrote down for Gideon the names of seventy-seven citizens of the town of Succoth ;[7] although even Isaiah suggests that a child might write down the few trees that would survive a forest fire[8]—all that does not justify the conclusion that reading and writing, in the literary sense, were

---

[1] Pape, *Handwörterbuch*, under the name.  [2] *Supra*, p. 129.
[3] 2 Sam. i, 18 ; Deut. xxxi, 22.  [4] *Supra*, p. 93 ff.
[5] The material written on was of various kinds : clay (Ezek. iv, 1), wood (Ezek. xxxvii, 16 ; Num. xvii, 17), stone (Exod. xxiv, 12), perhaps also metal (Job xix, 24), animal-skin, or papyrus. According to the material used the tool for writing was the hard style (Is. viii, 1) with diamond point (Jer. xvii, 1) or a reed (Jer. viii, 8 ; Ps. xlv, 2) and ink (Jer. xxxvi, 18). To dress the pen they used a penknife (Jer. xxxvi, 23). The writer carried his whole outfit in his girdle (Ezek. ix, 2, 11).
[6] *Supra*, p. 96.  [7] Judges viii, 14.  [8] Is. x, 19.

common accomplishments. Certainly the Siloam inscription, giving an account of the boring of the tunnel in Hezekiah's reign,[1] was not merely the chance scribbling of workmen in an idle hour. And although Isaiah[2] posted up a large placard with the portentous name of one of his sons, that does not mean that every passer-by could read it. It only means that every one would get to know what was written on it. Isaiah himself[3] expressly distinguishes between those who could read and those who could not. It is even, perhaps, not too much[4] to say that Jeremiah himself, who dictated his prophecies to Baruch, could not read. In order to understand Hebrew literature it is important to remember that the writings were mainly intended to be read aloud, so that those who thus heard them might convey their message to others by word of mouth. It could not be otherwise, if only for the reason that the ordinary individual could not have books of his own. That is the explanation of certain peculiarities of style in the narrative writings which must not be overlooked. For example, the neglect to mention the change of speaker is probably due to the fact that it was left to the person who read the writings aloud to make the meaning clear to his hearers by a suitable change of voice. Again, the recurrence of the same words, or collocations of words, was another means of bringing home impressively to the listeners the message of the writer. The effort to give point to the message is palpable ; for example, when a prose narrative reaches its climax it turns into poetry.[5]

It is not in all cases easy to draw the line between prose and poetry. There are transitions that are indefinite. But the infallible sign that we have poetry before us is found in what, since Robert Lowth, that acute student of Old Testament poetry,[6] has usually been called *parallelismus membrorum*. It is of three kinds, synonymous, antithetic, and synthetic. It is

---

[1] *Supra*, p. 208.

[2] Is. viii, 1. Similarly Hab. ii, 2, but this may be centuries later.

[3] Is. xxix, 12.

[4] Buttenwieser, *The Prophets of Israel from the Eighth to the Fifth Century* (1914), p. 133.

[5] See Gunkel's *Das Buch Genesis*. A similar feature is found in ancient Indian poetry. See Oldenberg, *Zur Geschichte der altindischen Prosa* (1917), p. 96.

[6] *Prælectiones de Sacra Poesi Hebræorum* (1753).

313

called synonymous parallelism when both parts merely express the same thought in different words :

> What is man, that thou shouldst think of him ?
> What is a mortal man, that thou shouldst heed him ? [1]

It is antithetic when the parts express a contrast :

> Good men's talk is like rare silver ;
> A bad man's views are little worth.[2]

It is synthetic when the parts supplement each other :

> Those who know what thou art can trust in thee,
> For never wilt thou abandon those who seek thee.[3]

A special variety of this last kind of parallelism is sometimes called " progressive." Words of the first part are resumed in the second part with increased effect :

> The Eternal is near to all who call on him,
> To all who call on him sincerely.[4]

A similar heightening of effect is exhibited in the numerical aphorisms ; for example :

> Aluka [5] has two daughters : give, give.[6]
> There are three things, that are never satisfied,
> Four never say : Enough ! [7]

The phenomenon of poetical parallelism is by no means confined to Hebrew poetry.[8] It grew out of the antiphonal singing of choirs, or of a choir and a soloist.[9] It has no doubt its psychological root as well, and Herder has attempted to define

---

[1] Ps. viii, 5. [Moffatt's translation.—TRANSLATOR.]

[2] Prov. x, 20. [Moffatt.—TRANSLATOR.]

[3] Ps. ix, 10. [Moffatt.—TRANSLATOR.]

[4] Ps. cxlv, 18. [Moffatt.—TRANSLATOR.] This progressive type is specially frequent in the " Pilgrim Psalms," Ps. cxx–cxxxiv. It is also found in Japanese poetry. See Florenz, *Geschichte der japanischen Literatur* (1906), p. 20.

[5] A female vampire-like demon.      [6] The text is perhaps corrupt.

[7] Prov. xxx, 15. For this parallelism based on numerical progression *cf*. Is. xvii, 6, Prov. xxx, 18, 21, 29, vi, 16, Amos i, 3–ii, 6. It is common in the *Kalevala*, the Finnish national epic.

[8] It occurs, for example, in Babylonian, Egyptian, Indian, and Chinese poetry. In view of its widespread occurrence, one should not at once read into it a dependence of Hebrew poetry on Babylonian.

[9] Thus the Hebrew word *'ānā*, ' to respond,' comes to mean in general ' to sing.' See Gunkel, *RGG*, vol. iv, p. 1642.

it thus : [1] " When the heart overflows, wave succeeds wave—that is parallelism. It never exhausts its message ; it always has something further to say. When the first wave gently subsides, or breaks with a splendid crash on the rock, the second wave returns. . . . The two members fortify, enhance, confirm each other in their teaching or their joy. In songs of rejoicing it is palpable ; in strains of woe the very nature of the sigh and the lament call for it. The breathing-space, so to speak, strengthens and comforts the soul. The other part of the choir shares our pain, and is the echo or, as the Hebrews call it, the ' daughter ' of the voice of our pain. In didactic odes one aphorism corroborates the other, as if a father were speaking to his son and the mother repeated the words. It is this that makes what is said so true, cordial, and intimate. In antiphonal love-songs the very nature of the subject produces such parallelism—love calls for sweet prattle, exchange of heart and thought."

The examples adduced exhibit very clearly a certain balance or equipoise of the lines. This rhythmic symmetry reveals another essential feature of Hebrew poetry. Some caution is still called for in answering the question how far the laws of metre extend, but certain principles may be laid down.

One thing is certain : Hebrew rhythm is not a matter of quantity, but of accent ; in other words, the metre does not depend on whether syllables are long or short, but whether they bear the stress. And as in Hebrew the tendency is to place the stress on the last syllable, Hebrew rhythm is a *rising* one. It is iambic-anapæstic in character.[2] What makes it difficult to determine the metre is that certain words, chiefly monosyllables, such as pronouns and particles, are considered ascending or descending according to the context in which they stand. The same can be seen in the *Nibelungenlied*. In the line *uns iſt in álten máeren* (I, i, 1) the *uns* is unaccented, but in the line *als úns daz iſt geséit* (v. 266, 2) the *uns* is accented. The *Nibelungenlied* further shows how the unstressed syllables between the stresses vary in number ; occasionally, indeed, two accented syllables come close together, with no unaccented syllable between them. Further, the symmetrical structure demands an approximately

---

[1] Herder, *Werke*, vol. x, p. 32 (Ausgabe des deutschen Verlagshauses).
[2] E. König, *Hebräische Rhythmik* (1914), p. 38.

equal number of descending syllables. This, of course, is not always strictly carried out, but probably the musical rendering produced the requisite symmetry by lengthening certain syllables. The same thing is found in modern Abyssinian poetry.[1]

This uniformity of metre can by no means be shown to exist in all cases in our texts. We must always take into account the possibility of mixed metres. These are found, especially in prophetical writings, when the surpassing force of the thought-content of a passage creates forms of expression for itself. Thus the close or climax of a prophetical passage is frequently distinguished by a change of metre. In fact, wherever opinions on metrical questions are divergent one can hardly ever go wrong in following the principle of greater freedom. The conformity to rule shown in these passages seems to be more of an ideal kind.[2] The same is true of the question of strophes. Certain poetical passages are without any doubt arranged in strophes. The occurrence of ' refrains '[3] proves this, even although these do not always occur at equal intervals. Strophes of from two to eight lines can be made out without any difficulty.[4] But, again, there are passages that defy any attempt to discover a strophe arrangement in them.

In Hebrew poetry, as in that of most nations, the system of rhythm is accompanied by a richer and more select style of expression, fond of images and metaphors and personification of inanimate things, and showing a preference for unusual, archaic forms of speech.[5] On the other hand, rhyme plays next to no part at all. In some of the few cases where it does occur it is merely a matter of inflection rhymes, such as are inevitable in an inflected language. A careful study of the forms of speech of Old Testament poetry will probably lead to the conclusion that, speaking generally (for a few alphabetic psalms are exceptions),

---

[1] So I have been told by Professor Littmann.

[2] In this sense König speaks (*op. cit.*, p. 12) of " ideal eurhythmic " ; see also König in *ZatW*, vol. xxxvii (1918), p. 145.

[3] *E.g.*, Ps. xlii f. ; Is. ix, 7–x, 4, v, 25. König, *Stilistik* (1900), pp. 346, 357.

[4] With two lines, Prov. x, 1, to xxii, 16 (the only exception—three lines, xix, 7—is due to text corruption) ; three lines, Ps. xxiv, 7–10, Lam. iii ; four lines, 1 Sam. ii, 1–10, and often ; five lines, Is. xl, 12–14 ; six lines, Ps. xxii, 2–22 ; seven lines, Ps. ii ; eight lines, Ps. cxix.

[5] See Sir George Adam Smith, *The Early Poetry of Israel in its Physical and Social Origins* (1913), p. 8.

the thought-content predominates over a mechanically strict construction of the form.[1]

From the point of view of style Hebrew literature differs from modern literature in one important point. Gunkel [2] has put it thus : modern literature for the most part is a matter of individual great poets or writers, so that modern literary history at its periods of climax cannot help assuming the form of biography ; whereas in the literary history of Israel the individual plays a far less important part. " This feature is due to the peculiar nature of ancient life. In antiquity individuals were differentiated to a far less degree, and tied down by custom to a far greater degree than in modern life ; and just as the individual in Israel considered it a wickedness to do ' what is not done in Israel,' so the writer wrote under the strong pressure of the style that was dictated by tradition and custom for his species of literature." Founding on arguments of this kind, Gunkel maintains that the history of the literature of Israel should take the form of a history of the literary types of Israel. No doubt such a treatment of the literature would open up many promising avenues of approach, but the more it confines itself to the purely formal sphere the less can we afford to forget how one-sided such a study of the history of style would be unless it were supplemented by a very profound regard for those things that are important for the civilization and personality of the Hebrew people.[3] And in the prophetical writings more than anywhere else we are bound to admit that " the living personality stands high above the mere word." [4]

With regard to the occasions that called forth Hebrew poetry, the simplest distinction is that between the public and private occasions.

Public poetry was in the service of political life. Above all it was war that called it forth, and seeing that war itself was looked upon as a holy thing religious notes are naturally often heard in this poetry ; either appeal is made to God to rise against the enemy,[5] or, when the victory has been won, a hymn of praise

---

[1] Cf. König, Hebräische Rhythmik, p. 72.

[2] Die israelitische Literatur, p. 52.

[3] See my review of Gunkel's paper in the Theologische Rundschau (1905), p. 149 ff.    [4] Duhm in the preface to his commentary, Das Buch Jesaias.

[5] Num. x, 35.

is raised to Him.[1]   There are also examples of later enlargements
of ancient hymnody of this kind.   The short ancient Song of
Miriam [2] was enlarged into the so-called Song of Moses,[3] the later
origin of which is shown by an allusion to the sanctuary on
Zion.[4]   Sometimes, however, specifically religious notes are lacking, as in the revolutionary song in which Sheba incited the
Israelites to desert the house of David [5] or in the triumphal song
with which the Hebrew women greeted the return of David,
" Saul has slain his thousands, but David his tens of thousands."[6]
In other cases the song of praise is put into the mouth of the
hero himself.[7]   Such songs, however, in the hands of a gifted
poet, might expand into an ode of the power of the Song of
Deborah,[8] in which quite a number of poetical themes meet.
One of these is the call addressed to Deborah to sing a song to
defeat the enemy.[9]   Evidently the poet is thinking of a lay like
the Arabic *higa* [10]—that is, a spell, an incantation or curse, by
which a poet was supposed to aid his side by his utterance, and
which was considered an element of war as important as, or even
more important than, the armed attack itself.   The idea was
that the prophet, in virtue of his personal gifts and his relation
to higher powers, could actually cause injury to the enemy.   To
this class of utterance belong the words of Balaam,[11] who, it is
important to notice, requires to have the enemy in view at the
moment when he utters his curse upon them.[12]   In a spell song
of another kind sun and moon are adjured to stand still in order
to give the victors a full opportunity to exploit the victory, and
the poet proudly claims that the spell was effective.   " The sun
stood still and the moon stayed until the people had avenged
themselves on their enemies." [13]   This song is taken from
*The Book of the Upright Man*.   This shows that there were

---

[1] Judges xvi, 24.      [2] Exod. xv, 21 ; cf. *supra*, p. 129.
[3] Exod. xv, 1–18.      [4] Verse 17.
[5] 2 Sam. xx, 1 ; cf. *supra*, p. 243.
[6] 1 Sam. xviii, 7, xxi, 12 ; cf. *supra*, p. 256.
[7] Judges xv, 16 ; *cf*. Gen. iv, 23.
[8] Judges v ; cf. *supra*, p. 144.      [9] Verse 12.
[10] *Cf*. Goldziher, *Abhandlungen zur orientalischen Philologie* (1896), p. 26.
[11] Num. xxiii f.
[12] Num. xxiii, 13, xxiv, 2, 20.   On this power of defeating the enemy by
a charmed word may be based the importance of Elisha, as expressed in the
phrase " the chariots of Israel and the horsemen thereof " (2 Kings xiii, 14).
[13] Josh. x, 12.

at that early time collections of songs ; and the title of a second one, *The Book of the Wars of Jahveh*,[1] indicates the tone that dominated them. Apparently the contents of *The Book of the Upright Man* were of a more general kind, for both the lay of the battle of Gibeon and the dirge of David over the death of Saul and Jonathan,[2] and perhaps also Solomon's speech at the consecration of the Temple,[3] were taken from it.

A second *motif* in the Song of Deborah is scorn—directed first against those tribes that absented themselves from the battle [4] and secondly against the fallen enemy and their disappointed hopes of booty.[5] Evidently the Hebrews loved to give rein to their scorn—at least, the scornful lay gradually evolved into a type by itself. That can be seen in the fear that was felt of becoming the target of such a lay.[6] This corroborates the opinion that there must have been a tremendous amount of " sins of the tongue " in Jewish society,[7] and it also explains the exhortation to the righteous not to sit in the circle of the scorners.[8] In any case, the fallen foe was a sure target for scorn ! Even in the lay on the fall of the city of Heshbon [9] this scornful note can be heard. It also dominates the poem attributed to Isaiah on the pitiful ending to the proud enterprises of Sennacherib,[10] as well as the lay on the descent to hell of the King of Babylon,[11] in which the shades in the underworld are joyously stirred at the downfall of this " angel of light," who now shares the humiliation of their own fate. " Even the cypresses rejoice at thee and the cedars of Lebanon." [12] On occasion scorn even borrows features from the dirge : " How hath the oppressor ceased ! " [13] " How art thou fallen from heaven ! " [14]

It is from the Hebrew word for ' how ' (*êk* or *êkā*), with which these poems usually begin, that the Hebrew dirge [15] or lamentation takes its name, *êkā*. These poems were sometimes occasioned by national disasters. Looking to the catastrophe which they saw steadily approaching, prophets adopted the actual dirge

---

[1] Num. xxi, 14.                          [2] 2 Sam. i, 18 ff.
[3] 1 Kings viii, 12 f. (*cf.* LXX), probable reading.
[4] Judges v, 15 ff.                       [5] Verse 28 ff.
[6] Ps. xliv, 15, lxix, 12 ; Job xxx, 9 ; Lam. iii, 14, 63.
[7] *Supra*, p. 232.            [8] Ps. i, 1.            [9] Num. xxi, 27 ff.
[10] Is. xxxvii, 22–29. The passage is not genuine.
[11] Is. xiv, 4 ff.        [12] Is. xiv, 8.        [13] Is. xiv, 4.        [14] Is. xiv, 12.
[15] 2 Sam. i, 19, 25, 27 ; Is. i, 21 ; Jer. xlviii, 17 ; Zeph. ii, 15.

form for their predictions,[1] and more than ever were such dirges sung when the threatened evil had passed into accomplishment. The lamentations over the fall of Jerusalem, which were collected in one roll and which tradition ascribes to Jeremiah, are the most perfect utterances of this kind. The dirge has a rhythm peculiar to itself, the so-called *kina* or lamentation metre, which Professor Budde detected. It consists of a longer half-line with (mostly) three rising accents, followed by a shorter half with (mostly) two:

> She féll, will néver ríse | the vírgin Ísrael,
> Full lów she liés on her lánd | líft her will nó one.[2]

Is it possible that, like the elegiac metre of the Romans, this rhythm is intended to represent the alternation of the flow and ebb of life ?[3] It probably arose from a processional pace. But this example shows with special clearness how the dirge over the national downfall grew out of the dirge over a deceased individual, and it may serve as a transition to poems which had their origin not in public, but in private occasions.

It would be natural to expect the dirge to play an important part among a people in whose midst the echoes of former ancestor-worship had not yet completely died away.[4] We must also remember what we read about the existence of a class of professional mourners, male and female.[5] Usually, no doubt, their utterances and cries were confined within narrow, conventional limits—" Alas, my brother ! alas, my sister ! alas for my lord, and alas for his glory ! "[6] The same impression of conventionality is conveyed by what we learn of Hebrew mourning for the dead.[7] But of course all such barriers are burst asunder by the direct, immediate feeling of a gifted personality like David, and the lamentations which he uttered over Saul and Jonathan[8] and again over Abner[9] are among the most precious things that

---

[1] Amos v, 1 ; *cf.* Ezek. xix, xxvii, xxviii, 11 ff., xxxii.    [2] Amos v, 2.
[3] König in *ZatW*, vol. xxxvii (1918), p. 148.
[4] *Supra*, p. 133 f.    [5] Amos v, 16 ; Jer. ix, 16, 19.
[6] Jer. xxii, 18 ; *cf.* xxxiv, 5. Possibly the form of the dirge is here influenced by the Adonis dirge. See my paper in the *Baudissin-Festschrift* (1918), p. 52.
[7] Zech. xii, 12 ff.
[8] 2 Sam. i, 18–27—the Song of the Bow, so called from the catchword in verse 22 ; but the text of verse 18 is perhaps corrupt. For the song see Gunkel's article in *RGG*, vol. i, p. 1284.
[9] 2 Sam. iii, 33 f.

Hebrew poetry has to show.   Side by side with David, as a poet of the dirge, must be ranked the prophet who wrote these moving lines :

> In at our windows death has come,
> Has entered even our palaces. . . .
> Men's bodies fall upon the field
> Like sheaves behind the reaper,
> And no one lifts them up.[1]

It is no wonder that a dirge over Josiah found in a collection belonging to the Chronicler's time [2] was attributed to Jeremiah, the author of these lines.

But in the life of the individual it was not only death, but life with its joys and sorrows that gave occasion for poetic activity.   How the spring-time rouses love into life finds magnificent expression in this lay : [3]

> Rise up, my love,
> My fair one, come away ;
> For lo ! the winter is over,
> The rain is past and gone.
> The land is all a-flower,
> The time for song has come.
> Hark to the ringdove's note ;
> The fig is showing red berries,
> And the vines are all a-bloom.

It is not often that we find so much delicate and deep feeling for nature in Old Testament poetry.   There are indeed a few other passages in this same Song of Songs ; [4] there is the Forty-second Psalm, whose author, apparently one of the exiles, feels, as he sits beside the waterfalls in the land of his exile, as if they were falling on him and overwhelming him in his hungry longing.[5]

In another respect also the Song of Songs shows to what heights Hebrew love-poetry could rise.   Suffice it to call to mind the " Vision of Delight " : [6]

---

[1] Jer. ix, 21, 22.
[2] 2 Chron. xxxv, 25.
[3] Song of Songs ii, 10–13.
[4] Song of Songs vi, 2, 11.
[5] Verse 8.   Deutero-Isaiah hears in nature notes of sympathy with the events which concern the people : he makes the trees clap their hands with joy over the return of the exiles (Is. lv, 12, and its echo in Ps. xcviii, 8).
[6] Song of Songs v, 2 ff.

X

I slept, but my heart was waking.
List ! there's my dear one knocking :
" Ope to me, dear one, open,
My love, my dove, my pure one.
For my head is wet with dew,
My hair with drops of the night."
" But I've put off my garment,
Why should I put it on again ?
My feet I have bathed,
Why should I soil them again ? "
Then my lover pushed his hand through
the opening,
And my whole heart went to meet him.

These are genuine love-notes ; and the poem contains even more powerful utterances of the same kind.[1]  It cannot be denied, however, that although the Song of Songs contains passages of unique beauty and charm, it also contains others which are undeniably trite and stereotyped.  Take as an example the stiff and wooden description of the charms of bride and bridegroom : [2]

His head is a crown of gold,
His curls, a bush of dates,
His eyes like doves beside the streams. . . .
His cheeks are beds of spice,
His lips are lilies
Dripping with liquid myrrh.
His hands are cylinders of gold,
Set with topaz stones,
His frame is a column of ivory,
Lined with sapphires,
His limbs are marble pillars,
Based on sockets of gold [and so on].

In every line the artificiality is glaring, and as a whole these songs, which were sung mostly at Hebrew weddings,[3] cannot be rated very highly.  One exception is the Forty-fifth Psalm, which is probably late, and was composed to celebrate the marriage of a king, probably not a Hebrew one.[4]  The inequality of these poems in poetical worth should, however, put us on our guard against overrating the importance of literary type as such.

We have already seen [5] that riddles and conundrums fre-

---

[1] *Supra*, p. 159.  [2] Song of Songs v, 11.
[3] Jer. vii, 34, xvi, 9, xxv, 10, xxxiii, 11 ; Ps. lxxviii, 63.
[4] A suggestion as to its origin is made by me in vol. ii of Stade's *Biblische Theologie des Alten Testaments* (1911), p. 273.  [5] *Supra*, p. 190.

quently formed a part of wedding festivities. As Samson's
riddle shows, these were often thrown into poetical form :

> What is sweeter than honey,
> And what has more strength than the lion ? [1]

And there is evidence that poetical riddles must have been
current on other occasions ; for example : [2]

> Who climbed up to heaven and came down again ?
> Who gathered the wind in his hands ?
> Who wrapped the waters in a cloth ?
> Who fixed the bounds of the earth ?
> What is his name, and his son's name ?
> Tell me, if you can.

We find the same literary type in Deutero-Isaiah's elaborate
description of the divine greatness,[3] and in the great speech of
the Almighty in Job.[4] In both cases the form is borrowed from
the riddle. There can be no doubt that it was frequently
amalgamated with the numerical aphorism, which, as we have
seen,[5] was a favourite form of artificial Hebrew poetry.

From love and marriage songs it is only a step to drinking
songs. Some of them seem to have been improvisations.[6] It
is perhaps such a song that Isaiah has handed down to us
in the words : [7]

> Let us eat and drink ; for to-morrow we shall die.

There are traces of others [8] till far into the late Jewish period,
for their praises were then still sung :

> A signet of carbuncle in a setting of gold
> Is good singing at a banquet of wine.
> Gold work around a signet of emerald
> Is a strain of music with pleasant wine.[9]

To people at the critical moments of life was ascribed some-

---

[1] Judges xiv, 18. The original answer was " Love."
[2] Prov. xxx, 4.     [3] Is. xl, 12 f.     [4] Job xxxviii, 5 ff.
[5] *Supra*, p. 314.     [6] Amos vi, 5.     [7] Is. xxii, 13.
[8] Is. lvi, 12 ; Prov. xxxi, 6.
[9] Ecclus. xxxii, 5, 6 ; *cf.* xlix, 1. A late Jewish drinking song is found in
the Wisdom of Solomon ii, 7 f. :

> " Fill we ourselves with costly wine and perfumes,
> And may no flower of spring escape us.
> Crown we ourselves with rosebuds, ere they wither."

thing like second sight. For example, a mother giving birth to a child could foresee its fate ; a father on his deathbed could foretell the fate of his descendants. To this belief we owe a special literary form—viz., the blessing or, as it might be, the curse—a type of composition that enjoyed great popularity. In the late Jewish period still another literary form grew out of it— viz., the testament. The popularity of these compositions was due to the fact that, in view of the great ease with which the Hebrew could represent national and tribal history using the metaphor of the life of an individual, an opportunity was thus provided for reflecting the political circumstances of nation or tribes. It is in this sense that we are to understand the blessing of Noah,[1] of Isaac,[2] of Jacob,[3] and of Moses.[4] They would thus form the bridge of return from the poetry of individual life back again to that dealing with public affairs, whereas the so-called " last words of David " [5] belong to the class of private literature.

The various songs of callings and work form an interesting class. In one we have the husbandman singing as he urges on his oxen,[6] in another a girl busy in the vineyard. One of this latter kind has been preserved :

> Catch for us the foxes,
> The tiny, little foxes ;
> For they ruin all our vineyards,
> When our vineyards are in bloom.[7]

To understand the point of these words it is necessary to know that this " vineyard " around which dangerous enemies prowl was a common metaphor for a girl's own person.[8] This may be part of the explanation of the great popularity of these vineyard songs, and it was probably of set purpose that Isaiah, on one occasion at least,[9] threw his earnest message into the form of such a song. Naturally the harvest songs had a specially glad-some note.[10] The merry cry of those treading the wine-press— *hêdâd*, 'hey'—was proverbial.[11] The builder also had his songs. They were sung at the laying of a foundation-stone,[12] at the

---

[1] Gen. ix, 25.
[2] Gen. xxvii, 28 f. ; *cf.* verse 39 f.
[3] Gen. xlix, 1-27.
[4] Deut. xxxiii.
[5] 2 Sam. xxiii, 1-7.
[6] Ecclus. xxxviii, 25.
[7] Song of Songs ii, 15.
[8] Song of Songs i, 6, viii, 12.
[9] Is. v, 1.
[10] Is. xvi, 10 ; Ps. lxv, 14.
[11] Is. xvi, 10 ; Jer. xxv, 30, xlviii, 33.
[12] Job xxxviii, 7.

placing of the keystone ;[1] and the ceremony of consecrating a house, especially a sanctuary, gave occasion for a poetical oration.[2] Out in the streets the wanton sang her strains to attract customers,[3] and a night-watchman's song is presupposed in the well-known prophetic passage [4] as an answer to the question, " Watchman, what of the night ? "

As each calling thus made its own songs in its own style, of course the intellectual man and the spiritually minded man would do the same ; and a special interest attaches to the prophetical style. Prophets had not always used the pen. Men like Elijah and Elisha and others whose names have been preserved in the ancient historical narratives did not write. Indeed, it is a sign of a general development of literary activity that we find the prophets, from Amos onward, committing their message to writing.[5] The real explanation of this development we learn from Isaiah. On one occasion [6] he declared his intention to collect his prophecies in his disciples as in a book, and seal them there like a legal document, so that, in face of the unbelief that confronted him in his lifetime, he might be justified in days to come by their fulfilment. From these living witnesses, as out of a book, people would read what he had prophesied, and be compelled to admit that he had been right. Thus his prophecies were actually put into written form in order to be " a testimony for the future."[7] " It was unbelief," says Duhm, " that caused this new practice to be begun ; it was faith that made it possible." [8] Seeing that the prophets thus took to writing in order to provide their own justification to future ages, we can understand why, in contrast to most other Old Testament writings, their literary work was not anonymous from the first.

The style of the prophets shows signs of its origin in the intense psychical excitement of its authors. It is a natural and a common mistake to try to understand the words of the prophets too exclusively with the intellect, as if they had their origin in pure intellect, and to overlook the fact that the intellect is only the latest born of human mental powers, while behind it and

[1] Zech. iv, 7.                [2] 1 Kings viii, 12 f. (LXX).
[3] Is. xxiii, 16.            [4] Is. xxi, 12.
[5] Cf. Hos. viii, 12, which presupposes great activity in this respect.
[6] Is. viii, 16.            [7] Is. xxx, 8, corrected reading.
[8] Duhm in Das Buch Jesaias on Is. viii, 16.

beneath it lies the original spring from which the prophetic words gush forth—emotional sensibility. Far down in these depths of inmost personal experience thought and word break forth ; and profound personal experience of this kind, even when it is a prophet who has it, has an element of incoherence, for it is only the echo, becoming audible to man, of a divine *melos* that moves high above the understanding of men, and of which even the most gifted man with his dull senses can only now and again catch a note and hand it on to others. Hence the utterance of prophetical experiences is bound to be fragmentary in character. This lends to the style of the prophets a strong element of disconnectedness and *anacoluthon*. In fact, the supreme experiences of life can never be put completely into words. The unutterable is sometimes more significant than that which can be put into speech—*omnis determinatio est negatio*—and literary art consists in suggestions that rather conceal than reveal. But by this concealment they convey a far better idea of the mystery that indwells in religion than can be given by the most exhaustive attempt, encumbered with all the resources of erudition, to describe it. In this respect Isaiah's brief account of his Call vision [1] need only be compared with the detailed account of Ezekiel's.[2] The contrast helps us to appreciate the great superiority of this literary reserve. In fact, extreme brevity is a distinguishing mark of the early prophetical style. The chapter-divisions of our Bible, and the name of 'preaching' which is usually given to the prophetical utterances, have created in our minds the impression that the prophetical 'units' are much longer than they really are. There are cases where the entire utterance is comprised in one verse, or even less—in one word. The lengthy address seems to have been a product of a later time.[3]

The aphorism or proverb was originally an oracle, for from the beginning the prophetical announcements referred to the future. Their first and last word was the coming change, the coming end. The thought *why* it is coming and must come— *i.e.*, the announcement of the nation's sin—is subordinated to the thought that it is coming. The announcement there-

---

[1] Is. vi.  [2] Ezek. i.
[3] *Cf.* König, *ZatW* (1918), p. 159, and see especially Gunkel in the third introductory essay to H. Schmidt's *Die grossen Propheten* (1915).

fore comes second, but it is indissolubly joined to the other. The fondness of the prophetical style for the obscure and the merely allusive is also a result of this close kinship with the oracular style, of which, of course, the dark, the mysterious, the enigmatical, has always been an essential feature. For the same reason the prophetical style prefers not to mention things by name, but to indicate them by image and metaphor. In keeping with the nimble mind of the Oriental, these images and metaphors, quickly changing, sometimes even actually jostling each other, lend to the style liveliness of movement and plastic strength. They were for the most part of a nature that thrilled and arrested their hearers, for their message of woe was so prominent in the minds of the ancient prophets that it is a question whether, in some of them, there is such a thing as a prophecy of salvation at all. Indeed, that is the burning question at the present time in the criticism of the Old Testament prophets.[1]

Behind this prophesying of woe there lies a mighty pathos. Isaiah's tone is one of extreme passionate force. At times it is violent—especially in his earlier utterances—and at other times repressed, finding relief in expressive sound-effects and biting plays on words, but always dignified and majestic. It is characteristic of his temperament that he loves comparisons with the phenomena of Nature in her excited and violent moods.[2] Amos is more matter-of-fact, harsher, but also cooler and more one-sided. And Micah resembles him. He too was a man from the country, to whose soul, with its healthy, incorruptible moral judgment, the ways and doings of the people of the great towns were an abomination. Hosea was gentler, more sensitive and more nervous, with a great range of feeling, but occasionally also showing a passionate fire. Gentlest of all was Jeremiah, whose heart-felt notes everywhere betray his lyrical nature, and whose tender heart was ground, as it were, to powder by the tragic fate that made him the prophet of destruction to his beloved nation.

The attempt has been made to demonstrate the existence of exact metrical forms in the prophetical writings. In view, however, of the originality of these men we should be wise to be

[1] *Cf.* Cornill, *Einleitung in das Alte Testament* (1912), p. 76.
[2] *Cf.* Is. xxviii, 2, ii, 12 ff.

on our guard against a too rigid application of literary rules. There is no doubt that prophetical utterance has a rhythmical arrangement ; but that does not imply that there existed a rigid mould into which the contents were poured. On the contrary, the contents were in every case the principal thing, and these created a suitable metrical form for themselves, at one time more variable, and at another more equable and consistent, so that the form really grows out of what the prophet has to say and what he wishes to achieve. It is incontestable that, speaking generally, prophetical utterance is poetical in form.[1] But the freedom with which the prophets made use of any and every means of expression that served their purpose is manifest from the fact that they laid under service the greatest variety of types and not only the poetical type. In the prophets that followed Ezekiel, who was the legislator among the prophets, and is fond of speaking in the ponderous " *torah* style," [2] prose-forms are more in favour, while the strongly lyrical Deutero-Isaiah [3] and his disciple Trito-Isaiah [4] seem to cling throughout to fixed metres. This increasing predominance of prose goes along with the adoption of elements which belong more or less to learned tradition. It indicates the arrival of the apocalyptic type of writing, which may be called scribal erudition standing on the shoulders of prophecy. The apocalyptic writer is to the prophet what the exegete and the commentator are to the original author.[5] It is just the difference between the epigone and the original. It is observable here that the visionary style is in an increasing degree wider than the visionary experience, of which it is, of course, a development. There is a great deal of writing in the visionary style that is not vision. When, for example, the author of the Book of Daniel, describing the clothing of the angel, tells how the angel's body (which was, of course, concealed by the clothing) was constituted, he is telling something that he did not actually see, but which he must have learned in some other way—viz., from learned tradition.[6]

With regard to the Wisdom literature,[7] a distinction must be

---

[1] A different view is taken by König, *ZatW* (1918), p. 161.
[2] *thora*, originally ' oral instruction,' later ' written law.'     [3] Is. xl–xlv.
[4] Is. lvi–lxvi.     [5] Dan. ix is particularly instructive in this respect.
[6] *Cf.* my *Daniel und die griechische Gefahr* (1907), p. 32 ff.
[7] [The so-called *Hochma* literature.—TRANSLATOR.]

drawn between popular proverbs and Wisdom in the narrower sense. The latter is altogether an artificial form of literature. The popular proverb can on occasion be in prose : " Where no oxen are, the crib is clean " ;[1] " Let not him that girdeth himself, boast as he that removeth his girdle " ;[2] " The fathers have eaten sour grapes, and the children's teeth are set on edge."[3] The popular proverb is essentially ' pithy.' Two or three words may suffice ; e.g., " Like mother, like daughter " ;[4] " As a man is, so is his strength " ;[5] or " Wickedness proceedeth from the wicked."[6] The rank of proverb may be attained by a familiar quotation which originated in a definite historical occasion, like " Is Saul also among the prophets ? "[7] Out of the large number of writers, mostly anonymous, who uttered sayings that thus became proverbial a few actual writers of Wisdom literature emerged, whose names are mentioned. Hebrew tradition found their embodiment on the royal throne. " Solomon was wiser than all men ; than Ethan the Ezrahite, and Heman, and Chalkol, and Darda, the sons of Mahol : and his fame was in all nations round about. And he spake three thousand proverbs; and his songs were a thousand and five. And he spake of trees, from the cedar-tree that is in Lebanon even unto the hyssop that springeth out of the wall : he spake also of beasts, and of fowl, and of creeping things and of fishes."[8] A statement like this implies the existence of a Wisdom literature dealing with nature, and the character of it is evident from the word used in Hebrew for ' proverb.' In keeping with its comparative, allegorical character it was called *māshāl—i.e.*, ' comparison.'[9]

Of this proverbial Wisdom none has come down to us. Our Book of Proverbs contains no mention either of the cedar of Lebanon or of hyssop, neither of fishes nor birds. As a whole, it is a book of practical, worldly wisdom, giving the result of a rich experience of life—after all, it is usually old people who are fond of adopting a tone of catechesis toward the young when giving them counsel and advice. Nor is the book at all confined

[1] Prov. xiv, 4.  [2] I Kings xx, 11.
[3] Jer. xxxi, 29 ; Ezek. xviii, 2.
[4] Ezek. xvi, 44 : Hebrew *ke'immah bittāh*.
[5] Judges viii, 21 : Hebrew *kā'ish gebûrātô*.
[6] I Sam. xxiv, 13 : Hebrew *mēreshā'îm jêsē resha*.
[7] I Sam. x, 11 ; *cf.* xix, 24.  [8] I Kings iv, 31-33.
[9] *Cf.* Eissfeldt, *Der Maschal im Alten Testament* (1913), p. 42.

to religious matters. Far from it. The purely secular character of many of the maxims shows that the aim of the righteous man was not merely to be on good terms with the Deity, but also to be popular with his fellow-men. There are numerous precepts on good manners and social etiquette, alternating with a great deal that goes deep into the moral life. There is an unmistakable kinship with maxims of Egyptian sages like Ptah-hotep, Ani, and others ; [1] and the Old Testament itself, as is shown by the quotation regarding Solomon given above, makes no attempt to conceal the fact that its wisdom is part of the international possession of the age. Agur [2] and Lemuel,[3] whose aphorisms are given in the Book of Proverbs, are said to have been kings of Massa, a North Arabian kingdom. Job belonged to the land of Uz, which is believed to have lain in Edom or Syria ; and his friends are also foreigners, Bildad of Suah being a Keturæan or Arab and Eliphaz a man from Teman, a district of Edom, famous for its wisdom. Under such circumstances it is impossible to say on which side the dependence lay, or who borrowed from whom.[4]

We can still to some extent follow the evolution of this Wisdom literature in Israel even in the matter of form. The core of the Book of Proverbs [5] is made up of two-line couplets,[6] which in each case exhaust the thought. By and by the units become longer, even double the length, and finally reach the compass of whole periods.

This type of literature is continued in larger works like the Book of Job and the Book of Koheleth or the Preacher (Ecclesiastes). For these works also parallels have been found outside Israel, such as the Egyptian composition of *The Man who was Tired of Life*.[7] The Book of Job is devoted to the problem, Why does the righteous man suffer and the wicked man prosper ? This universal problem, which occupied men's minds from Jeremiah [8] onward to such an extent that it formed the theme of other literature also,[9] presents itself to the author

[1] Cf. *TBAT*, vol. i, p. 201.  [2] Prov. xxx, 1.  [3] Prov. xxxi, 1.
[4] See Orelli's article in the *Proceedings of the Third International Congress for the History of Religion* (Oxford (1908), vol. i, p. 284), entitled " Religious Wisdom as cultivated in Old Israel in Common with Neighbouring Peoples."
[5] Prov. x, 1, to xxii, 16.  [6] *Supra*, p. 316, *note* 4.
[7] *TBAT*, vol. i, pp. 195–198.  [8] Jer. xii, 1 ff.
[9] Pss. xxxvii, xlix, lxxiii.

of Job as a problem of the individual. Why must Job, a man righteous above others, drain the cup of suffering to the dregs ? Job's story was told in an older popular book,[1] but the story as there told presented no problem.[2] The author of Job uses this story as a narrative framework into which he fits his own poem. The Book of Job was in its original form a sort of contest in argument. Beginning with a touching complaint of Job,[3] it developed in three cycles of speeches between him and his three friends [4] till, in reply to Job's challenge,[5] Jahveh Himself appears and, by a demonstration of the surpassing greatness of the divine sphere of action, forces Job back within the limits of humility.[6] The contrast between Job and his friends has been well expressed by saying that the friends find the reason of the misfortune in man, whereas Job sought it, at least in his own case, in God.[7] To the friends, who are whole-hearted champions of the traditional view,[8] it is beyond all cavil that suffering implies sin and that, in God's hand, it may be turned into a means of test and education for the righteous. In former days Job had believed God to be different from what in his illness he now thinks that He is; therefore his suffering can only be the result of divine caprice and abuse of power. But being, as he is, genuinely religious, he can find " no escape away from God other than to Him." [9] And what God teaches him—this is the poet's solution and Job's solution of the problem—is the thought that the world is greater than man, and God is greater than the world. This, of course, was a thought whose lofty flight could not be followed by every one, even within the Jewish pale. This is shown by the interpolation of the Elihu speeches,[10] which again come down to the lower standpoints of Job's friends.

With regard to the style of the Book of Job, the dialogue cannot be called first-rate ; it breaks down again and again

---

[1] Job i f., xlii, 7–17.

[2] Job's sufferings constitute merely an exception to the usual rule, and the explanation of them is supposed to be found in the prologue in heaven.

[3] Job iii.

[4] iv–xiv, xv–xxi, xxii–xxviii.

[5] xxix–xxxi.  [6] xxxviii–xlii, 6.

[7] Duhm's *Das Buch Hiob* (1897), p. 24.

[8] Bildad is outstandingly representative of the traditional view.

[9] Koran, Sure ix, 119. See also my work which forms vol. ii of Stade's *Biblische Theologie des Alten Testaments* (1911), p. 103 ff.

[10] xxxii–xxxvii.

into a series of monologues. Even these cannot be rated very highly, for they lack strict sequence of thought. There is an excessive lyrical element in the increasing complaints of the sufferer, or in his declarations of innocence, or in his acknowledgment of the Divine greatness—passages hymnic in character, which recur again and again both in Job's speeches and in those of his friends. But all through the book, in the wealth of metaphor, in poetic conception, in power of expression, in the fine knowledge of psychological motives and moods, there is displayed much beauty in detail, and the whole poem is a monument of the powerful wrestling not only of human thought, but of the human soul.

Similarly, it was out of inward discord, out of the contest between inherited belief and the new ideas of Greek philosophy,[1] that the pessimistic Book of Koheleth, the Preacher (Ecclesiastes), was born. It is introspective, and strikes in some respects the most subjective notes that are to be found in the Old Testament. It is interspersed with maxims of wisdom, some of which seem to be current expressions. The author must have incorporated these for the purpose of refuting them—unless they are due to redaction by another hand. Such redaction is undoubtedly evident in a number of passages,[2] which are meant to correct some extremely heretical views of the author. It is instructive to be told that the book belongs to a time—in all probability the Hellenistic period—when " of making of books there is no end." [3]

It is, however, one is inclined to think, in the Psalms that the most subjective poetry of Israel is to be found, and it must be remembered that there are psalms in the Old Testament outside the Psalter.[4] Speaking of the songs of praise and gratitude in the Psalter, Luther says : [5] " In these you can see into the hearts of all the saints, as into gardens of beauty and delight, nay, as into heaven itself. How choice and heartsome and beautiful are the blossoms of all kinds of beautiful gladsome thoughts opening there toward God and His goodness!" In these words

---

[1] See *supra*, p. 306.
[2] Eccles. iii, 17, vii, 18*b*, 29, viii, 11 ff., xi, 9*b*, xii, 13 f.
[3] Eccles. xii, 12.
[4] *E.g.*, 1 Sam. ii, 1–10 ; Is. xxxviii, 9–20 ; Jon. ii, 2–10.
[5] In his preface to the Psalter.

Luther reveals a fine perception of the fact that the subject who speaks in the Psalms is the individual. But in this he is only following in the line of the tradition that even claims to know the names of some of the psalmists. This view has been unreasonably disputed. It has been asserted that the " I " of the Psalms refers almost invariably to a collective, the community. Certainly there is some support for this position in the fact that the Hebrew was greatly given to individualize the collective.[1] It must be admitted that in cases where the author of a psalm held a leading, or at least a prominent, place in the community its concerns might become his, and, *vice versa*, his concerns might become those of the community, to such an extent that the line of division between the individual and the collective " I " might disappear. Think only of the numerous references in the Psalms to " the enemies."[2] And do not some of our Church hymns, such as " I will sing to Thee, my Rock," " Had I a thousand tongues to sing," show us that the utterance of an individual believing singer can be the expression of a collective feeling ? There is much in the Psalms, also, that supports the opinion that poems which were at first purely individual, though meant for liturgical use, were worked over and transformed into actual collective compositions. Nay, we may even go further, and arrange all the psalms in two classes—those which at first had no relation to the cultus and were only subsequently adopted for use in worship, and those which from the first were meant to be so used.[3] The former class would include morning [4] and evening [5] hymns, songs from the sick room,[6] laments over personal hostility [7] and distance from Zion,[8] personal expressions of gratitude for deliverance,[9] songs of personal faith in Jahveh,[10] assertions of innocence[11] or of personal penitence.[12] These " spiritual songs " owe their

[1] *Cf.* Gen. xxxiv, 30 ; Is. xli, 8 f.

[2] Passages like Jer. xvii, 18, xviii, 19 ff., and Amos vii, 17, show how illogical it is to find in the fierce curses against enemies an argument against individual origin.

[3] *Cf.* Gunkel, *Reden und Aufsätze*, pp. 92–123 ; his article " Psalmen " in *RGG*, vol. iv, p. 1927 ff. ; H. Schmidt, *Die religiöse Lyrik im Alten Testament* (1912).

[4] Ps. iii, lvii, 8–11 (cviii, 2–6).

[5] Ps. iv.

[6] Ps. vi, xxxviii, xli.

[7] Ps. lii, lv, lvii, 1–7.

[8] Ps. xlii, xliii.

[9] Ps. xxx, xl, cxxxviii.

[10] Ps. xxiii.

[11] Ps. xvii, xxvi.

[12] Ps. xxxii, li.

origin directly to the varying experiences and moods which make up the life of the religious man.[1]

The beginnings of literature actually meant for use in worship go far back, because, in the nature of the case, sacred rites are accompanied by words either spoken or sung, and such words readily assume the form of poetry. Thus the ancient utterance that accompanied the " setting forward " and the " resting " of the Ark [2] is poetical ; also the priestly blessing, whose origin probably lies far back. The lament of the Hebrew maidens for Jephthah's daughter [3] also points to literature of this kind, as does the song with which David brought home the Ark.[4] Isaiah mentions [5] the song which was sung to the sound of the flute on the solemn night of the procession to the Mountain of Jahveh ; that is to say, there existed in his time a sort of Song of Pilgrimage ; [6] and the song in the Temple, which he puts into the lips of the seraphs,[7] has all the features of an actual hymn. When we read how Amos detested the bawling of songs in the cultus of his day,[8] we should be loth to think that he meant earnest poems like those in our Psalter. In one of the psalms of the Exile [9] we hear of songs of Zion, to sing which by the waters of Babylon seemed to the exiles a profanation. Whether we have any of these songs in our Psalter is an open question, for it is impossible to date definitely the cult songs in the Psalter, including hymns,[10] songs of pilgrimage,[11] vigils,[12] prayers of confession and penitence,[13] vows,[14] public laments,[15] and thanksgivings.[16] The strongly marked individualism of their piety, and in particular the party spirit which forms the background of them, points on the whole to post-Exilic times. The feeling that certain psalms are most intelligible when they are taken as productions of the Maccabæan period [17] is too strong

---

[1] To maintain, as Gunkel does, that the " spiritual song " arose from the cult song seems to me unnatural. Of course, the spiritual singer uses many images taken from customs of worship, but in my opinion this does not take place by way of organic evolution, but by that of secondary borrowing.

[2] Num. x, 35, 36.    [3] Judges xi, 40.    [4] 2 Sam. vi, 5.
[5] 2 Sam. xxx, 29.    [6] Cf. Ps. xlii, 5.    [7] Is. vi, 3.
[8] Amos v, 23.    [9] Ps. cxxxvii, 3.
[10] Ps. xciii, xcv, cxiii, cxvii.    [11] Ps. cxx–cxxxiv.
[12] Ps. cxxxiv.    [13] Ps. cvi.    [14] Ps. cvii, cxvi.
[15] Ps. lxxiv, lxxix.
[16] Ps. c, cxviii, cxxxvi.
[17] Cf. especially Ps. lxxxiii with 1 Macc. v.

to be weakened by the objection that the rest of post-Exilic history is too little known to permit of their being dated in that period. But if some psalms do really belong to that period it is very doubtful indeed whether it is permissible to put centuries between them and a great many others, even those which were not originally used in the cultus. It is scarcely possible to shut one's eyes to the fact that the Psalms as a whole form a spiritual and literary unit. Further, it is very unsafe to assume on the one hand that some psalms are Maccabæan and on the other hand to ascribe royal psalms to pre-Exilic times, seeing that kings again sat on the Jewish throne in the days that immediately followed the Maccabæan revolt.[1] Nor can any argument for an earlier origin of the Hebrew psalms be based on the fact, remarkable in itself, that Egyptian and Babylonian psalms existed; for these Egyptian and Babylonian psalms are the product of a stage of civilization which Israel did not reach till after centuries of life in Palestine. The view that a comparatively late origin should be ascribed to psalm-composition in Israel [2] is confirmed by the fact that in some of the psalms, especially the so-called "eschatological" [3] psalms, we find echoes of the prophetical style, and in others, again, points of resemblance in style to the Wisdom literature, as when we find psalmists busying themselves with the problem discussed in the Book of Job.[4]

It is not only in respect of contents that the Psalms exhibit the greatest variety of composition. They also show great variety of style. A lament over some distressful experience is immediately followed by a vivid realization of its removal, which causes the poet to break forth into joy and praise, and then the poem closes with a prayer that the distress may be removed![5] Again, several hymns include a recollection of great things done by God, and thus assume an epic character.

[1] Of course, the title "king" in the Psalms may have been given in place of another title to the head of the post-Exilic community when the Psalms were used liturgically under the Asmonæan high-priest kings.

[2] Gunkel feels sure there must be a great interval between the canonical psalms and the uncanonical, the so-called Psalms of Solomon. I have exactly the opposite feeling. The similarity in form and mood proves to me that they come close to each other in time.

[3] See Kittel's *Die Psalmen* (1914), p. 185 ff.

[4] See *supra*, p. 330, *note* 9.     [5] *E.g.*, Ps. xxviii.

Such recollections are, in some cases, so numerous that the results are historical psalms, little other than versified prose.[1] Once more, we have splendid poems in praise of Jahveh as the Lord of Nature. Chief among these is the Hundred and Fourth Psalm, a kind of counterpart to the great sun-hymn of the Egyptian king Amenophis IV.[2] In some of the cult psalms there is clear evidence of a responsal character. The voice of the leader or priest alternates with the choir, or choir answers choir. In some instances also we can make out quite clearly the point in the poem where the act of worship is conceived as finished.[3]

The separate psalms were probably brought together in some such way as this. Definite bodies of singers, Korahites,[4] sons of Asaph,[5] etc., first formed collections of poems. The order of the psalms in these collections seems to have been determined frequently by cue-words. There was also a group of psalms put together for pilgrims.[6] Other collections, not meant for any special body, but simply for use in the Temple at Jerusalem, seem to have been called " Davidic," without regard to their authorship, because the later time regarded David as the spiritual founder of the entire cultus, and therefore also of the Temple-praise.[7] These various collections were finally brought together in the form of our Psalter. It was later divided into five books, after the fashion of the Pentateuch.[8]

Once again we are taken centuries back by other poetic types of literature—the fable, the parable, the allegory, the folk-tale, the saga, and the myth. If it is correct to say, as Gunkel does,[9] that the difference between the fable and the parable lies in this, that the *personæ* of the fable are taken from either the plant or the animal world, then Jotham's story of the trees who desired

---

[1] *E.g.*, Ps. lxxviii, cv.
[2] *TBAT*, vol. i, pp. 189–191. See *supra*, pp. 85, 113.
[3] Ps. xx, between verses 6 and 7.
[4] Ps. xlii, xliv–xlix, lxxxiv f., lxxxvii f.
[5] Ps. l, lxxiii–lxxxiii.
[6] Ps. cxx–cxxxiv. König (*Die Poesie des Alten Testaments* (1907), p. 17) refers to their liturgical use. These fifteen psalms were sung from the fifteen steps leading from the women's court to the inner court.
[7] See *supra*, p. 308, and Budde's *Geschichte der hebräischen Literatur*, p. 260.
[8] Ps. i–xli, xlii–lxxii, lxxiii–lxxxix, xc–cvi, cvii–cl.
[9] *Cf.* Gunkel, " Fabel und Parabel," in *RGG*, vol. ii, p. 803, and vol. iv, p. 1192.

a king,[1] or the answer of Jehoash, King of Israel, to Amaziah, King of Judah, about the thistle and the cedar,[2] must be classed as fables. The parable, which has not this restriction, has, however, one feature in common with the fable—viz., in keeping with its didactic purpose it represents reality in the form of a fictitious story. To this class belongs Nathan's story of the rich man who took the poor man's one ewe lamb,[3] or Isaiah's song of the vineyard on which his friend expended so much vain labour[4]—a story mirroring Jahveh's experience with ungrateful Israel. While the parable is a story complete in itself, illustrating one single main conception, the allegory attaches less importance to this compactness than to a continuous correspondence of detail. This makes it more artificial, and it is no mere chance that it belongs mainly to later literature. It was a favourite figure with Ezekiel.[5]

One thing militated strongly against the folk-tale in Israel—the exclusive character of its Jahvism. That did not harmonize well with the animistic world in which the folk-tale lives and moves. Therefore few finished folk-tales are to be found in the Old Testament—although the story of Joseph and Potiphar's wife is a counterpart of the Egyptian folk-tale of *The Two Brothers*[6]—but there is no lack of folk-tale *motifs*.[7] Gunkel has enumerated an amazing—perhaps an exaggerated—number of these.[8]

The same holds good of the myth.[9] The distinguishing feature between it and the saga is that in the myth gods are the actors, whereas in the saga the actors are human beings. In a book like the Old Testament, so completely pervaded by the Jahvistic spirit, it could not be expected that myths would occupy a large place, and, as a matter of fact, a comparison of the Biblical primeval sagas with those that were current in Babylonia shows

---

[1] Judges ix, 7–15. There is a parallel to the Jotham fable in a fragment from Assurbanipal's library. It takes the form of a dispute between the trees. The plant fable was borrowed from Babylonia and Assyria by the Greeks, among whom it was previously unknown. *Cf.* Diels' article in the *Internationale Wochenschrift für Wissenschaft*, vol. iv (1910), p. 993 ff.; Baudissin, *Adonis und Esmun* (1911), p. 436.

[2] 2 Kings xiv, 9.   [3] 2 Sam. xii, 1–7; *cf.* 2 Sam. xiv, 5–7.

[4] Is. v, 1–7.   [5] *E.g.*, Ezek. xvi, xvii, xxiii.

[6] *TBAT*, vol. i, pp. 223–225.   [7] *Cf.* von den Leyen, *Das Märchen*, p. 94.

[8] *Das Märchen im Alten Testament* (1917).

[9] *Cf.* "Mythen und Mythologie in Israel," in *RGG*, vol. iv, pp. 621–632.

to what extent Jahvism has repressed [1] the mythological element. At the same time, it is true that when the varnish of the faith of Jahveh which has been laid over so many narratives borrowed from foreign sources has been removed, the mythological element is everywhere manifest.[2] Take, for instance, the second verse of the Creation narrative. The Hebrew word *tehom*, translated by " the deep," at once reminds us of Babylonian mythology, according to which Marduk undertakes to contend with Tiamat (=Tehom), and splits the latter,[3] just as God divides the primeval sea. And things that appear in very faded hues in the Hebrew *prose* shine through a large number of *poetical* passages in the Old Testament in far coarser colours.[4] Recurring to the second verse of the Creation story, we find it speaks of the " brooding " of the spirit. This brooding is that of the bird hatching out its young, and it at once reminds us of the well-known conception, found in other mythologies, of the world-egg. These examples are sufficient to give some idea of the wealth of mythology that can be found in the Old Testament. Lying on the surface and palpable is the mythological element in the narrative of the marriages of the angels with the daughters of men, the unions from which the race of giants sprang.[5] There are other myths, of an ætiological kind—*i.e.*, they profess to explain the origin (αἰτία) of things. Whence came woman, and, in particular, what is the explanation of her desire to her husband ? The myth supplies the answer, by showing us God at work, taking woman actually out of man.[6]

Similarly, the sagas of Israel are to a large extent ætiological.[7] They are not merely due to sheer love of story-telling. There were all sorts of questions that called for answers. Why was Isaac so named, and how did the place Ebenezer get its name ? Why do the Ishmaelites live in the desert still, although they are

---

[1] See my little book *Die Eigenart der alttestamentlichen Religion*, p. 13.

[2] See *supra*, p. 93.  [3] *TBAT*, vol. i, p. 5 ff.

[4] *Cf.* Gunkel, *Schöpfung und Chaos* (1895), and my article " Drache," in *RGG*, vol. ii, p. 138 ; also *supra*, p. 289.

[5] Gen. vi, 1–4. That the giants were the fruit of these unions is to be read between the lines : it is not definitely stated. This is another example of the conscious repression in the Old Testament of the purely mythological element.

[6] Gen. ii, 21.

[7] *Cf.* Gunkel, " Sagen und Legenden Israels," in *RGG*, vol. v, p. 179 ff., and his commentary on Genesis.

descendants of Abraham ? Why does that rock in the south end of the Dead Sea bear such a resemblance to a woman ? Why does the serpent crawl on its belly and—as was popularly believed—eat dust ? Questions like these, etymological, ethnological, geological, and zoological, find answers in popular poetical narratives.[1] That is what saga is, and so it is legitimate to speak of etymological, ethnological, geological, and zoological sagas.[2] To say this is not to call in question their historicity. As to that, each case has to be judged separately, for, in contrast to the folk-tale, which from first to last is a child of the imagination, to describe a narrative as a saga is not to deny its historicity : it is only to say that it has been transformed into poetry. These sagas were usually associated with sacred places. As everybody knows, mankind has always been and is extremely conservative with regard to sites of worship. The Hebrew simply took over the places which were already sacred to the Canaanite.[3] But this laid on him the task of legitimizing their sacred character from the standpoint of Jahvism, and he did this by showing how God, or His angel, once appeared there to one of the national ancestors. A large number of narratives of this kind, cult-sagas (unless it is preferred to call them simply legends), are contained in the historical books, especially in Genesis. Customs and practices of the cultus were also frequently explained by ætiological cult-sagas. E.g., the prohibition against eating the sciatic nerve [4] was explained by the story of Jacob's wrestle with the demon. The original nucleus of all such stories is the separate saga, told in succinct, terse form ; by and by, as the people grow more able to receive it, its compass is enlarged ; the terseness is replaced by a more diffuse style, and a new type of literature is produced—viz., the romance. Simultaneously

---

[1] Isaac, from sachak, ' to laugh ' (Gen. xvii, 17, xviii, 12, xxi, 6, xxvi, 8) ; Ebenezer, " Stone of Help " (1 Sam. vii, 12). That this was merely a later explanation is clear from the earlier use of the name without question (1 Sam. iv, 1, v, 1). Ishmael's mother's flight is explained in Gen. xvi, 6, xxi, 9. The pillar of salt is explained in Gen. xix, 26, and the serpent in Gen. iii.

[2] Of course, these ætiological sagas are not specifically Hebrew. Grimm gives etymological, ethnological, and geological tales. Zoological examples are just as widespread : Why is the raven black ? Why has the hare a split lip ? Why is the thorax of the tortoise quite flat ?

[3] Supra, p. 146 f.

[4] Gen. xxxii, 33. [" The tendon of the hip," Moffatt.—TRANSLATOR.]

the separate sagas were united to form saga cycles.[1]  A splendid example of the romance, "the daintiest little cameo, either of epic or of idyll, that has come down to us,"[2] is the short Book of Ruth, which, in the guise of a charming romance, seeks to prove, as against zealots like Ezra and Nehemiah, who were inexorably opposed to marriages with foreign women, that even among the forbidden Moabite wives of the Jews there might be good and noble women, like Ruth.[3]

All these last-mentioned types of literature are in prose ; and this brings us to the uncertain boundary lines of the ancient historical writings.  In respect of subject-matter also the cult-sagas are the germs of historical writing, for the sanctuary is one of its sources of origin.  The account given by the priests of the sanctuary of the initial vision of the Deity to which it owed its being is followed up by information regarding other things that happened there.  That is what took place, for example, in connexion with the Temple at Jerusalem.  It was, no doubt, a priest or priests who described its erection and consecration, and the repairs that became necessary ; lists of priests were added, with statistics of offerings and income and the number of worshippers, and an account of the pillage and seizures of the Temple treasury at the hands of their own kings.  Then followed descriptions of events like the reform of Josiah, which so closely concerned the Temple.  This chronicle became one of the sources of our Books of Kings.[4]

A second source of material for the historian was the royal Court.  Royal inscriptions like that of Mesha, King of Moab,[5] are wanting, but, as at other Oriental Courts, such as that at Byblos in Phœnicia,[6] records were doubtless kept, both in Israel and in Judah, of the "events of the days."  It is extracts from this source that are meant by "the book of the chronicles of Solomon,"[7] "the book of the chronicles of the kings of Judah,"[8] and "the book of the chronicles of the kings of Israel,"[9] to which reference is made so often in our Books of Kings.  These

---

[1] This is the terminology suggested by Gunkel.      [2] Goethe.

[3] See these points expanded in my commentary on Ruth.

[4] No doubt it also contained the story of the Ark up to its arrival in the Temple at Jerusalem (1 Sam. iv-vi, 2 Sam. vi).      [5] *Supra*, p. 253.

[6] *TBAT*, vol. i, p. 227; also Eduard Meyer, *Die Entstehung des Judentums*, p. 48, *note* 2.      [7] 1 Kings xi, 41.

[8] 1 Kings xiv, 29, and often.      [9] 1 Kings xiv, 19, and often.

references imply that the actual author of our Books of Kings [1] drew his material from them. At least he took from them certain items that regularly recur. In connexion with the kings of Judah these items are the king's age when he ascended the throne, the duration of his reign, his mother's name, his death, and his burial. In the case of the kings of Israel they are merely the duration of the reign and the king's death. To the royal Court also are to be traced certain lists—e.g., lists of royal officials,[2] and of wars, and so on. Actual State documents, such as were issued by a royal Court, are incorporated in the Book of Ezra, but these came from a foreign Court, that of Persia.

A third starting-point for historical writing was the prophetic circles, which felt the importance of preserving the portrait of the outstanding figure of an honoured master. Such a portrait did not need to be far removed in time from the events to be strongly tinged with legendary features, for legend frequently follows hard on the heels of actual events.[3] It is in this light we must view the histories of Elijah and Elisha. The former [4] goes back in all probability to the ninth century B.C., and, in spite of these legendary elements, there can be no doubt that it reproduces something of the immediate impression which Elijah's forceful, choleric nature made on those who knew him. The history of Elisha,[5] on the other hand, has an even larger admixture of legend, and gives greater prominence to the magical doings of that "man of God." The narratives about Isaiah,[6] again, have a more historical ring, and that is still more true of the fuller biographical memoir of Jeremiah, which we owe to the hand of his faithful disciple Baruch, and which forms an important part of the Book of Jeremiah.

Even more important for us than these biographical sketches are the autobiographical notes which we have of men like Amos,[7] Hosea,[8] and Isaiah.[9] Emphasis has justly been laid on the difference between these writings and the State and tomb inscriptions with which we are familiar in Babylonia and Egypt.

[1] In the Hebrew Old Testament our Books of Kings constituted originally one book.
[2] 1 Kings iv.                          [3] Cf. *RGG*, vol. iii, p. 2004.
[4] 1 Kings xvii–xix, xxi ; 2 Kings i, 2–8, 17.
[5] 2 Kings ii–viii, 15, xiii, 14–21.     [6] Is. xxxvi–xxxix.
[7] Amos vii–ix, 1 ff.                    [8] Hos. iii.
[9] Is. vi–viii.

" The prophet does not write to draw attention to himself, to keep alive his own fame to after ages or in the world to come, but to preserve what he has seen and known of God. Not the man, but the experience is the main thing in these writings. Therefore the unpleasant feature of vanity which such memoirs so frequently exhibit is absent from the autobiographies of the prophets. They bear the impress of truth and sincerity." [1] And they have a further merit. These prophets were the first whose self-portraiture preserved for posterity, not external events, but inward, psychical experiences. " Their work in this respect is quite remarkable, when we remember that previous Hebrew narrative shows complete inability to express the experiences of the soul." [2] The " I " passages [3] of the Books of Ezra and Nehemiah, again, taken from autobiographies of these men, are more akin to the usual writings of the kind. They have that tang of self-complacency, especially the passages from the pen of Nehemiah, who, with all his helpfulness to his own people, lays before God with evident satisfaction all that he has accomplished, in order that God may " think upon " [4] him and his doings. In the memoirs of Ezra we hear the self-righteous tone of a rigorous legalism.

These biographical writings exhibit the tendency of incipient Hebrew historical writing to keep within a narrow compass. They start from the individual. This is the case with the originally independent stories of Judges and Kings, and here Hebrew writing reaches a really high level. The most beautiful blossom on this tree is a *Family and Court Life of David*.[5] The directness and graphic power of this narrative, and the convincing truth of its psychology, are equally admirable. Nowhere is there any trace of *Tendenz* or ulterior purpose in the writing, nor is there any gap in the narrative. The author has abundant material to work upon, and cannot have lived far, in either time or place, from the events he describes. After his time we find historical writing expanding into a history of tribe and nation. Of this

[1] Hans Schmidt, *Die grossen Propheten* (1915), p. 25.

[2] Hans Schmidt, *op. cit.*, p. 26.

[3] Ezra vii, 27, to viii, 34, ix, 1–15 ; Neh. i, 1, to vii, 73a, xii, 31, 32, 37–40, xiii, 4–31. But a good deal more than these comes from the autobiographical works : Ezra x, Neh. vii, 73b–ix, x, 1–xi, 24, xiii, 1 f.

[4] Neh. v, 19, xiii, 14, 22, 31.

[5] 2 Sam. ix–xx.

kind is the so-called " Jahvistic " work, *J*, produced in the southern kingdom in the ninth century, and also the " Elohistic " work, *E*, written in the northern kingdom in the eighth century. Both underwent numerous processes of addition and redaction, until they were combined into the so-called " Jehovistic " work, *JE*, but in their original form they were written by men of surpassing gifts, who were far from being mere collectors of the legendary traditions circulating among the people. We have already seen [1] how the writer of *J* succeeded in infusing a higher conception into his narrative. The author of *E* is, in comparison, more reflective. The then incipient prophetism seems to have affected his narrative and to have imbued it with its own spirit. But what is true of ancient historical Hebrew narrative generally holds good to a large extent in this case also. Its charm lies in its naïve objectivity, in its ingenuous attitude toward what is related. The writer tells his story from the sheer delight of telling it. He makes no attempt to conceal the weaknesses of his heroes. He even tells of a fib [2] or of cunning shepherd wiles [3] with evident gusto.

But as time passed all this was changed. The introduction of Deuteronomy in 621 B.C. meant that life was put under a law. This law laid down what was good and what was evil, provided a standard for judging what history must have been, and showed why at one time prosperity smiled upon the people and why at another time disaster fell. A felt belief in retribution began to permeate historical narrative,[4] and history itself came to be merely a medium to illustrate this theory of retribution. It was under the influence of this theory that the so-called Deuteronomists wrote. Deeply impressed by the dreadful events which were bringing about the downfall of Israel and Judah, they laboured to construct a theodicy. Their aim was to hold up as a warning both for their own day and for all time their conviction that it was the great load of guilt which had been growing from the time of their ancestors onward that was bringing destruction upon them. They not only produced original work, but collected what had been handed down—following in this the earlier

[1] See *supra*, p. 292 ff.   [2] Gen. xii, 11 ff., xx, 2, xxvi, 7 ff.
[3] Gen. xxx, 37 ff.
[4] A similar faith in retribution characterizes the view of history of the Chinese philosopher Shuking.

example of the men who had combined *J* and *E*—and used it to serve their own purpose. In the matter of style they used the terminology and the full, hortatory manner of the Deuteronomic legislator, so that there is little difficulty in identifying their share of Hebrew narrative.[1] Then, when in the year 444 or 432 the Priests' Code, introduced by Ezra, had become the *magna carta* of the Jewish community, the need was felt of a fresh version, brought into keeping with that law, of the entire history of Israel from the Creation of the world to the establishment of the Jewish community. That is what the Books of Chronicles are, with their continuation in the Books of Ezra and Nehemiah.[2] Being written from a one-sided point of view, and showing an interest only in what concerned the Temple and its worship, this account recasts the whole of the material that had been handed down. Secular history has become Church history—that is, the historical sense has been completely stifled by the sense for legality. It gives a picture of what the course of history would no doubt have necessarily been had the law been in force in days when it was utterly unknown. An equal lack of the historical sense is exhibited in the Book of Esther. Its object was to explain and recommend the keeping of a new feast, the Feast of Purim, but both in contents and in style [3] it bears the distinct stamp of the type of literature called romance.

But the sanctuary and the royal Court were points of departure not only for historical writing, but for legislative literature. In our section on law [4] we have already discussed the more important legal writings. The Book of the Covenant, probably composed at a sanctuary in North Israel, is made up of juridical [5] rules concerning both worship and morality.[6] These differ from each other also in style. The former take the form of discussions on the matter in hand and merely claim conditional validity, whereas the latter have a personal application and are unconditional in character. This leads to greater brevity ; *e.g.*, "Thou

---

[1] Read, for example, Judges ii, 11 ff., and 2 Kings xvii, 7 ff.

[2] The closing verses of Chronicles are identical with the opening verses of Ezra. As Ezra and Nehemiah come in the Hebrew Bible *before* Chronicles, they must have been received into the Canon before it, the reason being that the historical matter contained in Chronicles was already contained in the earlier historical books.

[3] *Cf.* Gunkel's analysis of the book in his *Esther* (1916).

[4] See *supra*, p. 280 ff.     [5] *mishpāṭim*.     [6] *debārim*.

shalt not suffer a witch to live." [1] A compromise between the priestly and the prophetical circles is believed to have led to the composition of the Book of Deuteronomy, which was introduced in 621, in the reign of Josiah. Its style is peculiar and unmistakable. It is the warm, heartfelt, urgent tone of the preacher, pouring forth at considerable length and with great verbosity and frequent repetition of stock phrases "judgments and commandments and statutes." It indicates the arrival of a style of language that could be used "when thou sittest in thine house and when thou walkest by the way and when thou liest down and when thou risest up." [2] The so-called Law of Holiness [3] has points of contact with Ezekiel, in both style and contents. We must not allow the name "Priests' Code" to mislead us into thinking that it was mainly a manual for priests. It is the later accretions that give it this character. The core of it is rather a "book for the people," [4] intended to exhort all readers, of every rank and class, to obey the Jewish law ; and to this end it seeks to demonstrate how this law took its rise in a special historical revelation to the Jewish people. As a result, the work is partly narrative and partly legal in content. In style it is characterized, both in the core and in the accretions, by a severe, dry tone of erudition and pedantry, by a juristic, systematic construction, by a formal schematism, with a continual reiteration of the same words and phrases. Now and again, as in the account of the Creation, [5] this monotonous evenness produces an impression of real solemnity. The Priests' Code has also a fondness for statistics and names, for the "bones" of history, but its narrative lacks life and colour.

How all this literature was gathered together to form our present Old Testament cannot be explained in detail here. One thing, however, may be said. It was not the result of one single act or *fiat*, as was formerly supposed. Both Christian and Jewish tradition believed that the Canon of the Old Testament was fixed by Ezra and his contemporaries, the men of the so-called Great Synagogue. In reality, it was the outcome of a process that lasted for centuries. In the interval learned scribes were zealously at work, enlarging and elucidating the text which they

---

[1] Exod. xxii, 17.    [2] Deut. vi, 7.    [3] Lev. xvii–xxvi.
[4] *Cf.* Wurster in *ZatW*, vol. iv (1884), pp. 112–133.
[5] Gen. i, 1, to ii, 4a.

had received. These early efforts at exposition, these more or less clumsy forerunners of present-day exegesis, have—and it is a fact that is too often overlooked—left their mark on the text itself, and constitute a tangled growth which in some passages almost stifles and hides from sight the simplicity and unadorned beauty of the original.

## 4. RELIGION [1]

We have seen that the civilization of Israel, in those aspects of it that have been before us, was a mixture, comprising elements which they had brought with them from the desert and elements which they found in the land where they settled. The same is true of Hebrew religion. Israel's entrance into Palestine meant, as we have seen in our chapter on the transition period,[2] a gradual change of their religion from that of the desert-dweller and nomad to that of the husbandman and city-dweller. During that transition time the religion inevitably showed very varied, and at times kaleidoscopic, features.

Speaking generally, the transition to settled life was accompanied by the substitution of territorial association for the ancient clan connexion. This does not mean, however, that the ancient religious bond which united all the members of a clan was altogether dissolved. Even in Palestine we still hear of special or separate sacrifices at which the clan members gathered. David, for example, had a perfectly good excuse for his absence from Saul's Court in the fact that he had been summoned to the annual sacrifice of his clan in his native city of Beth-lehem.[3] There is no need to doubt that Jahveh was the deity to whom the sacrifice was offered. In that case Jahveh has replaced the earlier clan god, perhaps the clan ancestor, of whose former worship relics may still have survived in out-of-the-way corners of the house. Many scholars, for instance, maintain that the teraphim which David's wife Michal found useful in an hour of need was an image of an ancestor.[4] It must have borne some

---

[1] The reader will not expect here anything like a full account of the religious thought of Israel. The author hopes to give such an account in another work. The present section is merely an attempt to describe the most important forms of expression and the most important conceptions of religious life in Israel.

[2] See *supra*, p. 146.     [3] 1 Sam. xx, 6, 29.     [4] See *supra*, p. 166.

resemblance to a human figure, for by placing it in the bed Michal deceived the men who had come to seek David.[1] It is probable also that the household god in whose presence a slave had to be attached to the house [2] was originally an ancestor-image. Indeed, it is more than probable, for the ordinance in question [3] expressly mentions together door and doorpost, meaning that the god was fixed over the door or to the doorpost.[4] It was natural that an ancestor should thus become the " house spirit," and such spirits preferred to live at the entrance to the dwelling. There is proof that Israel shared with other peoples the superstitious custom that a person crossing the threshold of a house did not tread upon it, but leaped over it.[5] This custom was rooted in the belief that a spirit dwelt beneath it.[6]

The protection of the house and of the family (which comes more and more to take the place of basal social unit [7] that was formerly occupied by the clan) was still entrusted to other powers than the tribal or clan god. Here we have proof already of the result of the new environment. The excavations reveal that when Israel entered into the Canaanite inheritance they also took over the custom of making free use of figures of Ashtaroth and Isis.[8] A passage in the Old Testament [9] indicates the kind of incident that might lead to the manufacture of an image—in this case an image of Jahveh.[10] A certain Micah stole money from his mother, but, impressed by the solemn curse which his mother pronounced upon the thief, he confessed his guilt. As an expiation the mother had an image made out of part of the recovered money. This image was set up in Micah's own private sanctuary, and was served by one of his sons. This case of a private cultus came to a violent end. Roaming Danites stole the image, and used it to found a tribal sanctuary of their own in the north of the country.[11] How far this practice of having household images went we do not know. As is well known, they

---

[1] 1 Sam. xix, 13 ff.          [2] See *supra*, p. 134.
[3] Exod. xxi, 6.     [4] Is. lvii, 8.     [5] Zeph. i, 9 ; 1 Sam. v, 5.
[6] Hence also the custom of announcing to this spirit one's intention of entering a closed apartment. *Cf.* p. 308 *supra*.
[7] *Supra*, p. 149.     [8] Thomsen, *Palästina* (1909), p. 70.     [9] Judges xvii.
[10] So many names are given to it that most scholars suppose several sources have been conjoined. It is called *ēphôd, terāphîm, pesel,* and *massēkāh* ; *ephôd* (also the name of part of the priest's dress) is probably the dressed image (*cf.* Is. xxx, 22) ; *pesel* is the image of wood or stone ; *massēkāh* that of cast metal ; for *terāphîm* see preceding page.          [11] Judges xviii.

are forbidden in the Decalogue. One form of the Decalogue, probably the older form, forbids " molten gods," [1] and the use of these must have been felt as a strong contrast to the simplicity of the desert worship. The other form of the Decalogue forbids images of all kinds.[2] To what extent such images were actually worshipped we cannot tell, nor is it easy to make out what form the worship took. Probably a portion of the blood of any animal killed in the house was smeared or sprinkled on the image.

The sheep-shearing still continued to be a real domestic festival.[3] We hear of cases which show that such gatherings were at times very lively. Guests were invited, and the wine flowed. The Passover, the Feast of the First-born, was also a family feast.[4] Whether this was in earlier times held in honour of the moon-god or not, it was now celebrated in honour of Jahveh. It was a reminiscence of the ancient desert custom that the flesh of the lamb that was eaten by those present had to be eaten roasted, not boiled, and that nothing of it must be left over till next morning. Nothing containing leaven was permitted at this meal. Evidently those who took part in the celebration were afraid of being somehow infected by the leaven. On the other hand, bitter herbs were to be eaten along with the Paschal lamb. That these were meant to recall the bitter sufferings of Israel in Egypt, as the later Rabbis taught, is a typical example of how historical explanations were invented for a practice whose original meaning had been forgotten. Similarly at the Greek festival of All Souls, when spirits were roaming about, bitter herbs were eaten as a preventative against demonic influence and to keep the demons from entering the mouth.[5] The care that was taken to preserve the bones of the lamb unbroken had also superstitious origin.[6] Its purpose was apparently to protect the rest of the flock, or perhaps the people present at the feast—perhaps both—that they might be kept unharmed from feast to feast.[7] Another

---

[1] Exod. xxxiv, 17.     [2] Exod. xx, 4 ; Deut. v, 8.

[3] *Supra*, p. 188.     [4] See *supra*, p. 137, and *cf.* Exod. xii.

[5] Beer, from whom this explanation is taken, suggests as another explanation that the herbs were meant to be a purgative and prevent the mixture of the sacred food with profane (*Die Mishna*, vol. ii, Part III, "Pesachim" (1912), p. 19).     [6] Exod. xii, 46 ; Num. ix, 12.

[7] *Cf.* Köhler in *AR* (1910), p. 153. He quotes from Curtis (*Ursemitische Religion*, p. 201) that when the fellaheen bring an offering for a newly born child they are careful not to break the animal's bones, " lest the child's bones should also be broken."

means of securing the safety of the house and the family was the
already-mentioned [1] practice of smearing the lintel and doorposts
with the blood of the Paschal lamb. The Paschal meal was
taken part in by the whole family, including the slaves.[2] If a
family were too small to have a lamb for themselves, they joined
a neighbouring family.[3] On this as on other occasions the offici-
ating priest was the father of the family.[4] This may be the
reason of the practice of addressing a priest as "father." [5] To
the preparations for worship that were customary in the desert [6]
was now added one that could hardly have been possible there
—viz., the clothing was changed.[7] Of course, everything had to
be carefully avoided that had any relation to alien cults. This is
the meaning of the ordinances forbidding sacrifices to the dead [8]
and certain foods,[9] prohibitions which were carried into daily life
also. Questions affecting " clean " and "unclean" cut deep into
family life. We need only recall that sexual intercourse, birth, leprosy, and many other things of the kind involved "uncleanness."[10]

The climax of family religious life was the annual visit to the
nearest sanctuary. Of Elkanah, Samuel's father, we read that
he went year by year to Shiloh,[11] with his two wives, taking the
children also as soon as they were old enough to go. Food and
drink were partaken of at the holy place. A special cell for
worship was assigned to the guests.[12] The fat of the sacrificial
animal was first burned to Jahveh, then the flesh was boiled in
the pot. But the priests in their greed and love of luxurious
ways (they preferred roasted meat to boiled meat) liked, if
possible, to secure their due portion before the Deity had been
propitiated by the burning of the fat.[13] The boiled meat was
then divided by the father among the members of the family,
and of course he occasionally betrayed natural failings—the
favourite wife occasionally received a larger share. Wine was

---

[1] *Supra*, p. 137. See other analogies in Marti, *Geschichte der israelitischen
Religion* (1907), p. 49. It is not an accident that the sprinkling has to be
done by means of a bunch of hyssop (Exod. xii, 22). Hyssop, which had
other uses in ceremonial purifications (Lev. xiv, 4 ; Num. xix, 6, 18 ; Ps. li, 9),
was credited with purifying qualities by the classical nations.

[2] *Supra*, p. 166.

[3] Exod. xii, 4. The codification of the law is late, but it contains old
custom.      [4] *Supra*, p. 152.         [5] Judges xvii, 10.

[6] *Supra*, p. 137.      [7] Gen. xxxiv, 2.      [8] Deut. xxvi, 14.

[9] *Supra*, p. 184.      [10] *Supra*, p. 72.      [11] 1 Sam. i.

[12] 1 Sam. i, 9, corrected text ; *cf*. ix, 22.      [13] 1 Sam. ii, 13 ff.

there also, and it was sometimes taken to excess.[1]   In any case, the character of these meals was a gladsome one.   To "rejoice before Jahveh" became, indeed, a synonym for performing this rite.   The attendance of the whole family seems to have been more a pious custom than a necessity.   The only ordinance on the subject was that every male should appear before Jahveh three times a year.[2]   That was in keeping with the fact that originally only the male was an independent unit privileged to take part in worship.

A sacrifice attended by men only is mentioned in the history of Samuel.[3]   At the high place of his native town thirty[4] men gather for the sacrificial meal.   It is an example of a ceremony attended by people territorially connected, people who lived in the same district.   Samuel, who conducts the ceremony, brings with him as guests Saul and his servant, who have just called upon him.   In this case also human traits are shown.   A cook has prepared the meal.   The guests not only get the place of honour, but also receive the best pieces, the shank and the fat tail of the sheep.[5]

Those who take part in such a meal are the guests of the Deity.   That is the meaning of the technical term applied to them, the "invited" or "bidden" ones.   It also brings out very clearly how sacrifice was understood—it was a meal in which the Deity was conjoined with his worshippers.   This view contains two conceptions, that the sacrifice was "the bread of the god"[6] and the ancient idea of a *communio* between the Deity and the sept[7] that worshipped him.   This second conception was an ancient one, and found its natural expression in the application of the blood.   The first requirement was to pour or smear the blood of the victim on the altar ; if there was no altar at hand one was provided by rolling along a large stone for this special purpose.[8]   Every slaughter of an animal was a sacrificial act. One and the same word was still used for both,[9] and the word for 'altar' is a derivative of it.   Whereas in connexion with smaller offerings (the usual offerings)[10] the worshipper shared the

---

[1] *Supra*, p. 183.          [2] Exod. xxxiv, 23.          [3] 1 Sam. ix, 19 ff.
[4] 1 Sam. ix, 22 (the Greek text says seventy men).
[5] 1 Sam. ix, 24 (corrected text).          [6] Lev. xxi, 8, 17.
[7] *Supra*, p. 130.          [8] 1 Sam. xiv, 33.          [9] *Supra*, p. 128.
[10] *zᵉbāchim*.   The relation of *zebach* to the sacrifice called *shelem* is obscure. Perhaps *shelem* was a more solemn sacrifice.

sacrifice with the Deity in such a way that only the blood and the fat were set aside for the Deity, in the case of the larger ones a whole beast was offered on the altar to the Deity, occasionally even several whole beasts, as " burnt offerings " [1] or "whole offerings." [2]  But as the people got accustomed to agricultural life more importance came naturally to be attached to the offering of bloodless sacrifices, [3] the firstfruits and tithes of the yield of the ground, [4] and the result of this was that the offering came to be regarded more in the light of a *gift* to the Deity.  This point of view was in turn transferred back to the bringing of sacrifices of blood, and in times of great distress, and perhaps also in times such as the reign of Manasseh, when alien cults were introduced in great profusion, there were cases where some even went the length of offering human life as a sacrifice. [5]  It must be said, however, that the practice of human sacrifice in Palestine seems to have become rarer and rarer. [6]  When once the offering had come to be looked upon as a gift, the tendency set in to offer things of increasing value and delicacy of material.  Luxurious people made great use of incense and spices, which came from abroad. [7]  It was in so many ways important to purchase the favour of the Deity, or to pay thanks by a " thank offering " [8] for some favour received.  Some worshippers, no doubt, made use of the opportunity offered by their visit to the sanctuary to put a question to the Deity, to " inquire of Jahveh," say, whether some sickness would be cured, and sought to receive an answer in a dream by sleeping in the holy place. [9]

The times and seasons which summoned the worshippers to the sanctuary were the same as they had been in the Canaanite period. [10]  First came the time "when thou puttest the sickle into the corn."  That was the Feast of *Massôth*, [11] the Feast of Unleavened Bread, named after the unleavened cakes which were

---

[1] 'ôlāh.   [2] kālîl.

[3] It is characteristic that *minhāh*, ' gift ' or ' tribute,' which in old time meant sacrifices generally, including bloody sacrifice (1 Sam. ii, 17), became later the technical name for bloodless sacrifice, " meal offering."  The shew-bread was an ancient meal offering, known as early as David's time (1 Sam. xxi, 6).

[4] *Cf.* Eissfeldt, *Erstlinge und Zehnten im Alten Testament* (1917).

[5] 2 Kings xvi, 3, xxi, 6; Mic. vi, 7.        [6] *Supra*, p. 138.

[7] Jer. vi, 20.        [8] *thôdāh*; *cf.* Amos iv, 5.

[9] *Cf.* 1 Sam. iii, perhaps also xxi, 7.

[10] *Supra*, p. 112.        [11] Exod. xxiii, 15, xxxiv, 18.

hurriedly baked in order that the Deity might receive as quickly as possible a share of the new yield. Until the Deity had been thus served no one might eat of it. Similarly, according to a later enactment no one might touch bread, or grain parched or unparched, without having carried the first sheaf to the sanctuary.[1] It is easy to understand that a feast of this kind would come to coalesce with the Passover, at which the firstlings of the flocks were offered. Like the beginning of the cereal harvest, so also the close of it was celebrated by a feast. This was the *Kāsîr*[2] or *Shābûôth*,[3] called the Feast of Weeks, from the seven weeks which lay between it and the Feast of Unleavened Bread.[4] It was, of course, inconceivable that the fruit harvest should not be likewise celebrated, and as this marked the close of the agricultural year it was so important that it was occasionally called simply "the Feast."[5] Other names for it were *Âsîph*,[6] "the Vintage," and more commonly later *Succôth*,[7] "Booths," a name derived from the booths constructed of leafy branches which it was the custom to erect in the vineyards. These occasions were marked by great rejoicings, and sometimes the high spirits of the people carried them away into excesses.[8] In a larger centre like Jerusalem the proceedings were probably more dignified. Isaiah refers to the procession, accompanied by song and flute, that took place on the night preceding the festival.[9]

Obviously these feasts were the natural outgrowths of agricultural life, and formed its joyous climax. On the other hand, the connexion of agriculture with the Sabbath and the new moon was of a merely negative kind—on these days all work ceased.[10] (When and how the Sabbath, which was originally a monthly festival,[11] became a weekly celebration it is impossible to say.[12]) The association of agricultural life with the place of worship led to the practice of associating Jahveh Himself more closely with the places of worship throughout the land—He being now regarded as the Giver of the products of the newly acquired soil.

---

[1] Lev. xxiii, 10, 14.    [2] Exod. xxiii, 16.
[3] Exod. xxxiv, 22.    [4] *Supra*, p. 199, *note* 5.    [5] 1 Kings viii, 2.
[6] Exod. xxiii, 16, xxxiv, 22.    [7] Deut. xvi, 13, 16.    [8] *Cf.* Judges ix, 27.
[9] Is. xxx, 29.    [10] Amos viii, 5 ; cf. *supra*, p. 186, *note* 1.
[11] *Supra*, p. 134.
[12] Exod. xxxiv, 21, denotes a step in this process.

" To see His face " [1] became the technical term for attendance at worship. This also led to the rise of those local differentiations within Jahvism itself of which we spoke in connexion with the Baal cult. [2] When Absalom wanted an excuse for going to Hebron, where he had numerous supporters, he left Jerusalem on the pretext that he had to pay a vow to Jahveh in Hebron. [3] As if a vow to Jahveh could not be paid just as well in Jerusalem ! The fact is, the Jahveh of Hebron was not the same deity as the Jahveh of Jerusalem. In a similar way, in Amos' time, people swore by the god of Dan, or of Beer-sheba, as if these were different deities. [4] As a matter of fact, Jahveh had taken the place of the locally differentiated gods of the country ; He had absorbed into Himself the various Baal deities. This transition is easier to understand when we remember that Baal was nothing but a generic name. [5] Jahveh thus became " the Baal "—*i.e.*, the lord and owner of the country—and this use of the name gave no offence to anyone till the time of the prophet Hosea. [6] The only possible exception is Elijah, whose importance lies in his contest for Jahveh against the Baal of Tyre. The name Baal even penetrated into proper names, and many of these were without any scruple compounded with that name. The close of the Judges' period and the early days of the monarchy supply numerous examples of such compounds, and these examples are not rendered less valuable by the fact that later tradition, to which the name Baal had become odious, made various clumsy attempts to tone them down. [7] The most instructive example is

---

[1] The phrase originated apparently in the Court style—see 2 Sam. xiv, 24, 28, meaning " admission " to the [king's] presence." The Massoretic text has instead " to appear before Jahveh," a dogmatic correction, due to the thought that no one could see Jahveh and live (Gen. xxxii, 30 ; Exod. xx, 19, xxxiii, 20 ; Judges vi, 22, xiii, 22 ; 1 Sam. vi, 19 (LXX) ; Is. vi, 5).

[2] *Supra*, p. 106 f.          [3] 2 Sam. xv, 7 ff.

[4] Amos viii, 14. Notice, too, the form of expression used in 1 Sam. i, 3. It is to the Jahveh at Shiloh that Elkanah offers sacrifice.

[5] *Supra*, p. 106.          [6] Hos. ii, 17 f.

[7] Jerub-Baal (the meaning is wrongly given in Judges vi, 32), the other name of Gideon, is changed (2 Sam. xi, 21) into Jerubbosheth ; Ish-Baal (1 Chron. viii, 33), a son of Saul, into Ishbosheth (2 Sam. ii–iv) ; Merib-Baal (1 Chron. ix, 40), a son of Jonathan and also a son of Saul (2 Sam. xxi, 8), into Mephibosheth (2 Sam. iv, 4) ; *bosheth* means ' shame.' Beeljada (1 Chron. xiv, 7), a son of David, is ' corrected ' into the more harmless Eljada (2 Sam. v, 16 ; 1 Chron. iii, 8). Baal-hanan (1 Chron. xxvii, 28), the name of an official of David, escaped correction ; *cf.* Hannibal.

the name Beal-Ja [1] (or the name Job-El, [2] although it only appears in the Greek translation). It contains clear evidence that " Jahveh *was* Baal." This fusion of Jahveh and Baal is additional proof that we were justified in including as sites of Canaanite Baal-worship the sites of Jahveh-worship in the Hebrew period. [3] Hosea's words are sufficient of themselves to show that in the course of time other sanctuaries were added to these :

> A wanton vine was Israel,
> And lavishly he bore ;
> The more his fruit increased,
> The more increased his altars ;
> The better his land prospered,
> The better he made his *massebas*. [4]

These *massebas*—i.e., sacred pillars of stones—and *asheras*—i.e., sacred poles of wood—were an indispensable accompaniment of sacrifice, and they betray the continued existence of the ancient conception that stone or tree [5] might be the dwelling-place of the Deity. Even in Jeremiah's day [6] there were people who said " to a stock, ' Thou art my father,' and to a stone, ' Thou hast brought me forth.' " As is easily understood, a cultus addressed to a deity who was conceived in such a strongly naturalistic way could not fail to have pronouncedly sensuous features, and in the account we have given [7] of Canaanite nature-worship we justly borrowed the colouring of Hebrew worship ; the latter is little other than a continuation of the former. There is occasional mention also of images of deity in public sanctuaries. We have already spoken of the one that was brought to Dan, [8] and when, in the reign of Jeroboam I, Dan and Beth-El together became the central seats of the cultus of the kingdom of Israel they both received their golden calves, [9] to which their worshippers paid the kiss of homage. [10] Among the names discovered in Samaria appears one Egel-Ja-u, " Jahveh is Calf " !

On the same level as the conception that Jahveh dwells in the material object, which had at first given to various places their sacred character, is the idea that the presence of the Ark meant

---

[1] I Chron. xii, 5.      [2] Judges ix, 26 (LXX).      [3] *Supra*, p. 105.
[4] Hos. x, 1. [After Moffatt.—TRANSLATOR.]      [5] *Supra*, p. 103.
[6] Jer. ii, 27.      [7] *Supra*, p. 99.      [8] *Supra*, p. 347.
[9] I Kings xii, 28.      [10] Hos. xiii, 2.

the presence of Jahveh. This idea finds its clearest expression
in the words which were put into the mouths of the Philistines
when they heard that the Ark had been brought into the camp
of the Israelites : " God has come into their camp." [1] The words
would be just as conceivable on Hebrew lips. Indeed, the context from which they are taken is an additional example of the
rule that Hebrew narrators make foreigners speak exactly as
they themselves would have spoken.[2] The usual dwelling-place
of the Ark was Shiloh, where there was a permanent temple. We
are not told what had become of the tent in which it was kept
during its desert wanderings.[3] The disastrous result of the battle
with the Philistines was the capture of the Ark and its removal
into the country of the enemy. But, owing to the evil effects of
its presence there, the Philistines sent it home. It was taken to
Beth-Shemesh, and because its presence there also had disastrous
results, it was sent to Kirjath-jearim—in the interval Shiloh seems
to have been destroyed. From Kirjath-jearim it was brought by
David to Jerusalem, where he constructed a special tent for it.
In the reign of Solomon it was brought into the Temple,[4] and
probably remained there till it was burned when the Temple was
destroyed by Nebuchadnezzar. It had outlived its day. By
this time people had become so unaccustomed to cult objects
of a pronouncedly material kind that one could already speak
expectantly of a time when no one would think of it, or remember
it, or miss it, or construct another one.[5] All the great venera-
tion that had been bestowed upon it had been an echo of the
ancient conception of Jahveh as the god of war. The fact that
it was in war that the religious life of the nation had reached its
zenith had been deeply imprinted on the national consciousness
through the centuries. But in this respect also a change took
place as days went by.[6]

Although the view had now come to prevail that Jahveh had
changed His abode to the land of Canaan, which could now be
called His " land," [7] or even His " house," [8] and that His special

---

[1] 1 Sam. iv, 7.

[2] 1 Sam. iv, 8. Notice how in 1 Sam. iv–vi God and Ark are used inter-
changeably.

[3] *Supra*, p. 137.

[4] For the history of the Ark see 1 Sam. iv–vi, 2 Sam. vi, 1 Kings viii, 1–9.

[5] Jer. iii, 16, but see Ps. cxxxii, 8.    [6] *Supra*, p. 156 f.

[7] Hos. ix, 3.    [8] Hos. viii, 1.

dwelling-places were the sacred localities of that country,[1] the ancient idea had not yet been abandoned that Sinai (or Horeb) was His peculiar dwelling-place. Thus it was to Horeb that Elijah found his way, and he had definite experience of Jahveh's presence there.[2] Jahveh Himself came at decisive moments in the history of His people specially to aid them.[3] And His progress is described with sufficient clearness to correct not inconsiderably the traditional view as to the situation of Sinai.[4] The educational value of this belief that Jahveh dwelt on Sinai is not to be underestimated. Other peoples, and especially the Canaanites with their Baal cult, had their gods close at hand. But Jahveh had always been in a sense a God from afar. Jeremiah came to be clearly aware of this contrast.[5] This fact that God dwelt far away became, for the faith of Jahveh, synonymous with Jahveh's power to work at a distance, but it was a feature which distinctly helped to restrict and spiritualize the conception of God, and which could not fail powerfully to promote faith in Jahveh's power to affect history. Jahveh was still a God who dwelt afar off when He was conceived as living in heaven, and there is no reason whatever for questioning the fact that already far back in the Hebrew time the thought of heaven as God's dwelling-place had become familiar.[6]

At the same time, however, people always like to think of their gods as near,[7] and although Jahveh was no longer conceived as actually walking among men, after the wondrously naïve fashion of the author of the Paradise story, people still clung to more or less material forms of manifestation. The most usual repre-

---

[1] Hence also the practice during prayer of taking up a posture toward the holy place (the *kibla* of the Arabs), 1 Kings viii, 29, 42, 44, 48, Ps. xxviii, 2, Dan. vi, 11 ; also the use of sanctuaries as refuges (p. 277).

[2] 1 Kings xix.

[3] Judges v, 4 ; Deut. xxxiii, 2 ; Hab. iii, 3 ; Ps. lxviii, 8.

[4] *Cf.* von Gall, *Altisraelitische Kultstätten*, p. 1.

[5] Jer. xxiii, 23 ; *cf.* Duhm, *Das Buch Jeremia*, on this passage.

[6] Gen. xi, 5, 7, xviii, 21, xix, 24, xxi, 17, xxii, 11, xxiv, 3, xxviii, 12 ; Exod. xix, 11, 20 ; 1 Kings xxii, 19.

[7] *Cf. A History of Civilization in Palestine* (1912), p. 40, where Macalister gives the following characteristic observation from modern Palestine : If in the district of Gezer anyone is accused of theft, he swears emphatically by Allah that he is innocent. But if he be taken to the sanctuary of Sheik Selman, which is in the neighbourhood, and challenged to place his hand on the grave and swear an oath to justify himself, his demeanour will reveal the truth.

sentative of Jahveh was the Angel of Jahveh. Suddenly he appears and talks to men as if they were his equals, but it is only reluctantly that he reveals his name.[1] This is not surprising, however, when we remember the universal belief that to know a name gave one power over the bearer of the name. Not till some word is spoken that betrays higher knowledge,[2] or some sign given that goes beyond the ordinary,[3] does the person perceive with whom he or she has to do. Unexpectedly as he had come, the strange visitant withdraws from sight. Alternating with this conception of the one angel who represents Jahveh's most intimate person, we find the conception of a plurality of angels.[4] This idea is conceived in a more popular way. Just as one of the great ones of the earth is surrounded by his servants, so Jahveh must have His retinue also. And, as Jahveh was conceived as dwelling in heaven, these servants of His ascend and descend by a ladder in order to carry out His will.[5] The conception of the angels hovering and flying is not found till the late Jewish period.[6] On some occasions their voice is audible, announcing to man this will of Jahveh.[7] One of these angels, an ancient demon of pestilence in a new Jahvistic dress, is the avenging angel, who brings pestilence.[8]

A more peculiar conception is that the " face " [9] of God, or His "name," [10] or His "glory" [11]—independent and separate embodiments of that element of the divine that *can* be seen and understood—may appear to men. These conceptions go back very far, but however far back they go they are rather the product of nascent theological speculation than the expression of naïve popular belief. They serve as bridges to unite local cults that were originally alien with Jahveh, the conqueror and new lord of the territory and soil. Corresponding conceptions are found elsewhere—*e.g.*, the so-called avatars of Vishnu, by means of

---

[1] Gen. xxxii, 29; Judges xiii, 6, 17 f.

[2] Gen. xvi, 8; Judges vi, 14, xiii, 3.    [3] Judges vi, 20, xiii, 19.

[4] *E.g.*, Gen. xxxii, 2.    [5] Gen. xxviii, 12.

[6] 1 Chron. xxi, 16. [The Angel of the Lord was " between the earth and the heaven."—TRANSLATOR.]

[7] Gen. xxi, 17, xxii, 11.

[8] Exod. xii, 23; 2 Sam. xxiv, 16; 2 Kings xix, 35.

[9] Exod. xxxiii, 14; cf. *Pene-Baal* (" Face of Baal ") as attribute of the Phœnician goddess Tanit.

[10] Is. xxx, 27, lix, 19; *cf.* proper names like Samu-El (" Name of God ").

[11] Is. lix, 19.

which other cults, even that of Buddha, were subsumed and adopted into the religion of Vishnu.[1] The cherubim, also, and the seraphim were originally independent beings, brought later into relation with Jahveh. The former were probably personifications of the thunderclouds,[2] and the latter of the jagged lightning. They were conceived as winged.[3] Herodotus' statement,[4] that he had seen in Lower Egypt numerous bones of winged serpents that inhabited the desert beyond the isthmus, and that, according to the current account of them, these tried to fly with the dawn over the isthmus to Egypt, but " are met by the birds called ibises, who forbid their entrance and destroy them all," suggests that Israel brought such conceptions with them from their desert life. There was a seraph in the Temple at Jerusalem. An ætiological saga [5] traced it back to Moses himself, and explained that Moses, by means of sympathetic magic and by the image of a brazen serpent, had saved the lives of those who had been bitten by serpents in the desert. Down to the time of Hezekiah offerings were made to this brazen serpent.[6] Isaiah, who received his Call vision in the Temple, saw seraphim in the retinue of the Deity Whom he saw in that vision [7]—that is to say, to his mind mental images like the serpent just named took on a visionary reality, and became the medium to convey to him a revelation of the surpassing sublimity of the God who was compelling him into His service. From his description of them they had a resemblance to the human figure.

But also the God who dwells in heaven has His living *entourage*, and the increasing subordination we find there reflects the gradual victory which Jahvism was gaining over other religions. Belief in the existence of other gods was not forthwith abandoned, but these deities were subordinated to Jahveh as spirits who came together to form his heavenly council.[8] This brings out all the more clearly Jahveh's supremacy. Even the Satan [9] is far from

[1] When Islam entered Palestine it preserved the sanctity of certain places by relating them to angels. In the local name Beth-gibrin it heard the name of Gabriel. It located his grave here, so that the place became sacred to the Mohammedan also. It is the town otherwise called Eleutheropolis.

[2] *Supra*, p. 211, *note* 3.    [3] Is. vi, 2, xiv, 29, xxx, 6.

[4] Herodotus II, 75 ; cf. *TBAT*, vol. i, p. 124.    [5] Num. xxi, 6 ff.

[6] 2 Kings xviii, 4.    [7] Is. vi, 2.

[8] 1 Kings xxii, 19 ; Job i, 6, ii ; Gen. i, 26, iii, 22.

[9] Job i, 6, to ii, 7 ; Zech. iii, 1 ; 1 Chron. xxi, 1.

being an adversary equal in rank to the Deity. He rejoices in all that is evil and frowns on all that is good, and therefore never rests till evil has its free course. In particular he neglects no opportunity of disclosing guilt, and hands over the guilty one to punishment. But the tribunal before which he urges his case is God's tribunal. It was not till a later period that the Satan became the actual author of evil. That was the period when angelology underwent great development,[1] and there emerge proper names for some of the angels.

There was still another special manner in which the Deity "dwelt among" men. He took possession of certain chosen ones, and these men went about as vehicles of His power and grace. Duhm[2] has finely said that in ancient times to meet a "man of God" was equivalent to visiting a holy place. Illustrations of this are supplied by the histories of Elijah and Elisha. The simple peasant who brought to Elisha twenty loaves of the firstfruits[3] would no doubt have given them to the house of God if he had not preferred to be in touch with the living vehicle of deity. And the way in which Saul and his servant went to Samuel's house in order to get information about his father's strayed she-asses[4] reminds us that, as a rule, it was at the sanctuary that such information was sought. Conversely, people felt the same awe at the too close proximity of the man of God as they felt in the presence of a higher being. The widow of Sarepta, who was saved from starvation by the coming of Elijah, and who suddenly lost her son by death, cried out in terror:[5] "What have I to do with thee, thou man of God? Thou art come to bring my sin to remembrance and to slay my son." That is to say, had Elijah not come the small sin would have been overlooked by the Deity and blotted out by the lapse of time. The presence of the man of God brought it as surely to light as if God Himself had come or the Satan had spied it out.[6]

These men of God were the heralds and pioneers of communion and fellowship between God and man. In their case eye and ear and heart have been opened so that they see and hear and know what no other " eye has seen, nor ear heard, nor hath

---

[1] Of the canonical books Daniel is instructive in this respect.
[2] Duhm, *Die Gottgeweihten in der alttestamentlichen Religion*, p. 15.
[3] 2 Kings iv, 22.      [4] 1 Sam. ix, 6 ff.
[5] 1 Kings xvii, 18.      [6] *Cf.* Luke v, 8.

entered into the heart to conceive." [1] Thus the prophets are in religion what creative artists are in art. That is to say, they constitute, albeit involuntarily and perhaps unconsciously, the progressive element in religion as against the holy places—these grow old. [2] Nay, the natural competition between the house of God and the man of God sometimes reaches the point of sharp conflict. Encounters like that between Amos the prophet and Amaziah the priest at Beth-El, [3] or between Jeremiah and the Temple fanatics at Jerusalem, [4] show this clearly. Over against these individual men of God, with whom the progress of religion is bound up, stand the many, the οἱ πολλοί (even if they are priests !), who are still untouched by the breath of the spirit, or merely perceive as much of it as their more restricted power of comprehension can receive. The spirit itself " blows where it listeth." Some it lays hold of violently, and people cannot understand how a Saul can be found " among the prophets " ; [5] others endeavour by the practice of consecration and abstinence to make for themselves a way to fellowship with God. Among the places and things and persons that have been consecrated to God Duhm [6] justly distinguishes between those whom God has consecrated to Himself and those who have consecrated themselves to Him, or have been consecrated by others.

In this connexion we should recall what we found [7] in Wen Amon's ancient notes of travel about the demeanour of an ecstatic in Byblos. What we read in the Old Testament about the Hebrew *nābî* ('prophet') reveals features that are absolutely identical. Of course, we must distinguish between these early *nebiim* ('prophets') and those whom *we* have in mind when we speak of "prophets." [8] A prophet like Amos expressly refuses to be classed with the *nebiim*. A *nābî* was an ecstatic, and his demeanour and behaviour remind us more of a madman [9] than of a mentally normal person. He falls into a state of wild frenzy, and becomes " another man," [10] but not in the sense of spiritual regeneration. He takes off his clothes and

---

[1] I Cor. ii, 9.      [2] See Duhm, *op. cit.*, p. 15 ff.
[3] Amos vii, 10.      [4] Jer. vii, 26.
[5] I Sam. x, 11, xix, 24.
[6] Duhm, *op. cit.*, p. 7.      [7] *Supra*, p. 100.
[8] The change of meaning of *nābî* is expressly admitted in I Sam. ix, 9.
[9] 2 Kings ix, 11 ; I Sam. xxi, 14.
[10] I Sam. x, 6.

lies for long periods naked or half-naked.[1] This type of *nābî* does not move about alone—in one case we read of fifty,[2] in another of four hundred.[3] They traverse the country in bands, working themselves up into passionate excitement and even sweeping outsiders into their frenzy. In order to whip up these sensuous impulses musicians precede them.[4] Even Elisha needs the music of a minstrel before " the hand of Jahveh comes upon him." [5] Dancing [6] and self-inflicted discomforts and wounds [7] were used for the same purpose. All this reminds us of the processions of dancers and flagellants of the Middle Ages, who similarly attracted ever-growing crowds of people.[8] We meet the *nebiim* at places of worship, or on the way thither, and we may therefore infer an organic connexion between them and the cultus of their time. This throws another bright light on the sensuous character of that cultus. These ecstatics were in the habit of gathering round a " master "—Elisha played the part of one,[9] whereas Elijah, the champion of Jahveh against Baal, stands in lonely grandeur at a greater distance from them.[10] Much has been said about " schools of the prophets " ; and the colonies where they are found—we even hear of branch colonies [11] —have been looked upon as a kind of seminary. But to use such terminology is to run the risk of encouraging a too intellectual and rational conception of these *nebiim*. If anything at all in the nature of instruction was given at these centres it was far more probably the study and practice of methods for producing the ecstatic condition than anything in the way of systematic instruction about God and the world. A society which conceives it possible that the spirit can suddenly snatch a prophet away to some mountain or cast him into some ravine [12] is not an environment from which calm, sober, intellectual work can come. Elijah sitting for hour after hour with his head between his knees [13] in order to induce the ecstatic state reminds

[1] I Sam. xix, 24.     [2] 2 Kings ii, 7.     [3] I Kings xxii, 6.
[4] I Sam. x, 5.     [5] 2 Kings iii, 15.
[6] *Supra*, p. 100.     [7] Zech. xiii, 4.
[8] See F. J. Bliss, *The Religions of Modern Syria and Palestine* (1912), p. 255 ff. ; H. Gelzer, *Geistliches und Weltliches aus dem türkischen Orient* (1900), p. 168 ff.     [9] 2 Kings ii, 15, vi, 5, ix, 1.
[10] I Sam. xix, 20, gives Samuel this position at the head of *nebiim*, but this is due to later and doubtful tradition.     [11] 2 Kings vi, 1 ff.
[12] 2 Kings ii, 16.     [13] I Kings xviii, 42.

us of the practices followed in the Indian *Yoga* system. The utterances of those seized by the ecstatic spirit are mostly such as defy intelligent comprehension. Probably they were characterized by the reiteration of similar sounds or groups of sounds.[1] As in the case of glossolalia, or "speaking with tongues," it must have been a hard task to separate the kernel from the useless shell. It is difficult to say what the positive contents of the preaching of these *nebiim* really were. It is remarkable that these men are mostly met with in times of political unrest, when the national idea was more than usually alive, and they may to some extent have been the vehicles of that nationalism. In any case, they are certainly found in the very centre of the life of the people. Their states of ecstasy were, of course, of short duration.[2] Many of them had wives and children and personal property.[3] They were distinguished from other men by their style of dress,[4] and, as it would seem, by tattooing[5] and by the tonsure—that is probably what is meant by Elisha's 'baldness.'[6]

On a level with these *nebiim* Amos mentions the Nazirites[7] as men "raised up" by God. Our information about them is scanty. They wore their hair long. Hair sacrifices played a large part in primitive cults, and it is possible that it was the fear of losing their hair to an alien cult that induced them to let it grow. These men were evidently in earnest in their service of Jahveh, and what they meant by such service is shown by their abstinence from the use of wine, an abstinence which was intended as a protest against the culture of the vine in the country.[8] In this they were at one with the Rechabites, who out of sheer zeal for Jahveh—it was their ancestor, Jonadab, who made common cause with Jehu in the extirpation of the cult of Baal[9]—went still further in their affirmation of nomadic ideals, and would neither build houses nor plant vineyards.[10] This of course put them outside the pale of ordinary life. There were other sects who, without going to such extremes, undertook

---

[1] *Cf.* Is. xxviii, 10, 13, and Hölscher, *Die Propheten*, p. 35.
[2] 1 Sam. x, 13.     [3] 2 Kings iv, 1 ff.     [4] *Supra*, p. 127.
[5] 1 Kings xx, 38–41.     [6] 2 Kings ii, 23.     [7] Amos ii, 11.
[8] *Supra*, p. 184.     [9] 2 Kings x, 15, 23.
[10] *Supra*, p. 140. Diodorus Siculus (XIX, 94) gives a similar account of the Nabatæans.

temporary vows of consecration to God. The Nazirite of later times was one of these. This special kind of consecration merely meant taking a vow for a time, and when the vow had been fulfilled the consecration came to an end.[1] The same was the case with the Temple prostitution,[2] and those who thus gave themselves brought the hire they received to the Temple treasury.

The priesthood was not, in ancient times, dependent on lineage. The Ephraimite Micah, who, as we have already seen, possessed an image of the Deity, appointed one of his sons to serve it.[3] Another Ephraimite was Samuel's father, and Samuel became a priest because his mother had dedicated him to that service.[4] David made two of his sons priests,[5] and there are other examples. The story of Micah is specially instructive, however, because it shows that, when it was possible to obtain a Levite for this office, the opportunity was gladly seized. When a man of that tribe came seeking employment Micah at once took him in place of his own son. We are also told the conditions attached to the appointment. In addition to food and clothing, Micah paid the priest ten silver shekels[6] per year.[7] When, later, the Danites stole the image they commanded the priest, who was a direct descendant of Moses,[8] to go with them.[9] This evident preference for Levites as priests may have been due to the fact that, being members of the tribe from which Moses sprang, they were expected to be familiar with the Mosaic traditions. If there ever really was a secular tribe of Levi, whose members were dispersed over the country by some catastrophe, we should have to assume that they had deliberately studied these traditions in order to gain a livelihood,[10] and that they must have succeeded sufficiently to enable them to raise up a new spiritual tribe of Levi,[11] which included all those who

[1] Num. vi, 1.  [2] *Supra*, p. 99.  [3] Judges xvii, 5.
[4] 1 Sam. i, 28.  [5] 2 Sam. viii, 18.
[6] Say, twenty-five shillings.  [7] Judges xvii, 10.
[8] Judges xviii, 30, in the original text. The present text has changed Moses into Manasseh, a sort of heretical name (2 Kings xxi, 2) which seemed more suitable than the name of Moses for the ancestor of a priest of a sanctuary outside of Jerusalem and a place forbidden to the faithful.
[9] Judges xviii, 19.
[10] The family of Eli also belonged to Moses' line ; *cf.* 1 Sam. ii, 27. Eli's son Phinehas (an Egyptian name, meaning " the Moor ") bore the same name as a grandson of Aaron.
[11] Deut. xxxiii, 8.

followed the priestly calling, many of them being of different descent.[1] Although as yet no special qualifications were necessary for the office of guarding and serving the image of the Deity,[2] some knowledge of the traditions must have been useful. In ancient time the main work of the priestly calling was the giving of the *torah*—i.e., the sacred instruction that was declared by the oracle of the lot.[3] This involved some considerable familiarity with the manipulation of the oracle,[4] and with the technique which had been developed in the course of long years. In addition to his qualifications for "giving the oracle" the priest would also have to be competent to give judicial decisions in the cases brought to the sanctuary for settlement.[5] The offering of sacrifice constituted no difficulty in olden time. Originally every one was entitled and qualified to do this. It was only when certain places of worship, especially the Temple at Jerusalem, gained importance, and when the ritual had become complicated, that specially trained men were required to carry it through. The menial services of the sanctuary, like those of the household, were usually done by slaves. Many of these were aliens;[6] most of them were captives taken in war, native Canaanites, who were well acquainted with the cultus as practised in the different localities. As yet no difficulty was felt in allowing these "uncircumcised in the flesh" to enter the sacred house.

The due performance of the cultus was believed to possess great efficacy in influencing the Deity. If He were angry "let him be propitiated by an offering."[7] If the land were afflicted by some disaster which could be traced to the divine displeasure a fast was proclaimed,[8] and deliverance was believed to be sure. The trust which the people placed in these measures may be estimated by the vigour displayed by the prophets in opposing them. Of course, the confidence of the individual was qualified by the vagueness of the conception of Jahveh. He was in the broad sense the Helper of His people. He had come to be in particular the husbandman's God, giving the rain and bestowing fertility upon the land,[9] and teaching the husbandman the best

---

[1] Deut. xxxiii, 9.  [2] 1 Sam. iii, 3.  [3] *Supra*, pp. 137, 139.
[4] *E.g.*, the use of the ephod; see *supra;* pp. 248, 255, 347, *note* 10, and 1 Sam. xiv, 3, 18.
[5] *Supra*, p. 265.  [6] Josh. ix, 27.  [7] 1 Sam. xxvi, 19.
[8] 1 Kings xxi, 9.  [9] Gen. xxvii, 27, xlix, 25; Deut. xxxiii, 13.

methods of tilling the soil.[1] It was He also who gave success in war [2] and protected the innocent before the judge.[3] To Him too were ascribed the blessings that had followed the institution of the monarchy.[4] It was He who watched over the welfare of the family, opened the mother's womb,[5] and healed the sick.[6] But His power to help had its limits, just as His knowledge had its bounds.[7] In some respects His power was limited by the frontiers of the land whose God He now was. Other lands, other gods.[8] To be forced to leave His land was equivalent to being forced to serve other gods.[9] Again, the individual was not free from the ties which united him with the larger whole, of which he was a part, and as we saw in the section on law [10] this idea of solidarity was in the Hebrew mind in one aspect or another. That is to say, the individual felt himself entangled in the fate of those with whom he was connected, either by blood or by territorial association, either as contemporary or as descendant. Who, then, could know whether good or ill had been appointed for him? Besides, God had His favourites [11]—at least, the motives of His actions were not always apparent. There was even at times a suggestion of arbitrariness on the part of the Deity,[12] and a suggestion of envy.[13] The conception of what we call chance [14] had also arisen in men's thoughts, but pious minds usually subsumed it into their faith in God, so that it became "a happening from on high."[15] All that happened, indeed, happened by the will of Jahveh. Nothing was impossible for Him,[16] and no man could resist His will.[17] Israel was very infertile soil for the growth of the idea of a magic that could force the hand of the Deity.

Seeing that everything came from God, evil also was His doing, and that too not only in the sense of harm, but even sin itself. He hardened men's hearts.[18] It was He who made Eli's sons

---

[1] *Supra*, p. 199.  [2] *Supra*, p. 254.  [3] *Supra*, p. 269 f.
[4] *Supra*, p. 242.  [5] Gen. xxix, 31, xxx, 22.
[6] Deut. xxxii, 39; also cf. *supra*, p. 300.
[7] Gen. vi, 5, xi, 5, xviii, 21; Job i, 7, ii, 2.
[8] Judges xi, 24; 2 Kings v, 17, xvii, 25.
[9] Gen. iv, 14; I Sam. xxvi, 19.
[10] *Supra*, p. 277.  [11] Exod. xxxiii, 19.  [12] I Sam. xv, 25.
[13] Gen. iii, 22.  [14] I Sam. vi, 9, xx, 26.
[15] Gen. xxvii, 20; Exod. xxi, 13.
[16] Gen. xviii, 14; I Sam. xiv, 6.  [17] Gen. xxiv, 50.
[18] Exod. iv, 21, vii, 3, x, 1, 20, 27, xi, 10; Deut. ii, 30.

disobey their father, and He did so because He had already determined to destroy them.[1] He sent the spirit of dissension between Abimelech and the citizens of Shechem,[2] and allowed the spirit of lying to befool Ahab.[3] It was He who tempted David to number the people.[4] And so on. The most succinct explanation of what was meant by sin is that it is " deeds that are not done and therefore ought not to be."[5] This shows very clearly the power of custom, whose unwritten law prescribes to each individual what to do and what not to do. And yet this code prescribed by custom was not immutable : it was just as variable as the moral conventions which were based upon it. This, of course, gave rise to a new uncertainty, for the individual never really knew how he stood toward God. From the religious point of view sin was disobedience to God's will,[6] a disobedience which God punished.[7] Only by his failure and his misfortune could the individual learn that things were not with him as they should be. Toward God only one attitude was possible—submission. Complete resignation to His will was the fundamental principle of Semitic piety, the same principle as is expressed by the name Islam. " Let God do as seemeth to Him good "—these were the words that rose to the lips of the pious Hebrew. Israel did not breed Promethean natures. In contrast to the ' theanthropic ' view of religion of the Indo-European peoples, in whose minds the dividing line between God and man comes very near to disappearing, the Semitic and Hebrew view was absolutely theocratic, in the sense that it placed man as toward God in the position of servant and slave, and dug between the two an impassable gulf. It is very significant that " the fear of God " was in Israel the common expression that corresponds most nearly to what we mean by " religion." Besides, what importance, after all, attached to the individual ? Ever and anon he is absorbed into the collective whole. The main interest lay in the prosperity of the family, the clan, the tribe, the nation, and it is, to us, astounding to think how little the individual demanded for himself.

For this collective whole a glorious future was in store, and men lulled themselves with dreams of a day when things would

---

[1] 1 Sam. ii, 25.　　　[2] Judges ix, 23.　　　[3] 1 Kings xxii, 20.
[4] 2 Sam. xxiv, 1.　　　[5] Gen. xx, 9, xxxiv, 7 ; 2 Sam. xiii, 12.
[6] *Cf.* the Paradise narrative and Gen. xxxix, 9.　　　[7] 1 Sam. xxvi, 23.

turn.[1] At that time, indeed, such dreams were universal throughout the Near East.[2] There is neither light nor colour in the future of the individual. On the brighter conceptions of an earlier age [3] with regard to existence after death and a lasting relationship between the living and the dead Jahvism laid an icy hand; and it did so with the deliberate purpose of extirpating worship of the dead. One could not serve two masters—Jahveh and the spirits of the dead. Therefore all that was connected with death was with increasing rigour laid under the curse of uncleanness, and all practices connected with it were as far as possible suppressed.[4] To extirpate them completely was impossible—their roots went too deep. This is the explanation of several mourning customs which led us to infer that worship of the dead did formerly prevail among the Hebrews.[5] How difficult it was to break entirely with long-established customs is clear from the case of Saul. The same man who is said to have expelled from the country [6] all necromancers himself runs in his hour of despair to a woman necromancer in order to get her to call up Samuel; [7] and even centuries afterward we still hear of the use of the oracle of the dead.[8] All the same, however, speaking generally, the dead were considered to be dead. Their existence in Sheol,[9] the Hebrew underworld, could hardly be called life. Wrapped in deep gloom and hopelessness [10] was the place " whence man shall not return." [11] Sheol was conceived to be a land, sometimes a city or a palace, fortified with gates and bolts.[12] In that land live together those that were together on earth. That was the after-effect of the ancient conceptions of the family grave, only they are projected on a larger surface. In one passage Ezekiel [13] describes how each nation with its members gathers round the

---

[1] Amos v, 18.

[2] See my article, " Eschatologie, israelitische und jüdische," in *RGG*.

[3] *Supra*, pp. 75 f, 132 f.      [4] *Cf*. Is. xxviii, 15; Ezek. xliii, 7.

[5] *Supra*, p. 132.      [6] 1 Sam. xxviii, 3.      [7] 1 Sam. xxviii, 5.

[8] Is. lvii, 9, lxv, 4; Lev. xix, 31, xx, 6, 27.

[9] The conception of Sheol probably arose outside of Israel. There is no acceptable Hebrew etymology of the name. See Beer, *Der biblische Hades* (1902), p. 3. See also *supra*, p. 289.

[10] Job xiv, 18–22.      [11] Job x, 21.

[12] Ps. cvii, 18; Is. xxxviii, 10. The gates and bolts correspond to the Babylonian conception expressed in Ishtar's descent into hell (cf. *TBAT*, vol. i, p. 65 ff.).      [13] Ezek. xxxii, 17–32.

one grave of its king, but Ezekiel himself nullifies this idea, which takes no account whatever of the moral character of the dead, by introducing the initial germ of a division into two classes. In the one class he places the mighty ones who found an honourable burial ; in the other the uncircumcised, who went down to the underworld in their shame, uncared for and unburied like those that fell by the sword. They lie in the furthest nooks and corners of Sheol, and when some mighty one, like Pharaoh, descends to them, scornful joy finds vent in the other camp.[1] It is worth noticing that these first hints of a separation within the Hebrew world of the dead are found at so late a period. It was the task of later centuries further to develop them.

In the interval, however, the religion of the Hebrews had undergone a radical transformation. Up to this point there was little in it to distinguish it from the religions of their immediate neighbours—the Moabites with their god Chemosh or the Ammonites with their god Milcom. But whereas these peoples have long disappeared, leaving no trace, Israel has outlived the centuries. In its encounter with the great world, whose dimensions and power it first really came to know in the mighty onset of Assyria, and later of Babylon, Israel was not destroyed. Men appeared who were able to include or subsume this world into their faith in Jahveh. To them God now became greater than His people, and His greatness shattered the ancient formulas " Jahveh and Israel," " Jahveh and Canaan." It was He Himself who was leading these mighty Assyrian and Chaldæan peoples and all their allies *against* His own people. These men took up their stand with the announcement, unprecedentedly bold, that destruction was coming upon Israel. In so doing they ran directly counter to the fondest expectations of the people. The preaching of Amos [2] turned the " Day of Light " for which they were longing into a Day of Darkness, and a century later it was described by Zephaniah [3] in these words :

A day of wrath, that day, of woe and anguish,
A day of stress and distress, darkness and gloom,
A day of cloud and thundercloud,
A day of trumpet-blast and battle-cry
Against towns fortified and ramparts high.

---

[1] Is. xiv, 9.      [2] Amos v, 18–20.
[3] Zeph. i, 15. [Moffatt's translation.—TRANSLATOR.]

A day of wrath that day, *dies iræ dies illa.* How many millions of human hearts have quailed at the sound of these words! What an impression they must have made when they fell at first on the ear of a joyous populace, free from care, holding high festival! Their effect is comparable with that produced when the day thus prophesied came.   As a later writer [1] puts it :

> No lilting now of tambourines,
> No lilting now of lutes,
> No sounds of revelry :
> No singing as the wine is drunk.
> For any liquor has a bitter taste :
> Gladness has gone from the earth,
> And pleasure is no more.

The inward struggles experienced by the prophets when, under divine compulsion, they forced themselves to utter such messages as these can be read between the lines of their writings. Only in the case of Jeremiah are they plainly told.   But they knew why it could not be otherwise.   Using the metaphor of God, the master-builder, laying the plumb-line to the wall, Amos [2] expressed the necessity in irrefutable words :  God requires straightforward, moral integrity, and will no longer suffer injustice and violence to go unpunished.   And Hosea, who ascribes to Him softer features, and emphasizes the love with which He took Israel to be His own, as a husband takes a wife, learned by personal experience what Jahveh had gone through with Israel, beholding their ingratitude and infidelity, their desertion of Him for idolatry, moral corruption, and false policy external and internal.   Isaiah, filled with the thought of Jahveh's surpassing majesty,[3] sees how in their doings the people and their leaders—he addresses the leaders specially, because he himself seems to have belonged to the upper class—mock that great thought by the trust they put in false supports and by the wickedness of their life.   And when, in spite of all that, the people still take pleasure in the mere forms of worship, the unanimous demand of the prophets, to which Micah [4] gives the

---

[1] Is. xxiv, 8 f., 11.   [Moffatt's translation.—TRANSLATOR.]

[2] Amos vii, 7–9.

[3] To Isaiah this majesty or sublimity means holiness, including, of course, the sphere of moral life.

[4] That is, if Mic. vi, 6–8, is from Micah's pen.

most decisive utterance, is, " Not worship, but righteousness of life." Jeremiah, who lived a century later, had a still lower opinion of the prevailing worship. We have only to listen a moment to the touching conversation of this the most sensitive of all the prophets with his God to see that he did not think any external forms of worship could bring about perfect fellowship with God. This prophet, who, in the attempt to reconcile his profound emotional nature with his strong, clear prophetic consciousness, felt more deeply than any other before him the personal nature of religion, has justly been styled the discoverer of the human heart.

By giving such a prominent place in their preaching to prophecies of disaster [1] the prophets of course came into opposition with their contemporaries, but their words did not all fall on stony ground. One result of Isaiah's labours seems to have been the abolition of the worship of the brazen serpent in the Temple at Jerusalem. This was apparently the sole tangible outcome of the reformation of King Hezekiah.[2] As another result of that prophet's ministry we hear of ' disciples ' of his [3] whom he himself regarded as the living vehicles and witnesses of his message. The remarkable fulfilment of some of his prophecies—e.g., the deliverance of Jerusalem from Sennacherib —would have been sufficient proof to these disciples of Isaiah's prophetic authority, if they needed any further proof than the force of the prophet's own personality. King Manasseh (698– 643), forced perhaps by political necessity, threw wide open the gates of the Temple at Jerusalem [4] to the pantheon of Assyria and Babylon, and thus drove into closer alliance all those people who clung uncompromisingly to their Jahvistic faith. The King ennobled them by considering some of them worthy of a

---

[1] The most disputed question to-day in the criticism of the prophets is how far the message of the ancient prophets contained an expectation of deliverance. Whatever decision may be reached on this matter, the main emphasis in pre-Exilic prophecy was on the announcement of disaster.

[2] 2 Kings xviii, 4.

[3] Is. viii, 16.

[4] Political alliances did sometimes lead to the entrance of the gods of the allies. This can be read between the lines of certain passages—e.g., Is. x, 4, xvii, 10, xxviii, 15, 18. The same cause also led to the introduction of foreign fashions—e.g., the foreign dress of royal princes and others, against which Zephaniah protested (i, 8). Budde deals with the attitude taken up by Manasseh in his *Auf dem Wege zum Monotheismus* (1910).

martyr's death in the good cause.[1] Meantime, the catastrophe foretold did not come. Did that mean that Jahveh was still giving them a respite ? Or might not the disaster be postponed, or even cancelled, if the people could only be made once more a people pleasing to God, or if such a people could be created, in anticipation of the holy people expected by Isaiah in the days to come ? This thought took possession of men's minds ; ways and means for its realization were found. If, as the prophets said, it was the sin of the people that was calling down the judgment, then the task before them was to restate as prohibitions and commands those things which the prophets declared to be the cause of the judgment, and to make them part of a regular constitution which the nation could be compelled to keep. The secular arm gave its aid to these spiritual pedagogues, and as a result Deuteronomy was solemnly introduced as the law of the land in the year 621.[2] Any accurate estimate of its import- ance and meaning must take into account this eschatological background. It was meant to be a means of warding off the threatened judgment. This also explains the part which the idea of retribution now began to play, and that is of fundamental importance for understanding the Jewish legal system as a whole. It built a direct bridge from prophetism to legalism.

There is one thing that seems to contradict this. We have seen that the prophets opposed the cultus, but is not the law, even the Deuteronomic law, to a large extent a law regulating the cultus ? That is certainly the case ; but when compared with the conditions that had been handed down, the require- ments of the law in the matter of worship were enormously reduced. Henceforth sacrifice was to be legitimately offered only in one place—the Temple at Jerusalem. All sanctuaries outside of Jerusalem were to be suppressed. That was the surest way to get under control the outward expressions of the people's religion. It seems, indeed, to be a concession to the public opinion that worship when duly and rightly performed secured acceptance with God. But have not compromises always been necessary when ideas were being embodied in institutional form? We may therefore fairly speak of a

[1] 2 Kings xxi, 16. According to tradition, Isaiah was sawn asunder in Manasseh's reign.
[2] 2 Kings xxii f.

compromise between the prophetical and the priestly circles. It meant a concession, too, on the part of the Jerusalem priests when the text of the law admitted the priests of the former sanctuaries outside Jerusalem to equal standing with the priests of the central sanctuary. The intention of the legislation is clear: it was to restrict the right to perform sacrifice to the members of the tribe of Levi and to exclude from that privilege all not belonging to that tribe. Compared with the practice that had hitherto prevailed, which permitted anyone and every one to perform sacrifice, that was an innovation, but it also was meant to help in bringing the cult observances under firm control. In actual fact, the circle of those who officiated at the sacrifice was even narrower. We can easily understand that when it came to carrying out the legal enactment the arrogant priests at Jerusalem would not welcome their brethren from the rural districts—who probably did not in all cases even look the part! In the sequel Ezekiel supplied the theory on which this practice was based. He declared [1] that it was just and right that these "Levites" should take a subordinate place. As priests of the former holy places throughout the country they had seduced Israel to idolatrous worship—the dogma of the centralization of worship was already thus rigidly fixed in Ezekiel's mind! They must bear their punishment for that by taking the place of the foreign Temple-slaves, and these latter, "uncircumcised in flesh and in heart," should never again be allowed to tread the courts of the sanctuary. And, lastly, Ezekiel was outdistanced by the legislation of the Priests' Code (444 or 432). Without any scruple it carries back this distinction between priests and the subordinate Levites to Moses' days; it does the same with regard to the one legitimate place of worship, only, keeping in mind the conditions of the desert period, it makes the one place of worship a movable one, a portable tent, the tabernacle of the wilderness.

The introduction of the Deuteronomic law made a deep cleft in Israel's religious life. That henceforth sacrifice was to be offered only at one place, that as a result the numerous places of worship throughout the land were suddenly suppressed, meant that Israel's religious life was apparently to be shorn at

---

[1] Ezek. xliv, 9 ff.

one stroke of its most sacred values. God, with whom they had had fellowship in the district where they lived, seemed now to be removed to a distance ; all sanctity was removed from the places where their homes lay ; the slaying of the victim, and the sprinkling of its blood on the soil of their own districts, had suddenly been reduced to a merely secular act. And that had been only one of the hundred threads which religion had woven into the daily round. All this meant a disenchantment of life ; in fact, it was now that such a thing as secular life began to be. The proceedings in the Temple at Jerusalem were now the only sacred item in life, either on holy days or on ordinary days, and to be present there involved a journey. The Temple was far away, and the road to it was long, and one had plenty of leisure *en route* to realize that paying vows to God was now something quite different from one's daily life. Thus the contrast between secular and sacred, between profane and holy—a contrast as old as the practice of religion itself—assumed a prominence it had never before possessed. The cultus became a thing apart, with an atmosphere, so to speak, entirely separated from one's calling as tiller of the soil. Then, again, the annual festivals had no longer any organic connexion with agricultural life.[1] They received a new, an artificial, an historical interpretation. Then this contrast between secular and sacred was reflected back on the persons concerned. A special class of men was required to study sacred things—a clergy as opposed to the laity. The laity were of course still entitled to take part in the sacrificial meal, but the trend of evolution could not fail to make the partaker soon become a mere spectator. The personal element diminished in proportion as the sacred apparatus increased, and the formal element as such gained greater meaning and importance.

But this contrast between clergy and laity was not the only contrast produced by this growth of a separate profession for dealing with holy things. There also arose the contrast between layman and theologian. The sacred element of life had now taken the form of a book, and special men were required to explain it and apply its rules to practical life. With the advent of the book religion became something that could be taught and learned. It took on a bent toward what was intellectual, and

---

[1] The law of tithes is instructive in this regard, Deut. xiv, 24-26.

this called for a new professional class, and gave birth at the same time to a new ideal. It is not accidental that people were now found saying, " *We* are the wise, for *we* have the *torah*." [1] These incipient scribes worked for a time hand in hand with the priests. Law code and Temple lent each other mutual support, and this brought about a fateful increase in the value attached to the externals of religion. [2] Pluming themselves on their familiarity with these externals, the scribes, to an extent never before known, looked upon themselves as the *élite* of humanity in comparison with all who were outside of their ranks. [3] It is instructive to see how the words 'nations' and 'countries' took on new meaning and became the equivalents for 'heathen' [4] and 'heathen lands.' This explains why the attitude of Israel toward non-Israel tended toward that view of an absolute separation which looked upon non-Israel as inferior and treated it as such—a particularism which is at bottom only a continuation of Hosea's conception of Jahveh's special marital relation to Israel. But the complacent confidence arising from such particularist exultation was held in check by the fear—which is a feature of all religions that come under the yoke of legalism—whether one had really kept all the commandments, and not left some undone. On the other side, the fulfilling of the law viewed from the standpoint of retribution or requital gave rise to a type of piety characterized by a readiness to enter into reckoning with God. [5] That is in keeping with the view of the religious relation as one governed by an agreement, a constitutional arrangement, a relation that more and more replaces the natural relationship based on blood and descent. Piety then becomes synonymous with obedience, observance. [6] One's task is to "observe" and "keep" [7] the commandments. When these are kept the task is done. King Josiah's bold march against Pharaoh Necho is an eloquent expression of this frame of mind. In that march Josiah met his death. After the greater mis-

---

[1] Jer. viii, 8.   [2] Jer. vii, 4.   [3] Deut. xxvi, 19.   [4] *Cf.* Hos. ix, 1.
[5] Deut. xxvi, 13, and later ; Neh. xiii, 14, 22-31.

[6] It is instructive here to notice how the old phrase "to see Jahveh's face" (*supra*, p. 353) becomes, by a change of pointing, "to appear before Jahveh." "The older phrase raises the act of worship to a reception of the highest favour that religion knows ; the later one reduces it to the level of a duty" (Duhm's *Das Buch Jesaias* on i, 12).

[7] The frequent use of the corresponding word *shāmar* is characteristic.

fortune had overtaken the State we still find echoes of this state of mind. The people felt that they were suffering undeservedly, and entrenched themselves, in their endeavours to explain what had happened, behind the ancient thought of solidarity : " The fathers have eaten sour grapes, and the children's teeth are set on edge." [1]

The severance of Israel's ancestral religion from the soil of the country which had become their home was completed by the deportations in the years 597 and 586. How could they serve Jahveh in a strange land ? It was the fulfilment of Hosea's warning words : [2]

> No libations to the Eternal then !
> No sacrificing victims for Him then !
> All food shall be like mourners' food,
> Defiling all who eat it :
> Their food shall only be for their own table ;
> None can be offered in the Eternal's house.

Without doubt the people felt this keenly. All the more zealously they clung to those parts of the cultus which could be performed without regard to their connexion with the native soil, and the Sabbath and circumcision gained a significance that was completely new. [3] The attitude to the Sabbath now took the tendency toward strict observance which it was to retain all down the centuries, and which still survives in a certain view of Sunday entertained in Christian countries.

In their exile the people also gathered round the sacred writings which had been saved out of the ruins, and seized with eagerness on all the words of promise that they found in the prophetic writings. Seeing that the prophecies of disaster had been fulfilled, the promises of deliverance would surely come to fulfilment also. A new "faith in Scripture" must have arisen at that time. It was nourished by the institution of the synagogue. The beginnings of the synagogue are shrouded in obscurity, but they must go back to a fairly early date. [4] One

---

[1] Jer. xxxi, 29 ; Ezek. xviii, 2.

[2] Hos. ix, 4, corrected text. [Moffatt's translation.—TRANSLATOR.]

[3] Ezek. xx, 12, 20, xxxi, 18 ; *supra*, pp. 112, 139.

[4] The oldest inscriptional mention of the synagogue in Egypt goes back to the time of Ptolemy III (247–221). In the Old Testament Ps. lxxiv, 8, undoubtedly refers to synagogues. *Cf.* my remarks in Stade's *Biblische Theologie des Alten Testaments*, vol. ii, p. 338 ff.

fruit of this faith in Scripture, which bore in itself the seed of its own continuance, was a literature that spoke of comfort, hope, and justification. "My former predictions have now been fulfilled, and now I foretell new things," says the God of Deutero-Isaiah,[1] and the first words put into the lips of God by that prophet are, "Comfort ye, comfort ye my people."[2] And even if they were not suffering undeservedly, were they not, compared with the heathen around them, righteous? God could not but recognize Israel's claim and help them to realize it. It was in this light that they now began to view God's righteousness, full of help for them, but so one-sided that a later psalmist could utter the prayer that God should punish the wicked and "let them not come into thy righteousness."[3]

The Exile contributed powerfully to the "dividing of the spirits," and, in particular, to the full growth of the contrast between Israel and the 'heathen.' But Israel itself was no longer a compact unit. The nation was broken into pieces—the exiles dwelt together in comparatively small groups. Involuntarily their thoughts turned more than ever to the individual. We see this change in Ezekiel. Unlike the earlier prophets, he no longer envisages the nation collective and entire. His task lay among individuals, and in fulfilling his task he became the express advocate of that individualism which had been begotten in men's minds by Jeremiah's teaching. In a new sense, it is true, he leads the way back from the individual to the collective whole by drawing up a finished and detailed plan of a constitution—the theocratic community of the future made up of individuals.[4] He is thus the connecting link between Deuteronomy and the Priests' Code, in which latter we find the completed transition to a religion of law. Ezekiel's attitude is proof that compensation for the interruption of the ceremonial worship was being found in the intellectual study of it. Jewish literature after the fall of Jerusalem and after the second destruction of the Temple in 70 A.D. exhibits the same phenomenon—satisfaction was being found in thought.

After the Return from Exile these thoughts were translated into action. On the ancient soil there arose, not a nation, but

[1] Is. xlii, 9.   [2] Is. xl, 1.
[3] Ps. lxix, 28.
[4] See my small book, *Der Verfassungsentwurf des Hesekiel* (1896).

a religious community, and that community clung to its beautiful cultus.[1] It also provided itself with a hierarchical leadership. It is no mere chance that the first mention of a high priest appears in a writing of the Exile, the so-called Law of Holiness,[2] and then reappears in the post-Exilic prophets Haggai and Zechariah. The difference between the periods is reflected in the expectations of these two prophets that with the building of the Temple the fullness of the eschatological blessing would descend upon the people of the Return. What a contrast to the attitude of the earlier prophets toward the cultus ! This keen eschatological expectation, which reminds us of similar phenomena among Christian chiliastic sects, was the only thing that made the conditions bearable. The life of the returned exiles was spent under miserable conditions, and they passed through one disappointment after another. But the less satisfaction they found in the present, the more the centre of gravity of religious interest shifted away from it, and the prevailing mood became one of expectant looking to the future. This mood pervades the entire post-Exilic history, and—strangely enough—after every reverse it waked anew, to stronger life than before. In Duhm's fine words : " In this expectant attitude, this ceaseless anticipation of fulfilment, there lives an inextinguishable impulse of humanity to reach the highest goal. The impatience, the shortsightedness, the precipitancy in it are the transient—though ever-recurring —admixtures of human immaturity. But in that impulse is revealed the divine force by which humanity is being raised from the dust to the eternal." [3]

The opposite pole of Jewish piety was, as is well known, legalism. It was based on the Priests' Code, introduced by Ezra in the year 444 or, perhaps more correctly, 432. Its introduction gave expression to the reaction against a renewed secularization of life which had found its way into the young community on the heels of a relaxation of the original exclusiveness of the returned exiles.[4] In the words of a contemporary writer,[5] the community was like a cluster of grapes which at first

---

[1] Ps. xxvii, 4.  [2] Lev. xxi, 10.
[3] *Das Buch Habakuk* (1906), p. 45.
[4] The resumption of a fixed Temple service from 516 seems to have heralded an expansive movement ; see my book, *Die Stellung der Israeliten und der Juden zu den Fremden*, p. 126 ff.  [5] Is. lxv, 8.

sight one was tempted to destroy, but which nevertheless contained good wine. Righteous and wicked were found together. Here we already see the division of the community into two camps [1] which runs through all the after-time, and which also forms the foundation on which the literature of Proverbs and the Psalms is built.[2] The striking thing is that the contrasts were more and more felt to be definitive and absolute. The boundary lines were fixed, and there was no middle position. The parties hated each other with a deadly hatred, and the religious ideal became more and more a separatist one. This is seen with special clearness in the fanatical rigorism with which Ezra took action against the mixed marriages of his day.[3] A ruthless objectivity, based only on the rigid letter of the commandment, stifled in Ezra that warm feeling of humanity which pulsated through Hosea's touching message, and which is again felt—a proof that it could not be entirely suppressed—in the Books of Ruth and Jonah. In the spirit of this new religious ideal of Ezra men sought to work out their salvation in fear and trembling,[4] encouraged by the conviction that it was only in a return to obedience to the law that " life " was to be found.[5]

The new law—the Priests' Code—separates the Jews as a holy people from all the rest of the world, in order to unite them to their God by the rule of obedience to a rigidly constituted ritual. In its entirety this cultus was the outstanding means of propitiation, the one way to regain a good standing with God. Here we see again victoriously breaking through the ancient idea of the efficacy of the cultus. But it is not the same as it formerly was. The experiences of the national downfall and of the Exile had not been without result. The point of view of atonement or expiation, to which the entire cultus was now subordinated, had the effect of bringing new sacrifices—sin offerings and guilt offerings—into the forefront, and making a new feast—the Day of Atonement—the crown of all the services of the cultus.[6] It also gave the cultus a different character. Instead of the festal

---

[1] This comes out in Trito-Isaiah (Is. lvi–lxvi) and especially in Malachi.
[2] *Supra*, pp. 232 f., 334 f.
[3] Ezra ix f.
[4] Ezra ix, 4, x, 3 ; Is. lxvi, 2, 5.  [5] Neh. ix, 29.
[6] Other new feasts were the New Year (Lev. xxiii, 23 ; Num. xxix, 1), Purim (Esther ix, 29), the Dedication of the Temple (1 Macc. iv, 56 ; John x, 22), and the Day of Nicanor (1 Macc. vii, 49).

joy which had hitherto found expression in eating and drinking before Jahveh we have now the terrible earnestness of a difficult obedience, which runs to excess in the bringing of all kinds of offerings, in fasts and in penances, and in blood ceremonies. Now that the laity could no longer offer these, they continually increased in number and value in the hands of the priests.[1] The paraphernalia of sacrifice and cultus grew more and more complicated, and the more perfect it became the more efficacy was attributed to it in itself. It became an *opus operatum*, independent of the personal participation of the individual. This also was a direct development of germs found in Deuteronomy.[2] In this respect it is instructive to find that the burnt offering now received a superior position to that of the bloodless meal offerings, and that *pari passu* with this more attention was now given to the collective sacrifices than to private offerings. As a result of all this there came both into life and into the cultus a large number of practices which were non-Jewish in origin. The best method of making heathenism harmless was to absorb it! Even the gods of alien peoples had to do duty in helping to enlarge the Court of Jahveh and act as His angels.[3] Indeed, in all that Judaism absorbed from heathenism it saw a kind of spiritual tribute paid by other faiths to that of Jahveh ; and it received it as readily as it received at a later time those sacrifices with which foreigners did homage to the God of the Jews in the Temple at Jerusalem.[4] In the Book of Malachi [5] we meet the thought that all the worship in the world belongs to Jahveh.

The religion of the post-Exilic community, however, comprised more than legalism and cult-observances. It was far more complex than that. Their "teachers of Wisdom" re-echo the ancient prophetical teaching—not cultus, but *ethos*. And the urgency and the emphasis with which they invite men to listen to their instruction, and praise its blessings as contrasted with all religion

---

[1] The annual sacrifices of the community required 1093 lambs, 113 bulls, 37 rams, 32 goats ; also 150·6 *epha* of fine flour, 342·08 *hin* of wine, and an equal amount of oil (*cf.* my *Biblische Theologie des Alten Testaments* (Stade, vol. ii), p. 30).      [2] *Supra*, p. 374.

[3] Dan. x, 13, 20 ; Ps. lviii, 2, lxxxii, 1, 6 ; and *supra*, p. 359.

[4] See my *Das religionsgeschichtliche Problem des Spätjudentums*, p. 20.

[5] Mal. i, 11.  *Cf.* the saying of Vishnu, " Even those who sacrifice to other gods are really sacrificing to Me " (Hopkins, *The Religions of India* (1895), p. 395, *note* 1).

that confines itself to the practices of the cultus, create the impression that there was a competitive struggle between influences trying with unequal means, but with equal zeal, to bring the community into a condition pleasing to God, both equally conscious of having their roots in the faith of God. To pass muster before God (but before men also[1]), that was what Wisdom undertook to teach ; and whereas the cultus, with at bottom the same object in view, was more a matter for the collective community, Wisdom directed its efforts *ad hominem* [2] with a more pastoral purpose. It thus took a far deeper grip of daily life, permeating it with instruction and counsel. He who attends to it is not only good, but wise, for Wisdom also shows the path to happiness and prosperity.

But, it was asked, is it the case that the good man prospers ? Is not the teaching of experience rather that innocent men suffer ? Of course, appearances might be deceptive—no eye can see into the secret places of the heart. Thus there was always the possibility of secret sins, or of sins which one had committed in the ignorance of early youth, and the validity of the dogma of retribution was thus saved. It is also beyond question, it was said, that in spite of everything there is a very great amount of inward righteousness. And yet was it not still true that the wicked man prospered and the good man fared ill ? We have already seen in our section on literature how greatly this " Job's problem" occupied men's minds, and how it became a theme of literary treatment.[3] A resonant ' yet ' shows that the good did not doubt their God.[4] And this brings us to what is best in post-Exilic religion. In the main the Psalter, which is the child of the post-Exilic period, is the Song of Songs of faith in God. Having their origin in a sense of need, in persecution and oppression, the Psalms are the living witnesses that their authors sought help in God because they were irrefragably certain that in Him, and in Him alone, was help to be found. The main source of this certainty was the consciousness that the good man can ever and anon turn to God in prayer ; and in its best forms this

---

[1] *Supra*, p. 330.

[2] Of course, the priests had to remit much pastoral care out of fear of being rendered " unclean." They dared not approach a dead body except in the case of their own nearest kin. *Cf.* Lev. xxi, 1 ff.

[3] *Supra*, p. 335.  [4] Ps. lxxiii, 26.

consciousness reached the level of true inward delight in God.[1] There is another thing. We read God's word and find in it promises which God must make good. And the fact that an indissoluble tie binds God to His people is for the individual such an inexhaustible source of comfort that he eagerly turns to the history of the nation to strengthen himself with the thoughts of selection and election, guidance and preservation. In addition to history there is nature, in whose greatness and orderliness one sees evidence of God's strong hand and of His goodness. That is the thought of Deutero-Isaiah. The Creator becomes the Helper. And in its turn personal experience of the kindly leading of God becomes the strongest motive to faith in His providence. And in the further thought of God's forgiving grace, and the cessation of His anger, there is opened up a new aspect of faith in God— an aspect rich beyond others in comfort to the good man, and one on which his longing hopes are fixed.

The traits of gentleness and mercy in the idea of God, so welcome to men who need help in so many different ways, also colour practical religion. Righteous living is mainly comprised in benevolence and charity.[2] The ideal of life is seen embodied in a man like Job, who could say of himself : [3]

> I delivered poor men, when they cried,
> The fatherless and helpless ;
> Perishing people gave me their blessing,
> I gladdened the heart of the widow ;
> I wore the robe of charity and kindness,
> My justice was a tunic and a turban :
> I was eyes to the blind, I was feet to the lame,
> I was a father to the poor,
> Taking up their case, though I knew them not ;
> I broke the jaws of the oppressors,
> And forced their prey out of their teeth.

These last words strike another note, which is heard to excess in the Psalms, and which introduces a grating discord into this whole conception of religion—the thought of the enemies. It culminates in the constant prayer that all their malice and

---

[1] Ps. iv, 8. With what follows *cf.* § 24 of vol. ii (by me) of Stade's *Biblische Theologie des Alten Testaments.*          [2] *Supra,* p. 239.
[3] Job xxix, 12–17 ; *cf.* xxxi, 16 ff. [Mainly Moffatt's translation.—TRANSLATOR.]

wickedness may be avenged upon them. This finds its explanation in the cleavage of the community, for in most cases, though not in all, the enemies are of the Jewish race. Here faith in God comes near to being degraded. Frequently God is degraded into a national and a party God. It is even one of His claims to the praise of His people that He destroys their enemies.[1] Once more there breaks through here a thought that lay at the basis of the ancient national religion—that the nation's foes were God's foes, and must be destroyed. This expectation is the truest expression of the eschatological frame of mind. Apart from this the individual still expects little for himself in the future. The ideas of the state after death continued to be pitched in a low key. Sheol was still the land of silence and forgetting.[2] There all relationship to Jahveh was broken off.[3] This note rings out at times in the hopeless scepticism of Ecclesiastes : " A live dog is better than a dead lion. The living know that they must die ; but the dead know nothing, they have nothing for their labour." [4] Profounder natures, like the author of Job, battled their way to a more idealistic solution of the irrational element in life. Yet what we find in Job [5] is only a kind of gleam of the hope of resurrection, and nothing more. But born of the soul's need and confident faith that hope emerges and breaks forth victoriously out of the specific faith in a Messianic future, in which the dead pious hearts shall share.[6] It is probable that a foreign faith, a Persian faith, had some influence on the development of this Jewish conception.[7]

It may strike some readers that our study of Israel's religious growth and achievement has revealed far less dependence on other peoples than we have found in any other aspect of its civilization. That indicates where Israel's originality lay. It exhibited dependence in almost all other directions. Even when it gained the political mastery over Canaan it became subject

---

[1] Ps. cxliii, 12 ; cf. xli, 11.

[2] Ps. xciv, 17, lxxxviii, 13.

[3] Ps. vi, 6, xxx, 10, lxxxviii, 6, 12—perhaps an indication that the belief in Sheol and the faith of Jahveh were originally unconnected (supra, p. 367, note 9).    [4] Eccles. ix, 4 f.

[5] Job xix, 25. Unfortunately the text is doubtful.

[6] Dan. xii, 2 ; Is. xxvi, 19.

[7] See my paper " Zur Frage des Verhältnisses von persischem und jüdischem Auferstehungsglauben " in Festschrift für F. C. Andreas (1916), pp. 51–62.

to that people in its civilization.[1]  But in the sphere of religion, in spite of much initial admixture, it succeeded in asserting its independence, and it finally prevailed.  Nothing shows this more clearly than a glance at the much-discussed question of "Babylon *versus* the Bible."  It may suffice, going back for a moment again over some centuries, to take as illustration one typical instance. Every one now knows that much of the material of the early Biblical narratives was borrowed from other sources, and specially from Babylon.[2]  For example, the dependence of the Biblical narrative of the Flood on the Babylonian account of it is unmistakable.  But compare the two.  The Babylonian version tells [3] how the great gods were moved to bring about a flood.  The actual motive that animated them is left unmentioned.  The god Ea, however, anxious to save his favourite Ut-napishtim (the Babylonian Noah), betrays to him what is imminent.  Out of fear of the other gods he does this by stealth, whispering the plan of rescue at night at the house of reeds in which Ut-napishtim is asleep.  When the waters which they have themselves summoned actually begin to rise fear seizes on the gods.  They retreat and ascend to heaven, where they cower like frightened dogs.  After the flood has abated the rescued Ut-napishtim offers sacrifice.  The gods, smelling the sweet savour, gather round him like flies, and endeavour to prevent Bel, who was the prime mover in causing the flood, from enjoying any share.  Bel comes forward, however, and when he hears that one soul has been saved he is angry with the gods—especially with Ea, who contrived the rescue.  In return Ea covers him with vehement reproaches for having foolishly caused a flood instead of some other catastrophe !  Where is there anything like this in the Hebrew narrative ?  Here all notes of mistrust and fear, petty resentment and repulsive disputes among the gods, are absent. Everything has been gathered up, of course with a wondrous anthropomorphism, in the moral will of the one sole Jahveh. When He sees the wickedness of men on the earth He repents that He created man, and in the bitterness of His heart He resolves to destroy them.  At the same time, however, He devises the deliverance of Noah—a deliverance dictated solely by ethical considerations, for Noah was found righteous.

[1] *Supra*, p. 147.    [2] *Supra*, p. 92.    [3] *TBAT*, vol. i, p. 55.

This deliverance of the patriarch is, as it were, a prophecy. Whereas those religions from which of old the Hebrew religion borrowed have been swept away in the stormy waters of historical catastrophes, the Hebrew religion, changed indeed in many ways, has endured all down the centuries ; and it is this fact that constitutes the abiding interest of Israel's entire civilization.

# INDEX

# INDEX

# INDEX

# INDEX

Huleh, plain of, 24
Human sacrifices, 102, 138, 350 f.
Humanity, growing tendency toward, 51, 238, 261, 266, 271
Hunting, 203
Hyacinth, 177
Hyksos, 50
Hymns and hymnody, 317 f., 334 f.
Hyssop, 241, 349, *note* 1

" I " (of the Psalms), 333
Ibex, 60, 180
Ibzan, 111, *note* 4
Idols, 38
*Ilani*, 86, *note* 1
Ili-milki, 108, *note* 3
*Iliad* (quoted), 231, 256, *note* 10
Illness, 72, 298 f., 365
*Ilu*, 86, *note* 1
Images, 347 f.
Imhotep, 94
Immanuel, 16, *note* 1
Incense, 218 ; -stands, 210
India, 134, 304, 358, 379
Individualism, 370, 376
Indo-Germans, 44, 170
Indra, 44, *note* 2
Inheritance, rights of, 154, 161, 163 f., 241
Ink, 96, 312, *note* 5
Inns, 187
Inscriptions, 209, 214, 313
Instruments, musical, 307 ff.
Intermarriage, 145, 378
Ir-Shemesh, 66
Irak, 240
Irbid, 43
Irby, traveller, 42
Iron, 22, 90 f., 211
Isaac, meaning of name, 339 ; blessing of, 324
Isaiah, 327
*Ish chajil*, 262, *note* 2
Ish-Baal, 353, *note* 7
Ishbosheth, 353, *note* 7
Ishmael, 153, 338
Ishtar, 99, *note* 5
Isis, 347
Islam, 138, 147, 224
Ivory, 61, 214 f., 219

*Jaar*, 25
Jabbok, river, 23
Jabesh, 105, 254, 260
Jabne-El, 107, *note* 16
Jachin, 205, *note* 4
Jacob, 103, 151, 324
Jacob-El, 108, *note* 4
Jael, 119, 158

Jaffa, 26
Jahveh, 352 ; Ark of, 137 f., 205, 211
Jahveh-zebaoth, 129, 254
Jahvist, the, 290, 343
Jair, 111, *note* 4, 142
Japanese poetry, 314, *note* 4
Japhia, 84, *note* 1
Jarmuth, river, 86, *note* 5
Jasper, 177
Jebel Mirad, 23
Jebusites, 56
Jeduthun (minstrel clan), 308
Jehoash, 337
Jehoiakim, 252
Jehoiakin, 294
Jehoram, 295 *and notes*
Jehosadak, 295
Jehosaphat, 210
Jehosheba, 65, *note* 4
Jehovistic writer, 343
Jehu, 295, *note* 9, 362
Jeketi, 81, *note* 5
Jephthah, 154
Jephthah-El, 72
Jerahme-El, 165, *note* 4
Jeremiah, 230, 327
Jericho, 13, 55
Jeroboam I, 214
Jeroboam II, 214
Jerome, 68
Jerub-Baal, 353, *note* 7
Jerusalem, 29, 108, *note* 3, 207 ff., 251 ff., 273, 352 f., 371
Jesse, 243, 247
Jesus, son of Mary, 223
Jesus, son of Sirach, 232, 302
Jethro, 265
Jewellery, 177 ff.
Jezebel, 159, *note* 7
Jezreel, plain of, 12, 143
Jibleam, 56
Jirpe-El, 72
Joab, 245
Job, Book of, 330 f.
Job-El (the name), 354
*Jôbel*, 310, *note* 12
Jochabed, 136, *note* 3
Joel, 20
Jonadab, 362
Jonah, 131, 378
Jonathan, 172, 231
Jordan, river, 13 f. ; the land east of the, 14
Joseph, 25, 137, 142, 272, 302, 337
Joseph-El, 108, *note* 4
Joshua, 25, 265
Josiah, 268
Jotham (king), 207

# INDEX

# INDEX

# INDEX

397

# INDEX

399